A GUIDE FOR
GIVING

...

A GUIDE FOR
GIVING

• • •

250 CHARITIES
AND
HOW THEY USE YOUR MONEY

HOWARD GERSHEN

PANTHEON BOOKS • NEW YORK

All rights reserved under International and Pan-American Copyright Conventions. Published in the United States by Pantheon Books, a division of Random House, Inc., New York, and simultaneously in Canada by Random House of Canada Limited, Toronto.

Library of Congress Cataloging-in-Publication Data

Gershen, Howard.
   A guide for giving : 250 charities and how they use your money /
Howard Gershen.
      p. cm.
   Includes index.
   ISBN 0-679-73275-6
   1. Charities—United States—Handbooks, manuals, etc.   I. Title.
HV97.A3G47   1990   90-52562
361.7′6′0973—dc20

Book Design by Robert Bull Design
Manufactured in the United States of America

First Edition

To the entire Family Tree:
roots, trunk, branches, and buds,
but most of all,
to Bugsy and Shoil.

□ CONTENTS □

□ ACKNOWLEDGMENTS □

The long, circuitous route this project has taken began over three years ago, when I was a writer and researcher for the Democracy Project, a nonprofit public policy group in New York. *Esquire* magazine needed someone to research and write an article on how fifty American charities spend their money. Mark Pinsky, executive director of the project, recommended my services to his friend Adam Moss, then deputy editor of *Esquire*, and I was hired to write the original article for the December 1987 issue.

Joe Vallely of Flaming Star Literary Enterprises (now my agent) saw the article, contacted me, and suggested turning the article into a book. David Sternbach, an editor and one of the pillars of the old Pantheon Books, bought the idea and soon I was on my way.

I thank each of them for their faith in this project, their input, and their confidence in my abilities even when I felt snowed under with all the work to be done to complete this book to my own satisfaction. I must also thank several people and institutions without whose knowledge and assistance this book would have had gaping holes:

At *Esquire:* Larkin A. Warren (chief of research) and Ellen Fair (deputy editor).

At Pantheon: Frances Jalet-Miller and Diane Wachtell, editor and interim adviser, respectively, who helped shape and push along the book in its final stages; Altie Karper (managing editor), Fearn Cutler (art director), and Kathy Grasso (production manager), who contended with all my missed deadlines but nevertheless did a superb job; and Luisa Siepi, who checked mountains of source material to confirm that all of the figures I quoted in the profiles were correct.

I also thank, in scattered order, Howard D. Leib (legal, comedic, and junkmail help); Chris Radin (our man in San Francisco); Stan Edelman (computer wizardry and advice); Margery Heitbrink and Frank Driscoll (both from the National Charities Information Bureau); Bennett Weiner (Philanthropic Advisory Service); at various state offices of charities registration: Carole Palmer and Howard Carr (New York), Peggy Catalano (Tennessee), Betty Blakemore (Virginia), and Julie Langford (California); Cecelia Hilgert, Michael Alexander, and Milton Cerny (Internal Revenue Service); Herb Chao Gunther (Public Media Center); Len Levitt (Sierra Club); James S. Briggs, Jr. (United Cancer Council); Lambert Franklin (VISA); Mac-Donald Architects; and the research facilities and reference librarians at: the Columbia University School of Journalism Library; the Direct Marketing Association; the Foundation Center; Harborfields Public Library; Huntington Public Library; New York Public Library; and last, but certainly not least, the West Islip Public Library.

In addition to the documents and articles noted in the profiles and footnotes, my work was also aided by two books from the National Center for Charitable Statistics, a division of Independent Sector: the *Yearbook of New York State Charitable Organizations* (1987) and the *Yearbook of California Charitable Organizations* (1989). Also of enormous help were *Charity U.S.A.* by Carl Bakal, *And the Band Played On* by Randy Shilts, and the *Encyclopedia of Associations* (1990 edition).

Lastly, I must thank David Frederickson, my copy editor. More than anyone else, he shaped this book into a readable manuscript. His perceptive questions, clear sense of organization, attention to detail, and superhuman endurance and patience in the face of a project that never seemed to end have earned my eternal gratitude . . . despite the fact we still disagree over which words should've been capitalized.

Giving and Getting

□ INTRODUCTION □

■ THE 1980S WERE a decade of federal budget cuts, personal computers, and global mass media, and the world of nonprofit fundraising responded to these changes with changes of its own.

Reductions in federal outlays for social services hit nonprofit and charitable groups across the nation. In 1974 these groups had received about $16 billion from government sources, and $25 billion from private contributions. Yet by 1980 government financing had soared to nearly equal the amount of private giving ($45 billion).[1]

Then came the budget cuts of the Reagan years. No longer guaranteed government grants, even for epidemics of AIDS and homelessness, many organizations died out. In 1981, the number of nonprofits closing down operations jumped almost 75 percent, to 19,000 from 11,000 the previous year. One year later, the number of nonprofits ceasing operation (33,000) exceeded the number of start-ups. But by 1983 the rate of closing was decreasing: only about 15,000 groups shut their doors for good. By 1986 the trend had reversed: the number of nonprofits grew twice as fast as at the beginning of the Reagan years.[2]

Surviving nonprofits were required to shift priorities and aggressively raise funds, filling some or all of their budget gaps with increased individual contributions, foundation grants, or corporate gifts.

Although nonprofit and charitable organizations are granted tax-exempt status largely because they are not commercial businesses, the 1980s saw many nonprofits tiptoeing or rushing into the marketplace. A century ago Joseph Pulitzer sold more newspapers by printing the names of contributors to the fund to build a base for the Statue of Liberty, but in the past decade commercial licensing agreements and alliances with banks and corporations provided new sources of income for the statue's restoration. Kitchen cupboards and refrigerators bulged with products whose manufacturers

3

donated a portion of the purchase price to charity, sometimes as an inducement to buy the product (cause marketing).

Unfortunately, the marketplace was not always beneficial. Some corporations reduced contributions to their own foundations, preferring to keep their cash at hand to fight off hostile takeover attempts. Recipients of corporate largesse were therefore affected by the very market forces from which their tax-exempt status sought to protect them.

Door-to-door fundraising continued, but other methods were needed to make better use of scarce resources, hunt down new sources of funding, and reduce fundraising costs. Direct-mail fundraising, which can be very expensive and often inefficient, emerged as a key tool in the development offices of charities. Advances in computer technology, including the widespread availability of personal computers with mail-merge word processing and Zip-code-sort database programs, increased the use of direct-mail fundraising in the 1980s.

The basic tool of this kind of fundraising, a sorted mailing list, dates back at least forty years. Walter Weintz, a direct-mail specialist who worked for the subscription department of the *Reader's Digest* in the 1940s, tells of hiring people to check his subscription lists by hand against telephone books, and then using home typists to type labels from the "clean" telephone lists, all to avoid duplicate mailings. Today, direct-mail companies use the latest computer equipment to combine mailing lists with census information, purchasing patterns, and subscription and donation lists to create detailed information-pictures of the kinds of people likely to live at a given address. This type of information can increase direct-mail efficiency by permitting more accurate targeting of materials to the people most likely to respond to a given solicitation—to buy a magazine or give money to a major health organization. And such mailing lists were behind the creation of a new tool for giving—and selling: affinity cards. These special credit cards, offered to people on a group's mailing list, form a symbiotic relationship between card issuer and nonprofit: the card issuer gets an efficient preselected mailing list for solicitation (it pays the mailing costs), and the group earns a royalty on each purchase charged on its affinity card.

Personal computers, first available in the 1980s, expanded direct-mail capability. Smaller nonprofit organizations can now perform limited direct-mail operations in-house through software that creates "personalized" letters (mail-merge) and sorted mailing lists (by name, donation size, or Zip code). As a result, more and more organizations are reaching into homes through the mailbox.

Nonprofits and charities also continued to get their message into homes through the airwaves. There were radio fundraising marathons half a century ago, followed by telethons, such as those featuring Jerry Lewis (Muscular Dystrophy Association) and Lou Rawls (United Negro College Fund). Benefit records and concerts, with part of the proceeds going to a charity, have long been used to raise money. However, it was not until 1984 that these elements were joined together.

Irish rock star Bob Geldof, sitting at home watching news reports of the devastating famine in Ethiopia, decided something must be done to alleviate the suffering. He proceeded to organize Band Aid, the group of British rock stars who donated their talent for the benefit single and album, *Do They Know It's Christmas?* Then he organized Live Aid, the first global telethon; it's estimated that a billion people saw the July 1985 concerts and pleas for funds broadcast from London, Philadelphia, Moscow, Australia, and other points around the Earth.

Over the years nonprofit researchers, advocates, and service-providers have achieved great results for many worthy causes. Their successes and the need for more aid to continue their work has spurred greater giving. During the past decade, total giving in America more than doubled, from $48.73 billion in 1980 to $104.37 billion in 1988.[3]

It's not hard to see why Americans of all income levels have answered the call to give more. (Poorer families were proportionately more generous. According to a 1988 survey conducted for Independent Sector, a Washington-based national coalition of nonprofit and charitable groups, households earning less than $10,000 gave 2.8 percent of their income to charitable and other nonprofit causes, while households earning $75,000–$90,000 gave 1.7 percent and those earning over $100,000 gave 2.1 percent.[4]) The concept of charity is an ancient practice in human history, enshrined in most of the great religions, from Jewish *tzedakah* and Christian tithing to almsgiving traditions in Islam, Hinduism, Buddhism, and other Eastern religions. In the 1830s, French author Alexis de Tocqueville, in his famous study *Democracy in America*, commented on the American tendency to set up committees to raise money for the common good. And today we have a president who campaigned on the idea of "a thousand points of light," indicating people helping people.

This is a book about how the charity that began at home is now influenced by sophisticated new fundraising techniques, and how the resulting contributions are used by individual charities and nonprofit groups.

This is also a book about how to be a knowledgeable contributor to those worthy causes. There are hundreds of thousands of tax-exempt groups recognized by the Internal Revenue Service, and it is certainly difficult to choose between effective and ineffective groups. Unfortunately, many people surrender their wallets to guilt and give blindly.

Too often emotions color contributions. When corporations consider appropriate groups with which to link their products through cause marketing, or banks search for affinity-card partners, they often speak of "sexy causes." By this they mean those causes that will engender the broadest, deepest response from consumers. Cancer, missing children, and terminally ill youngsters are just a few of these "sexy causes"; obscure diseases, unpopular political views, and highly technical problems or solutions are too complicated to produce immediate responses in a consumer-contributor. Even direct-mail specialists, who tweeze out minute, specialized samples of the population, are also succumbing to the tendency toward strong, across-the-board emotional responses. With the rise of the New Right, this has become especially true in direct-mail political fundraising campaigns—sent out by both the Right and the Left.

Of course sympathy, one of the most important of emotions, lies at the heart (literally and figuratively) of charity and will always play a role in any decision to donate to a worthy cause. However, effective giving can work only if a sympathetic contributor makes an intelligent choice about where to give a donation. For instance, which is a more effective means of fighting famine and hunger—buying grain to feed bloated stomachs or buying research to fight bloated rhetoric? Both have their place in the world, but sometimes one may be more useful than the other.

The organizations profiled in this book cover a wide range of activities and interests. Their concerns are today's headlines and tomorrow's. Their budgets range from a few thousand dollars up to nearly a billion dollars in a given year, but size is deceiving: there are definitely some highly effective Davids profiled next to the Goliaths.

Ideally, the information in this book will not only increase contributions to solid, deservedly well-known groups, but also lead many contributors to worthy smaller organizations tackling lesser-known problems. As always when selecting a new charity to support, it's important to do some extra research before signing a check or a volunteer sheet. In the long run it will help you support worthy groups making a real difference in the world, and will help prevent misguided generosity.

Several years ago, a reporter who was curious about how generous

Americans were to unknown causes created his own charity and started collecting money. Had he not stopped after proving his point that people will give to just about anything they're asked, he might have ended up a very rich man.

And today we might be writing generous checks to him and the Fund for the Widow of the Unknown Soldier.

□ 1 □

A GUIDE FOR GIVING

■ **T H E   P H O N E   R I N G S .** It's a representative of the Fund for the Widow of the Unknown Soldier asking you to contribute.

Should you give?

If you took a moment to consider, you'd probably realize that the group's premise doesn't make any sense and say no.

Or say you get a phone call asking you to help a group of terminally ill children attend a circus. Or a letter arrives, seeking your help in the fight against AIDS or homelessness, yet this is the first time you've ever heard of the group asking for your hard-earned money.

Same question as above: should you give?

The 250 organizations profiled later in this book are a mere fraction of the hundreds of thousands of charities and nonprofit groups operating and soliciting money across the country. Undoubtedly several of them have already appealed for your help, and you've had to decide if they were worth a donation.

How do you decide?

■ **FIRST, MAKE SURE YOU UNDERSTAND AND AGREE WITH THE GROUP'S PHILOSOPHY AND PROGRAM.** A group's philosophy, no matter how controversial, does not enter into the Internal Revenue Service's decision to designate it as nonprofit and tax-exempt. Decisions are based on a determination that the organization will work for the common good, rather than for personal profit.

A group's purpose is crucial for deciding the best means to achieve your own goals when you contribute. A charity may spend 95 percent of its income on its program (the work it does to achieve its mission), but if it's spending that money on public education when you feel it should go to direct action, your money's not being effectively used—at least not according to your own personal set of standards.

Over time, however, a group's purpose may change. The March of Dimes, for instance, was originally formed to fight polio. When a vaccine for that disease was developed in 1955, the charity could have dissolved. Instead, it expanded its purpose to encompass a fight against birth defects. Likewise, CARE began its life just after World War II as a consortium of several charities formed to distribute leftover military food rations to the starving in Europe. The rations are long since gone, but hunger and starvation persist—more in the Third World than in Europe—so CARE's purpose has evolved to cover long-term development as a preventive measure.

On the other hand, Bob Geldof's Band Aid Trust, which disbursed the funds raised through his efforts to fight the Ethiopian famine of 1984–85, was planned from the start to be a temporary organization and worked to spend all its money and dissolve itself as soon as possible. Some spending priorities had to change, however, when it was discovered that food shipped to Ethiopia could not be moved to famine-plagued areas due to the lack of roads that could support trucks laden with supplies; some Band Aid Trust funds ended up paying for road construction.

■ **REQUEST SOME PRINTED MATERIAL ABOUT THE ORGANIZATION, SUCH AS AN ANNUAL REPORT.** Legitimate groups will be only too happy to supply literature describing their work. Find out if the group's officials include specialists in the field. Confirm that your contribution is deductible for *your* tax purposes; contributions to some groups are not, though the organizations are themselves worthy and tax-exempt (more about that later).

■ **ASK FOR A PHONE NUMBER TO CALL IF YOU HAVE MORE QUESTIONS.** *No responsible organization will pressure you to contribute immediately.*

■ **DEMAND IDENTIFICATION.** Be suspicious of any charity or fundraiser that won't supply such information on request. Ask for the group's and the professional fundraiser's state registration number, and contact the appropriate office (addresses are given in Appendix C of this book). Make certain that both group and fundraiser are legally entitled to solicit money in your area.

■ **FIND OUT WHERE YOUR MONEY GOES.** How many of those children will get to see the circus? What percentage of your donation will go to the group's program? What percentage will pay for fundraising? These figures can change from year to year, and vary with the fundraising method. The Supreme Court has ruled that state governments cannot *compel* fundraisers to limit these percentages or reveal them at the point of solicitation (when you're asked to contribute), but it is certainly within your rights to ask for the figures.

An organization's age may be useful for judging some fundraising expenses. Older groups tend to have lower fundraising costs because they've had time to make their name known to the general public. Newer organizations, however, must contend with the burden of obscurity: their fundraising must take into account the added expense of getting their name and their cause known by the public. Keep this in mind when considering expense categories.

Most charities will gladly supply potential contributors with a wealth of detail about their financial health. Besides the annual reports most contributors request, independently audited statements are available, and, due to special provisions of the Revenue Act of 1987, even the groups' own tax returns (IRS form 990) are open to public inspection. These documents can also be obtained (often for a nominal photocopying charge) either directly from the IRS or through a state charity-registration office (see Appendix C).

In addition to your questions, beware of these tricks of the trade:

■ **THE TEAR-JERKER.** A hard-luck story is a familiar ploy of a phony operator. Don't succumb to guilt or emotional blackmail.

■ **THE VARIANT NAME OR ADDRESS.** A less-than-reputable organization may try to "piggy-back" on the fame of a better-known group by adopting a similar name or logo, or by having an address close to the larger group.

■ **THE MAIL-SOLICITATION TRINKET.** Federal law states that, unless you requested the item, you can keep it without making a contribution. Likewise, sweepstakes cannot demand a contribution with an entry.

■ **THE FAKE BILL.** It is illegal to mail a fake bill, invoice, or statement of account when it is really an appeal for funds. A disclaimer must appear on the solicitation, stating that you are under no obligation to pay.

If you're still unsure whether to give any money:

■ **CONTACT A CHARITIES WATCHDOG GROUP.** The National Charities Information Bureau or the Philanthropic Advisory Service of the Better Business Bureau can tell you more about nationwide organizations. For smaller groups, contact your local Better Business Bureau. The national addresses are:

National Charities Information Bureau
19 Union Square W., 6th Fl.
New York, NY 10003
(212) 929-6300

Philanthropic Advisory Service
Council of Better Business Bureaus, Inc.
4200 Wilson Blvd.
Arlington, VA 22209
(703) 276-0100

Generally, although their purpose is *not* to make judgments as to which groups are worthy of your contributions, both NCIB and PAS have certain minimal standards to which they hold the groups they analyze (NCIB's standards are reprinted in Appendix B).

■ **ASK PUBLIC-SERVICE AGENCIES IN YOUR AREA FOR INFORMATION** about the charity or nonprofit in question.

When you finally decide to contribute, be generous to a worthy cause, but keep the following in mind:

■ **DON'T COMMIT DONATIONS OVER THE PHONE.**

■ **NEVER USE A CREDIT CARD** to contribute to an unknown group.

■ **CONTRIBUTE BY CHECK, AND MAKE IT OUT TO THE CHARITY OR NON-PROFIT—NEVER THE PERSON SOLICITING YOUR DONATION.** Use the check as a receipt to claim a deduction, if possible, at tax time. Be sure to find out if your contribution is tax-deductible.

Most charities or nonprofit groups are designated as tax-exempt under either section 501(c)(3) or 501(c)(4) of the tax code. Contributions to (c)(3) groups are generally tax-deductible. Groups described in 501(c)(4), however, usually spend most of their time lobbying or otherwise working for partisan political causes, so contributions to these groups are *not* tax-deductible, though they are still exempt from paying taxes themselves.

Often an organization segregates lobbying functions from other functions, and sets up two related groups: one designated (c)(3), the other (c)(4). Each group may share office space and even officers, and funds from one organization may be shifted to the other, as needed. In this book, separate but related (c)(3) and (c)(4) groups are sometimes given separate profiles.

Another concern about contributions is whether you can actually claim a deduction on your own tax return. Tax reform made it more difficult (those who don't itemize, for instance, can't deduct). Check with the IRS or your accountant for the latest rulings, and remember that only the charitable-donation portion of fees paid for goods or services can be deducted (that is, if the benefit concert tickets cost $100 but would usually cost $30, you're only allowed to deduct $70).

■ **CONSIDER WHETHER YOU WOULD PREFER TO HAVE SOME CONTROL OVER THE DESTINATION OF YOUR CONTRIBUTION.** You might specify that the money should go for a particular program or service. Groups don't encourage this, but some will honor requests that donations not go to overhead expenses. Bear in mind, however, that while you might specify that your contribution pay only for program expenses (say, food for a homeless shelter), *someone* will have to pay for the overhead (board meetings, reception, accounting, and preparation of the annual report) and fundraising (the cost of finding you and getting you to write the check in the first place).

The United Way, the Federation of Protestant Welfare Agencies, and the United Jewish Appeal–Federation of Jewish Philanthropies are just three of the "umbrella" groups that collect and distribute funds to other agencies. Donations to these umbrella organizations are lumped with others and then distributed according to the group's decision. Although there is power in numbers, you may wish to give more money to one nonprofit in particular. The Combined Federal Campaign and similar payroll-deduction plans may also provide you with less control over your donation than you might wish.

■ **MOST IMPORTANT, CONSIDER VOLUNTEERING.** Good charities not only need your money, they can also use your time. Beyond stuffing envelopes and helping to raise funds, you can help out charities in any number of ways, including (but certainly not limited to):

- Tutors are needed by literacy groups.
- Cooks and servers are needed by homeless shelters.
- Buddies are needed by AIDS patients too weak to shop for food or get prescriptions refilled, and sometimes they're needed just to listen and offer a hug.
- Computer specialists are sometimes needed to program computer databases that keep track of donations and projects.
- Bookkeepers, clerical workers, and managers can help groups become more efficient in providing services.
- Docents are often needed by museums.
- Big Brothers and Big Sisters, and volunteers for Boys Clubs and Girls Clubs, are needed by youths who need role models, confidants, and alternatives to gangs.
- Attorneys, accountants, doctors, dentists, architects, real-estate agents, and writers can help by supplying their skills *pro bono* to groups.
- People with good listening skills are needed to handle hotline calls.
- Job-skills training is needed for youth and the unemployed.

Potential volunteers may also be interested to know that recent medical studies have suggested that volunteers can gain real, measurable physical benefits from helping. Lower blood pressure, reduced risk of heart disease, increased immunoglobulin counts, and other signs of diminished risk of stress-related illness have been discovered in people who volunteer or help with others' needs.

The list of ways to help is endless and the need is great. Independent Sector, a coalition of 650 nonprofit and corporate groups, advocates that you "Give Five"—contribute 5 percent of your time and 5 percent of your income. You may have your own amount in mind—perhaps a tithing figure recommended by a synagogue, church, or mosque.

But by all means contribute *something.* Every organization profiled in this book needs your money, and most of them can also make good use of your time and energy. Thousands of others can, too. You might not change the entire planet, but each pebble thrown in a pond produces ripples that affect everything else.

☐ 2 ☐

CHARITY BEGINS AT HOME—HOW DIRECT-MAIL APPEALS WORK

■ YOU'VE PROBABLY GOT a typical mailing list—the people you send greeting cards to. Over the years, you've created and pruned this list with a special purpose in mind: to share holiday joys with relatives and friends.

You could have randomly selected a page from the local phone book and sent cards to thirty names, but would those strangers respond? Probably not.

Your own list, however, will usually bring responses. If people don't send cards to you, you'll take them off your list. And if someone marries, moves, or dies, you'll also update the list.

Now imagine a million-name mailing list trying to accomplish the same sort of result (a response) with the same degree of predictability. That's the sort of work that goes into creating a professional mailing list that would be useful for a nonprofit group.

And imagine, out of the million names on a "prospecting" list, only thirty thousand people (3 percent) actually responding. If each letter costs a quarter to print and mail, this organization has just spent $250,000—and *wasted* about $242,500 of it.

And that's considered a success.

The amount of money sent in by those thirty thousand first-time contributors or consumers should at least pay for the entire mailing, and the names of those who responded to the mailing can be repackaged and resold as a new list, a grouping of respondents to a particular appeal. The cycle that began with the original list (perhaps created from just such a previous mailing) continues, and your name and address migrate to another set of mailing labels. Your name and address will be compiled, coded, indexed, cross-indexed, merged, purged, sorted by sex, age, income, zip code, etc.,

.

and packaged for sale as part of something that might be called "Star Wars: The List"[1] or "Lincoln's Revenge."[2]

Getting your name on a mailing list is easier than falling off a log. In fact, given the high degree of specialization in targeted mailing lists, it wouldn't be surprising to find a list composed entirely of people who fall off logs: log-rolling contestants who'd buy stronger cleats or who'd support efforts to keep rivers clean.

Nearly every magazine subscription, mail-order purchase, sweepstakes entry, refund coupon, or piece of paper or computer file containing names and addresses is a potential source of names for a new mailing. Like your greeting-card list, most of these sources are already a step or two away from raw data (randomly selected names). They contain some valuable piece of information about you, your interests, your needs, and the likelihood you will respond to a given appeal or advertisement. This is true whether one is using direct mail to sell Hong Kong suits or support class-action suits.

The *Whole Earth Review,* a quarterly publication put out by the same people who in the 1960s created the *Whole Earth Catalog* (a collection of tools and informational materials considered useful for lifestyles outside of the mainstream), is one of many magazines that rent out their mailing list of subscribers. However, unlike most magazines, *WER* prints the names of organizations that have used the list. From its Winter 1985 to Winter 1989 issues, *WER* rented its list to such for-profit companies as Barnes and Noble, the *Christian Science Monitor,* the Calvert Social Investment Fund, and the magazines *Garbage* and *Reality Hackers.* Nonprofit renters during that period included the American Friends Service Committee, Amnesty International, Common Cause, Greenpeace USA, Public Citizen, and the Sierra Club. These renters determined there is something about readers of the *Whole Earth Review* that makes them likely to respond, for some reason, to a particular appeal or sales pitch.

Walter Weintz, the direct-mail specialist who worked for the *Reader's Digest,* was hired by the Republican Finance Committee in 1969 to help set up a system for soliciting contributions from existing contributors and to solicit new donors.[3] In 1972, when funds were being raised for the election, the head of the Finance Committee to Reelect the President suggested soliciting the national list of registered Republican voters.

Weintz knew better. It was "probably the worst list we could use," he said. The Republican list included both high and low donors, and did not segregate those who would *not* respond to a direct-mail appeal. A lot of money would be wasted in printing and postage if the list was used, even though it was readily available and would not cost a penny to rent. Weintz suggested instead using a list called "Ruby Red Grapefruit."

The Grapefruit Theory went as follows: "Anybody who could afford to pay $110 for a supply of grapefruit ordered by mail on the strength of a promotion letter had to be both well-to-do and *very* mail-order susceptible."

Four hundred lists were tested for the GOP mailing. Ruby Red Grapefruit came out among the top winners. Registered Republicans came out last.

Once a mailer selects the best lists for a solicitation, the first hurdle is cleared—but not the biggest one. Millions of dollars have been spent on research to determine why the pieces of direct mail sent to your home get opened (Hurdle 2) and, most important, get a response (Hurdle 3).

Every last detail of a mailing is choreographed to produce the maximum yield, both in terms of number of respondents and total dollars per response. In their quest to squeeze a last dollar per response, direct mailers often see neither the forest *nor* the trees: they're concerned with the color of the bark, the tilt of the branches, and the size of the leaves.

For example, research has determined the following will increase the response rate for a mailing:

- affixing the stamp to the envelope at a slight angle
- using more than one color ink in the letter itself
- using the addressee's name in the first paragraph of the letter
- using "you" rather than "we" in the letter
- using a poster girl instead of a poster boy
- using a one-page letter instead of a three-page letter (30 seconds and about 50 words of copy are the endurance limit for the average reader[4])
- using a computer "telegram" instead of a computer letter
- using a self-stamped reply envelope instead of a postage-paid envelope

Even typestyles can affect response: Garamond Light beats Formal Script and Carbon.[5]

Weintz, in his work for the *Reader's Digest,* was one of the first to discover the effectiveness of sending letters in envelopes that resemble those used for IRS refund checks or telephone bills: people are conditioned to believe that what comes in a yellowish envelope is important and should be opened immediately. Nowadays, this technique has evolved (as the public caught on) to imitation of Federal Express and other overnight mail envelopes. Same good response.

Just as the famous yellow envelope or imitation FedEx grabs someone's attention, so do oversize envelopes. Third-class nonprofit mail that came in an envelope larger than letter-size was read by 49.1 percent of household recipients in 1987. Only postcards and flyers produced a better readership rate.[6] This finding was taken to an extreme in 1988 when the National Committee to Preserve Social Security and Medicare sent out a mailing that measured 14″ × 17″.

Printed copy on the front of an envelope can also increase response, but it must be something that will create a reaction. The Paralyzed Veterans of America sent out mailings in envelopes imprinted with the words, "How many paralyzed veterans does it take to change a lightbulb?" CARE ran into some trouble when it tried to raise money for a program that would supply Third World businesspeople with needed capital to expand their shops and employ more people (thus aiding CARE's long-term development goals of removing more people from poverty). The outside of the envelope for the CARE fundraising letter was plain white, imprinted with a red stamp that read CREDIT DENIED. It was a reference to the Third World businesses, but this wasn't clear until you read the letter. Two thousand people complained to CARE about their embarrassment and fear that neighbors might believe the letter was about their own credit rating; one woman threatened to sue CARE for defamation of character and demanded the charity send letters to credit agencies informing them that her credit was still good. Ironically, even though some of those 2,000 people wanted their names removed from CARE mailing lists, the CREDIT DENIED mailing produced a better-than-average response.

Part of the problem with the CARE mailing was that there was no return address on the front of the envelope. A return address, especially from a celebrity, can spark interest and cause envelopes to be opened. (A return address or logo similar to that of a better-known organization can also cause a letter to be opened, although by mistake.)

The American Foundation for AIDS Research, actively supported by actress Elizabeth Taylor, has frequently sent out fundraising letters purportedly coming from her, with her signature on the envelope. Common sense rules out the possibility that she, or anyone else whose name and signature are found on fundraising literature, could send out a million letters, much less sign each one. Nevertheless, this false personalizing continues to be used because it produces better responses.

The letter inside the all-important envelope should also have a signature, preferably in an ink of a different color than the body of the letter (again, to give the impression that a real person signed the letter even though the signature is actually drawn by a signature machine or a laser printer, or printed with the letter; a real person would have a fatal case of writer's cramp). The signature need not be that of a real person. A false name can help direct responses to the appropriate department: letters addressed to "John Smith" might deal with memberships; mail for "Jane Doe" could contain donations.

False names in fact play another, more important role in direct mail. Owners "seed" their mailing lists with some randomly placed false names with real addresses (perhaps the home address of someone the list owner knows) to track usage. If Group A rents a mailing list for a single use, but two separate mailings are sent to the same fake name, that means Group A is using the list for a second time without authorization. This practice prevents copying of lists, and can be useful for checking your own name's usage.

Sometimes, your name and address are typed into a computer with a wrong letter or number. Often special software will correct the error (for instance, a typed "Daivd" will probably be corrected to "David"—or perhaps to "Baird") but sometimes the extra middle initial or odd spelling of your name will persist. By collecting all the direct mail you get, you can see who's trading or renting your name. You could also intentionally misspell your name or address to track usage, but this would only cause more money to be wasted on direct-mail solicitation by creating duplicate listings. Therefore, do *not* use a false name when contributing to a nonprofit; you'd only be increasing fundraising expenses and taking away from money that should go to the charity's programs.

Extra copies of direct-mail solicitations not only increase an organization's fundraising expenses, they are also a waste of paper. To *remove* your name from mailing lists, send a letter to that effect (with your name and address) to:

DMA Mail Preference Service
Direct Mail Association
6 E. 43rd St.
New York, NY 10017

Your name will be put on a master purge program that mailers rent. Future mailing lists that are traded or rented will not include your name. To remove your name from existing lists, you must write each organization or company separately.

By stating your preference, you are aiding the mailer by reducing their costs for sending solicitations which would otherwise be ignored. Direct mail is an expensive fundraising method when it doesn't work, and only slightly less expensive when it does. Lists must be continuously tested to ensure accuracy.

One major reason why mailing lists must be constantly tested and updated is that Americans move. According to the U.S. Postal Service, nearly one American in five moves each year. Changes in addresses create havoc with a mailing list. The Postal Service forwards mail for only a limited period of time, and although they can supply direct mailers with computerized files of address changes, updating a mailing list adds to the expense of mailings.

Direct-mail operations can reduce costs by presorting mail, to take advantage of lower postal rates. A Zip-code sorting can be performed when the mailing list's address labels are printed by computer. Address labels that carry the code CAR-RT SORT indicate mail that's been through an even finer sort: they're organized by postal-carrier routes, through computer programs which recognize the individual streets and house numbers in a given carrier route. The extra computer sorting costs are balanced by the benefits to a mailer. Even fractions of a penny shaved off the postage of one letter can mean big money saved over the course of an enormous mail solicitation.

The money saved on the outside of the envelope can pay for a more effective message inside the envelope. A good fundraising letter will be even better if it features Interest, Desire, Explanation, Action, and a P.S. for a Summary. It will also take into account the sex of the reader. The professional fundraising firm of Huntsinger, Jeffer, Van Groesbeck reported in 1984 that "for national nonprofit organizations, approximately 80 percent of donors are women. This should be considered in writing your appeal."[7]

One way to grab a reader's interest is to include a survey requesting input. Everyone wants to feel his or her opinion is important, and so Greenpeace, the National Organization for Women, Sierra Club, and the presidential campaign of George Bush were among those sending out surveys in 1988.

Yet the results of those "surveys" can hardly be considered objective. They are sent to members or others who already have some interest in the group's cause. While these people are very likely to fill out and return the forms, any statistics derived from the survey are biased. If the survey was sent to a truly random sample, many forms might never be completed, let alone returned, and the results would be biased in an entirely different direction (remember the problems with getting people to complete and return their 1990 U.S. Census forms).

The survey is often just another device to induce someone to open the envelope, absorb the message, and support the organization. A simple brochure describing a group's programs and successes might be just as effective, and more reputable, but brochures tend to be put away for future reading.

It is very important that once someone opens an envelope and reads the message, she or he acts upon it—ASAP. That's one of the reasons why, since 1948, contribution forms have suggested dollar figures (rather than leave blank spaces). When a social service agency's mailing listed a specific amount for a suggested contribution, the average gift rose by 47 percent.[8]

Another method to increase response is timing. With so many other pieces of direct mail competing for your attention, it's important for a mailer to know when is the best time to send a letter. Some mailings, such as urgent pleas for disaster relief or help for an upcoming battle in Congress, appear regardless of the date on the calendar. Major fundraising, on the other hand, primarily occurs during December and February: December, because it's the end of the year (time to think of last-minute charitable deductions) and because of the tradition of giving during the holidays; February, because by that time holiday bills are paid and year-end bonuses are being included in paychecks. The summer, when many people are away from their homes and on vacations, is traditionally the time for the least amount of all types of direct mail.

Finally, the most obvious means for increasing fundraising response: trinkets.

Ever since the *Reader's Digest* started sending out a penny in each subscription solicitation, and the Disabled American Veterans began sending keyrings, direct mailers have resorted to sending cheap trinkets with their letters as a way of ensuring a response.

Trinkets of whatever type—address labels, matches, keyrings, pens, membership cards, bumperstickers, etc.—are *gifts*. It is against the law to charge someone for an item they received in the mail but for which they did not pay. Don't be taken in by guilt when you receive in the mail a cheap pen that doesn't write or an extra calendar. You are under absolutely no obligation to pay for a trinket. A charity or nonprofit group cannot charge you anything; your decision to contribute must be your own.

Fundraising solicitations doubled from 1977 to 1987, when the average household received about thirty-five solicitations.[9] As mailing costs go up, those solicitations will become slicker and slicker. You should learn to recognize the tools of manipulation appearing regularly in your mailbox. By being aware of the ways a simple piece of mail can be constructed to increase the likelihood that you will open it, heed its message, and send back some money, you can make better, more objective contributions.

You can also gain a new understanding of the clever minds behind what may be the most amazing direct-mail fundraising solicitation of 1988: a letter from the Alzheimer's disease research charity that included either the most ingenious or the sickest trinket of all—a packet of seeds for forget-me-nots.

BURIED BY DIRECT MAIL—
THE DEATH OF A CHARITY

■ O N J U N E 1, 1990, the United Cancer Council, at one time the fourth-largest cancer charity in the nation, filed for bankruptcy. It listed no assets.

At a final board meeting held on March 17, members were presented with a range of options to resolve the charity's financial difficulties. L.W. Robbins Associates, a professional fundraiser hired by the UCC as of June 1, 1989,[1] had worked on a pay-as-you-go basis. However, according to board secretary James S. Briggs, Jr., the UCC only "got a dime for each dollar we spent."[2] Eventually, the UCC settled its debts with L. W. Robbins Associates for a dime on the dollar. Briggs explained, "Time caught up with us. Our name was spoiled."

The board voted unanimously to declare bankruptcy.

The United Cancer Council had begun in 1959 as a collection of local American Cancer Society affiliates that broke off from the ACS in a dispute over fundraising. A couple of years later UCC had formally begun operations as a small Indiana charity aiding both cancer patients and cancer researchers. In addition to public education, UCC helped families experiencing cancer to live longer, better, and more fulfilling lives by providing up to $500 in assistance per patient (forty-seven patients received aid in 1988). Researchers were awarded yearly grants (maximum $7,500) to fund various research projects.[3]

It was a simple, noncontroversial program with contributions totaling $240,380 in 1984.[4] The UCC could have survived, but expenses were growing faster than income. A massive fundraising effort was needed, so a professional fundraiser was sought.

In 1984, the UCC hired the professional, for-profit direct-mail fundraising firm of Watson and Hughey Company of Alexandria, Virginia. They had raised money for other cancer charities, and agreed to pay the huge initial costs of direct mailings for UCC, in anticipation of future profits.[5] Thus UCC could start raising money without a substantial investment.

Watson and Hughey's mailings, including sweepstakes offerings suggesting optional contributions to be sent in with entry forms, were being sent all across the country. The charity formerly known just in Indiana was now making a national name for itself as a funder of cancer-patient services and cancer research. Money began to pour in. In 1985, UCC's contributors sent $5,087,453; in 1986, $7,869,015.[6]

In New York, the National Charities Information Bureau (NCIB), one of two major charities watchdog groups in the country, was beginning to take notice. Its researchers were reviewing figures supplied by UCC and coming to their own conclusions about where the money was going.

On April 13 and 14, 1987, the wire services reported that NCIB had determined *97 percent* of UCC's income was being spent on fundraising costs.[7] The mailings for the United Cancer Council were almost like a cancer themselves: they grew and grew, their expenses sapping money that should have gone to the main purposes of the group. In 1985, the year examined by NCIB, the United Cancer Council sent out mailings to 15 million households—and spent only $20,170 on research (including one grant of $15,638) out of $5.2 million spent by UCC in 1985.

It was astounding, but it was not a violation of any federal law.

Interestingly, it was not the first time that the fundraising costs and methods of a Watson and Hughey client had come under public scrutiny.

In 1983 Maine's attorney general, James E. Tierney, announced an agreement between his state and the American Institute for Cancer Research—another W&H client. Officials of the state's Consumer and Antitrust Division had found "several serious inaccuracies and misstatements concerning the nature of [AICR's] activities." Among the "various misrepresentations" made in the AICR fundraising letter was a statement that the group conducted research; it only gave financial support to research done by independent scientists. Under the agreement, more than seven hundred Maine residents who had received a solicitation mailing from AICR would be offered refunds of their donations.[8]

The American Institute for Cancer Research has had a long association with the Watson and Hughey Company. In fact, the fundraisers *founded* AICR in 1981 to sponsor cancer-prevention educational programs and fund cancer research projects. This purpose was expanded in fiscal 1987 to "provide funding to support research into the relationship between nutrition, diet, and cancer and to expand public knowledge of the results of recent research as it relates to cancer prevention, detection, and treatment."[9] Many of AICR's educational publications feature recipes or lists of foods said to reduce the risk of cancer. Until late 1983, Messrs. Watson and Hughey retained the power to appoint and remove AICR directors;[10] they are now nonvoting members of the institute, but *not* members of the board.[11]

Despite the potential for conflict of interest, AICR retains W&H as its direct-mail consultant. In terms of money raised, AICR has reaped enormous benefits: contributions in fiscal 1988 were *more than four-and-a-half times* what they were in fiscal 1983[12] and the AICR mailing list earned the group $799,141 in rentals during fiscal 1988.[13] For their work that year, W&H received $367,136 in direct compensation (not including reimbursements for expenses).[14]

This success has not been without its controversy. There was the trouble in Maine. Officials in New York and California also investigated AICR's finances, and required the group to make fuller disclosure of its handling of donations.[15] Of particular concern was the percentage of money going to fund actual research. During the year ending September 30, 1988, only about 18 percent of AICR's income went for research.[16]

Most of AICR's program expenses are said to be for "public education." Solicitation mailings that include a "Survey on Diet and Cancer" or resemble a billing notice for the "Annual Fund" (including a "Payment Requested By" date and a "Suggested Voluntary Contribution") are imprinted with four "Dietary Guidelines" for lower cancer risk. In spite of the mailings' apparently primary goal of raising money, the dietary guidelines are considered public-education expenses. (A similar allocation of costs for United Cancer Council fundraising materials was based on inclusion of the nine warning signs of cancer in that group's mailings.) According to AICR's independently audited statement for fiscal 1988, more than half of the $7.9 million spent on dual-purpose mailings (informational materials including an appeal for funds) was allocated to education.

By splitting solicitation mailing expenses between fundraising and education, fundraising percentages can be made to look smaller. A better measure of real fundraising expenses can be found in the contracts between the Watson and Hughey Company and their clients. The 1987 W&H contract with AICR provides for the following schedule of payment (not including postage) for letters to people who've never previously responded to an AICR mailing:

$18.00 per thousand prospect letters for the first 10 million letters mailed; $9.00 per thousand prospect letters mailed, for the next 5 million prospect letters mailed; $4.50 per thousand for the next 9 million prospect letters mailed. It is anticipated that W&H will not be requested to mail in excess of 24 million prospect letters.[17]

For mailings to previous AICR contributors, the fee was set higher: $30 per thousand pieces mailed for the first 400,000, $10 per thousand for the next 400,000, and no charge for further contributor mailings.

AICR's donor base grew to more than 3 million individuals in 1988.

Project CURE (a.k.a. Center for Alternate Cancer Research), another Watson and Hughey client, had a much more expensive arrangement. Their five-year contract, which began June 1, 1987 (four days before the charity, along with the National Emergency Medicine Association, yet another W&H client, was banned from raising any more money in West Virginia pending their proper registration in that state*), called for payment of $50 per thousand prospect letters mailed and $100 per thousand contributor letters—plus $60 for each thousand names W&H supplies from its subsidiary, the Washington List Company. No less than seven mailings would be made annually; no less than 500,000 prospect letters would be mailed.[18]

A contract Watson and Hughey made on July 19, 1984, with the Committee against Government Waste was slightly better: $40 per thousand prospect letters mailed, and $80 per thousand contributor letters. Contributor mailing costs would also include a creative fee for each Contributor File Package created, depending on how many contributors were in the file: $2,500 for under 25,000 contributors, up to $6,000 for contributor files of 100,000 and over.[19] The better contract terms, however, could not prevent disaster in 1987: direct mailings brought in $60,768, but payments to W&H were $31,069 and the total expense of the mailings was $88,379—the committee lost $27,611 on its fundraising mailings.[20]

*West Virginia state charity officials reported in July 1990 that Project CURE and NEMA were still not registered to solicit in that state. The decision not to solicit in West Virginia was apparently made by the nonprofits themselves and was not due to any state action.

The United Cancer Council's five-year contract with Watson and Hughey (dated June 11, 1984) called for fees of $50 per thousand prospect letters mailed and $100 per thousand contributor letters mailed. Creative costs were limited to $2,500 for files under 50,000 contributors and $5,000 for files of 50,000 and up.[21]

As with several other W&H contracts, solicitation costs would be paid out of gross receipts from the mailing itself. W&H therefore had a financial incentive to send out more and more mailings to help pay for expenses. According to Briggs of the UCC:

> In 1986, I recall discussions that UCC donation envelopes were warehoused, unopened, at Washington Intelligence Bureau for six weeks or more. That, and other items discussed in correspondence between UCC and W&H, would seem to indicate that the UCC campaigns were generating more numbers of responses than the "caging house" was able to handle and that W&H procedures, in-house, for handling the volume of business weren't up to the challenge. The same series of letters show a trend toward better staff and procedures, as W&H grew to be able to perform.[22]

About 15 million households had received the 1985 mailings, according to the UCC.[23]

While "stridently" urging UCC to adopt other fundraising methods,[24] W&H tried several techniques to ensure large response rates. Bill-like "Fund Statements," like those used in AICR mailings, were sent out. In 1986 a mailing was sent out on stationery resembling a federal government letterhead, with a return address of "Treasurer's Office, 665 Fifteenth St., NW, Washington, D.C." It was a dummy mail drop.[25] Jerry Watson (the Watson of Watson and Hughey) reportedly said of the technique, "It works. It's better than not doing it."[26]

The mailings that seemed to draw the greatest response were sweepstakes offers. They were also, however, the mailings that drew the greatest negative response—from UCC member agencies; a few resigned UCC in protest, while others expressed misgivings.[27]

The sweepstakes at first offered chances to win a mink coat or a Chrysler LeBaron. Later versions of the sweepstakes featured instant cash prizes. Most people who entered the contest offering $5,000 sent in their suggested contribution of five dollars and thought that they had a chance at winning a top prize of $5,000. In fact, the cash prizes *totaled* $5,000 per mailing. "The top prize of $10 was given to five people," Randall Grove, executive director of UCC at the time, told a reporter for the *Washington Post*. "Everyone else gets something. It could be just a check for a few cents."[28]

Similar sweepstakes mailings were sent out by W&H for Project CURE and the Committee Against Government Waste. In the case of the latter, at least one name on the mailing list was shared with the United Cancer Council mailing list.[29] Interestingly, UCC's mailing list was the property of W&H and it was "free to use the names and addresses . . . in any way it so desires and for any purpose it may so determine."[30]

In late 1988 the sweepstakes idea was used with a new twist: millions of households received letters from a lawyer informing them that they had "won a cash prize in the . . . $5000 sweepstakes." These lawyer notification letters, prepared by Watson and Hughey, were sent out under the names of the Cancer Fund of America (Knoxville, Tennessee), the Cancer Association of Tennessee, the Walker Cancer Research Institute (Aberdeen, Maryland), and the Pacific West Cancer Fund (Seattle, Washington). As with the controversial UCC sweepstakes mailings of 1986 and 1987, the $5,000 figure referred to was an award total; those who received the lawyer notification letter most often received a check for *forty cents* after sending in the suggested voluntary contribution.

Outraged recipients of checks worth less than the cost of an airmail stamp contacted their state charities offices, and investigations began around the country. More than a dozen states initiated some kind of proceedings, either administrative actions or lawsuits, against Watson and Hughey, the charities that sent out their sweepstakes mailings, or lawyers who had signed the prize-notification letters. The charges often involved alleged violation of various consumer-protection and charity laws. A House transportation subcommittee held hearings on the deceptive fundraising practices, a Senate antitrust subcommittee also investigated, and inspectors of the U.S. Postal Service impounded reply letters, alleging that the letters misrepresented the sweepstakes.

On June 20, 1989, the U.S. Postal Inspection Service reached a consent agreement with the four charities, one of the lawyers who signed some of the letters, the Watson and Hughey Company, and Byron C. Hughey and Jerry C. Watson, whereby donors would receive a refund of their donation upon request.[31] The consent agreement also ordered the charities to hire an escrow agent who would send each contributor a letter outlining the procedure for requesting a refund. The charities sent out identical letters; the Cancer Fund of America letter said in part:

> You recently responded to a letter . . . notifying you that you had won a prize in the "Cancer Fund of America $5,000 Sweepstakes." It has been brought to our attention by the U.S. Postal Service that the mailing may have been misleading. While we do not agree, we want to make you aware of several facts. The . . . mailing was mass mailed to millions of people and the cash prizes awarded were between $100 and $.10, with most of the prizes being $.40. No person receives a check for $5,000; that is the total amount distributed to all who respond.[32]

Errol Copilevitz, an attorney for Watson and Hughey, points out that "if there's anything fascinating with the cases, it's that the packages that Watson and Hughey were using are not uncommon in a for-profit arena." He says that the W&H charity-sweepstakes mailings were similar to a magazine-sweepstakes mailing he's discovered, which was sent out on bank stationery. The central question, he feels, is "Do you treat a promotion by a nonprofit differently than one by a commercial concern? There is no answer to that."[33]

The states that took actions in response to the sweepstakes mailings judged the charities using a standard based on distribution of funds received. The Minnesota attorney general's office determined that in 1987 most of the health charities involved in W&H sweepstakes had spent less than 3 percent of revenues on research or patient services.[34] Copilevitz, who argued and won a case before the Supreme Court that overturned a state law requiring fundraisers to reveal how they spent the money they raised, finds fault with this standard: "If you valued everything on dollar efficiency, you'd never have any new groups." He also takes issue with the idea of using a blanket set of standards without taking into account the method of fundraising or the history of the group: "I think it takes a charity three to five years to build a donor base, and the groups were within that."[35]

Most of the cancer charities involved in the sweepstakes cases were relatively new or were embarking on their first large-scale direct-mail fundraising campaigns. The Cancer Fund of America was established in 1988; the Pacific West Cancer Fund was incorporated in the fall of 1987; and the Walker Cancer Research Institute was begun in January of 1981.[36] Although the United Cancer Council was begun in 1959, its highest fundraising expenses occurred during the second year of direct-mail solicitations.

Citing "all of the legal challenges by attorneys general," the board of the American Heart Disease Prevention Foundation, another W&H client, terminated its contract with Watson and Hughey in January 1989.[37] In July of 1990, a year and a half later, Copilevitz said, "I would look for the bulk of it [the state cases] to be settled by the end of the year."[38] Most of the states that took action had banded together in a "global settlement project" to reach a common agreement.[39]

One of the charities involved in the sweepstakes, the Cancer Fund of America, had an unusual arrangement with another charity which had ended its association with Watson and Hughey a year earlier, the American Health Foundation. Under a February 1988 agreement, the Cancer Fund of America agreed to assume the American Health Foundation's fundraising debts to Watson and Hughey, in return for CFA getting exclusive rights to the trade name "Cancer Prevention Project," a fundraising device created by Watson and Hughey for the foundation.[40] Apparently money raised by CFA was applied to the debt incurred by AHF; one charity was substituted for another, but the fundraising mechanism continued and Watson and Hughey got the money due them. According to James T. Reynolds, president of CFA: "We did mail in 1988 using the CPP name. To the best of my knowledge, we mailed to approximately 127,000 of the American Health Foundation names . . . having only a 5 percent response."[41]

Of particular concern to several states was the Pacific West Cancer Fund, which was named in the Missouri suit. It was incorporated in Delaware, used a telephone answering service in Seattle, and contracted with a Louisiana management consultant—yet it had no staff. The fund's management consultant was Donald G. Tarver, who was listed as president of the United Cancer Council in the Council's 1987 annual report.[42]

Coincidentally, in October 1988 the United Cancer Council's board of directors voted not to renew their contract with Watson and Hughey.[43]

During 1988 UCC paid W&H $999,527 for their work: contributor-file mailings elicited contributions totaling $11,215,016 and, after expenses, provided UCC with $1,930,909; donor-acquisition mailings elicited contributions totaling $16,533,347 and, after expenses (which were lumped with administrative costs), resulted in a *deficit* of $78,020 which W&H was to pay UCC.[44] By the end of 1988, over 7 million households had received UCC mailings, but the largest single donor contribution was $6,000—from W&H.[45]

It was only a matter of time before the UCC's demise. Margery Heit-brink of the National Charities Information Bureau says one factor may be UCC's methods of raising funds. She points out that many of the solicitations used to build up its mailing list were sweepstakes. "Our understanding is that these people are not very good renewal prospects," she said.[46] They're more interested in the prize than in the sponsoring group's cause.

Nearly thirty years after the United Cancer Council was formed as a result of a dispute between the American Cancer Society and some of its affiliates, UCC board secretary Briggs sees sinister forces at work, saying that "the 'fine Italian hand' of other cancer groups might be detectable in the surge of negative publicity that at first hit UCC and later involved other W&H clients."[47] Copilevitz seems to agree: "Don't ever underestimate the fact that many of [the W&H clients] were set up as alternate cancer-treatment programs." He also distances Watson and Hughey from the fate of the United Cancer Council. "You understand that their financial troubles came about after they left Watson and Hughey."[48]

Briggs, too, doesn't fault the for-profit professional fundraising firm that made a name for the UCC. "If we'd spent $25,000 and hired a lobbyist" to counter the watchdog groups and bad publicity, "we might now be an eight- or nine-figure agency. It's not fair to say Watson and Hughey caused the death of the United Cancer Council."[49]

☐ 4 ☐

USING PLASTIC FOR A GOOD CAUSE—HOW AFFINITY CARDS WORK

■ BY THE 1980S, issuers of charge cards were running up against the law of diminishing returns in their direct-mail solicitations. By 1988, the average American owned 7.8 credit cards.[1] With little to distinguish one card from another, apart from fees and charges, there was no firm way to predict if Customer A would choose one card over another. Customers were fickle and might cancel one card if a solicitation for a more promising piece of plastic appeared in the mail; only constant solicitation and offers of new and better gimmicks and benefits could hold some customers.

That's why many card issuers sat up and took notice when the American Express Company used a little-known marketing method to raise money for the restoration of the Statue of Liberty. It was a sort of profit-sharing called cause-related marketing, and the vehicle they used was something called an affinity card.

An affinity card is a charge card marketed to a group of people who share a defined interest or hobby, perhaps members of an organization or customers of a company. The card often sports the group's name or logo, and provides the affinity group's beneficiary with a financial reward.

In 1983, American Express announced it would begin a program to benefit the Statue of Liberty restoration through the use of its charge cards. A penny was to be set aside from every charged purchase, and a dollar would be donated for most new cards issued in the United States.

Nearly $2 million was raised by this means. It was a windfall for the statute, and bankcard (VISA and MasterCard) issuers saw it as a torch lighting the way to prosperity: AmEx card usage had risen 28 percent in one quarter over the same quarter a year before, and the number of new cardholders shot up by over 45 percent.

The race to sign up or create affinity groups began, and it was to be a fast race. Between 1985 and July 31, 1988, the number of VISA and

31

MasterCard affinity-card programs shot up from 23 such programs to 2,599.[2]

It's easy to see why. Affinity-card arrangements are a symbiotic relationship between all three parties in the transaction: the nonprofits, the banks and other companies that issued the cards, and the consumer-contributors:

■ *Nonprofits* are able to raise money without having to hire another staff member. The group's financial reward is proportional to the number of new cardholders enrolled (a percentage of the annual fee) or to actual card usage (a royalty payment for each transaction using the card), or both. In some cases, membership dues can be collected automatically by billing member cardholders' accounts, thus increasing membership renewal and reducing its expenses.

■ The *card issuers,* which had watched acquisition costs for new card accounts rise higher and higher over the previous few years, had a way to break the law of diminishing returns and get away with it. Their solicitation expenses for new customers are greatly reduced by the use of the nonprofit's targeted mailing list.

■ *Consumer-contributors* had a way to donate to their favorite causes "painlessly." In fact, the affinity group's clout could sometimes gain the consumer a waiver of the first year's annual fee, lower interest rates, or even a longer grace period.

In a typical affinity-card program, the nonprofit group provides a copy of its membership or contributor list to a card issuer (often a bank). The people on the list are sent a solicitation mailing, at the card issuer's expense, offering a special new charge card.

Merchants who accept credit cards pay a fee of 3 percent on credit-card transactions, which is split between the merchant and the card-issuing bank. Generally, the merchant builds this fee into the price of the items you buy.

Affinity cards differ from ordinary charge cards in one key respect. The card-issuing bank splits its 1.5 percent cut three ways—a half of a percentage point each goes to itself, to the affinity group, and to a marketer who has brokered the deal and done the promotion. (The affinity card offered by Working Assets, a for-profit firm specializing in socially responsible investing, pays five cents per transaction to a collection of thirty charitable groups; UNICEF and Special Olympics get twenty-five cents per transaction for their cards.)[3] In addition to (or instead of) the transaction royalty, nonprofits may receive a portion of each annual fee, a set amount per transaction, or a set amount per new card issued.

The card issuers, despite having their fee income cut by two-thirds, benefit from the affinity programs. According to a VISA Custom Mark Program promotional booklet, not only do typical responses to affinity solicitations of all types (nonprofit and for-profit) range from 3 to 8 percent (a tremendous success for any direct-mail solicitation), but "Affinity group members typically are more affluent, use their bankcards more often, and charge more on them than traditional cardholders." This is borne out in the case of the Sierra Club affinity program, whose cardholders charge an average of $3,600 per year, as compared with an average of $2,000 per year charged by cardholders using regular bank cards.[4]

There's another, unexpected benefit, according to Juanita Beasley, senior vice-president at NCNB Texas National Bank: people pay their bills on time. "There is a perception among people that someone in this affinity group, which they love and feel dearly about, will know if they pay late," said Beasley. "That's not true, but they still have a lower delinquency rate."[5]

Who started it all? While American Express's 1983–86 Statue of Liberty campaign was certainly the first large-scale, fully publicized effort, Affinity Group Marketing, Inc., claims that its founder, David C. Mann, created the first true affinity card sporting a group's logo (the American Express cards whose use supported the Statue looked like any other AmEx cards). Mann's creation was the VISA "Educard," issued in 1984 for the benefit of the American Federation of Teachers.[6] Daniel G. Finney, a spokesman for MNC Financial Inc., parent company of Maryland National Bank, claims that since 1982 MNC has made agreements with more than 700 affinity groups (about 95 percent of their 4 million credit-card customers are members of these affinity groups).[7] American Express pushes its claim back to 1981 by pointing out an attempt to increase its market share in California that year by offering donations to a local charity as an incentive to use its card not just for foreign travel but for local use as well.[8] But that claim is predated by an American Automobile Association VISA card offered in 1978.[9]

Whoever proves to be the originator of the idea, its continued application seems assured. Stephen Bartell, director of MasterCard's ID Plus Program, predicts that "by the year 2000 there will *only* be affinity cards." MasterCard itself added 233 affinity-card programs in 1986, and signed on 628 more in 1987, for a total of 13 million new cardholders serviced by

175 banks in 1988. VISA was equally successful, having gone from 63 new programs in 1986 to 825 in 1987, and bringing in an additional 13 million cardholders through its 1,100 individual programs in 1988.[10]

No small part of VISA's growth was due to its affinity program with the International Olympic Committee, begun in 1987. The boost from the Olympics affinity program gave VISA five successive quarters of increased growth for the first time since 1983.[11] VISA sales in the Christmas season rose 28 percent over 1986. The goal was a total contribution of $2 million to the IOC, based on one to two cents per transaction.[12]

MasterCard's major affinity effort was the "Choose to Make a Difference" campaign, which donated $2.8 million to six national causes in 1987. It was revived the following year to donate in the fourth quarter of 1988 (October 1 to December 31) a guaranteed minimum of $150,000 to each of six groups: the Alzheimer's Association, Just Say No International, the American Red Cross, the American Heart Association, the National Committee for Prevention of Child Abuse, and the American Cancer Society.[13] Seven-tenths of 1 percent of each transaction would be donated by Master-Card, raising its contribution to $3 million. Cardholder balloting would determine the distribution of contributions to the six groups.

Who is gaining the most from these affinity-card programs? MasterCard and VISA certainly experienced huge jumps in their national enrollment figures, and MasterCard pledged to devote almost its entire fourth-quarter advertising budget of $15 million to publicizing its program.[14] But that advertising budget is *five times as much* as what they intended to contribute to all six groups. So MasterCard could have cut its advertising budget by a fifth and contributed an equivalent amount directly to the nonprofits in their affinity programs—doubling the amount the charities got.

"The line separating marketing and philanthropy in some corporations is beginning to get blurred," observes Warner J. Canto, Jr., a vice-president for marketing communications at American Express. "Building your business on the shoulders of human suffering is kind of iffy. That should be part of a philanthropic program, not a marketing campaign."[15]

Notice also that the causes embraced by the VISA and MasterCard national affinity programs are what might be called "sexy causes."* The

*The IOC and "Choose to Make a Difference" programs were for *all* VISA cards and MasterCards, whether or not they had a special imprint or logo. Smaller affinity programs for each card are often associated with lesser-known causes.

MasterCard program linked itself with fights against drug abuse, child abuse, cancer, heart disease, and Alzheimer's disease, and in favor of disaster relief. Likewise, the VISA program is associated with international sports competition. Each of those causes calls to mind an instant association—visual and, perhaps, personal. That "sexiness" is fodder for emotional "image" advertising which can be used to differentiate one credit card from another by linking it to something other than interest rates and annual fees.

Keeping the consumer's attention off interest rates and annual fees is crucial, because interest rates and annual fees are the Achilles heel of affinity cards. In 1988 the average rate for regular credit cards was 18.5 percent; affinity cards came in somewhat lower, at 17.8 percent.[16] Annual fees, which are often waived as an enticement to acquire a particular affinity card, resume after the first or second year, at the standard amount. Yet at that time there were two nationally available bankcards (Simmons First National in Arkansas, and People's Bank of Connecticut) with interest rates below *twelve* percent, and charging an annual fee of less than $25.[17]

Some affinity cards arrange to contribute to an organization only a portion of the interest collected on unpaid balances. In other words, the charity benefits only if members go into debt; it collects nothing from "convenience" users (those who pay off their bills in full each month). Approximately 40 percent of all credit-card users fall into that category.[18]

Another matter to consider is the proliferation of affinity cards. For affinity programs which base their charitable contribution on the number or amount of transactions, a consumer with more than one affinity card is a big problem. Imagine an individual who makes ten charges a month over the course of a year, earning a charitable contribution of five cents per transaction. At the end of the year, that charity sponsored by the card earns six dollars. It's not much, but it was gained without any fundraising cost to the nonprofit. If those ten charges a month were split between eight affinity cards (remember, the average American has 7.8 charge cards of all sorts), each nonprofit would only get seventy-five cents.

One danger of a reliance on affinity products for fundraising is that contributors may feel they've already made their donation to a group and need not give any more. Unfortunately, six dollars—let alone seventy-five cents—would never appear as a suggested gift on any contribution form sent out by a charity or nonprofit.

Then there's the matter of the charitable tax deduction a cardholder can take on the amount of money contributed through an affinity program: *there is no deduction.* Technically, the card issuer is the party making the contribution to charity. The cardholder never takes possession of the money generated in the affinity-card transaction, so she or he cannot consider the six dollars a personal contribution to charity when it comes to paying taxes.

For most people, then, affinity cards are not exactly the "win-win" product advertised. If an affinity card doesn't offer tangible benefits greater than or equal to other cards, it's probably better to find a less expensive charge card and contribute the difference to your favorite organization. "Convenience" users of charge cards who pay off each bill completely at the end of the month, and therefore don't worry about interest rates, might have reason to get an affinity card, but only if the card's annual fee is reasonable and the group is not earning money *only* on account-debt interest. Those who do get affinity cards should limit their number to make certain each beneficiary will get a respectable percentage of total spending (an additional "conscious" contribution, charged on the card, is also a good idea).

Despite the problems for contributors and some pitfalls for the nonprofits themselves, the continued success of affinity programs breeds competition and new programs, even for for-profit groups.* By 1990 there were affinity cards in circulation for American Airlines, AT&T, Subaru, the NFL, the NHL, the New York Yankees, the AFL-CIO, various county Republican or Democratic parties, *Star Trek,* and USA Wrestling. There's even an Elvis MasterCard, offered by the Memphis-based Leader Federal Savings & Loan (featuring a photo of Elvis singing, it donated a portion of the revenues and fees to the Elvis Presley Memorial Foundation).[19]

American Express, which opened the affinity-group floodgates, now rarely engages in cause-related marketing in the United States, where the market appears saturated. There's also the matter of card acceptance: American Express is at a fundamental disadvantage, as VISA or MasterCard are each accepted at about four times as many establishments. So, American Express has turned from America and shifted its attention to fresher horizons through programs in foreign countries. The latest affinity campaign from the company that helped finance the restoration of the Statue of Liberty is in Mexico, where American Express expects to raise at least $50,000 toward restoration of the Aztec pyramids at Teotihuacan.[20]

*This is surprising, considering a September 30, 1988, VISA Custom Mark Tracking Report. It said that the 1,346 programs approved by that time had resulted in 6,072,406 accounts by second quarter 1988. However, this was less than one-third of the total number of accounts *projected* for year 2 of these programs.

For sheer fundraising ambition, though, the champion appears to be the proposal for an affinity card to help fund the U.S. Space Station. Given a present cost estimate of $30 billion for the spacecraft, and a typical affinity group's 0.5 percent cut of each charge, a total of *$6 trillion* would have to be charged on the affinity cards. That's about $24,000 charged by every man, woman, and child in America.

Talk about astronomical spending.

□ 5 □

CAUSE MARKETING
AND THE "BAND AID" SOLUTION

■ **WHILE DIRECT MAIL** and affinity cards raised money from carefully defined slivers of the population, charities and nonprofits also benefited from mass marketing techniques. In particular, "cause-related" or "joint-venture" marketing took the idea behind affinity cards—turning normal consumer purchasing into a source of contributions—and applied it to the *object* of the transaction. In cause marketing a company donates to a charity a part of the price of every product or service sold. The marketing effort (paid for by the company, not the charity) is *not* limited to the organization's membership list; anyone who buys the product or service aids the program.

Like affinity cards, cause marketing is said to be a win-win situation: charities get more money; companies get greater sales; consumers contribute painlessly while getting something they'd probably buy anyway.

Although informal local promotions have existed for years, Kentucky Fried Chicken took it national in May 1979 with a formal cause-marketing program: 50 cents was donated to the March of Dimes for every bucket of chicken bought.[1] By 1985, when General Foods distributed coupons for Tang breakfast drink and promised to donate 10 cents per proof-of-purchase to Mothers Against Drunk Driving, cause marketing was an established success for both cause and market. The Tang program produced $100,000 for MADD and increased sales of Tang by 13 percent.[2]

Cause-marketing efforts continue to multiply. Quality International's program contributes $2 to the American Lung Association every time a room is booked through its special no-smoking number: 800-228-LUNG.[3] Working Assets, a for-profit firm which administers a socially responsible money-market fund, puts money into a pool shared by over thirty organizations. The donation pool includes money from affinity cards, 2 percent of travel reservations made on an 800 telephone number, and 1 percent of all long-distance telephone calls made by customers of a special Sprint program.[4] Sales of Ben & Jerry's Ice Cream contribute 1 percent for peace projects. And several smaller companies have voluntarily imposed a "Green Tax" on their products to raise money for environmental concerns.

Some operations exist almost solely for charitable purposes. Since August 1982, Paul Newman and A. E. Hotchner's Salad King Inc. and Newman's Own Inc. foods (salad dressing, popcorn, lemonade, and spaghetti sauce) have donated all profits to charity. By 1986 profits had totaled about $15 million.[5]

Scott Paper Company developed a separate product line, called Helping Hand: for each item sold, a nickel goes into a fund for the southwestern U.S. affiliates of six national charities fighting children's diseases. One-fourth of the money is split evenly among the groups; the rest is divided in proportion to the amount of money each affiliate raised in public contributions for the year.[6]

Coupon programs, however, still seem to be the favorite. In October 1988 a Sunday newspaper advertisement with six coupons for Stayfree feminine hygiene products offered the opportunity to help the Shelter Aid program: ten cents per redeemed coupon would be donated to support a toll-free hotline operated by the National Coalition against Domestic Violence, up to a total of $525,000.[7] That same year, 3M promised a quarter per coupon redeemed (maximum $300,000) to benefit the U.S. Olympic Team; V8 Vegetable Juice and Campbell's Soup promised up to $150,000 to support the March of Dimes by donating fifteen cents per coupon; Johnson and Johnson gave five cents per coupon to the Association for Retarded Citizens; and the Jimmy Dean Meat Company promised $50,000 to Reading Is Fundamental in a program that donated books when buyers sent in proofs of purchase. The Easter Seal Society stood to gain up to $1 million in cause-marketing contributions from Glenbrook, makers of Bayer aspirin, Midol, and Phillips milk of magnesia, in a program that had produced $300,000 or more each year since 1983.[8]

At first the numbers are impressive, but don't let them obscure the true nature of the contributions. The money to promote cause-marketing programs typically comes from advertising and marketing budgets, and the advertising produces sales, upon which the contributions depend. Meanwhile, total corporate giving (of all types) in the United States was *down*, in fact, during the second part of the decade: corporate contributions, measured in constant 1982 dollars, fell from $3.83 billion to $3.56 billion between 1985 and 1988 (but figures for individual, bequest, and foundation giving all *increased*).[9] According to Jerry C. Welsh, executive vice-president of American Express, "Cause-related marketing is not philanthropy. It is marketing in the public interest."[10] Maurice G. Gurin, president of the Gurin Group, a fundraising counseling firm, concurs: "A corporate contribution is a philanthropic gift because it involves no quid pro quo and entails some sacrifice. A philanthropic gift should cost the donor something; it should not provide the donor with a profit." Cause marketing is "a business transaction, since it is based on a financial return to the corporation."[11]

Cause marketing is being used by corporations trying to hold onto or increase their market share, or penetrate new markets. Just as affinity cards increase bankcard usage by capitalizing on a predisposition of contributors to help a particular cause, so cause marketing uses high ideals to increase bottom lines. Unfortunately, nonprofits are then tied to the vicissitudes of the marketplace, depending not only on the popularity of the product or service with which they are linked but also on the popularity of their own particular cause. "When marketing determines philanthropy," asks Jon Pratt of the Philanthropy Project in Minneapolis, "will only the marketable causes get help?"[12]

Worse, will some groups co-opt their goals when faced with the lure of easy money and publicity? Burt Knauft, executive vice-president of Independent Sector (and formerly head of Aetna's corporate social-responsibility program) fears groups "may sacrifice their ideals to fit the image this corporation has in mind for 'its' charity."[13] As Donald Sexton, a professor at the Columbia Graduate School of Business, puts it, a nonprofit must ask itself, "Will we lose more in image than we gain in income?"[14] Some environmental organizations have responded to this concern by turning down corporate contributions from polluters.

So far, cause marketing hasn't taken over. A 1988 Independent Sector survey of seventeen businesses and thirteen nonprofits found that less than 10 percent of total nonprofit revenue came from cause marketing.[15] Still, the questions about this risk to charities' independence can't be ignored: Why cause marketing?

More important, Why *now*?

The answers lie in a tangle of demographics relating to givers. People aged 55 to 64 give more than any other group, and those who are 65 to 74 give more than average.[16] However, due to a fifteen-year dip in the U.S. birthrate during the 1930s and early 1940s, these groups face less than average growth.[17] They will also be faced with increasing medical costs, which could cut into the amount of money available for contributions.

The age group that appears to hold the greatest future potential for giving and volunteering is the baby-boomers. At present, according to a survey from Yankelovich, Skelly, and White, adults aged 30 to 55 give only 1.7 percent of their pretax income to charity, as compared with the 2.4 percent given by all adults. However, according to a survey by Mediamark Research, people in the 45–54 age group volunteer 42 percent more than the average adult.[18] Projections from the Gallup Organization estimate that boomers' donations will increase from $361 billion in 1985 to $387 billion in 2000.[19]

The problem for nonprofits is that much of the boomer generation is in transition. Contributions by a given age group tend to increase only after they have put down roots in a community, but, having delayed marriage and children, boomers are only now settling down. Debts from college loans and high-interest mortgages still burden many of them.

Cause marketing, affinity cards, and other such efforts are ideal for attracting this constituency. In place of contributions solicited from a fixed location (as is the case with direct mail or even door-to-door solicitations), cause-marketing donations occur in the normal course of buying, regardless of location. They're also "painless" donations: you don't have to consciously sign a check or make a pledge. It's an extra "value" to consider when making a purchase, and an extra benefit from a product or service. Given the buying power of the boomer generation and its media savvy, cause marketing is a natural way for nonprofits to capture the interest of new donors as they age into the prime giving years.

There is another boomer characteristic which was exploited seriously by the nonprofit world during the 1980s: love of rock music.

Toward the end of 1984, Irish rocker Bob Geldof saw something on TV that broke his heart and boiled his blood: pictures of famine in Ethiopia. He decided to do something about it. He and Midge Ure wrote a song called "Do They Know It's Christmas?" gathered a group of British music stars (dubbed Band Aid), and recorded the single. Sales of the benefit record raised money to feed the famine victims.

Within two years of Geldof's first, modest effort, pop charities had brought in $242.9 million in contributions.[20] According to Harvey Goldsmith, England's most important concert promoter and one of the catalysts behind Live Aid, Geldof's worldwide benefit concert, "Live Aid has changed the face of causes and music. Organizations call us every day for help because they know rock is an effective way to reach young people . . . that there is a receptiveness."[21]

Peter Gabriel, a performer who has appeared at many benefit concerts, agrees. "There is a radical change between the peace events of the sixties—which were idealistic, but impotent—and the eighties, which are much more physical and practical and, I think, better anchored. It has a much better chance of making a difference."[22]

One reason for the increased effectiveness is that the technology was ready. By the 1980s global satellite telecasts, a novelty when the Beatles performed "All You Need Is Love" during a 1967 transatlantic broadcast, were commonplace. Music videos had turned rock music into a daily feature of television, which was increasingly being programmed by boomers. Fund-raising techniques pioneered by Jerry Lewis's Muscular Dystrophy Telethon and Lou Rawls's Parade of Stars for the United Negro College Fund were well established and pointed the way to mass appeals with corporate sponsors and cause-marketing programs.

There was also the very real power of mass media to encourage contributions. Radio and television preachers weren't the only ones to recognize this ability to influence audiences. Back on New Year's Day in 1965, Soupy Sales, host of a live New York children's TV program, was left on the air with about a minute to go and no more material. He started to ad-lib and asked his young viewers to go into their sleeping, hung-over parents' rooms and retrieve "green pieces of paper" from their wallets without waking them. He directed the kids to send the money to him at the station, and he promised to send them "a postcard from Puerto Rico."

He got $80,000. It was all play money, except for one dollar from a twenty-eight-year-old girl who had seen his show and wrote, "You oughta go to Puerto Rico."

In 1988, Ron Chapman, a Dallas disk jockey, made a similiar on-air request: "Write a check payable to KVIL Fun and Games. in the amount of $20 and mail it to this address." KVIL got $244,240—in *real* money. According to the FCC, there was no fraud because no promises were made. The station donated the money to charities and civic projects.[23]

With such technological factors on his side, Geldof's success was almost inevitable. "Band Aid didn't need to raise money," says Michael Norton, who heads London's Directory of Social Change. "The news media, especially TV, raised it for them. Band Aid just needed to provide a channel for the money to flow in."[24]

Geldof's famine-relief efforts provided vast channels for that money. Proceeds from sales of records, tickets, T-shirts, souvenir books, and other merchandise quickly piled up. The initial Band Aid recording raised almost $10 million worldwide. Two Live Aid concerts, in London and Philadelphia on July 13, 1985, brought in $65 million from Britons and Americans and $17 million from people in twenty-one other nations. Then Geldof organized Sport Aid, a May 1986 effort by athletes around the world, which raised an estimated $15 million.[25] Other musical fundraising efforts inspired by Band Aid ranged from Classical Aid (classical musicians in Geneva) to Hear 'N' Aid (hard rock musicians).

Shortly after Geldof's first effort, Harry Belafonte, Quincy Jones, and Kenny Rogers assembled forty-five of America's biggest names in pop music after the 1985 American Music Awards ceremony to sing "We Are the World" under the banner of the trio's newly formed USA for Africa Foundation. That record grossed $51 million. The next year USA for Africa produced Hands Across America, a charity event that benefited U.S. programs for the hungry and homeless, and which unfortunately was held the same day in May 1986 as Geldof's Sport Aid.[26]

Live Aid was an unprecedented worldwide outpouring of charity. Although Joan Baez, a performer at the event, likened the global concert to Woodstock, it had stronger ties to Woodstock's predecessor, the nonprofit Monterey Pop festival of June 16–18, 1967, a benefit concert for the Los Angeles Free Clinic.[27]

There were many precursors of Band Aid and Live Aid throughout the previous two decades of rock music. A late 1960s benefit record for the World Wildlife Fund sported a Beatles contribution, "Across the Universe." George Harrison's August 1971 Madison Square Garden Concert for Bangladesh raised millions for famine relief, but lost much of the money to American and British taxes. John Lennon was headliner at a benefit concert in the early 1970s to raise money for One-to-One, a charity benefiting retarded children in New York, and Paul McCartney headlined a late 1970s benefit concert for Kampuchea. British comedians and musicians performed together in the late 1970s (The Secret Policeman's Ball) to benefit Amnesty International. In America, the No Nukes concerts of 1980 (featuring Jackson Browne, James Taylor, and Bruce Springsteen) raised money to support safe energy.[28] In 1984, during his Born in the USA tour, Springsteen made a point of visiting local food banks and Vietnam veterans' groups and leaving generous donations. But perhaps the real godfather of it all was Harry Chapin. Famous from his mid-1970s song "Taxi," Chapin soon became interested in hunger issues. He founded World Hunger Year, performed numerous benefit concerts to raise money for local hunger-relief efforts, and lobbied Congress for more domestic food aid.

Live Aid's telethon of fifty-two acts, beamed to 500 million TV sets in 100 countries, helped spur contributions to other groups. In Britain, more established charities were at first skeptical of Geldof's efforts. However, the generosity unleashed by Band Aid also filled their coffers: figures compiled by the Charities Aid Foundation showed that fifteen British-based "international agencies" raised nearly three times as much—£179 million—in 1984–85 as eleven had raised in 1983–84.[29]

The pop charities expanded into other concerns. Following a comment from Bob Dylan* during the Live Aid concert about the need to help farmers in America, a Farm Aid concert was organized later in 1985 in Champaign, Illinois. Money raised by the benefit set up food banks and shelters, and helped retrain displaced farmers. That same year a mix of artists from Miles Davis, Bob Dylan, and David Ruffin to Rubén Blades, Lou Reed, Bono, and Bruce Springsteen were gathered by Springsteen's former bandmate, Little Steven, to record the "Sun City" benefit single to help aid anti-apartheid efforts in South Africa.[30]

In 1986, Amnesty International staged the "Conspiracy of Hope" concert tour in the United States to raise money and awareness of that group's human-rights efforts. The concerts brought 100,000 new members to Amnesty. Two years later, the 1988 Human Rights Now! world tour traveled to five continents and many cities that rarely see major Western rock concerts (such as New Delhi, India, and Harare, Zimbabwe), celebrating the fortieth anniversary of the Universal Declaration of Human Rights.[31]

In March 1986, the first annual Comic Relief concert to help the homeless was organized in Los Angeles. Besides its array of comedy talent and the fact that Home Box Office picked up the entire $2 million production tab, Comic Relief was unusual among pop charities in that its vice-president, Dennis Albaugh, actually had some experience raising funds for an established charity, United Way.[32]

Britain's 1988 Comic Relief Day, which sought funds for African famine relief and London's sick and homeless, raised more than $3.5 million by selling millions of red plastic clown noses. Everyone from prison guards and milk carriers to BBC broadcasters and Prince Andrew sported

*Dylan has also contributed money to worthy causes through his Seacoast Foundation.

a scarlet schnoz. Even an airplane leaving Belfast on a morning flight to London wore a huge red nose.[33]

But not all such concert or record efforts are so much fun. Some Amnesty International directors around the world were uncomfortable with the idea of corporate underwriting of the $20 million cost of their Human Rights Now! informational concert tour.* The corporate sponsor (eventually Reebok put up the money) had to agree to strict guidelines and endure a lengthy examination of its business practices. "We didn't want to go into a country and have someone get up and say, 'Did you know that company does so and so?'" said Franca Sciuto, chair of Amnesty's international executive committee. "That kind of incident could really damage us as an organization."[34]

The 1988 Freedomfest concert was faced with a different problem. It was staged in London's Wembley Stadium as a seventieth-birthday party for Nelson Mandela. Proceeds would be split between the Anti-Apartheid Movement's campaign to free the imprisoned Mandela and seven children's charities in South Africa. Several performers complained when the Fox network, which broadcast the concert in America, deleted all references to the South African government's system of apartheid. Still, the Anti-Apartheid Movement doubled its membership to more than 15,000.[35]

Even USA for Africa had problems. On December 24, 1986, seven months after its Hands Across America project, USA for Africa received a public "demand" from the National Coalition for the Homeless to release $15 million of the project's net income. The 5.5 million Americans who participated in the effort to form a transcontinental line of linked hands (there were gaps in the line) were asked to contribute $10 apiece, but HAA grossed $33 million, and had $16 million in expenses.[36]

Pop charities, like cause-marketing efforts and affinity cards, aren't always a godsend. It's important to consider the beneficiaries of any of these efforts. First and foremost, the charity or nonprofit should truly gain from the use of a particular fundraising method. If cause marketing is being used as a substitute for corporate philanthropy, or if a ticket for a benefit concert is bought with no thought of further contributions to the cause, then the nonprofit is not getting maximum benefit. Likewise, a million-dollar adver-

*Proceeds from the tour paid for expenses. By design no money was earmarked for Amnesty, so the tour events were *not* benefit concerts. However, the group did sign up new members at concerts and publicized the fortieth anniversary of the Universal Declaration of Human Rights.

tising budget to support a program which will ultimately give away only half that amount has its priorities mixed. The corporate sponsor seems more interested in keeping its own name in the news than in truly helping the charity. The ideal would be to combine purchases of cause-marketed goods and services or use of affinity cards with concerted giving.

But whatever happens, cause marketing and benefit concerts and records seem to be here to stay. By the end of 1989 Bob Geldof was said to be re-recording "Do They Know It's Christmas?" to aid another famine crisis in Africa; another Farm Aid concert was held in early 1990; and in May 1990 (about four months before his Labor Day telethon), Jerry Lewis appeared in a Sunday color supplement ad for Sanka coffee, promising to donate 25 cents per redeemed coupon to the Muscular Dystrophy Association, up to $500,000.

□ 6 □

CHARITY GOES ABROAD—
LEARNING A NEW TRADE

■ SOME INTERNATIONAL CHARITIES and nonprofits are making their dollars go further by swapping red ink for green. They're buying up portions of Third World debt in exchange for local currency to help with their projects in those countries.

Debt-swapping is an innovative method of cooperation most often carried out between First World banks, Third World governments, and international environmental or development groups. The swaps arose out of the desire of many Third World nations to keep their currency within their own borders. Any money sent out of the country might be used to call in some of the nation's scarce reserves of hard Western currency to pay off the billions of dollars of debt the nation owes in loans.

There are actually three main debt-swapping deals being negotiated by brokers for various nonprofits these days: blocked-fund purchases; debt-for-development; and debt-for-nature.

Blocked-fund purchases, the simplest procedure, involve an American corporation operating in a Third World country and avoid banks completely. Because of the desire of a given cash-starved nation to keep its money in its borders, it may block the transfer of the local profits (or other funds) of an American corporation. A charity with a program within the same country may approach the American corporation with the following deal: the corporation's foreign operation will pay the charity's foreign operation all of the money in question; in return, the charity will pay the American corporation the discounted face value of the currency in U.S. dollars. The corporation is able to repatriate some of its funds (where before it had all but written off any hope of seeing the money), and the charity earns a profit in the transaction and doesn't have to worry about losses due to unfavorable exchange rates. And the money stays in the Third World country.

Debt-for-development deals involve American and Third World banks. As in the example above, the Third World nation is not releasing its money. It is in debt to American banks for loans, however, and the banks here are anxious to retrieve the money they lent out. A charity can offer a deal to buy up a portion of the Third World nation's debt (at a discounted rate) in exchange for money made available for the charity for its work in that country. American banks, faced with vague promises by the nation to pay sometime in the future, are willing to take less than face value on debts to get U.S. dollars now. The difference in the dollar values goes to the charity involved in the deal, minus a fee charged by the nation involved in the swap. Once again, the local currency stays within the Third World nation. And American banks have an added incentive: the Internal Revenue Service has ruled that they can write off a portion of their donations of debt as a charitable deduction.

Debt-for-nature swaps take the process one step further. Many Latin American debtor nations are trying to achieve economic growth and pay off their debts by destroying tropical rain forests and other delicate ecosystems in their development of land. This destruction will render many rare species of plants and animals extinct, and since the forests use up carbon dioxide and release oxygen in great quantities, will ultimately contribute to the greenhouse effect. In a debt-for-nature swap, the Third World bank provides funds either to fund conservation programs or to buy up parcels of land for parks and wildlife refuges within the country.

In 1988 the U.S. branch of the World Wildlife Fund arranged a $3 million three-year debt-for-nature swap in Costa Rica to support the country's national parks. The Costa Rican government's Central Bank agreed to exchange the debt for local-currency bonds to be held by Fundación Neotrópica, a Costa Rican conservation group, and similar local conservation groups. Interest from the bonds will support the parks.[1]

"Debt-swapping is the most important tool to achieve conservation," Mario Boza, executive director of the Fundación, told *Science* magazine. "You multiply money by five. It's a lot of money that's free. We can use it to buy land, pay personnel, and do everything. It's an incredible scheme." At the time of the deal (March 1988), the going rate for Costa Rican debt was 17 cents on the dollar (by the end of the year it was down to 12.5 cents). The bonds issued to the Fundación and other groups were worth 75 cents for each dollar of debt retired. The bonds could then be used as collateral by the groups, and draw 25 percent interest.

The transactions provided the World Wildlife Fund with up to six times as much value for its dollars—your dollars—as would direct investment in the local economy.

Similar successes have been noted by debt-for-nature deals involving the Nature Conservancy in 1988 ($9.2 million for efforts in Costa Rica, Ecuador, the Andes, the Amazon, and the Galapagos Islands), WWF in 1989 (about $6 million for projects in Ecuador and the Philippines), and Conservation International in 1987 ($650,000 worth of Bolivian debt bought for $100,000 for nature reserves in that country).[2] The largest arrangement considered so far has been a 1988 proposal by a Brazilian environmental group (Fundação SOS Pro Mata Atlántica) to swap $100 million of that country's debt (funded by U.S. foundations) to protect 772 square miles of estuary and lagoon on Brazil's southern coastline.[3]

Other debt-related transactions have produced extra income for child sponsorship and other international charities. Debt-for-development deals, primarily in Brazil, provided nearly 3 percent of the Christian Children's Fund's $92 million budget in the year ending June 30, 1988.[4] A single 1988 debt-for-development swap with Citibank produced a net "profit" of $228,000 for use by Foster Parents Plan in the Philippines, the equivalent of signing up about 863 new $22-a-month sponsors for a year.[5] Techno-Serve and the Salvation Army have worked with blocked funds. Nearly 6 percent of the Salvation Army's 1988 overseas budget was funded through debt and blocked currency deals.[6]

There are, of course, dangers to debt arrangements. Changes in governments can negate promises for long-term funding for a nature park, and desperate governments might just print more money (raising inflation) to solve their debts. USA for Africa reportedly pulled out of a currency deal in the Sudan because they were afraid of giving foreign companies a means of withdrawing their investments totally from that country.[7]

However, as governments of debtor nations stabilize and interest continues to add up, debt-related transactions involving charities (only a tiny portion of the total number of deals) will probably increase. New debt-related deals may even arise in Eastern Europe. Poland was considering proposals with Citicorp in 1988.[8] As details emerge about industrial pollution throughout Eastern Europe, we may see proposals to fund clean-up efforts through deals benefiting emerging democracies now looking for the means to retire their debts.

The possibilities seem as large as the mountains of debt.

250 Charities
and
How They Use
Your Money

□ 7 □

HOW TO READ THE PROFILES

■ E A C H O F T H E 2 5 0 profiles that follow aims to help potential donors make informed decisions about their contributions. The group's name, address, and phone number are listed, and whether contributions are tax-deductible. Often there's also an indication of the group's size (e.g., number of members, offices, or people served) and a "Little-Known Fact," plus a summary of the opinion of the National Charities Information Bureau (a major charity watchdog group) and a partial list of state charities-registration offices to contact for more information. Appendix A lists groups by their cause.

Most of the groups chosen for this section are national or international organizations. They were selected from the lists of national organizations producing the most inquiries at two charity watchdog groups, from direct-mail solicitations, from news reports, and from the *Encyclopedia of Associations, 1990 Edition.* Your own favorite charity may not be among the groups profiled, but omission from this list *in no way* has a negative significance.

Nearly all of the profiles appear in alphabetical order. However, there are three notable exceptions: (1) If a group is named for a person (say, the Will Rogers Memorial Fund), it's alphabetized under the last name of the individual rather than the first letter of the organization's name. (2) In the interest of showing the relationship between two separate-but-related groups (like Sierra Club and Sierra Club Foundation), profiles of these groups are shown face-to-face. This has caused some profiles to be moved up in the alphabetical ordering to make room for the change in layout. (3) Groups are listed under their proper names (for instance, the Red Cross is actually listed as "American National Red Cross"). If a group seems to be missing, look under *American* so-and-so or *National* so-and-so. If it still can't be found, it's probably not listed at all.

Generally, religious groups, hospitals, educational institutions, and cultural organizations such as museums and theaters are not profiled in this book. Most of them have local constituencies (or, like colleges, restricted ones) and don't make nationwide appeals for funds. A few that do, however, are included.

A few words about the category headings used in the profiles and what they mean:

■ **CONTRIBUTIONS** are tax-deductible for most of these groups, but not for a few of them. This distinction will be important to you only if you itemize your deductions on your tax return.

■ **PURPOSE.** When considering any organization, you should know some background. Here's where you'll find the group's founding date, a little history, and the basics of its reason for existing.

■ **SIZE.** Sometimes the budget doesn't give a clear idea of a group's size, and it is helpful to know something about number of chapters, countries, or whatever.

■ **INCOME.** Figures for total income in a given year (either a calendar year or a fiscal year different from the calendar year) include contributions from *all* sources. Your dollars are added to donations and grants from corporations, foundations, federal and state agencies, and income deferred from a previous year.

Information in these profiles comes from public sources, as openly available to you as to the author. The IRS requires all nonprofit groups to submit form 990—except for religious groups, and even some of them file. Although the financial information listed on the 990 form often does not conform to "generally accepted accounting principles," it is a commonly defined system of presenting data about the finances of charities and nonprofits. For most of these profiles, the main source of financial data was their form 990. In certain cases, the main source was the independently audited statement, next the annual report, or third, New York State form 497 (another financial disclosure form available to the public).

The document listed in parentheses after the income amount is the source for that figure and nearly all of the expense figures, too. A fuller listing of sources of income and expense figures can be found under the heading "Financial Data."

■ **HOW THEY USE YOUR MONEY: PROGRAM, PAYMENTS TO AFFILIATES, OVER-HEAD, AND FUNDRAISING.** These four expense categories are crucial to understanding the priorities a group places on the use of your contributions. Bear in mind that their relationship to each other varies from year to year, and one expense may even be intertwined with another.

PROGRAM: Most of your money should go to carrying out the program of your charity, the work it does to accomplish its mission. But program expenses are not as clearly defined as you might think. A cancer charity that sends out a fundraising letter on stationery imprinted with the seven warning signs of the disease might consider part of the production costs of the letter a public-education expense. After all, readers of the letter will see the warning signs of cancer, and publication of that health information helps further the goals of the charity. The American Institute of Certified Public Accountants (AICPA) issued a ruling in 1987 (SOP-87) outlining how the joint allocation of costs for such a mailing could be determined, but not all charities follow the AICPA ruling. Fundraising mailings that occasionally take advantage of the presence of an interested audience to educate the public make business sense; so do educational newsletters or magazines that include a coupon for contributions. However, contributors should be aware that extreme allocations of the costs of such dual-purpose mailings exist. Details of the joint allocation of costs for a given group are included in a footnote at the end of the profile.

PAYMENTS TO AFFILIATES: IRS form 990 has a separate category for such expenses, distinct from program, but many national headquarters raise funds for an entire network of affiliates. The situation is similar to the relationship between the federal and state governments: your federal income taxes fund the federal government, but on occasion, some money is sent down the line to state governments to work on problems at *their* level. (Affiliates of charities and nonprofits, like state governments, can also raise money on their own.)

Much and in some cases most of what is listed as "payments to affiliates" is in fact funds used for programs at the affiliate level. A group's national headquarters can be more effective in funding research, for instance, while a state or local affiliate might be better for direct services. Both functions advance the purpose of the group, but in different ways. Therefore, payments to affiliates are grouped with program expenses in the pie charts, but appear as a separate paragraph after the program-expenses section of the profiles.

OVERHEAD: Management and general expenses, administrative costs, and many other items used for the day-to-day functioning of the organization are listed as overhead costs. For the most part, this category includes items that are not associated directly with programs, payments to affiliates, or fundraising efforts. Depreciation, plant costs, losses on sales or liquidations of assets, relocation costs, and any other extraordinary items (often one-time expenses) are usually given separate expense-category headings both in the text of the profile and in the pie chart.

FUNDRAISING: You have to spend money to get money. The efficiency with which this fact of nonprofit life is handled is often the gauge most people use to judge a group's effectiveness. Direct-mail fundraising, as seen in Chapter 2, is an expensive method of raising funds. Yet some groups, usually newer charities and nonprofits without name recognition, prefer this means of raising money to grassroots, door-to-door soliciting. It's a gamble for many groups, but when it pays off, the income is great. Affinity cards, cause marketing, and benefit records and concerts require little or no fundraising expense, yet their effectiveness varies even more than that of direct mail.

As seen above, sometimes fundraising efforts can have part of their cost allocated to program expenses. Membership-development costs are also a gray area. Informing present and potential members about a group's work could be considered part of public education, and therefore a program expense; but membership fees are also part of income, so the costs of material sent to members might be considered fundraising expenses. Should membership-development costs be considered part of program or of fundraising? In cases where a group specifically includes membership development as a category of program expenses, that practice is honored in the profiles; where it is a separate category, the dollar figures are noted separately in both text and pie chart.

■ **EXCESS OR DEFICIT.** Ideally, an organization's budget would be balanced, with income equaling expenses. A modest excess or deficit is normal in the real world, but a large one needs an explanation.

Organizations planning for major future expenses may hold off some spending for a given year, leaving an excess of funds at the end of a fiscal year. The construction of a new headquarters or the planned purchase of land will often lead a group to raise more money than it intends to spend in a single year. For example, the Nature Conservancy purchases land for conservation. Each year it buys and maintains thousands of acres of ecologically significant land, but it also keeps in reserve money to buy lands unexpectedly put on the market. By maintaining an excess, the group is actually aiding its purpose, even though it's not spending all its income for a given year.

If a group's excess is greater than 25 percent of total income for the year, an explanation is offered in the profile. A new organization, for instance, may have a large excess if it raised a lot of money before settling into routine operations. Older groups may register large excesses if their income figures include money put aside for an endowment rather than day-to-day operational expenses.

Deficits, on the other hand, may appear when a major program expense (such as a sudden natural disaster or an unpredicted political confrontation) occurs during one year, while the fundraising campaign to offset its cost doesn't bear fruit until the following fiscal year. Deficits may also arise from: changes in interest rates, exchange rates, or fiscal years; depreciation due to sale of unprofitable assets; or the start-up costs of a new office or fundraising campaign.

An appreciable deficit (or an appreciable excess figure) should not be taken as an automatic sign of fiscal mismanagement. Unlike commercial establishments, which can adjust inventories or sales to fit market conditions, nonprofits rely to a certain extent on secondhand market forces (inflation, for instance, affects personal income and that, in turn, may affect contributions) and often cannot make adjustments in income as quickly. However, if you find what you feel is a significant deficit or excess in an organization's financial statement, it is perfectly correct to make inquiries.

■ **LITTLE-KNOWN FACTS.** This optional profile category provides room for that unusual background material usually buried in an annual report or in the closing paragraphs of a news article—sometimes amusing, sometimes telling.

■ **RATINGS:** The National Charities Information Bureau (NCIB), one of two charity watchdog groups (the other is the Philanthropic Advisory Service of the Better Business Bureau), has permitted us to publish a summary of their findings in the profiles of groups they examine. These reports are regularly updated, but aren't necessarily based on figures for the latest fiscal year. Therefore, note the year for which the group was analyzed: what's true in 1990 may not be true for 1991.

NCIB reports are current as of the date they are released, but are subject to change at any time. Contact NCIB for the latest report on an agency covered in this book. (NCIB's address is listed in Chapter 1.) Keep in mind that exclusion of a group from NCIB's, PAS's, or this book's list of nonprofit groups does not *in any way suggest a negative significance.*

On July 1, 1988, NCIB began using a revised set of their standards, so some report summaries refer to the eightfold (old) standards and some to the ninefold (new) ones; both sets of standards are included in Appendix B. On January 1, 1991, NCIB will begin to apply a similar set of nine standards, with further revisions to ensure greater accuracy of reporting. These standards are an extension of those listed in Appendix B; an example of the greater accuracy of the 1991 standards is noted in Appendix B. *None of the reports cited in this book use the 1991 standards.*

■ **REGISTRATION.** Most states have Freedom of Information Acts or other laws that make registration forms and charities' IRS form 990 or independently audited statements available to the general public. Further information about the groups discussed in this book (including, in some cases, copies of the documents noted above) can be obtained from the states noted here. State registration numbers are given, when known, for the groups. Refer to them when contacting the state offices listed in Appendix C.

For most groups this is only a *partial* list of states where they are registered. A state affiliate, rather than the national office, may be registered in a given state, and not mentioned here. Revisions of state charities laws, changes in a group's fundraising territory, or the opening or closing of state affiliates may also affect registration in a particular state. If there is no listing for your state, contact your state charities-registration office to discover if the group is registered under an affiliate's name.

If the registration category for a group has no listing at all, contact the charity itself or the Internal Revenue Service for information. (Generally, requests for information from the IRS take longer than requests from a state office.)

■ **FINANCIAL DATA.** Here is a more complete listing of the sources for financial data found in the text of a given profile and in the pie-chart illustration. Footnotes, and some Little-Known Facts dealing with money, may have a different source than the other expense figures listed in the profile. (Readers should be aware of this distinction, as figures for those sections may come from the use of slightly different accounting methods.)

■ **THE PIE CHARTS.** Financial data are presented a second time in each profile, in graphic form. The pie charts show the percentage of total income for each expense category when there is an excess, and the percentage of total spending when there is a deficit; the deficit is given in a caption as a percentage of total spending. NCIB and PAS have certain standards as to the minimum percentage a group should spend on program. The U.S. Supreme Court, on the other hand, has ruled three times in the last decade (most recently in 1988)[1] that it is unconstitutional for such standards to be established in law. When considered in context, along with the other information provided in the profiles, the pie-chart percentages can be a useful tool for making a decision. For instance, NCIB recommends at least 60 percent of total spending should be for program expenses. This figure can serve as a benchmark to compare two groups' spending during the same year (as long as you remember that percentages can vary from year to year). You should note, however, that the percentages in some pie charts will not add up to 100 percent. (They have been rounded off to the nearest one-tenth of a point.) Also note that the IRS form 990 and NYS form 497 have different ways of looking at "payments to affiliates": the IRS considers this expense a separate line-item (the pie chart shows a new piece); NYS adds this line to other "program" figures for "total program expenses" (so the pie chart has a larger "program" slice). The sum of program and payments-to-affiliates expenses, therefore, appears in a small box next to the chart. Very large excesses will also be briefly explained in a small box.

Finally, when examining financial data, remember the difference a year can make in income and spending. Consider the effect of the Supreme Court's July 1989 decision in *Webster v. Reproductive Services,* one of the most important abortion cases heard by the court in recent years and a direct challenge to the 1973 *Roe v. Wade* decision, which had legalized abortion. Both pro-choice and pro-life forces actively campaigned for their views to be heard, filed briefs, and raised much money on fears and hopes.

Webster's repercussions on the 1989 revenue of the National Abortion Rights Action League, a pro-choice organization, were impressive. The first big jump in revenues occurred in May, probably due to publicity surrounding massive pro-choice rallies in April, when the case was argued at the Supreme Court. At the biggest rally, in Washington, D.C., NARAL volunteers made a "census" of attendees and increased their mailing list significantly in the process (all names and addresses collected at the rally were for people who were friendly to an appeal from groups like NARAL). The next big jump occurred in July, when the court rendered its opinion on *Webster,* limiting the availability of abortion and returning many policy prerogatives to the states (thus money was needed by forces on both sides of the abortion debate to influence opinion in states where existing laws might be in jeopardy). The last jump in revenues occurred in November, an election month and soon after the Court's announcement in October that it would accept three more abortion cases during the new term. Total revenues for NARAL, NARAL Foundation, and the NARAL Political Action Committee nearly *tripled,* from $4,345,298 in 1988 to $12,174,259 in 1989.

So, be mindful that while the financial information in the profiles can be helpful in your decisions as a contributor, the picture can change drastically within a single year.

But, by all means, give.

Account for POW/MIAs, Inc.
280 Wheatley Rd.
Old Westbury, NY 11568
(516) 626-0800

- **CONTRIBUTIONS** are tax-deductible.
- **PURPOSE:** Founded in 1984 by former Long Island Congressman John LeBoutillier, Account for POW/MIAs (also known as Skyhook II Project) seeks an accounting of the fate of Americans missing in action or made prisoners of war in Southeast Asia, and humane treatment for them.
- **INCOME:** $524,789 (year ending 1/31/89, NYS form 497).
- **HOW THEY USE YOUR MONEY:**
  PROGRAM: $264,217.
  OVERHEAD: $85,097.
  FUNDRAISING: $138,915.
- **EXCESS:** $36,560.
- **RATINGS:** As of June 1, 1990, NCIB had requested but not received sufficient information for a report.
- **REGISTRATION:** NY (53381).
- **FINANCIAL DATA:** Text and chart source was their NYS form 497 covering the year ending 1/31/89.

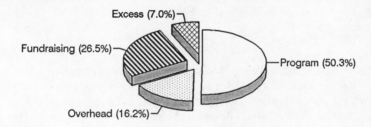

61

Accuracy in Media
1275 K St., N.W., Suite 1150
Washington, DC 20005
(202) 371-6710

- **CONTRIBUTIONS** are tax-deductible.
- **PURPOSE:** Accuracy in Media was founded in 1969 to monitor accuracy (and liberal or left-wing bias) of news-reporting activities by the media. Some members of the AIM board also sit on the boards of the Council for the Defense of Freedom and Accuracy in Academia. AIM performs certain services free of charge and pays certain expenses (some of which are reimbursed) for these groups.
- **SIZE:** Over 28,000 members in 1988, but Executive Secretary Donald Irvine reports that "If there is any problem that we face it is in retaining members, as some 40 percent neglect to renew."
- **INCOME:** $1,841,700 (year ending 4/30/89; accrual accounting, IRS form 990), of which $1,468,778 came from direct mail. Apart from a slight dip in 1985, during the preceding four fiscal years support had been increasing.
- **HOW THEY USE YOUR MONEY:**
PROGRAM: $883,018: spent on disseminating information on "the deficiencies of news media reporting." The AIM Legal Aid Fund, intended to finance litigation against news media for deficient or biased reporting, was closed during the year; its $3,719 was transferred to the AIM general fund.
OVERHEAD: $579,188.
FUNDRAISING: $339,894.
- **EXCESS:** $39,600.
- **LITTLE-KNOWN FACTS:** During 1989 *AIM Report,* the group's semimonthly newsletter, criticized what it perceived as biased news reporting on several other nonprofit groups, including the Christic Institute, the Consumers Union of the United States, and the Natural Resources Defense Council. As a regular feature, *AIM Report* provides names, addresses, and pre-addressed postcards to send to individuals, advertisers, editors, publishers, and network officials who are mentioned.
- **RATINGS:** NCIB reported (12/4/87, using figures from the year ending 4/30/87) that AIM met old standards 2, 3, 5, 6, and 8, but not standards 1 and 7, and that "there is inadequate information on which to make a determination with respect to standard 4."
- **REGISTRATION:** NY (49427).
- **FINANCIAL DATA:** Text and chart source was their IRS form 990 covering the year ending 4/30/89.

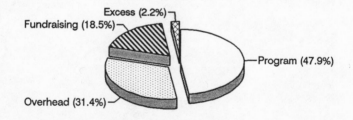

Excess (2.2%)
Fundraising (18.5%)
Program (47.9%)
Overhead (31.4%)

The Africa Fund
198 Broadway
New York, NY 10038
(212) 962-1210

- **CONTRIBUTIONS** are tax-deductible.
- **PURPOSE:** Founded 1966 to support the struggle for African freedom by informing Americans about apartheid and southern Africa generally, working for concerned U.S. policy, and aiding victims of apartheid, South African political
prisoners, and refugees in Africa and the United States.
- **INCOME:** $810,034 (calendar 1988; accrual accounting, IRS form 990), includ-
ing an unspecified amount in royalty payments from Artists United against
Apartheid, a musical collaboration that produced the album and single *Sun City*
in 1987, for a restricted anti-apartheid fund.
- **HOW THEY USE YOUR MONEY:**
  PROGRAM: $560,365*:
  - $136,961* on research and education to produce and disseminate informa-
  tion on topical African issues.
  - $371,404 for aid for African causes ($362,465 in the form of grants and
  allocations to several organizations).
  - $52,000 for aid to war refugees in the form of medicines, food, clothing,
  and other materials.
  OVERHEAD: $31,135.
  FUNDRAISING: $28,464.
- **EXCESS:** $190,070.
- **LITTLE-KNOWN FACTS:** The fund sponsors the weekly half-hour TV news pro-
gram *South Africa Now,* seen on PBS and cable stations across the country, to
supply news about South Africa despite government censorship in that nation.
- **RATINGS:** NCIB reported (5/6/86, using figures from calendar 1984) that the
fund met all eight of NCIB's old evaluation standards.
- **REGISTRATION:** IL, NJ, and NY (40544).
- **FINANCIAL DATA:** Text and chart source was their IRS form 990 covering 1988.

*The Africa Fund allocated $3,141 for some publicity costs (allocated to program expenses) and a
portion of the $50,181 allocated to research and education was used for temporary help and a brochure
for the *Sun City* project. (Little Steven Van Zandt, an organizer of the project, is a member of the fund's
advisory committee.)

Excess (23.5%)
Fundraising (3.5%)
Overhead (3.8%)
Program (69.2%)

Africare, Inc.
440 R St., N.W.
Washington, DC 20001
(202) 462-3614

■ **CONTRIBUTIONS** are tax-deductible.

■ **PURPOSE:** Established in 1971, Africare carries out development projects throughout Africa—first in western Africa (Mali and Niger), later in southern Africa (1978), eastern Africa (1980), and central Africa (1983). Education and outreach programs have also been undertaken in the United States since 1971.

■ **SIZE:** More than 200 programs in twenty-one African nations.

■ **INCOME:** $12,105,655 (year ending 6/30/88; accrual accounting, IRS form 990). During the preceding four fiscal years support had been increasing.

■ **HOW THEY USE YOUR MONEY:**
PROGRAM: $9,837,035:
  • $3,049,292 for agriculture and small-scale irrigation.
  • $2,020,158 on water-resources development.
  • $1,657,200 on integrated rural development.
  • $1,386,568 on relief and refugee assistance.
  • $1,091,194 on health programs (malnutrition, immunization, medical supplies and treatment).
  • $632,624 on general support of program activities.
OVERHEAD: $2,446,644.
FUNDRAISING: $126,317.

■ **DEFICIT:** $304,341.

■ **LITTLE-KNOWN FACTS:** Ever wonder whatever became of the money raised by Band Aid and USA for Africa? Several Africare projects in FY88 were supported by those two musical fundraisers: Burkina Faso (4 USA), Chad (2 USA), Mali (3 USA, 2 BA), Niger (1 USA), and Senegal (1 USA).

■ **RATINGS:** NCIB reported (4/17/87, using figures from the year ending 6/30/85) that Africare met all eight of NCIB's old evaluation standards.

■ **REGISTRATION:** DC, NY (44975), PA, and VA (11).

■ **FINANCIAL DATA:** Text and chart source was their IRS form 990 covering the year ending 6/30/88.

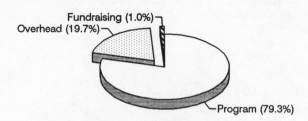

Fundraising (1.0%)
Overhead (19.7%)
Program (79.3%)

Due to deficit of 2.5%, chart is based on spending, not income.

AIDS Project Los Angeles
6721 Romaine St.
Los Angeles, CA 90038
(213) 962-1600

- **CONTRIBUTIONS** are tax-deductible.
- **PURPOSE:** Active since 1982; provides and promotes vital human-support services to persons diagnosed as having AIDS or AIDS-related complex, as well as training and technical assistance to professionals and educational programs and information to the general public.
- **SIZE:** Receives more than 5,000 calls a month on its hotline.
- **INCOME:** $8,899,091 (year ending 6/30/89; independently audited statement). During the preceding four fiscal years, support increased—over 500 percent between FY84 and FY85.
- **HOW THEY USE YOUR MONEY:**
  PROGRAM: $7,141,736: support for persons with AIDS or AIDS-related complex, and to public and professional education.
  OVERHEAD: $560,272.
  FUNDRAISING: $1,116,339.
- **EXCESS:** $80,744.
- **LITTLE-KNOWN FACTS:** Two out of the four people who began AIDS Project Los Angeles have themselves died of AIDS.
- **RATINGS:** No NCIB report.
- **REGISTRATION:** CA (51766).
- **FINANCIAL DATA:** Text and chart source was their independently audited statement covering the year ending 6/30/89.

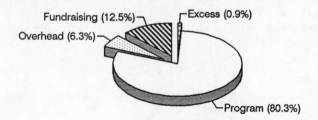

Fundraising (12.5%)
Overhead (6.3%)
Excess (0.9%)
Program (80.3%)

ALSAC–St. Jude Children's Research Hospital
Box 3704
Memphis, TN 38173
(901) 522-9733 • (800) USS-JUDE

- **CONTRIBUTIONS** are tax-deductible.
- **PURPOSE:** ALSAC (American Lebanese Syrian Associated Charities) was founded by Danny Thomas in 1957 to raise funds to operate and maintain St. Jude Children's Research Hospital (they have a common board of directors). St. Jude conducts basic and clinical research on catastrophic childhood diseases (primarily childhood cancer), and provides all patient care associated with its work. ALSAC and the St. Jude Hospital Foundation (formed in 1951 to solicit funds to build the hospital) are affiliated fundraising organizations, solely concerned with raising money to operate and maintain the hospital. No child has ever been refused admission for financial reasons.
- **INCOME:** $126,782,035 (year ending 6/30/89; annual report).
- **HOW THEY USE YOUR MONEY:**
  PROGRAM: $56,355,398.
  OVERHEAD: $13,157,637.
  FUNDRAISING: $17,082,972.
- **EXCESS:** $40,186,028. In addition to the money spent on program expenses, the hospital spent $21,662,000 in 1989 on construction of facilities and equipment used in providing program services. About $91,200,000 will ultimately be required to complete the current construction.
- **LITTLE-KNOWN FACTS:** St. Jude's infectious-diseases department is conducting research on pediatric AIDS.
- **RATINGS:** As of June 1, 1990, NCIB was preparing a new report.
- **REGISTRATION:** NY (46722), TN, and VA (64).
- **FINANCIAL DATA:** Text and chart source was their annual report covering the year ending 6/30/89.

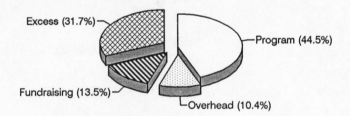

Excess (31.7%)
Program (44.5%)
Fundraising (13.5%)
Overhead (10.4%)

ALS Association
21021 Ventura Blvd., Suite 321
Woodland Hills, CA 91364
(818) 340-7500 • (800) 782-4747

- **CONTRIBUTIONS** are tax-deductible.
- **PURPOSE:** In 1985 the National ALS Foundation (founded in 1972) and the Amyotrophic Lateral Sclerosis Society of America (founded in 1975) merged to form ALS Association, now the only national organization dedicated solely to fighting amyotrophic lateral sclerosis (also known as Lou Gehrig's disease), a progressive fatal neuromuscular disease. The association engages in research and education, and it helps ALS patients and families through referrals for counseling, training, and support.
- **SIZE:** 140 chapters and support groups nationwide.
- **INCOME:** $2,722,859 (year ending 1/31/90; annual report covering the national headquarters only).
- **HOW THEY USE YOUR MONEY:**
PROGRAM: $1,969,629:
  - $767,944 for research.
  - $732,900 for patient and community services.
  - $468,785 for public and professional education.
OVERHEAD: $229,673.
FUNDRAISING: $388,785.
- **EXCESS:** $134,772.
- **LITTLE-KNOWN FACTS:** Next to Lou Gehrig himself, the most famous ALS patient is Dr. Stephen Hawking, a British theoretical astrophysicist whose work has been compared with that of Albert Einstein. Dr. Hawking, who has miraculously survived twenty-five years of progressive loss of motor functions, visited the ALS Association support group in Santa Barbara, California, on its first anniversary.
- **RATINGS:** NCIB reported (9/21/89, using figures from the year ending 1/31/89) that the ALS Association, national headquarters only, met all nine NCIB standards.
- **REGISTRATION:** NY (49817) and VA (2733).
- **FINANCIAL DATA:** Text and chart source was their annual report (for the national headquarters *only*) covering the year ending 1/31/90.

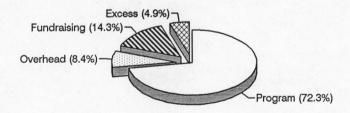

Excess (4.9%)
Fundraising (14.3%)
Overhead (8.4%)
Program (72.3%)

Alzheimer's Association
70 East Lake St., Suite 600
Chicago, IL 60601
(312) 853-3060 • (800) 621-0379 • (800) 572-6037 (in Illinois)

- **CONTRIBUTIONS** are tax-deductible.
- **PURPOSE:** Founded in 1980 to combat Alzheimer's disease and related disorders through research (to find the cause, treatment, and cure for the disease), public education, and professional education; and by representing, before government and social service agencies, the continued-care needs of the affected population.
- **SIZE:** More than 30,000 volunteers in nearly 200 U.S. communities.
- **INCOME:** $11,037,212 (calendar 1987; restricted fund by cash accounting, all other funds by accrual accounting; IRS form 990). During the preceding four fiscal years support had been increasing.
- **HOW THEY USE YOUR MONEY:**
  PROGRAM: $6,850,025:
  - $2,640,772 (including $2,240,037 in grants and allocations) for research.
  - $2,340,467 for public awareness and education.
  - $1,158,708 (including $76,804 in grants and allocations) for chapter services.
  - $439,020 (including $80,500 in grants and allocations) for patient and family services.
  - $271,058 for public policy.

  OVERHEAD: $535,744.

  FUNDRAISING: $1,564,807. The Alzheimer's Association has begun offering MasterCard affinity cards.
- **EXCESS:** $2,086,636.
- **LITTLE-KNOWN FACTS:** In 1987 Yasmin Aga Khan, daughter of actress Rita Hayworth, who suffered from Alzheimer's disease in her final years, was one of four vice-chairmen of the association.
- **RATINGS:** NCIB reported (3/31/89, using figures from calendar 1987) that the Alzheimer's Disease and Related Disorders Association (the old name for the group) met all nine NCIB standards.
- **REGISTRATION:** IL, NJ, NY (54700), VA (2503).
- **FINANCIAL DATA:** Text and chart source was their IRS form 990 covering 1987.

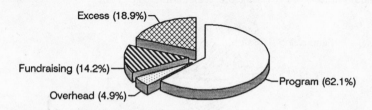

Excess (18.9%)
Fundraising (14.2%)
Overhead (4.9%)
Program (62.1%)

AMC Cancer Research Center
1600 Pierce St.
Denver, CO 80214
(303) 233-6501

- **CONTRIBUTIONS** are tax-deductible.
- **PURPOSE:** The Jewish Consumptives' Relief Society was founded in 1904 in Denver; it merged with the Ex-Patients Sanatorium for Tuberculosis and Chronic Disease, and took its present name in 1955.
- **INCOME:** $7,298,444 (year ending 6/30/89; accrual accounting, IRS form 990). $904,644 resulted from a MasterCard affinity program.
- **HOW THEY USE YOUR MONEY:**
  PROGRAM: $7,544,825:
    - $3,811,382 for the laboratory cancer program.
    - $2,431,332 for the clinical cancer program.
    - $1,302,111 for the national community cancer control programs.
  OVERHEAD: $794,613.
  FUNDRAISING: $886,547.
- **DEFICIT:** $1,927,541.
- **RATINGS:** NCIB reported (4/1/87, using figures for the year ending 6/30/86) that the center met all eight of NCIB's old evaluation standards.
- **REGISTRATION:** CO, NY (12732), and VA (29).
- **FINANCIAL DATA:** Text and chart source was their IRS form 990 covering the year ending 6/30/89.

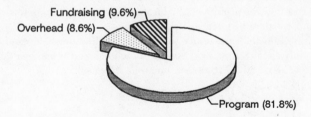

Fundraising (9.6%)
Overhead (8.6%)
Program (81.8%)

Due to deficit of 20.9%, chart is based on spending, not income.

American Cancer Society
3340 Peachtree Rd., N.E.
Atlanta, GA 30026
(404) 320-3333 • (800) ACS-2345

- **CONTRIBUTIONS** are tax-deductible.
- **PURPOSE:** Established in 1913, dedicated to eliminating cancer as a major health problem. Through research, education, and service, the ACS seeks to prevent cancer, save lives of patients, and reduce suffering. During 1988 it spent $12,736,000 to move its national headquarters from New York to Atlanta. By August 31, 1988, $3,500,000, including an Emory University donation of land valued at $2,500,000, had been received to help pay that cost.
- **SIZE:** Besides its national headquarters, the ACS has 57 separately incorporated divisions. Public education efforts reached 50 million Americans, and 631,864 individual patients received services in FY88.
- **INCOME:** $335,758,000 (national headquarters and all divisions, year ending 8/31/88; annual report). During the preceding four fiscal years support for the divisions had been increasing. In 1988 the ACS participated in a MasterCard affinity program, but no specific figures were noted.
- **HOW THEY USE YOUR MONEY:**
PROGRAM: $238,747,000:
  - $89,188,000 for research.
  - $56,973,000 for public education (prevention programs).
  - $42,642,000 for patient services (information, home-care supplies, transportation, rehabilitation and counseling, etc.).
  - $29,144,000 for professional education (for prevention, detection, diagnosis, and treatment of cancer patients).
  - $20,800,000 for community services (rehabilitation, detection, improving community health practices; supporting clinics and other health facilities).
RELOCATION COSTS: $12,736,000 (a one-time expense)
OVERHEAD: $23,821,000.
FUNDRAISING: $48,605,000.
- **EXCESS:** $11,849,000.
- **LITTLE-KNOWN FACTS:** For three years running, ACS-sponsored research resulted in a Nobel Prize for medicine. George Hitchings and Gertrude Elion won in 1988; Susumu Tonegawa and Stanley Cohen won in the two previous years.
- **RATINGS:** NCIB reported (12/14/88, using figures for the year ending 8/31/87), that ACS had met all nine of its standards.
- **REGISTRATION:** NY (4526), headquarters; branches may be registered locally.
- **FINANCIAL DATA:** Text and chart source was their annual report covering the year ending 8/31/88.

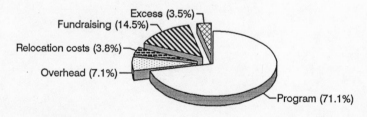

Excess (3.5%)
Fundraising (14.5%)
Relocation costs (3.8%)
Overhead (7.1%)
Program (71.1%)

American Civil Liberties Union
ACLU Foundation
132 W. 43rd St.
New York, NY 10036
(212) 944-9800

■ **CONTRIBUTIONS** to the ACLU are *not* tax-deductible; contributions to the ACLU Foundation are.

■ **PURPOSE:** Founded in 1920, the ACLU has championed a variety of rights included in the Declaration of Independence and the U.S. Constitution—freedom of inquiry and expression; due process; the right to a fair trial; and equality before the law regardless of race, creed, color, national origin, or political opinion. The ACLU defends these rights through court cases, opposition to repressive legislation, and, when necessary, public protests. The ACLU Foundation was established in 1966.

■ **SIZE:** 250,000 members support groups in every state and 200 local communities.

■ **INCOME:** $8,512,403 (ACLU); $8,755,087 (foundation). (Both for calendar 1988; annual report covering both groups.)

■ **HOW THEY USE YOUR MONEY:**
PROGRAM (ACLU): $6,340,607:
  • $4,115,047 for affiliate support.
  • $1,211,361 for education.
  • $679,648 for legislative.
  • $334,551 for civil liberties policy formulation.
PROGRAM (FOUNDATION): $6,542,446:
  • $5,153,207 for legal.
  • $1,197,064 for education.
  • $192,175 for affiliate support.
OVERHEAD: $406,335 (ACLU); $1,352,142 (foundation).
FUNDRAISING: $1,627,434 (ACLU); $753,306 (foundation).

■ **EXCESS:** $138,027 (ACLU); $107,193 (foundation).

■ **RATINGS:** As of June 1, 1990, NCIB was preparing a new report.

■ **REGISTRATION:** MA, NY (9697), PA, and VA (41).

■ **FINANCIAL DATA:** Text and chart source for both groups was their common annual report covering 1988.

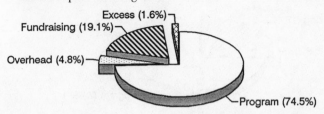

Excess (1.6%)
Fundraising (19.1%)
Overhead (4.8%)
Program (74.5%)

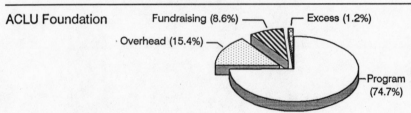

ACLU Foundation
Fundraising (8.6%)
Excess (1.2%)
Overhead (15.4%)
Program (74.7%)

American Cultural Traditions, Inc.
701 E. Main St.
Grand Prairie, TX 75050
(214) 642-6000

- **CONTRIBUTIONS** are tax-deductible.
- **PURPOSE:** Founded in 1981 to "help restore the historic American cultural consensus of traditional Judeo-Christian values, specifically the sanctity of human life, the right to liberty, and the freedom to pursue happiness within the bounds of moral responsibility." ACT works to achieve its goals through the American Coalition for Life (founded 1984; its "Adopt-a-Congressman" project began the following year); *The Washington Report* (founded 1984); and Teen Suicide Prevention Taskforce (founded 1985).
- **SIZE:** ACT's *Washington Report* is broadcast daily over 100 radio stations in 35 states.
- **INCOME:** $2,632,788 (calendar 1988; accrual accounting, IRS form 990). During the preceding four fiscal years support had been increasing.
- **HOW THEY USE YOUR MONEY:**
  PROGRAM: $1,957,360:
  - $1,780,219 for a teen suicide prevention taskforce.
  - $52,653 for the American Coalition for Life (concerned with a wide variety of "human life issues," such as abortion, infanticide, and euthanasia; meets with government leaders on legislative concerns and facts regarding "challenges to the sanctity and value of life").
  - $85,276 for *The Washington Report* (news, commentary, and analysis; broadcasts nationally and distributes a free newsletter):
  - $30,538 for "Adopt-a-Congressman" (educates national leaders "about life issues and coordinating prayer for those same leaders").
  - $8,674 for additional, unspecified grants and allocations.

  OVERHEAD: $147,609.
  FUNDRAISING: $459,062.
- **EXCESS:** $68,757.
- **RATINGS:** No NCIB report.
- **REGISTRATION:** VA (2424).
- **FINANCIAL DATA:** Text and chart source was their IRS form 990 covering 1988.

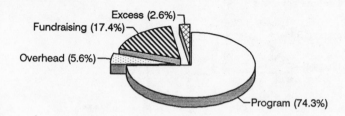

Excess (2.6%)
Fundraising (17.4%)
Overhead (5.6%)
Program (74.3%)

American Enterprise Institute for Public Policy Research
1150 17th St., N.W.
Washington, DC 20036
(202) 862-5800

- **CONTRIBUTIONS** are tax-deductible.
- **PURPOSE:** Founded in 1943, a research and education organization that analyzes issues of national and international concern—economics, foreign policy, defense, political and social processes.
- **SIZE:** Staff of about 100 people.
- **INCOME:** $10,006,541 (calendar 1988; NYS form 497).
- **HOW THEY USE YOUR MONEY:**
  PROGRAM: $5,029,851.
  OVERHEAD: $3,183,398.
  FUNDRAISING: $421,506.
- **EXCESS:** $1,371,786.
- **RATINGS:** As of June 1, 1990, NCIB had requested but not received sufficient information for a report.
- **REGISTRATION:** NY (3903).
- **FINANCIAL DATA:** Text and chart source was their NYS form 497 covering 1988.

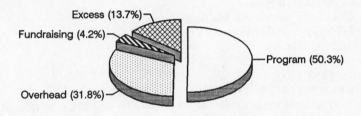

Excess (13.7%)
Fundraising (4.2%)
Program (50.3%)
Overhead (31.8%)

American Foundation for AIDS Research
5900 Wilshire Blvd., 2nd Fl.
Los Angeles, CA 90036
(213) 857-5900
1515 Broadway, Suite 3601
New York, NY 10036
(212) 719-0033

- **CONTRIBUTIONS** are tax-deductible.
- **PURPOSE:** AmFAR, which raises funds for AIDS research and education in the clinical, biological, and social sciences, was created in 1985 as a result of the merger of the AIDS Medical Foundation (founded 1983) and the National AIDS Research Foundation. It does not provide primary ongoing patient care. In June 1990 AmFAR announced two major new programs: one to teach doctors how to conduct local trials of experimental AIDS treatments, and one to fight AIDS in developing countries.
- **INCOME:** $10,334,970 (year ending 6/30/89; independently audited statement).
- **HOW THEY USE YOUR MONEY:**
  PROGRAM: $8,013,500:
  - $3,320,596 for research grants.
  - $2,710,658 for education.
  - $1,412,056 for clinical trials.
  - $570,190 for other program expenses.
  OVERHEAD: $769,628.
  FUNDRAISING: $988,452.
- **EXCESS:** $563,390.
- **LITTLE-KNOWN FACTS:** Much of the initial funding for AmFAR came from a $250,000 advance against royalties for the posthumous autobiography of actor Rock Hudson, who died of complications from AIDS in 1985.
- **RATINGS:** NCIB reported (4/5/89, using figures from the year ending 6/30/88) that AmFAR met all nine NCIB standards.
- **REGISTRATION:** CA (60392), NY (54346), and VA (2371).
- **FINANCIAL DATA:** Text and chart source was their independently audited statement covering the year ending 6/30/89.

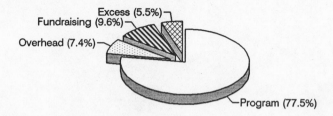

Excess (5.5%)
Fundraising (9.6%)
Overhead (7.4%)
Program (77.5%)

American Foundation for the Blind, Inc.
15 W. 16th St.
New York, NY 10011
(212) 620-2000 • (212) 620-2158 (TDD)
Hotline: (800) 232-5463

■ **CONTRIBUTIONS** are tax-deductible.

■ **PURPOSE:** Established 1921; advocates, develops, and provides programs and services that help blind and visually impaired people achieve independence with dignity in all sectors of society.

■ **SIZE:** In October 1988 the foundation's toll-free hotline received nearly 2,000 calls, the highest monthly total since it began operations in January 1986.

■ **INCOME:** $12,893,392 (year ending 6/30/89; accrual accounting, IRS form 990), including $1,751,546 earned through the sale of aids and appliances developed to help blind persons (e.g., braille watches), and the sale of pamphlets, journals, and textbooks on blindness for the general public and professionals in the field, and $2,480,025 earned through recorded materials manufactured under contract (Talking Books).

■ **HOW THEY USE YOUR MONEY:**
PROGRAM: $11,159,181.
OVERHEAD: $1,579,370.
FUNDRAISING: $1,081,671.

■ **DEFICIT:** $926,830.

■ **LITTLE-KNOWN FACTS:** In May 1989 the foundation entered into an agreement with Xerox Corporation to provide financially deserving blind individuals with low-interest four-year loans (financing 90 percent of the purchase price) to buy Kurzweil Reading Machines, which translate written words into voice.

■ **RATINGS:** NCIB reported (1/22/90, using figures from the year ending 6/30/89) that the foundation did not meet standard 6b, but that it met all other new NCIB standards.

■ **REGISTRATION:** NY (7856) and VA (52).

■ **FINANCIAL DATA:** Text and chart source was their IRS form 990 covering the year ending 6/30/89.

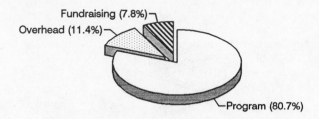

Due to deficit of 6.7%, chart is based on spending, not income.

American Friends Service Committee
1501 Cherry St.
Philadelphia, PA 19102
(215) 241-7000

- **CONTRIBUTIONS** are tax-deductible.
- **PURPOSE:** Established in 1917; engages in religious, charitable, social, and relief work, here and abroad, on behalf of the Religious Society of Friends in the United States (the Quakers), to bring about change through nonviolence.
- **SIZE:** AFSC has a national office, nine regional offices, and over thirty international project offices.
- **INCOME:** $23,028,858 (year ending 9/30/88; accrual accounting, annual report; as an association of churches, the AFSC files no IRS form 990).
- **HOW THEY USE YOUR MONEY:**
  PROGRAM: $15,241,872:
  - $5,733,703 for overseas efforts promoting economic and social justice, international understanding, human rights, and the relief of human suffering.
  - $4,144,716 for efforts toward peace, reconciliation, and disarmament.
  - $3,850,586 for programs examining the causes of violence due to poverty, exclusion, and denial of rights.
  - $1,512,867 for special programs, including $403,207 in grants and allocations to other service agencies.

  OVERHEAD: $3,498,718.
  FUNDRAISING: $2,101,830.
- **EXCESS:** $2,186,438.
- **LITTLE-KNOWN FACTS:** In support of its commitment to broad public education on Middle East issues, the committee joined in the successful legal challenge to the closing of the PLO Observer Mission at the United Nations, and also brought Israeli peace activists to speak in the United States.
- **RATINGS:** NCIB reported (10/6/88, using figures from the year ending 9/30/87) that the AFSC met all nine NCIB standards.
- **REGISTRATION:** VA (54).
- **FINANCIAL DATA:** Text and chart source was their annual report covering the year ending 9/30/88.

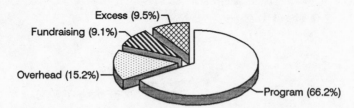

Excess (9.5%)
Fundraising (9.1%)
Overhead (15.2%)
Program (66.2%)

American Heart Association
7320 Greenville Ave.
Dallas, TX 75231
(214) 373-6300

- **CONTRIBUTIONS** are tax-deductible.
- **PURPOSE:** Established 1924; "dedicated to the reduction of disability and death from cardiovascular disease and stroke."
- **SIZE:** There are about 1,800 divisions nationwide.
- **INCOME:** $248,776,142 (all divisions, year ending 6/30/89; accrual accounting, IRS form 990). During the preceding four fiscal years support had been increasing.
- **HOW THEY USE YOUR MONEY:**
  PROGRAM: $172,318,204*:
  - $70,671,177 (including $66,659,919 in grants and allocations) for research.
  - $46,246,316* (including $350,404 in grants and allocations) for public health education.
  - $24,308,115 (including $865,731 in grants and allocations) for professional education.
  - $31,092,596 (including $495,205 in grants and allocations) for community services, such as training in emergency aid, blood-pressure screening, etc.
  OVERHEAD: $19,038,333.
  FUNDRAISING: $29,091,281.*
- **EXCESS:** $28,328,324.
- **LITTLE-KNOWN FACTS:** Since 1949 the association has invested more than $754 million in research. One research project, studying the oxygen-releasing mechanisms in hemoglobin of Amazon fish like the piranha, resulted in a "chemical cocktail" used in blood transfusions during the Vietnam War to increase the recovery rate of wounded soldiers.
- **RATINGS:** NCIB reported (5/5/89, using figures for the year ending 6/30/88) that the American Heart Association met all nine NCIB standards.
- **REGISTRATION:** CT, NY (8098), OH, PA, and WV.
- **FINANCIAL DATA:** Text and chart source was their IRS form 990 covering the year ending 6/30/89. Footnote source was their 1989 annual report, covering the same year.

*A joint allocation of costs, for $5,597,000 in informational materials that included fundraising appeals, gave $3,296,000 to fundraising, $1,526,000 to public health education, and $775,000 to other program expenses.

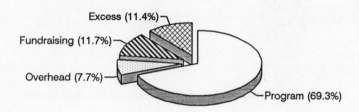

Excess (11.4%)
Fundraising (11.7%)
Overhead (7.7%)
Program (69.3%)

American Health Assistance Foundation
15825 Shady Grove Rd., Suite 140
Rockville, MD 20850
(301) 948-3244 • (800) 227-7998

■ **CONTRIBUTIONS** are tax-deductible.

■ **PURPOSE:** Since 1973 has funded scientific research of age-related and degenerative diseases, sought to educate the public about these diseases, and provided financial assistance to Alzheimer's-disease patients and their caregivers.

■ **SIZE:** In FY89 more than 1.5 million newsletters were distributed to the public, and over 4,500 calls were received by the toll-free number (whose operators do *not* attempt to provide medical answers).

■ **INCOME:** $10,785,711 (year ending 3/31/89; accrual accounting, IRS form 990). During the preceding four fiscal years support had been increasing.

■ **HOW THEY USE YOUR MONEY:**
PROGRAM: $6,529,131:
  • $2,202,582 for public education.
  The remaining money supported four projects, each of which raises money separately and with the foundation:
  • $3,489,488* (including $3,115,800 in grants and allocations) for the Alzheimer's-disease research program.
  • $376,655* (including $341,250 in grants and allocations) for the national glaucoma research program.
  • $348,971* (including $320,352 in grants and allocations) for the coronary heart-disease research program.
  • $111,435* (including $25,000 in grants and allocations for emergency respite care to the Alzheimer's patient or caregiver) for the Alzheimer's family relief program.
OVERHEAD: $819,103.*
FUNDRAISING: $3,687,050.*

■ **DEFICIT:** $249,573.

■ **LITTLE-KNOWN FACTS:** Certain fundraising, public-education, list-brokering, printing, and mailing services are provided to AHAF by companies at least 48 percent owned and operated by persons directly related to the executive director and president of AHAF. (The executive director and president own no stock, nor have any other interest in any of these companies.) Due to various questionable activities, including failure to report related-party transactions, AHAF was banned (1986) by West Virginia from soliciting money in that state, and Maryland also investigated the group that year. Eventually, stipulation agreements were reached with Maryland (1987) and West Virginia (1988), allowing solicitations to continue in those states.

■ **RATINGS:** As of June 1, 1990, NCIB was preparing a new report.

---

*A joint allocation of costs of $3,290,687 incurred during the year was split by the foundation's own guidelines as follows: $170,824 for overhead; $2,046,781 for fundraising; and the remaining for program expenses—$782,605 for Alzheimer's-disease research; $105,128 for coronary heart-disease research; $98,442 for the Alzheimer's family relief program; and $86,907 for national glaucoma research.

- **REGISTRATION:** CA, CT, DC, FL, GA, IL, KS, KY, MA, MD, MI, MN, NC, NH, NJ, NM, NY (46401), OH, OR, PA, RI, SC, TN, VA (58), WA, WI, and WV.
- **FINANCIAL DATA:** Text and chart source was their IRS form 990 covering the year ending 3/31/89. Footnote source was their annual report for the same year.

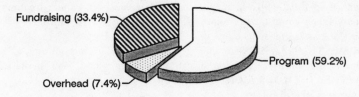

Fundraising (33.4%)

Program (59.2%)

Overhead (7.4%)

Due to deficit of 2.3%, chart is based on spending, not income.

American Institute for Cancer Research
1759 R St., N.W.
Washington, DC 20009
(202) 328-7744 • (800) 843-8114

- **CONTRIBUTIONS** are tax-deductible.
- **PURPOSE:** Established in 1981 to "fund cancer-research projects and to sponsor educational programs in the area of cancer prevention." This purpose was expanded in fiscal 1987 to include research projects in cancer treatment, the primary focus being on the relationship between diet and cancer.
- **SIZE:** Donor base grew to more than 3,000,000 in 1988.
- **INCOME:** $15,993,999 (year ending 9/30/88; accrual accounting, IRS form 990). During the preceding four fiscal years support had been increasing.
- **HOW THEY USE YOUR MONEY:**
  PROGRAM: $10,394,891:
  - $7,514,119* for education (distribution of booklets, brochures, calendars, cookbooks, reference books, a quarterly newsletter, and a video on diet and cancer).
  - $2,880,772 (including $2,403,959 in grants and allocations) for research (including twenty-seven new cancer-research grants).
  OVERHEAD: $1,476,019.*
  FUNDRAISING: $3,522,926.*
- **EXCESS:** $600,163.
- **LITTLE-KNOWN FACTS:** In a related-party transaction, the Watson and Hughey Company provides fundraising and other professional services to AICR and several other cancer charities. Messrs. Watson and Hughey, owners of the company, are also nonvoting members of AICR (not members of the board). Compensation to W&H and related companies during the year amounted to $367,136 (the AICR audited statement says about $383,000); AICR earned $799,141 on rental of its mailing list during that same period.
- **RATINGS:** As of June 1, 1990, NCIB was preparing a new report.
- **REGISTRATION:** AL, AK, AR, CA, CO, CT, DC, DE, FL, GA, HI, IA, ID, IL, IN, KS, KY, LA, MA, MD, ME, MI, MN, MO, MT, NC, ND, NE, NH, NJ, NM, NV, NY (51307), OH, OK, OR, PA, RI, SC, TN, UT, VA (62), VT, WA, WI, WV, and WY.
- **FINANCIAL DATA:** Text and chart source was their IRS form 990 covering the year ending 9/30/88. Source of footnote and one figure in Little-Known Facts was their independently audited statement covering the same year.

*A joint allocation of costs of $7,938,263 for informational materials and activities that included fundraising appeals divided funds thus: $3,053,807 for fundraising, $4,218,796 for education, and $665,660 for overhead.

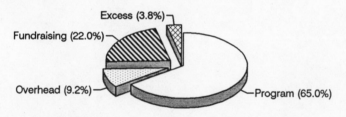

Excess (3.8%)
Fundraising (22.0%)
Overhead (9.2%)
Program (65.0%)

American Jewish Committee
165 E. 56th St.
New York, NY 10022
(212) 751-4000

■ **CONTRIBUTIONS** are tax-deductible.
■ **PURPOSE:** Established 1906, "the pioneer human-relations agency in the United States." The AJC protects the rights and freedoms of Jews and others worldwide; combats bigotry and anti-Semitism; works for the security of Israel and greater understanding between Americans and Israelis; defends democratic values and seeks their realization in American public policy; enhances the creative vitality of the Jewish people.
■ **SIZE:** 50,000 members; headquarters in New York City, an office in Washington, area offices in thirty major U.S. cities, and an office in Jerusalem.
■ **INCOME:** $19,629,692 (year ending 6/30/88; annual report).
■ **HOW THEY USE YOUR MONEY:**
PROGRAM: $15,423,024.
OVERHEAD: $1,528,814.
FUNDRAISING: $2,507,869.
■ **EXCESS:** $169,985.
■ **LITTLE-KNOWN FACTS:** Amid numerous reports, studies, surveys, articles, committee work, community liaisons, and political and religious lobbying on such issues as anti-Semitism, the intifada, Kurt Waldheim, Supreme Court cases challenging civil rights laws, abortion rights, and the future of the Jewish people in America (to name just a few topics), AJC still found time to consider *humor.* In September 1987 AJC and *Lilith* magazine released a report on the problem of the proliferation of "Jewish American Princess jokes" and the "cruelty and destructiveness of this stereotype, even when it is propagated by Jews." AJC chapters in Chicago, Philadelphia, Portland, and St. Louis held public meetings on the issue and the hostility it evokes. On the other hand, AJC's Washington representative co-authored *The Jokes of Oppression: The Humor of Soviet Jews,* a look at "how Soviet Jews use humor to cope with the tensions they endure."
■ **RATINGS:** No NCIB report.
■ **REGISTRATION:** NY.
■ **FINANCIAL DATA:** Text and chart source was their annual report covering the year ending 6/30/88.

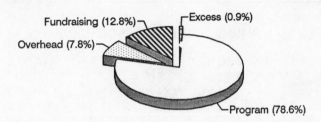

Fundraising (12.8%)
Excess (0.9%)
Overhead (7.8%)
Program (78.6%)

American Jewish World Service, Inc.
1290 Avenue of the Americas, 11th Fl.
New York, NY 10104
(212) 468-7380

- **CONTRIBUTIONS** are tax-deductible.
- **PURPOSE:** Founded in 1985, "the only American Jewish relief and development organization totally dedicated to alleviating poverty and hunger in the Third World." Assists poor families, regardless of religion, by supporting programs in small-scale agriculture and primary health care.
- **SIZE:** Projects in nineteen countries.
- **INCOME:** $2,469,114 (calendar 1988; cash accounting for contributions, accrual for all other items, IRS form 990).
- **HOW THEY USE YOUR MONEY:**
  PROGRAM: $2,136,949, to support self-help projects in agriculture and health care throughout Asia (including Armenia, India, the Philippines, and Sri Lanka), Africa (including Ethiopia and Mozambique), and Latin America (including Colombia), and to rebuild communities struck by natural disasters.
  OVERHEAD: $47,411.
  FUNDRAISING: $403,354.
- **DEFICIT:** $118,600.
- **LITTLE-KNOWN FACTS:** *No* projects active in Israel.
- **RATINGS:** No NCIB report.
- **REGISTRATION:** MA and NY (54210).
- **FINANCIAL DATA:** Text and chart source was their IRS form 990 covering 1988.

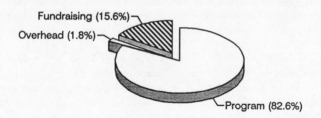

Fundraising (15.6%)
Overhead (1.8%)
Program (82.6%)

Due to deficit of 4.6%, chart is based on spending, not income.

American Lung Association

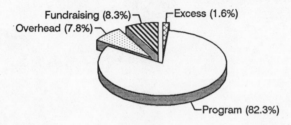

Fundraising (8.3%) Excess (1.6%)
Overhead (7.8%)
Program (82.3%)

American Lung Association
1740 Broadway
New York, NY 10019
(212) 315-8700

■ **CONTRIBUTIONS** are tax-deductible.

■ **PURPOSE:** The National Tuberculosis Association was established in 1904; the present name was adopted in 1973. ALA is dedicated to promoting lung health through the prevention and treatment of such lung diseases as asthma, emphysema, cancer, bronchitis, and tuberculosis, in addition to informing the public as to the health hazards of smoking, air pollution, and occupational lung hazards.

■ **SIZE:** Fifty-nine "constituent" associations "which have jurisdiction over specific geographic areas or over certain of the seventy-six affiliated lung associations."

■ **INCOME:** $17,145,851 (national headquarters, year ending 6/30/89; accrual accounting, independently audited statement). Each constituent or affiliated lung association is required to remit 10 percent of its sharable income to ALA; in return ALA provides (approximately at cost) Christmas Seal and health-education materials, plus certain services.

■ **HOW THEY USE YOUR MONEY:**

PROGRAM: $14,102,845:

- $8,022,290 (including $2,784,314 in awards and grants) for lung-disease programs.
- $2,826,157 for programs on smoking and health.
- $1,912,069 for community-health programs.
- $740,075 for air-conservation programs.
- $602,254 for occupational-health programs.
- Since lung disease accounts for the majority of AIDS deaths, the ALA conducts educational programs on AIDS and is developing recommendations for comprehensive health care of patients with AIDS and HIV infection.

OVERHEAD: $1,335,289.

FUNDRAISING: $1,429,093.

■ **EXCESS:** $278,624.

■ **LITTLE-KNOWN FACTS:** The double-barred cross, the emblem that has appeared on Christmas Seals since 1920, is adapted from the Cross of Lorraine, which was used by medieval Crusaders and was adopted by the association to symbolize the crusade against tuberculosis.

■ **RATINGS:** An NCIB report (11/22/89, on the ALA's national service center *only*, using figures for the year ending 6/30/88) stated that the center met all nine NCIB standards.

■ **REGISTRATION:** NY (7212).

■ **FINANCIAL DATA:** Text and chart source was their independently audited statement (for the national headquarters *only*) covering the year ending 6/30/89.

American Mental Health Fund
3299 Woodburn Rd.
Annandale, VA 22003
(703) 573-2200 • (800) 433-5959

- **CONTRIBUTIONS** are tax-deductible.
- **PURPOSE:** Formed in 1983 by Jack and Jo Ann Hinckley (parents of John Hinckley, who shot President Ronald Reagan in March 1981) through amendment of the name and purpose of a Colorado organization founded in 1977. The fund provides public education about mental health and conducts fundraising campaigns to further promote this education and to expand psychiatric research.
- **SIZE:** Staff of seven.
- **INCOME:** $710,733 (calendar 1988; accrual accounting, IRS form 990). During the preceding four fiscal years support had been increasing.
- **HOW THEY USE YOUR MONEY:**
  PROGRAM: $626,447* for educational programs related to developing an awareness of mental illness, including a single $25,000 research grant.
  OVERHEAD: $30,965.
  FUNDRAISING: $92,175.*
- **DEFICIT:** $38,854.
- **LITTLE-KNOWN FACTS:** According to the independently audited statement for 1988, the fund bought (at publisher's cost) 2,940 copies of a book written by the president of the fund, and distributed free copies to contributors and interested parties.
- **RATINGS:** NCIB reported (9/6/89, using calendar 1988 figures) that the American Mental Health Fund met all nine NCIB standards.
- **REGISTRATION:** NY (52487).
- **FINANCIAL DATA:** Text and chart source was their IRS form 990 covering 1988. Footnote source was their independently audited statement covering 1988.

*In 1988 a joint allocation of costs of $55,310 for informational mailings that included educational materials and fundraising appeals attributed $20,497 to educational (program) expenses, while $34,813 was considered as part of fundraising expenses.

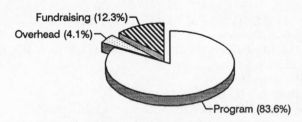

Fundraising (12.3%)
Overhead (4.1%)
Program (83.6%)

Due to deficit of 5.2%, chart is based on spending, not income.

American National Red Cross
430 D St., N.W.
Washington, DC 20006
(202) 737-8300

- **CONTRIBUTIONS** are tax-deductible.
- **PURPOSE:** In 1881 Clara Barton established the American Association of the Red Cross. Granted a congressional charter in 1900, the American Red Cross works to improve the quality of human life; enhance self-reliance and concern for others; help people avoid, prepare for, and cope with emergencies; and further the principles of the International Red Cross movement.
- **SIZE:** The ratio of volunteers (1,152,393) to paid staff (23,357) is an amazing *50 to 1.* Of the 2,817 chapters of the American Red Cross, 1,560 are staffed entirely by volunteers.
- **INCOME:** $985,175,000, total for all 2,817 chapters, 56 regional blood services, and the national sector (year ending 6/30/88; annual report).
- **HOW THEY USE YOUR MONEY:**
  PROGRAM: $886,248,000:
  - $572,417,000 for blood services.
  - $93,166,000 for disaster programs.
  - $80,618,000 for services to members of the armed forces, veterans, and their families.
  - $79,158,000 for health services.
  - $47,050,000 for community volunteer programs.
  - $7,379,000 for youth programs.
  - $6,460,000 for international programs.

  OVERHEAD: $64,854,000.
  FUNDRAISING: $26,701,000.
- **EXCESS:** $7,372,000.
- **LITTLE-KNOWN FACTS:** Collects, tests, and distributes more than 6,000,000 units of blood—half of the nation's blood supply.
- **RATINGS:** An NCIB report on the American Red Cross (6/29/89, using figures for the year ending 6/30/88) stated that it met all nine NCIB standards.
- **REGISTRATION:** VA (78).
- **FINANCIAL DATA:** Text and chart source was their annual report covering the year ending 6/30/88.

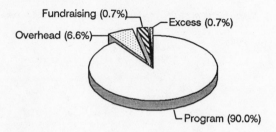

Fundraising (0.7%)
Excess (0.7%)
Overhead (6.6%)
Program (90.0%)

American Refugee Committee
2344 Nicollet Ave. S., Suite 350
Minneapolis, MN 55404
(612) 872-7060

- **CONTRIBUTIONS** are tax-deductible.
- **PURPOSE:** Established 1979; works for the survival, health, and well-being of refugees, and helps them gain skills to rebuild productive lives of dignity and purpose.
- **SIZE:** ARC says that its programs affected nearly a quarter-million refugees in Thailand, the Sudan, and the United States in 1988.
- **INCOME:** $2,197,387 (calendar 1988; accrual accounting, IRS form 990).
- **HOW THEY USE YOUR MONEY:**
  PROGRAM: $1,961,833:
    - $1,565,697 for international programs (primarily health-care programs in the Sudan, in Thailand, along the Thai-Cambodian border, and in Malawi).
    - $396,136 for U.S. programs (five programs to help refugees become self-sufficient and integrated into American society).
  OVERHEAD: $220,570.
  FUNDRAISING: $264,146.
- **DEFICIT:** $249,162.
- **LITTLE-KNOWN FACTS:** Originally, ARC worked only with Indochinese refugees, but work expanded to encompass Ethiopian refugees in the Sudan (1985) and Mozambican refugees in Malawi (1988).
- **RATINGS:** NCIB reported (1/18/89, using calendar 1987 figures) that ARC met all nine NCIB standards.
- **REGISTRATION:** CA, IL, MN, NY (48789), OH, VA (79), and WI.
- **FINANCIAL DATA:** Text and chart source was their IRS form 990 covering 1988.

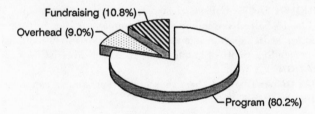

Fundraising (10.8%)
Overhead (9.0%)
Program (80.2%)

Due to deficit of 10.2%, chart is based on spending, not income.

American Society for the Prevention of Cruelty to Animals
441 E. 92nd St.
New York, NY 10128
(212) 876-7700 • (212) 876-7711

- **CONTRIBUTIONS** are tax-deductible.
- **PURPOSE:** Established in 1866, the ASPCA was the nation's first humane society; in 1988 it directly cared for more animals than any other humane society in this country. It also engages in legislative initiatives, humane-law enforcement, litigation, and educational programs.
- **SIZE:** The ASPCA's New York hospital and clinic handled 43,373 animals in 1988, and the NYC Animal Control Shelters and ambulances provided care for 69,220 lost, stray, and homeless animals.
- **INCOME:** $15,010,623 (calendar 1988; accrual accounting, IRS form 990). During the preceding four fiscal years support had been increasing. There is an ASPCA VISA affinity card.
- **HOW THEY USE YOUR MONEY:**
  PROGRAM: $10,347,389:
  - $4,902,196 for NYC Animal Control Shelters and ambulances.
  - $2,195,390 for the hospital.
  - $1,087,178 for licensing 199,648 dogs in NYC.
  - $903,000 for humane education.
  - $736,906 for humane-law enforcement.
  - $400,977 for special shelter service for animals in transit.
  - $121,742 was spent on influencing and initiating animal-welfare legislation (national, state, and local).
  OVERHEAD: $1,847,039.
  FUNDRAISING: $2,903,542.
- **DEFICIT:** $87,347.
- **LITTLE-KNOWN FACTS:** In 1988 the ASPCA, disturbed by the implications genetic engineering has for humane animal-research practices, joined the Animal Legal Defense Fund in a suit against the U.S. Commerce Department and Patent Office for granting a patent on a genetically engineered mouse.
- **RATINGS:** No NCIB report.
- **REGISTRATION:** NJ and NY (7632).
- **FINANCIAL DATA:** Text and chart source was their IRS form 990 covering 1988.

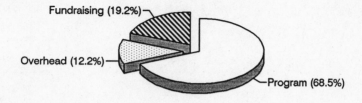

Fundraising (19.2%)
Overhead (12.2%)
Program (68.5%)

Due to deficit of 0.6%, chart is based on spending, not income.

Americans for Peace Now
27 W. 20th St., 9th Fl.
New York, NY 10011
(212) 645-6262

- **CONTRIBUTIONS** are tax-deductible.
- **PURPOSE:** Informs the American public about the activities and purposes of Peace Now *(Shalom Achshav)*, a broad-based, nonpartisan Israeli peace movement that seeks solutions to Middle East problems posed by continued Israeli occupation of the West Bank and Gaza Strip.
- **SIZE:** Representatives in New York, Washington, DC, and Los Angeles.
- **INCOME:** Chicago Friends of Peace Now, Inc. (the former parent organization of Friends of Peace Now—see Little-Known Facts) recorded total revenues of $354,706 for the year ending 5/31/88 (accrual accounting, IRS form 990).
- **HOW THEY USE YOUR MONEY:**
  PROGRAM: $243,783 (including, $98,000 to Peace Now in Israel).
  OVERHEAD: $44,834.
  FUNDRAISING: $41,953.
- **EXCESS:** $24,136.
- **LITTLE-KNOWN FACTS:** For several years various unregistered organizations in the United States had solicited money as "Friends of Peace Now." The Chicago Friends of Peace Now, however, incorporated as a 501(c)(3) group, and its Peace Now Education Fund was predecessor to Friends of Peace Now (which reincorporated in May 1989). In 1990, FPN changed its name to Americans for Peace Now.
- **RATINGS:** No NCIB report.
- **REGISTRATION:** NY.
- **FINANCIAL DATA:** Text and chart source was the IRS form 990 for Chicago Friends of Peace Now, Inc., covering the year ending 5/31/88.

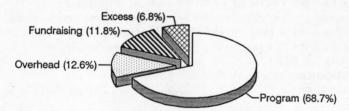

Excess (6.8%)
Fundraising (11.8%)
Overhead (12.6%)
Program (68.7%)

Americans United for Separation of Church and State
8120 Fenton St.
Silver Spring, MD 20910
(301) 589-3707

- **CONTRIBUTIONS** are tax-deductible.
- **PURPOSE:** Since 1947 the organization has worked, through litigation, education, and communication, to protect the constitutional guarantees of religious liberty.
- **SIZE:** National membership of more than 50,000, plus offices in Washington, DC, and California, and volunteers in all fifty states.
- **INCOME:** $1,851,877 (Americans United for Separation of Church and State and the AUSCS Fund, year ending 9/30/88; accrual accounting, independently audited statement).
- **HOW THEY USE YOUR MONEY:**
PROGRAM: $1,000,978:
  - $415,375 for education (including publication of *Church and State Review*).
  - $246,659 for the legal division.
  - $115,470 for general services (such as membership).
  - $88,602 for field services.
  - $76,909 for the national conference.
  - $57,963 for regional offices.
OVERHEAD: $414,563.
FUNDRAISING: $417,792.
- **EXCESS:** $18,544.
- **LITTLE-KNOWN FACTS:** Supreme Court Justice John Paul Stevens, in a dissenting opinion in the case of *Webster v. Reproductive Health Services,* cited the *amicus curiae* brief of Americans United. AU took no position on the advisability of abortion, but took issue with the law's definition of life beginning at conception as an unconstitutional endorsement of one religious view.
- **RATINGS:** No NCIB report.
- **REGISTRATION:** VA (2597).
- **FINANCIAL DATA:** Text and chart source was their independently audited statement (for both Americans United *and* the AUSCS Fund, Inc.) covering the year ending 9/30/88.

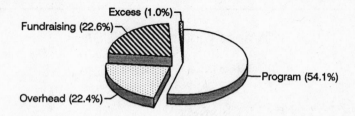

Excess (1.0%)
Fundraising (22.6%)
Program (54.1%)
Overhead (22.4%)

89

AmeriCares Foundation, Inc.
161 Cherry St.
New Canaan, CT 06840
(203) 966-5195 • (800) 666-HOPE

- **CONTRIBUTIONS** are tax-deductible.
- **PURPOSE:** Established 1979, an international humanitarian organization that provides long-term medical and emergency disaster aid worldwide.
- **SIZE:** AmeriCares, which has a staff of sixty (forty of them volunteers), has worked in forty-one countries worldwide.
- **INCOME:** $22,811,257 (six-month period ending 6/30/89; accrual accounting, IRS form 990; the shortened accounting period reflects a change in fiscal year from the previous December 31). AmeriCares says that it "is able to deliver at least $51 worth of humanitarian aid for each dollar donated."
- **HOW THEY USE YOUR MONEY:**
  PROGRAM: $21,522,225, including cash grants of $50,000 to Covenant House (New York) and $5,000 to Covenant House (Florida).
  OVERHEAD: $302,991.
  FUNDRAISING: $379,327.
- **EXCESS:** $606,714.
- **RATINGS:** NCIB reported (1/26/90, using figures for calendar 1988) that Ameri-Cares met all nine NCIB standards.
- **REGISTRATION:** NY (51719).
- **FINANCIAL DATA:** Text and chart source was their IRS form 990 covering the six-month period ending 6/30/89.

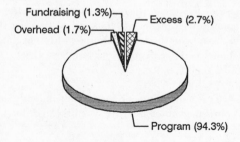

Fundraising (1.3%)
Overhead (1.7%)
Excess (2.7%)
Program (94.3%)

Amnesty International USA

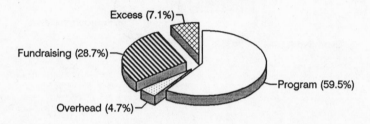

Excess (7.1%)
Fundraising (28.7%)
Overhead (4.7%)
Program (59.5%)

Amnesty International of the U.S.A., Inc.
322 Eighth Ave., 10th Fl.
New York, NY 10001
(212) 807-8400

- **CONTRIBUTIONS** are tax-deductible.
- **PURPOSE:** Established in 1966 in Britain, Amnesty International won the Nobel Peace Prize eleven years later for its work as an independent, impartial, world-wide movement that seeks to protect fundamental human rights. AI works for the release of all prisoners of conscience (provided they have neither used nor advocated violence), fair and prompt trials for political prisoners, and an end to torture and executions. The basis for much of AI's work is the United Nations' 1944 Universal Declaration of Human Rights. In the United States in 1988 AI focused its attention on death-penalty cases, possible political aspects of treatment of a Black Panther Party leader and a member of a Puerto Rican independence organization, and prison conditions.
- **SIZE:** More than 800,000 members in 150 countries—306,000 in the United States.
- **INCOME:** $17,030,682 (year ending 9/30/88; accrual accounting, IRS form 990). During the preceding four fiscal years support had been increasing.
- **HOW THEY USE YOUR MONEY:**
PROGRAM: $10,138,467:
  - $3,428,141 for international support of the research of Amnesty International, Ltd., in London for "country campaigns, international co-group meetings, prisoner research, relief, and U.N. mission support."
  - $1,642,118 for campaigns and actions (work associated with specific countries and special campaigns and actions).
  - $2,268,677 for membership programs (the development, training, and support of local, campus, and country coordination groups working on Amnesty's behalf).
  - $2,799,531 for communications and publications (the dissemination of information relating to human rights and Amnesty's concerns and organizational methods to members as well as the general public).
OVERHEAD: $798,645.
FUNDRAISING: $4,888,785.
- **EXCESS:** $1,204,785.
- **LITTLE-KNOWN FACTS:** Today Amnesty International is most often associated with benefit rock concerts like the 1988 Human Rights Now! tour, and such performers as Peter Gabriel, Bruce Springsteen, Sting, and U2. But when AI first began operations in America, William F. Buckley, Jr., was a member of the board of directors.
- **RATINGS:** NCIB reported (2/10/89, using figures for the year ending 9/30/87) that Amnesty met all nine NCIB standards.
- **REGISTRATION:** NY (42098) and VA (93).
- **FINANCIAL DATA:** Text and chart source was their IRS form 990 covering the year ending 9/30/88.

AMVETS National Service Foundation
4647 Forbes Blvd.
Lanham, MD 20706
(301) 459-6181

- **CONTRIBUTIONS** are *not* tax-deductible.
- **PURPOSE:** The AMVETS National Service Foundation, a subsidiary of AMVETS, Inc., was established in 1944 and offers Americans the opportunity to support programs to serve veterans as well as "community and youth-oriented programs designed to promote unity and patriotism." The foundation's national service officers counsel and represent veterans (regardless of whether they are members of AMVETS) and their dependents before the Veterans Administration without charge.
- **SIZE:** 200,000 members in 37 state and 1,100 local groups.
- **INCOME:** $12,616,082 (year ending 8/31/88; accrual accounting, independently audited statement).
- **HOW THEY USE YOUR MONEY:**
  PROGRAM: $6,478,068:
  - $3,932,736 for service to veterans.
  - $1,525,075 for "Americanism."
  - $893,600 for grants, awards, and scholarships.
  - $126,657 for the carillon program.

  OVERHEAD: $1,540,705
  FUNDRAISING: $3,666,198.
  LOSS ON SALE: $70,963 loss on sale of property.
- **EXCESS:** $860,148.
- **RATINGS:** As of June 1, 1990, NCIB was preparing a new report.
- **REGISTRATION:** TN and VA (95).
- **FINANCIAL DATA:** Text and chart source was their independently audited statement covering the year ending 8/31/88.

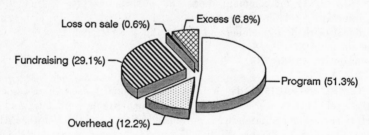

Loss on sale (0.6%) — ⌐ Excess (6.8%)
Fundraising (29.1%) —
Program (51.3%)
Overhead (12.2%)

Animal Welfare Institute

Box 3650
Washington, DC 20007
(202) 337-2332

- **CONTRIBUTIONS** are tax-deductible.
- **PURPOSE:** Founded in 1951 to "reduce the sum total of pain and fear inflicted on animals by man." It advocates the humane treatment of lab animals (and the development of nonanimal testing), the reform of cruel trapping methods, a ban on the importation and sale of wild-caught exotic birds, the preservation of threatened species, and the "humane slaughter" of food animals.
- **SIZE:** About 20,000 receive the *Animal Institute Quarterly.*
- **INCOME:** $403,998 (year ending 6/30/89; annual report).
- **HOW THEY USE YOUR MONEY:**
  PROGRAM: $368,374:
    - $282,002 for public education and projects.
    - $49,389 for the elephant program (work against ivory-poaching).
    - $36,983 on the Save the Whales Campaign.
  OVERHEAD: $84,805.
  FUNDRAISING: $14,790.
- **DEFICIT:** $63,971.
- **RATINGS:** NCIB reported (7/14/89, using figures for the year ending 6/30/88) that the Animal Welfare Institute met all nine NCIB standards.
- **REGISTRATION:** NY (5479).
- **FINANCIAL DATA:** Text and chart source was their annual report covering the year ending 6/30/89.

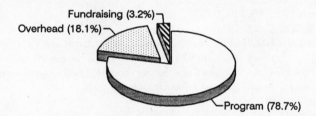

Due to deficit of 13.7%, chart is based on spending, not income.

Anti-Defamation League of B'nai B'rith
823 United Nations Plaza
New York, NY 10017
(212) 490-2525

- **CONTRIBUTIONS** are tax-deductible.
- **PURPOSE:** Formed in 1913 in the wake of the Leo Frank case, the Anti-Defamation League of B'nai B'rith defends democratic ideals and works to eliminate anti-Semitism and bigotry worldwide, while providing knowledgeable leadership for the American Jewish community.
- **SIZE:** Headquarters in New York, thirty-one regional offices throughout the United States, plus offices in Jerusalem, Paris, and Rome.
- **INCOME:** $32,330,639 (year ending 6/30/88; accrual accounting, IRS form 990). During the preceding four fiscal years support had been increasing.
- **HOW THEY USE YOUR MONEY:**
  PROGRAM: $21,018,402:
  - $11,161,266 for community service (regional operations of ADL).
  - $2,489,545 for publications and communications.
  - $2,437,371 for national affairs.
  - $1,218,301 for Mideast programs (including a liaison in Israel).
  - $991,352 for foreign affairs.
  - $951,970 for education.
  - $646,311 for legal and discrimination programs (litigation relating to civil rights, church-state matters, and all forms of discrimination).
  - $635,745 for leadership programs (recruiting and developing new leaders).
  - $486,541 for interreligious programs.

  OVERHEAD: $2,454,284.
  FUNDRAISING: $8,829,449.
- **EXCESS:** $28,504.
- **LITTLE-KNOWN FACTS:** The Jewish Foundation for Christian Rescuers, a division of the Intergroup Relations Division of ADL, has instituted monthly grants to needy Gentiles who rescued Jews during the Holocaust. About ninety people in seven countries are assisted through this program.
- **RATINGS:** No NCIB report.
- **REGISTRATION:** NY.
- **FINANCIAL DATA:** Text and chart source was their IRS form 990 covering the year ending 6/30/88.

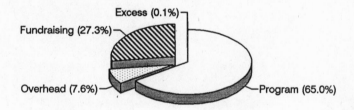

Excess (0.1%)
Fundraising (27.3%)
Overhead (7.6%)
Program (65.0%)

Asian-American Legal Defense and Education Fund
99 Hudson St., 12th Fl.
New York, NY 10013
(212) 966-5932

- **CONTRIBUTIONS** are tax-deductible.
- **PURPOSE:** Founded in 1974; uses law and education to deal with problems of the Asian-American community in areas such as immigration, employment, housing, voting rights, and racially motivated violence. Provides bilingual counseling and representation, litigates, and monitors and reports on incidents of racial discrimination.
- **INCOME:** $183,509 (calendar 1988; IRS form 990).
- **HOW THEY USE YOUR MONEY:**
  PROGRAM: $123,463:
  - $31,743 for legal access.
  - $14,125 for student internships.
  - $70,836 for programs on Japanese-American redress, voting and employment rights, anti-Asian violence, immigration, and community education.
  - $6,759 for development coordination, capital campaign, development grants, back wages, and brochures.
  OVERHEAD: $24,035.
  FUNDRAISING: $18,866.
- **EXCESS:** $17,145.
- **LITTLE-KNOWN FACTS:** Publishes pamphlets in Chinese, Japanese, Korean, and English.
- **RATINGS:** No NCIB report.
- **REGISTRATION:** NY (47587).
- **FINANCIAL DATA:** Text and chart source was their IRS form 990 covering 1988.

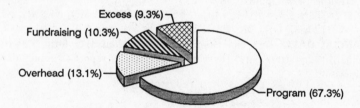

95

Association for Retarded Citizens of the United States
2501 Avenue J
Arlington, TX 76005
(817) 640-0204

- **CONTRIBUTIONS** are tax-deductible.
- **PURPOSE:** Organized in 1950; adopted present name in 1980. The group works to promote the welfare of all persons who are retarded (an estimated six million people in the United States) and their families, to prevent retardation, and to search for cures.
- **SIZE:** 160,000 members in 1987; 1,300 local and state chapters nationwide.
- **INCOME:** $6,167,430 (national headquarters, calendar 1988; accrual accounting, IRS form 990). During the preceding four fiscal years support had been increasing.
- **HOW THEY USE YOUR MONEY:**
  PROGRAM: $4,838,567:
  - $3,730,232 for community and supporting services.
  - $422,345 for professional health education and training.
  - $353,100 (including $62,125 in grants and allocations) for research.
  - $332,890 for public health education.

  OVERHEAD: $607,828.
  FUNDRAISING: $128,485.
- **EXCESS:** $592,550.
- **LITTLE-KNOWN FACTS:** Since 1966, the U.S. Department of Labor has funded the association's National Employment and Training Program. Over the years, NETP has matched more than 40,000 workers with mental retardation with employers—more than 2,500 in 1988 alone.
- **RATINGS:** NCIB reported (4/12/89, using figures for calendar 1987) that ARC met all nine NCIB standards.
- **REGISTRATION:** CA, CT, FL, IA, ID, KS, MD, ME, MI, MN, NE, NH, NJ, NM, NV, NY (12463), OH, OK, PA, RI, SC, TN, VA, and WI.
- **FINANCIAL DATA:** Text and chart source was their IRS form 990 (for the national headquarters *only*) covering 1988. NCIB's report examines the *entire* organization.

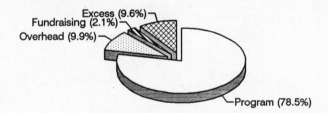

Excess (9.6%)
Fundraising (2.1%)
Overhead (9.9%)
Program (78.5%)

Bankcard Holders of America, Inc.
460 Spring Park Pl., Suite 1000
Herndon, VA 22070
(703) 481-1110 • (800) 638-6407

- **CONTRIBUTIONS** are tax-deductible.
- **PURPOSE:** Founded in 1980 to educate the American public about the wise and careful use of credit, and inform consumers of their rights and responsibilities as credit users.
- **SIZE:** 100,000 members and a staff of ten.
- **INCOME:** $1,168,616 (year ending 6/30/87; NYS form 497).
- **HOW THEY USE YOUR MONEY:**
  PROGRAM: $850,468.
  OVERHEAD: $539,964.
  FUNDRAISING: $89,412.
- **DEFICIT:** $311,228.
- **LITTLE-KNOWN FACTS:** BHA's quarterly publication, *BankList,* publishes the names of banks that do not charge an annual fee or that charge low interest rates for their credit cards. It also lists banks that offer cards for people trying to establish or reestablish a positive credit history.
- **RATINGS:** No NCIB report.
- **REGISTRATION:** NY (51959).
- **FINANCIAL DATA:** Text and chart source was their NYS form 497 covering the year ending 6/30/87.

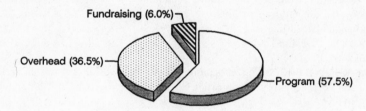

Fundraising (6.0%)

Overhead (36.5%)

Program (57.5%)

Due to deficit of 21.0%, chart is based on spending, not income.

97

Alexander Graham Bell Association for the Deaf, Inc.
3417 Volta Place, N.W.
Washington, DC 20007
(202) 337-5220 (voice or TDD) • (800) 255-4817

- **CONTRIBUTIONS** are tax-deductible.
- **PURPOSE:** Founded in 1890 by Alexander Graham Bell, the Bell Association promotes the teaching of language, speech, and lipreading, and encourages the use of residual hearing by deaf individuals. It also works for better educational facilities for all deaf children, and disseminates information on deafness to parents of deaf children and to the general public.
- **SIZE:** Members in over thirty-five countries.
- **INCOME:** $1,285,097 (calendar 1988; accrual accounting, independently audited statement). During the preceding four fiscal years support had been increasing.
- **HOW THEY USE YOUR MONEY:**
  PROGRAM: $813,881:
  - $261,325 for educational publications.
  - $191,006 for membership services.
  - $109,355 for scholarships.
  - $79,126 for the international parents' organization.
  - $66,946 supported an international organization for the education of the hearing-impaired.
  - $61,409 for library and information services.
  - $34,947 for the oral deaf adults section.
  - $9,767 for children's rights.
  OVERHEAD: $272,302.
  FUNDRAISING: $170,332.
- **EXCESS:** $28,582.
- **LITTLE-KNOWN FACTS:** The association's Volta Bureau Library has an archival collection of the history of education of the deaf going back to the sixteenth century.
- **RATINGS:** No NCIB report.
- **REGISTRATION:** DC and NY (8950).
- **FINANCIAL DATA:** Text and chart source was their independently audited statement covering 1988.

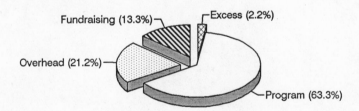

Fundraising (13.3%) — Excess (2.2%) — Overhead (21.2%) — Program (63.3%)

Big Brothers/Big Sisters of America
230 North 13th St.
Philadelphia, PA 19107
(215) 567-7000

- **CONTRIBUTIONS** are tax-deductible.
- **PURPOSE:** The first Big Brothers organization was established in 1903, in Cincinnati, Ohio. Local groups joined together as Big Brothers of America in 1945, and received a congressional charter in 1958 and merged with Big Sisters International (created in 1970) in 1977. BB/BSA provides quality volunteer and professional services for children and youths, mostly through individual relationships between an adult volunteer and a child (usually from a single-parent home) to help the child achieve his or her highest potential. A 1987 five-year plan set a goal of serving 50 percent more youngsters by 1992.
- **SIZE:** 483 affiliated, independent agencies in forty-nine states.
- **INCOME:** $2,976,529 (national headquarters only, calendar 1988; accrual accounting, IRS form 990). A cause-marketing effort with Arby's Restaurants netted over $500,000 in cash to local agencies and BB/BSA, and $100,000 worth of in-kind contributions.
- **HOW THEY USE YOUR MONEY:**
  PROGRAM: $2,152,373:
  - $1,068,105 on field services and new-agency coordination.
  - $691,962 for program development for member agencies.
  - $392,306 for training conferences and meetings, information services (dissemination of data to members), and communication.
  - Special programs include AIDS education and child sexual abuse education and prevention.
  OVERHEAD: $302,927.
  FUNDRAISING: $296,607.
- **EXCESS:** $224,622.
- **LITTLE-KNOWN FACTS:** More than 61,000 children are now matched with adult volunteers, but nearly 40,000 more are on the waiting list.
- **RATINGS:** NCIB reported (2/5/90, using figures for calendar 1988) that the BB/BSA national service center met all nine NCIB standards.
- **REGISTRATION:** CA, NJ, NY (5405), and PA.
- **FINANCIAL DATA:** Text and chart source was their IRS form 990 (for the national headquarters *only*) covering 1988.

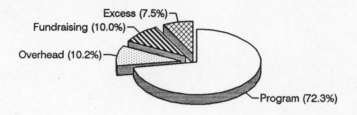

Excess (7.5%)
Fundraising (10.0%)
Overhead (10.2%)
Program (72.3%)

Bowery Residents' Committee Human Services Corporation
191 Chrystie St.
New York, NY 10002
(212) 533-5700

■ **CONTRIBUTIONS** are tax-deductible.

■ **PURPOSE:** Founded in 1970, BRC serves "the poorest of the poor" through outreach programs to street- and subway-dwelling homeless people, offering nonmedical alcohol detox, and providing food and a day respite center for homeless adults. BRC owns a community residence in Brooklyn and three buildings in Manhattan.

■ **SIZE:** Serves 3,500 people a year with a staff of about 150.

■ **INCOME:** $4,793,413 (year ending 6/30/89; IRS form 990). During the preceding four fiscal years support had been increasing.

■ **HOW THEY USE YOUR MONEY:**

PROGRAM: $3,757,337:

- $1,602,799 for housing services for psychiatrically disabled individuals.
- $1,131,317 for around-the-clock alcoholism services.
- $382,401 for mental health services (serving homeless and deinstitutionalized former mental patients).
- $640,820 for senior-citizens and homeless program (social, recreational, nutritional, and emergency-care services).

OVERHEAD: $603,180.

FUNDRAISING: $7,190.

■ **EXCESS:** $425,706.

■ **RATINGS:** No NCIB report.

■ **REGISTRATION:** NY (45842).

■ **FINANCIAL DATA:** Text and chart source was their IRS form 990 covering the year ending 6/30/89.

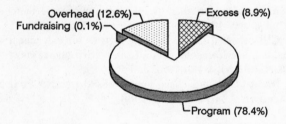

Overhead (12.6%)
Fundraising (0.1%)
Excess (8.9%)
Program (78.4%)

Boys and Girls Clubs of America
771 First Ave.
New York, NY 10017
(212) 351-5900

- **CONTRIBUTIONS** are tax-deductible.
- **PURPOSE:** The first Boys Club was established in Hartford in 1860; in 1906 fifty-three separate clubs merged as the Boys Clubs of America. Now a federally chartered national organization formed "to promote the health, social, educational, vocational, and character development of young people throughout the United States." The New York headquarters helps form new clubs and provides training, management consulting, and materials to all member clubs. In the fall of 1990, the group changed its name to Boys and Girls Clubs of America.
- **SIZE:** In 1988 local clubs served 1.3 million boys and girls from ages six to eighteen.
- **INCOME:** $16,594,337 (national headquarters only, calendar 1988; accrual accounting, IRS form 990).
- **HOW THEY USE YOUR MONEY:**
  PROGRAM: $10,292,391:
  - $6,648,584 in services to member clubs and extension of clubs.
  - $3,643,807 for training of leadership and development and maintenance of programs for youth.
  OVERHEAD: $1,536,741.
  FUNDRAISING: $1,643,772 (the 1988 annual report gave a larger overall figure for fundraising, including $502,509 spent on a sweepstakes program that raised $645,007 and contributed "over $250,000 to the operating budget").
- **EXCESS:** $3,121,433.
- **LITTLE-KNOWN FACTS:** BGCA has a five-year plan to "increase by 56 percent the number of boys and girls served" and to upgrade the quality of services by 1991. In the plan's first two years, BGCA helped establish 99 new club service locations, and laid the groundwork for new clubs in 204 more communities to open by 1991.
- **RATINGS:** NCIB reported (3/4/86, using figures for calendar 1984) that the national service center met all eight of NCIB's old evaluation standards.
- **REGISTRATION:** NY (6686) and VA (225).
- **FINANCIAL DATA:** Text and chart source was their IRS form 990 (for the national headquarters *only*) covering 1988. Fundraising expense details came from their 1988 annual report.

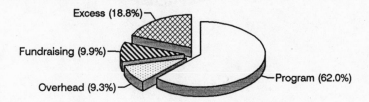

Excess (18.8%)
Fundraising (9.9%)
Overhead (9.3%)
Program (62.0%)

Boys Town/Father Flanagan's Boys' Home
14100 Crawford St.
Boys Town, NE 68010
(402) 498-1111

- **CONTRIBUTIONS** are tax-deductible.
- **PURPOSE:** Established in 1917, Father Flanagan's Boys' Home (also known as Boys Town) is a nonsectarian organization devoted to providing housing, care, support, educational, and medical services to homeless, abused, handicapped, and learning-disabled youth.
- **INCOME:** $64,778,763 (calendar 1988; accrual accounting, IRS form 990).
- **HOW THEY USE YOUR MONEY:**
  PROGRAM: $41,207,124:
  - $23,269,474 (including $386,319 in grants and allocations) for the home campus residential care and education.
  - $11,993,625 for the National Institute for Communication Disorders in Children.
  - $2,386,735 for three off-campus residential programs (Boys Town USA; the National Family Home Program; and the Family-Based Programs).
  - $2,184,717 (including $2,750 in grants and allocations) for the Father Flanagan High School.
  - $1,372,573 for the youth information and research services.
  OVERHEAD: $5,906,557.
  FUNDRAISING: $5,120,675.
- **EXCESS:** $12,544,407.
- **LITTLE-KNOWN FACTS:** Boys Town has unrelated-business income from a farm located in Green County, Iowa, and from the Sadie, Fred, and Steve Copulos Ranch, Inc.
- **RATINGS:** As of June 1, 1990, NCIB was preparing a new report.
- **REGISTRATION:** CA, CT, GA, IL, MA, MI, MN, NJ, NY (43998), OH, OK, VA (530), WI, and WV.
- **FINANCIAL DATA:** Text and chart source was their IRS form 990 covering 1988.

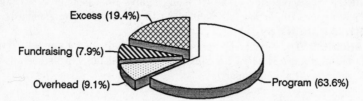

Excess (19.4%)
Fundraising (7.9%)
Overhead (9.1%)
Program (63.6%)

Braille Institute of America, Inc.
741 N. Vermont Ave.
Los Angeles, CA 90029
(213) 663-1111

- **CONTRIBUTIONS** are tax-deductible.
- **PURPOSE:** Provides free educational and adjustment training, programs, and services to blind and visually impaired people of all ages, enabling them to lead full and productive lives. Founded in 1919 to provide brailled reading material for those who are blind (published brailled King James Bible in 1924); incorporated in 1929 as Braille Institute of America, Inc.
- **SIZE:** More than 200 programs and services in personal development, rehabilitation, and adjustment at nineteen Southern California locations.
- **INCOME:** $22,815,946 (year ending 6/30/89; annual report).
- **HOW THEY USE YOUR MONEY:**
PROGRAM: $8,496,233:
  - $6,303,612 for educational services and student services.
  - $1,649,157 (including $695,083 in grants and allocations) for the Braille Institute Press and Library (a regional branch of the Library of Congress that circulated 565,111 units in braille and recorded format).
  - $543,464 for public education and public relations.
OVERHEAD: $1,123,994:
  - $713,369 for support services.
  - $410,625 for administration.
FUNDRAISING: $832,849.
DEPRECIATION: $946,368.
- **EXCESS:** $11,416,502. (In 1988 construction began in Los Angeles on a library and conference center, which includes expanded regional-library and braille-press facilities, and a regional educational center in Rancho Mirage, California. Both are due for completion in 1990 at a cost of $20 million.)
- **LITTLE-KNOWN FACTS:** Will produce more than 3 million brailled pages in 1989–90. More than 26,000 service recipients. Library services also available to reading-disabled persons.
- **RATINGS:** No NCIB report.
- **REGISTRATION:** CA and NY (11209).
- **FINANCIAL DATA:** Text and chart source was their annual report covering the year ending 6/30/89.

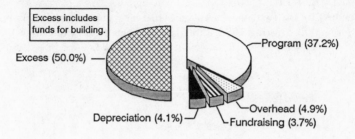

Excess includes funds for building.

Excess (50.0%)

Program (37.2%)

Depreciation (4.1%)

Overhead (4.9%)

Fundraising (3.7%)

Bread for the World, Inc., and
Bread for the World Institute on Hunger and Development
802 Rhode Island Ave., N.E.
Washington, DC 20018
(202) 269-0200

- **CONTRIBUTIONS** for the parent group are *not* tax-deductible; contributions to the institute are.
- **PURPOSE:** Bread for the World was founded in 1974, as "a nationwide Christian movement that seeks justice for the world's hungry people by lobbying the nation's decision-makers." The institute "seeks justice for hungry people" through impartial, scientific research and analysis of the causes, nature, and prevention of poverty and hunger in America and worldwide, and education on policies related to hunger and development.
- **SIZE:** 40,000 members, more than 400 local chapters, and four regional offices.
- **INCOME:** $2,711,727 (parent group); $383,606 (institute; both calendar 1988; IRS form 990).
- **HOW THEY USE YOUR MONEY:**
  PROGRAM (PARENT GROUP): $2,091,004:
  - $890,880 for outreach.
  - $617,808 for organizing.
  - $281,980 for issues (promoting research and legislation of hunger-related issues).
  - $300,336 for information systems (servicing and maintaining membership).
  PROGRAM (INSTITUTE): $276,123: for educating the public on issues relating to hunger by publishing books and materials, holding seminars and conferences, and promoting research.
  OVERHEAD: $685,108 (parent group); $46,687 (institute).
  FUNDRAISING: $93,533 (parent group); $31,087 (institute).
- **DEFICIT:** $157,918 (parent group).
- **EXCESS:** $29,709 (institute).
- **LITTLE-KNOWN FACTS:** Bread for the World and the BFW Institute share offices, have a common board of directors, and have engaged in fund transfers. During 1988, according to the institute's audited statement, "administrative, program, and consulting services were performed" by BFW for the institute in the amount of $130,134.
- **RATINGS:** No NCIB report.
- **REGISTRATION:** DC, IL, MN, NC, NJ, NY, and VA.
- **FINANCIAL DATA:** Text and chart sources (parent group and institute) were their IRS forms 990 covering 1988. Little-Known Facts figure came from the institute's independently audited statement covering 1988.

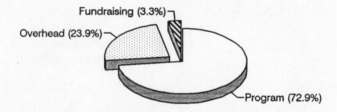

Fundraising (3.3%)
Overhead (23.9%)
Program (72.9%)

Due to deficit of 5.5%, chart is based on spending, not income.

Brookings Institution
1775 Massachusetts Ave., N.W.
Washington, DC 20036
(202) 797-6000

- **CONTRIBUTIONS** are tax-deductible.
- **PURPOSE:** The result of a 1927 merger between the Institute for Government Research (the first think tank, it was established by Robert S. Brookings in 1916) and the Robert Brookings Graduate School of Economics and Government. The institution studies problems in economics, foreign policy, and government.
- **SIZE:** About 50 full-time scholars, plus a staff of nearly 200.
- **INCOME:** $16,634,228 (year ending 6/30/89; accrual accounting, operating fund *only,* independently audited statement).
- **HOW THEY USE YOUR MONEY:**
  PROGRAM: $12,780,871 (excluding $3,769,367 allocated to supporting services): for economic studies; the Center for Public Policy Education; foreign policy studies; publications; the computer center; governmental studies; and fellowships.
  OVERHEAD: $2,350,583 for institutional administration.
  FUNDRAISING AND PUBLIC AFFAIRS: $931,619.
- **EXCESS:** $571,155.
- **LITTLE-KNOWN FACTS:** As in the 1970s and early 1980s, the Brookings Institution will publish an edition of *Setting National Priorities* in 1990, focusing on the budget, taxes, the environment, and defense spending.
- **RATINGS:** No NCIB report.
- **REGISTRATION:** NY (8040) and VA (241).
- **FINANCIAL DATA:** Text and chart source was the Operating Fund figures found in their independently audited statement covering the year ending 6/30/89.

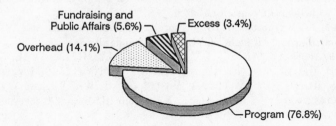

Fundraising and Public Affairs (5.6%)
Excess (3.4%)
Overhead (14.1%)
Program (76.8%)

Bread for the World Institute

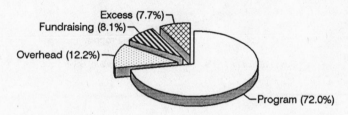

Excess (7.7%)
Fundraising (8.1%)
Overhead (12.2%)
Program (72.0%)

Pearl S. Buck Foundation
Box 181
Perkasie, PA 18944
(215) 249-0100 • (800) 242-BUCK

- **CONTRIBUTIONS** are tax-deductible.
- **PURPOSE:** Established in 1964 by author Pearl Buck, winner of both the Nobel and Pulitzer prizes, for the education and general welfare of the displaced children of the world, "to publicize and eliminate injustices suffered by children who, because of their birth, are not permitted to enjoy the educational, social, economic, and civil privileges normally accorded to children." Particular attention is given to Amerasian (half-American) children in Southeast Asia. Programs assist and educate Amerasians so they may become self-sufficient adults in their homelands. Social services include citizenship adjustment, permanent U.S. foster-home placement, and reunification.
- **SIZE:** 6,956 children were assisted in Korea, Japan, Taiwan, Thailand, and the Philippines in 1988.
- **INCOME:** $3,778,073 (calendar 1988; accrual accounting, IRS form 990).
- **HOW THEY USE YOUR MONEY:**
  PROGRAM: $3,586,832:
  - $3,157,258 for education and support of children through centers in Asia.
  - $148,862 for public education (radio and TV, newsletters, press releases, educational programs).
  - $280,712 to maintain the Pearl S. Buck House (a registered historic site open to the public).
  OVERHEAD: $321,654.
  FUNDRAISING: $367,986.
- **DEFICIT:** $498,399.
- **LITTLE-KNOWN FACTS:** In 1988 the foundation reunited fourteen American fathers with their Amerasian children.
- **RATINGS:** NCIB reported (3/18/87, based on figures from calendar 1985) that the foundation met all eight of NCIB's old standards.
- **REGISTRATION:** AK, AR, AZ, CA, CT, DE, FL, GA, HI, IA, ID, IL, KS, LA, MA, MD, ME, MI, MN, NC, ND, NE, NH, NJ, NM, NY (12506), NV, OH, OK, OR, PA, RI, SC, SD, TN, TX, UT, VA (1460), VT, WA, WI, and WV.
- **FINANCIAL DATA:** Text and chart source was their IRS form 990 covering 1988.

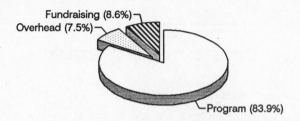

Fundraising (8.6%)
Overhead (7.5%)
Program (83.9%)

Due to deficit of 11.7%, chart is based on spending, not income.

106

Cancer Care, Inc., and the
National Cancer Care Foundation, Inc.
1180 Avenue of the Americas
New York, NY 10036
(212) 221-3300

- **CONTRIBUTIONS** are tax-deductible.
- **PURPOSE:** Founded in 1944, Cancer Care, Inc. (described as a "service arm" of the National Cancer Care Foundation), provides services and supplemental aid (including limited reimbursement for chemotherapy and radiation treatments) to cancer patients and their families in the New York Tri-State area. Services are provided free of charge.
- **SIZE:** Over 11,483 new requests for services were received and 15,404 individuals were helped in FY88.
- **INCOME:** $8,633,904 (CC); $392,366 (foundation; both year ending 6/30/88; accrual accounting, IRS form 990). Support has been increasing since FY86.
- **HOW THEY USE YOUR MONEY:**
  PROGRAM (CC): $4,425,711:
  - $3,487,014 for social services (including professional social work, counseling, and financial help).
  - $810,381 for community services (more than 8,000 volunteers were kept informed about the service program and the needs of cancer families).
  - $128,316 for public affairs (responses to legislative proposals that might affect the nationwide population of cancer patients and their families).

  PROGRAM (foundation): $392,366 (all income). Salaries of professional social-work staff, who consulted with cancer patients and their families.
  OVERHEAD: $497,104.
  FUNDRAISING: $1,945,414.
- **EXCESS:** $1,765,675.
- **LITTLE-KNOWN FACTS:** Cancer Care also offers specialized support groups, such as those for women with breast cancer, people with Hodgkin's disease or lymphoma, parents of children with cancer, Spanish-speaking patients and families, and people with AIDS-related cancer.
- **RATINGS:** NCIB reported on Cancer Care and the National Cancer Care Foundation (2/15/89, using figures from the year ending 6/30/87) that the groups met all nine NCIB standards.
- **REGISTRATION:** CT, NJ, NY (7858), and VA (255).
- **FINANCIAL DATA:** Text and chart sources (CC and foundation) were their IRS forms 990 covering the year ending 6/30/88.

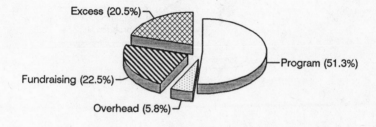

Excess (20.5%)
Fundraising (22.5%)
Overhead (5.8%)
Program (51.3%)

CARE USA
660 First Ave.
New York, NY 10016
(212) 686-3110 • (800) 242-GIVE

- **CONTRIBUTIONS** are tax-deductible.
- **PURPOSE:** Established 1945 as the Cooperation for American Remittances to Europe to deliver food packages to individuals in Europe during the postwar famine. CARE (now the Cooperative for American Relief Everywhere) says its present purpose is "to help the developing world's poor in their efforts to achieve social and economic well-being through processes that create competence and become self-sustaining over time."
- **SIZE:** CARE USA is a member of CARE International, an umbrella coordinating the work of donor organizations in Australia, Austria, Britain, Canada, Denmark, France, Germany, Italy, Japan, and Norway. Worldwide, CARE has 7,200 employees and thousands of volunteers.
- **INCOME:** $329,126,000 (year ending 6/30/89; independently audited statement). Chase Manhattan offers a CARE VISA affinity card.
- **HOW THEY USE YOUR MONEY:**
  PROGRAM: $302,702,000: on development (e.g., agriculture, agroforestry, food-assisted maternal and child health, health education and training, integrated primary health care, natural resources, small enterprise development, and water supply and sanitation), and on disaster and emergency relief.
  PAYMENTS TO AFFILIATES: $1,804,000.
  OVERHEAD: $8,082,000.
  FUNDRAISING: $12,603,000.
- **EXCESS:** $3,935,000.
- **LITTLE-KNOWN FACTS:** CARE signed an agreement with the People's Republic of China in December 1987, becoming the first major private development group to operate there.
- **RATINGS:** NCIB reported (4/27/89, using figures for the year ending 6/30/87) that CARE met all nine NCIB standards.
- **REGISTRATION:** AR, CA, CT, GA, IL, KY, MA, MD, MI, MN, NC, NE, NH, NJ, NM, NY (3539), OH, OK, OR, TN, TX, VA (262), and WV.
- **FINANCIAL DATA:** Text and chart source was their independently audited statement covering the year ending 6/30/89.

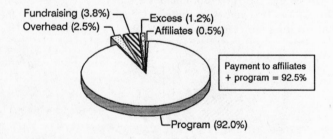

Fundraising (3.8%)
Overhead (2.5%)
Excess (1.2%)
Affiliates (0.5%)
Payment to affiliates + program = 92.5%
Program (92.0%)

Catholic Relief Services
1011 First Ave., 13th Fl.
New York, NY 10022
(212) 838-4700

- **CONTRIBUTIONS** are tax-deductible.
- **PURPOSE:** Established 1943 to assist the "poor and disadvantaged outside of this country." CRS serves as the overseas relief and development agency of the U.S. Catholic Church, operating in 74 countries worldwide.
- **SIZE:** 1,600 staff members.
- **INCOME:** $288,296,000 (calendar 1988; accrual accounting, independently audited statement).
- **HOW THEY USE YOUR MONEY:**
  PROGRAM: $280,562,000:
  - $183,884,000 for human development.
  - $62,136,000 for disaster and emergency relief.
  - $22,171,000 for general welfare.
  - $12,371,000 for refugee relief and resettlement.

  OVERHEAD: $11,119,000.
  FUNDRAISING: $4,326,000.
  PUBLIC AWARENESS: $838,000.
- **DEFICIT:** $8,549,000.
- **RATINGS:** No NCIB report.
- **REGISTRATION:** VA (3041).
- **FINANCIAL DATA:** Text and chart source was their independently audited statement covering 1988.

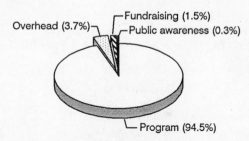

Overhead (3.7%)

Fundraising (1.5%)
Public awareness (0.3%)

Program (94.5%)

Due to deficit of 2.9%, chart is based on spending, not income.

Center for Auto Safety
2001 S St., N.W., Suite 410
Washington, DC 20009
(202) 328-7700

■ **CONTRIBUTIONS** are tax-deductible.

■ **PURPOSE:** Founded in 1968 by Ralph Nader and the Consumers Union; seeks to "reduce the human and economic losses wrought by the automobile and the auto industry." Programs include highway safety, mobile homes, product-liability research service, and vehicle safety. The center participates in the rule-making procedures of the National Highway Traffic Safety Administration and the Federal Highway Administration.

■ **SIZE:** 14,000 members.

■ **INCOME:** $742,201 (year ending 6/30/89; accrual accounting, IRS form 990).

■ **HOW THEY USE YOUR MONEY:**
PROGRAM: $520,612:
- $176,181 for highway safety project.
- $140,676 for vehicle safety project.
- $122,227 for publications.
- $81,528 for product liability research service for attorneys and engineers.

OVERHEAD: $36,326.
MEMBERSHIP SERVICES: $100,822.

■ **EXCESS:** $84,441.

■ **LITTLE-KNOWN FACTS:** Among the center's publications are the *Car Book,* an annual guide to buying new and used cars, which includes ratings on crash safety, fuel economy, maintenance, insurance, tires, and child seats, as well as a chart summarizing state lemon laws.

■ **RATINGS:** No NCIB report.

■ **REGISTRATION:** DC, NY (49851), and VA (271).

■ **FINANCIAL DATA:** Text and chart source was their IRS form 990 covering the year ending 6/30/89.

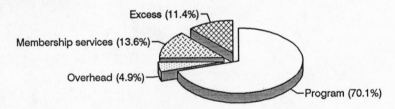

Excess (11.4%)
Membership services (13.6%)
Overhead (4.9%)
Program (70.1%)

Center for Community Change
1000 Wisconsin Ave., N.W.
Washington, DC 20007
(202) 342-0519

- **CONTRIBUTIONS** are tax-deductible.
- **PURPOSE:** Founded 1968; helps empower poor people to improve their communities and change policies and institutions that affect their lives, primarily through helping them develop strong organizations controlled by community people.
- **SIZE:** During 1988 the center assisted more than 200 low-income community organizations, 60 of them intensively.
- **INCOME:** $3,675,239 (year ending 9/30/88; IRS form 990).
- **HOW THEY USE YOUR MONEY:**
  PROGRAM: $2,884,203; the three largest program expenditures were:
  - $356,283 for the Campaign to End Hunger and Homelessness.
  - $344,683 for the National Committee for Responsive Philanthropy.
  - $241,260 for the National Coalition on Human Needs.
  OVERHEAD: $669,242.
  FUNDRAISING: $125,069.
- **DEFICIT:** $3,275.
- **LITTLE-KNOWN FACTS:** Thanks to a 1988 co-sponsorship donation of 120 computer systems from Apple Computer (worth $245,549), the center began a project to create a nationwide information and communication network for community organizations.
- **RATINGS:** As of June 1, 1990, NCIB had requested but not received sufficient information for a report.
- **REGISTRATION:** CA and NY (43008).
- **FINANCIAL DATA:** Text and chart source was their IRS form 990 covering the year ending 9/30/88.

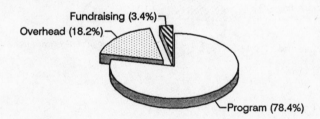

Fundraising (3.4%)
Overhead (18.2%)
Program (78.4%)

Due to deficit of 0.1%, chart is based on spending, not income.

Center for Constitutional Rights
666 Broadway, 7th Fl.
New York, NY 10012
(212) 614-6464

■ **CONTRIBUTIONS** are tax-deductible.
■ **PURPOSE:** Founded in 1966; works against the "steady erosion" of civil liberties in the United States. Particular interests include abuses of the grand-jury process, women's rights, civil rights and affirmative action, freedom of the press, racism, electronic surveillance, and criminal trials.
■ **SIZE:** Twenty-four staff members.
■ **INCOME:** $2,107,902 (calendar 1988; accrual accounting, IRS form 990).
■ **HOW THEY USE YOUR MONEY:**
PROGRAM: $1,324,270:
  • $899,973 for litigation.
  • $424,297 for education (publishing and distributing materials regarding constitutional rights).
OVERHEAD: $212,941.
FUNDRAISING: $258,375.
■ **EXCESS:** $312,316.
■ **LITTLE-KNOWN FACTS:** CCR cases have ranged from the defense of the Chicago Seven to representing the Philippine government of Corazón Aquino in its attempts to recover the U.S. portion of money spirited out of the country by deposed dictator Ferdinand Marcos.
■ **RATINGS:** No NCIB report.
■ **REGISTRATION:** NY (42927).
■ **FINANCIAL DATA:** Text and chart source was their IRS form 990 covering 1988.

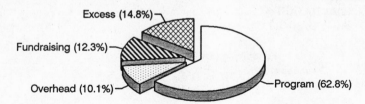

Excess (14.8%)

Fundraising (12.3%)

Overhead (10.1%)

Program (62.8%)

Center for Democratic Renewal
Box 50469
Atlanta, GA 30302
(404) 221-0025

- **CONTRIBUTIONS** are tax-deductible.
- **PURPOSE:** Formerly known as the National Anti-Klan Network, founded in 1979 following the KKK-related murders of five persons in Greensboro, NC. It serves as a national clearinghouse for efforts to counter hate-group activities.
- **SIZE:** Offices in Atlanta, Kansas City, and Seattle.
- **INCOME:** $287,920 (year ending 6/30/89; independently audited statement).
- **HOW THEY USE YOUR MONEY:**
  PROGRAM: $162,434 on public education, research, community response (and victim assistance), and leadership training.
  OVERHEAD AND FUNDRAISING: $103,259 combined total.
- **EXCESS:** $22,227.
- **LITTLE-KNOWN FACTS:** During the 1990s the center plans to focus on youth, and expand its own concerns to include gay-bashing and anti-Semitism.
- **RATINGS:** No NCIB report.
- **REGISTRATION:** IRS.
- **FINANCIAL DATA:** Text and chart source was their independently audited statement covering the year ending 6/30/89.

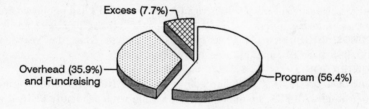

Excess (7.7%)

Overhead (35.9%) and Fundraising

Program (56.4%)

Center for Science in the Public Interest
1501 Sixteenth St., N.W.
Washington, DC 20036
(202) 332-9110

- **CONTRIBUTIONS** are tax-deductible.
- **PURPOSE:** Formed in 1971, CSPI investigates and seeks consumer-oriented solutions for problems related to science and technology. In the future, CSPI intends to work toward obtaining clear, informative food labeling, and "alerting consumers to the dangers of saturated fats hidden in over 500 processed foods."
- **SIZE:** Staff of more than 30; more than 140,000 members.
- **INCOME:** $3,506,459 (year ending 6/30/89; accrual accounting, IRS form 990).
- **HOW THEY USE YOUR MONEY:**
  PROGRAM: $2,616,918:
  - $1,167,903* for public education.
  - $625,845 for the *Nutrition Action* newsletter (a periodical on nutrition, diet, and related health issues).
  - $823,170 for special projects on nutrition and related health areas.

  OVERHEAD: $62,888.
  FUNDRAISING: $208,506.
  MEMBERSHIP DEVELOPMENT: $582,455.*
- **EXCESS:** $35,692.
- **LITTLE-KNOWN FACTS:** Well before the early-1990 controversy over plans to market a cigarette specifically to African-Americans, CSPI had published *Marketing Disease to Hispanics: The Selling of Alcohol, Tobacco, and Junk Foods.*
- **RATINGS:** NCIB reported (4/25/90, using figures from the year ending 6/30/89) that CSPI met all nine NCIB standards.
- **REGISTRATION:** DC, NY (47860), and VA (272).
- **FINANCIAL DATA:** Text and chart source was their IRS form 990 covering the year ending 6/30/89. Footnote source was their independently audited statement covering the same year.

*Informational materials used in membership development cost $1,377,438; $812,227 of this expense was allocated to public education and the rest to membership development.

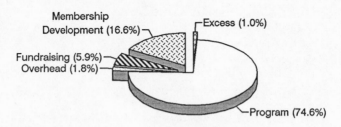

Membership Development (16.6%)
Excess (1.0%)
Fundraising (5.9%)
Overhead (1.8%)
Program (74.6%)

Central Committee for Conscientious Objectors
2208 South St.
Philadelphia, PA 19146
(215) 545-4626

- **CONTRIBUTIONS** are tax-deductible.
- **PURPOSE:** Founded in 1948, CCCO provides draft and military counseling and counterrecruitment counseling. In addition, CCCO assists other attorneys with draft and military cases.
- **SIZE:** Eight staff members and one regional group.
- **INCOME:** $277,734 (year ending 8/31/89; IRS form 990).
- **HOW THEY USE YOUR MONEY:**
  PROGRAM: $177,729:
  - $160,167 for counseling, training, and outreach to conscientious objectors.
  - $17,562 for periodicals, such as handbooks and newsletters.
  OVERHEAD: $74,762.
  FUNDRAISING: $26,112.
- **DEFICIT:** $869.
- **RATINGS:** No NCIB report.
- **REGISTRATION:** NY (54550) and PA.
- **FINANCIAL DATA:** Text and chart source was their IRS form 990 covering the year ending 8/31/89.

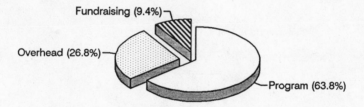

Fundraising (9.4%)

Overhead (26.8%)

Program (63.8%)

Due to deficit of 0.3%, chart is based on spending, not income.

115

Child Find of America
7 Innis Ave.
New Paltz, NY 12561
(914) 255-1848
Hotlines: Mediation: (800) A-WAY-OUT; Location: (800) I-AM-LOST

- **CONTRIBUTIONS** are tax-deductible.
- **PURPOSE:** Founded in 1980 by the parent of a missing child, for the purpose of "finding missing children, preventing child abduction, and offering counseling support and mediation." The present name was adopted in 1986.
- **SIZE:** Fourteen staff members.
- **INCOME:** $539,252 (year ending 5/31/89; accrual accounting, IRS form 990).
- **HOW THEY USE YOUR MONEY:**
  PROGRAM: $401,093.
  OVERHEAD: $65,976.
  FUNDRAISING: $43,582.
- **EXCESS:** $28,601.
- **LITTLE-KNOWN FACTS:** CFA maintains a registry of missing children.
- **RATINGS:** NCIB reported (7/8/87, using figures for the year ending 5/31/86) that Child Find met all eight of NCIB's old evaluation standards.
- **REGISTRATION:** NY (51409) and VA (2173).
- **FINANCIAL DATA:** Text and chart source was their IRS form 990 covering the year ending 5/31/89.

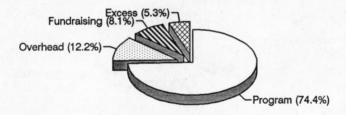

Excess (5.3%)
Fundraising (8.1%)
Overhead (12.2%)
Program (74.4%)

Child Welfare League of America
440 First St., N.W., Suite 310
Washington, DC 20001
(202) 638-2952

- **CONTRIBUTIONS** are tax-deductible.
- **PURPOSE:** In 1909 President Theodore Roosevelt called a White House conference on children, and the Child Welfare League was organized in 1920 to
  improve the lives of abused, neglected, and troubled children. In 1976 the
  Florence Crittenton Association merged with CWLA, which added prevention of
  adolescent pregnancy and assistance to adolescent parents to its concerns. Ten
  years later Generations United, a joint project with the National Council on the
  Aging, was formed to promote intergenerational cooperation.
- **SIZE:** 535 member agencies; CWLA Children's Campaign, a national network of
  individual child advocates, nearly tripled in 1988 to 35,000 members.
- **INCOME:** $3,819,513 (year ending 9/30/88; accrual accounting, IRS form 990).
- **HOW THEY USE YOUR MONEY:**
  PROGRAM: $2,989,470.
  OVERHEAD: $476,192.
  FUNDRAISING: $227,614.
- **EXCESS:** $126,237.
- **LITTLE-KNOWN FACTS:** A CWLA task force developed and published the first
  North American guidelines for the care of HIV-infected children, children at
  risk, and their families.
- **RATINGS:** NCIB reported (7/20/89, using figures for the year ending 9/30/88)
  that the CWLA met all nine NCIB standards.
- **REGISTRATION:** NY (8777).
- **FINANCIAL DATA:** Text and chart source was their IRS form 990 covering the
  year ending 9/30/88.

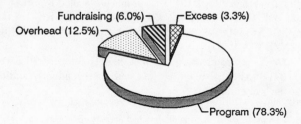

Fundraising (6.0%) Excess (3.3%)
Overhead (12.5%)
Program (78.3%)

Children's Aid International
Box 480155
Los Angeles, CA 90048
(213) 519-8923 • (800) 842-2810

- **CONTRIBUTIONS** are tax-deductible.
- **PURPOSE:** Formed in 1977 "to help relieve the suffering of children, promote village self-sufficiency, and rescue refugees through programs of relief, development, and child sponsorship." The nondenominational organization is dedicated to "Giving children a chance . . . to live . . . to grow . . . to dream."
- **INCOME:** $3,414,339 (year ending 7/31/89; accrual accounting, IRS form 990).
- **HOW THEY USE YOUR MONEY:**
  PROGRAM: $2,955,083,* including:
  - $2,766,008 in cash and in-kind grants (the independently audited statement for this period provides more detail of some expenses: $963,810 for school supplies in Jamaica; $956,070 for agricultural supplies in Haiti; $569,378 for food and milk in Brazil, Haiti, Honduras, Mexico, and the Philippines; $125,800 for clothing in Mexico; $115,000 for building materials in Mexico; and $11,500 for medical supplies in Armenia and Jamaica).
  - $45,947 for child sponsorship ("two projects that sponsored the health, nutrition, and education of children," apparently in Bangkok, Thailand, and Jakarta).
  OVERHEAD: $51,880.
  FUNDRAISING: $361,274.*
- **EXCESS:** $46,102.
- **LITTLE-KNOWN FACTS:** CAI intends to expand its child-sponsorship program into Latin America and Africa. New projects are being developed and implemented for Guatemala and Mexico. By 1991, CAI will be able to enter payroll-deduction plans offered to state and county employees.
- **RATINGS:** As of June 1, 1990, NCIB was preparing a new report.
- **REGISTRATION:** AR, CA, CO, CT, DC, FL, GA, HI, ID, IL, KS, LA, MA, MD, ME, MI, MN, MO, NC, ND, NE, NH, NJ, NM, NV, NY (46896), OH, OK, OR, PA, RI, SC, TN, UT, VA (310), VT, and WI.
- **FINANCIAL DATA:** Text and chart source was their IRS form 990 covering the year ending 7/31/89. Footnote source was their independently audited statement covering the same year.

*During the year, CAI adopted SOP 87-2 on joint allocation of costs; no fundraising costs have been allocated to program expenses. In the past, CAI says, "28 percent of the costs of fundraising materials and actvities were allocated to program services" because management felt they provided useful information. During FY89, $25,657 out of $314,303 spent on "production fees and services has been recorded as program expense representing costs of informational materials that did not include an appeal for funds."

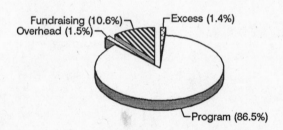

Fundraising (10.6%)
Overhead (1.5%)
Excess (1.4%)
Program (86.5%)

Children's Defense Fund
122 C St., N.W.
Washington, DC 20001
(202) 628-8787

- **CONTRIBUTIONS** are tax-deductible.
- **PURPOSE:** Established in 1973 as an outgrowth of the Washington Research Project, Inc. (founded 1969), CDF was the sole project of WRP until 1978, when it became the Children's Defense Fund. Acts as an advocate for children (primarily poor, minority, and handicapped) at the federal, state, and local levels in such areas as child development, education, health care, child welfare and mental health, and prevention of adolescent pregnancy.
- **SIZE:** At the end of 1988, CDF had an eighty-three-member staff in Washington and four state offices. The Mississippi office was due to close in 1989.
- **INCOME:** $6,331,474 (calendar 1988; accrual accounting, IRS form 990). During the preceding four fiscal years support had been increasing.
- **HOW THEY USE YOUR MONEY:**
PROGRAM: $5,019,752:
  - $1,407,967 for public affairs and publications.
  - $737,056 for state and local affairs.
  - $617,544 for state offices (Ohio, Mississippi, Virginia, Texas, Minnesota).
  - $455,906 for health programs (advocacy work).
  - $350,048 for child development.
  - $278,448 for research.
  - $253,184 for legal programs.
  - $250,954 for education.
  - $238,753 for youth employment.
  - $234,792 for child welfare and mental health.
  - $195,100 for government affairs.
  - Included in all CDF program services are costs of about $1,700,000 for their adolescent-pregnancy prevention program.

OVERHEAD: $566,624.
FUNDRAISING: $631,413.
- **EXCESS:** $113,685.
- **LITTLE-KNOWN FACTS:** In 1988 CDF published *Teens and AIDS: Opportunities for Prevention.*
- **RATINGS:** NCIB reported (7/9/90, using figures from calendar 1989) that CDF met all nine of NCIB's standards.
- **REGISTRATION:** DC, NY (45046), and VA (3221).
- **FINANCIAL DATA:** Text and chart source was their IRS form 990 covering 1988.

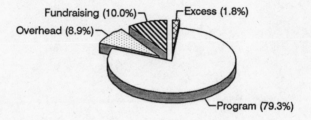

Fundraising (10.0%) Excess (1.8%)
Overhead (8.9%)
Program (79.3%)

Christian Anti-Communism Crusade
Box 890
Long Beach, CA 90801
(213) 437-0941 • (213) 775-2006

■ **CONTRIBUTIONS** are tax-deductible.

■ **PURPOSE:** An educational organization "devoted to the battle against Communism, and the propagation of the Christian faith," founded 1953. Activities involve lecturing in schools, civic clubs, churches, and servicemen's organizations, and publishing books and literature for distribution at home and abroad.

■ **SIZE:** Works in the United States and twenty-three foreign countries.

■ **INCOME:** $1,638,004 (calendar 1988; accrual accounting, IRS form 990).

■ **HOW THEY USE YOUR MONEY:**
PROGRAM: $1,387,167*; on education to "combat communism by . . . distributing information through publications and radio and TV broadcasts."
OVERHEAD: $319,849.
FUNDRAISING: $47,748.

■ **DEFICIT:** $116,760.

■ **LITTLE-KNOWN FACTS:** To "diminish the effectiveness of the accusations that they are agents of U.S. Imperialism," the group does not open branches abroad; instead it encourages local organizations through education, training, literature, and essential financial support.

■ **RATINGS:** No NCIB report.

■ **REGISTRATION:** CA (3624), NY (10908), and OH.

■ **FINANCIAL DATA:** Text and chart source was their IRS form 990 covering 1988. Footnote source was their independently audited statement covering 1988.

*The group's independently audited statement notes that $34,874 was paid to affiliates.

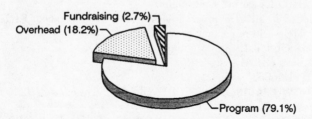

Fundraising (2.7%)
Overhead (18.2%)
Program (79.1%)

Due to deficit of 6.7%, chart is based on spending, not income.

Christian Children's Fund
203 E. Cary St.
Richmond, VA 23261
(804) 644-4654 • Sponsor Communications: (800) 776-6767

- **CONTRIBUTIONS** are tax-deductible.
- **PURPOSE:** Established in 1938 as the China's Children Fund to aid Chinese children after the Sino-Japanese War, CCF is a nonsectarian, international organization dedicated to "serving the needs of children worldwide through person-to-person assistance programs." CCF adopted its present name in 1951.
- **SIZE:** Over 420,000 children served through the fund's children's support in family program.
- **INCOME:** $101,743,506 (year ending 6/30/89; accrual accounting, IRS form 990). During the preceding four fiscal years support had been increasing.
- **HOW THEY USE YOUR MONEY:**
  PROGRAM: $75,883,769:
  - $65,070,332 (including $3,126,238 in grants and allocations) for children's support in family.
  - $10,259,485 (including $492,906 in grants and allocations) for children's education.
  - $553,952 (including $26,615 in grants and allocations) for homeless-children services (orphanages).

  OVERHEAD: $8,901,156.
  FUNDRAISING: $8,681,707.
- **EXCESS:** $8,276,874.
- **RATINGS:** NCIB reported (7/24/89, using figures for the year ending 6/30/88) that the CCF met all nine NCIB standards.
- **REGISTRATION:** NY (8962) and VA (323).
- **FINANCIAL DATA:** Text and chart source was their IRS form 990 covering the year ending 6/30/89.

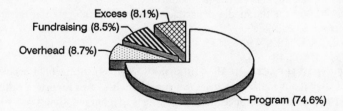

Excess (8.1%)
Fundraising (8.5%)
Overhead (8.7%)
Program (74.6%)

Christic Institute
1324 N. Capitol St., N.W.
Washington, DC 20002
(202) 797-8106

- **CONTRIBUTIONS** are tax-deductible.
- **PURPOSE:** Founded in 1980 by the attorneys, educators, and organizers who launched and directed the Karen Silkwood lawsuit against the Kerr-McGee Nuclear Corporation, the Christic Institute is an interfaith center for law and national policy in the public interest, with offices in Washington, Los Angeles, and San Francisco. The Christic Institute–South office was opened in North Carolina in 1985 to work primarily on civil rights. "Christic" was a term used by Jesuit philosopher and scientist Pierre Teilhard de Chardin (1881–1955) to describe his conception of the historical process by which creation is drawn toward a future unity.
- **SIZE:** In 1987 and 1988, the institute's base of supporters grew from 28,000 to 72,000.
- **INCOME:** $2,621,330 (calendar 1988; accrual accounting, IRS form 990). Apart from a slight dip in 1985, during the preceding four fiscal years support had been increasing. The institute received unspecified earnings from sales of baseball-type trading cards, depicting the principals named in the lawsuit described below.
- **HOW THEY USE YOUR MONEY:**
  PROGRAM: $1,760,606:
  - $613,022 for litigation.
  - $278,353 for investigations (used in litigation).
  - $306,379 for public education.
  - $164,367 for Christic Institute–South (which provides legal and organizing assistance to groups working to achieve social justice).
  - $142,741 for field offices in Los Angeles and San Francisco.
  - $134,882 for outreach and organizing.
  - $120,862 for the media department (to provide information to reporters).
  OVERHEAD: $328,097.
  FUNDRAISING: $422,079.
- **EXCESS:** $110,548.
- **LITTLE-KNOWN FACTS:** In May 1986 the Christic Institute filed a civil RICO lawsuit in Miami Federal District Court on behalf of two reporters injured in a May 1984 press-conference bombing. The suit charged that twenty-nine individuals were allegedly part of a widespread conspiracy consisting of former military and intelligence officers. (Several of the defendants, including Major General Richard Secord, became household names later in 1986 when their roles in the Iran-contra scandal were revealed.) In June 1988 the court granted summary judgment to the defendants and in February 1989 entered over $1 million in sanctions against the institute, which posted a surety bond and appealed both judgment and sanctions. In August 1988, the institute collected its highest one-month total of contributions in its history.
- **RATINGS:** No NCIB report.
- **REGISTRATION:** DC.
- **FINANCIAL DATA:** Text and chart source was their IRS form 990 covering 1988.

City Harvest, Inc.
159 W. 25th St.
New York, NY 10001
(212) 463-0456

- **CONTRIBUTIONS** are tax-deductible.
- **PURPOSE:** Founded in 1982, City Harvest collects donated food from many of New York City's retailers, wholesalers, corporate cafeterias, and restaurants and distributes it by its own vans to homeless shelters, soup kitchens, and food pantries.
- **SIZE:** Each day City Harvest provides food for more than 8,110 meals served at participating facilities throughout New York—about 2,320,000 pounds in FY89.
- **INCOME:** $1,178,652 (year ending 6/30/89; accrual accounting, IRS form 990).
- **HOW THEY USE YOUR MONEY:**
  PROGRAM: $620,495: on picking up and transporting donated food to social-service agencies, soup kitchens, food pantries, and homeless shelters. Net cost per distributed meal is 39 cents.
  OVERHEAD: $157,473.
  FUNDRAISING: $282,789—over five times as much as the previous year. (Income grew by over $370,000 during the period.)
- **EXCESS:** $117,895.
- **LITTLE-KNOWN FACTS:** In 1986, after a party celebrating the centennial of the Statue of Liberty, City Harvest was given a 14-foot, 4,000-pound chocolate replica of the statue. The group worked all night to break it into pieces that were then distributed to drug-rehabilitation centers, where sugar must be taken with some medications.
- **RATINGS:** No NCIB report.
- **REGISTRATION:** NY (52588).
- **FINANCIAL DATA:** Text and chart source was their IRS form 990 covering the year ending 6/30/89.

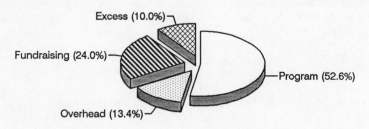

Excess (10.0%)
Fundraising (24.0%)
Overhead (13.4%)
Program (52.6%)

Christic Institute

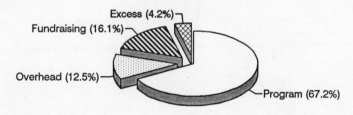

Excess (4.2%)
Fundraising (16.1%)
Overhead (12.5%)
Program (67.2%)

City of Hope
1500 E. Duarte Rd.
Duarte, CA 91010
(818) 359-8111 • (800) 826-4673

- **CONTRIBUTIONS** are tax-deductible.
- **PURPOSE:** Established in 1913, the City of Hope provides patient care and studies diabetes, Alzheimer's disease, AIDS, Huntington's disease, genetics, and brain and nerve functions. It also supports the National Pilot Medical Center and the Beckman Research Institute, centers for treatment, research, and medical education concerning catastrophic diseases such as cancer, leukemia, heart and lung diseases, certain hereditary maladies, and metabolic disorders such as diabetes.
- **SIZE:** Over 500 chartered auxiliaries in over 230 cities (thirty-two states and the District of Columbia).
- **INCOME:** $44,849,964 (year ending 9/30/88; accrual accounting, IRS form 990).
- **HOW THEY USE YOUR MONEY:**
  PROGRAM: $1,724,261:
  - $1,315,398 for social services (such as assistance to patients and their families).
  - $408,863 for public information and education (including free patient services, medical research, and medical education conducted at the City of Hope National Medical Center and the Beckman Research Institute).
  DONATIONS TO AFFILIATES: $33,919,438:
  - $21,783,000 to the City of Hope National Medical Center.
  - $12,136,438 to the Beckman Research Institute.
  OVERHEAD: $8,238,223.
  FUNDRAISING: $0.
- **EXCESS:** $968,042.
- **RATINGS:** No NCIB report.
- **REGISTRATION:** CA (50010), NY (8528), TN, and VA (346).
- **FINANCIAL DATA:** Text and chart source was their IRS form 990 covering the year ending 9/30/88.

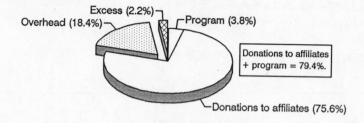

Excess (2.2%)
Overhead (18.4%)
Program (3.8%)
Donations to affiliates + program = 79.4%.
Donations to affiliates (75.6%)

Coalition for the Homeless
105 E. 22nd St.
New York, NY 10010
(212) 460-8110

- **CONTRIBUTIONS** are tax-deductible.
- **PURPOSE:** Formed in 1980; opened its doors in 1982. The coalition's founder, Robert M. Hayes, led the legal battle to establish the right to shelter for New York's homeless. The coalition has three priorities: serving as an aggressive advocate for New York City's homeless population; operating (with closely allied organizations) model direct-care service programs for the homeless, and working with other organizations to end homelessness. In 1983 the National Coalition for the Homeless was formed, and it opened its offices in Washington, D.C., in 1985. The New York State Coalition for the Homeless opened its Albany office in 1986.
- **SIZE:** National Coalition operations are divided into ten different regions.
- **INCOME:** $1,361,238 (six months ending 6/30/89; accrual accounting, IRS form 990). During the preceding four fiscal years support had been increasing.
- **HOW THEY USE YOUR MONEY:**
  PROGRAM: $1,128,236 (six months):
  - $473,859 for advocacy (legal assistance to the homeless and technical assistance to nonprofit groups regarding housing for the homeless).
  - $435,330 for food (feeding homeless people at hotels for the homeless and various other locations).
  - $219,047 for direct services (publications, public education, transportation, clothing, and building maintenance).
  OVERHEAD: $98,356.
  FUNDRAISING: No fundraising expenses during the six months considered. During 1988 private support for the coalition was greatest in December (27 percent), January (22 percent), and November (16 percent).
- **EXCESS:** $134,646.
- **LITTLE-KNOWN FACTS:** A plea bargain in a tenant-harassment case resulted in three single-room-occupancy buildings (forty units, total value appraised at $2,200,000) being donated by the defendants, five former landlords, to the coalition in 1988. The landlords were ordered to fund the buildings' rehabilitation, start-up costs, and first year's operating expenses.
- **RATINGS:** No NCIB report.
- **REGISTRATION:** NY (50274).
- **FINANCIAL DATA:** Text and chart source was their IRS form 990 covering the six-month period ending 6/30/89.

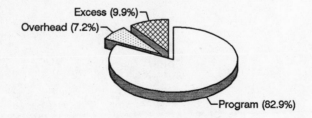

Excess (9.9%)
Overhead (7.2%)
Program (82.9%)

Coalition to Stop Gun Violence
100 Maryland Ave., N.E.
Washington, DC 20002
(202) 544-7190

- **CONTRIBUTIONS** are *not* tax-deductible.
- **PURPOSE:** Founded in 1975 as the National Coalition to Ban Handguns; present name adopted in 1989 to reflect its larger concerns (such as banning semiautomatic weapons). Studies and researches the use and effects of firearms in the United States; educates the public on the effects of firearms safeguards and control; and advocates legislation banning importation, manufacture, sale, transfer, ownership, possession, and use of handguns by the general public.
- **SIZE:** An affiliation of thirty-four organizations, with total membership of 14 million.
- **INCOME:** $494,070 (calendar 1988; cash accounting, IRS form 990).
- **HOW THEY USE YOUR MONEY:**
  PROGRAM: $221,976:
    - $164,891 for public education.
    - $40,452 for research.
    - $12,509 for lobbying expenses.
    - $4,124 for community services.
  OVERHEAD: $74,575.
  FUNDRAISING: $217,088.
- **DEFICIT:** $19,569.
- **LITTLE-KNOWN FACTS:** The coalition notes that, since its eventual goal is to change federal law, "everything we do can be construed as lobbying. But not all of our work is done in the halls of Congress."
- **RATINGS:** No NCIB report.
- **REGISTRATION:** NY (48518) and VA (1311).
- **FINANCIAL DATA:** Text and chart source was their IRS form 990 covering 1988.

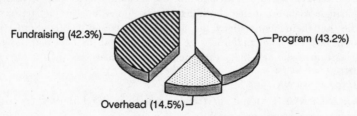

Fundraising (42.3%) — Program (43.2%) — Overhead (14.5%)

Due to deficit of 3.8%, chart is based on spending, not income.

126

Comic Relief, Inc.
2049 Century Park E., Suite 4250
Los Angeles, CA 90067
(213) 201-9317 • Donations: (800) 528-1000

- **CONTRIBUTIONS** are tax-deductible.
- **PURPOSE:** Formed in 1986 to solicit, receive, and administer property through the production of their comedy concerts, and disburse property and income to provide aid for America's homeless. Funds are granted to relief projects through two advisors: the Robert Wood Johnson Foundation and the Department of Community Medicine of St. Vincent's Hospital and Medical Center. The National Health Care for the Homeless Program, designated recipient of Comic Relief monies, provides primary and secondary medical care and related health, mental-health, and social services to homeless people across the country.
- **SIZE:** The National Health Care for the Homeless Program has projects in twenty-three major U.S. cities.
- **INCOME:** $4,540,897 (year ending 5/31/88; accrual accounting, independently audited statement). About $1,500,000 came from Home Box Office for broadcast rights to the show.
- **HOW THEY USE YOUR MONEY:**
PROGRAM: It's not easy to determine Comic Relief's true program expenses, which the group gives as $3,004,746:
  - $1,574,672 for show expenses ($1,111,916 for production costs; $425,019 for administration support; and $37,737 for advertising).
  - $1,430,074 for grant expenditures.
    However, Comic Relief says that the HBO money was used to defray all production costs and administrative overhead, as well as 85 percent of all remaining operating expenses, so "100 percent of all pledge funds received and 85 percent of all revenues generated other than business license and production fees" were used for grants.
OVERHEAD: $722,730 (processing donations and premium expense).
FUNDRAISING: Although the show expenses might be considered fundraising costs, Comic Relief identifies production of its shows as part of its program. Therefore, no funds were spent on fundraising expenses.
- **EXCESS:** $813,421.
- **LITTLE-KNOWN FACTS:** Comic Relief paid $935,000 for production of Comic Relief II to a company controlled by two members of its board of directors.
- **RATINGS:** No NCIB report.
- **REGISTRATION:** CA (59782).
- **FINANCIAL DATA:** Text and chart source was their independently audited statement covering the year ending 5/31/88. HBO figures source was the Comic Relief *Activities Report 1987–88*.

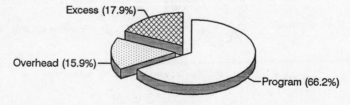

Excess (17.9%)
Overhead (15.9%)
Program (66.2%)

127

Common Cause
2030 M St., N.W.
Washington, DC 20036
(202) 833-1200 • Legislative Hotline: (202) 833-1319

- **CONTRIBUTIONS** are *not* tax-deductible.
- **PURPOSE:** Formed in 1970 by John Gardner, a former secretary of HEW, Common Cause is a nonprofit citizen's lobby that has lobbied federal and state officials on such national issues as: winning eighteen-year-olds the vote; extending the Voting Rights Act; passing "sunshine" laws to open the workings of government to the public; passing financial-disclosure laws and tough ethics codes; and ethics investigations of both Attorney General Edwin Meese III and House Speaker Jim Wright.
- **SIZE:** At December 31, 1988, membership was 273,337.
- **INCOME:** $11,302,705 (calendar 1988; accrual accounting, IRS form 990). This includes $63,000 from renting the CC membership lists.
- **HOW THEY USE YOUR MONEY:**
PROGRAM: $6,893,839:
  - $3,738,468* for national lobbying, issue management, and communications.
  - $2,180,684 for state lobbying, issue management, and communications.
  - $974,687 for program development and management (including lawsuits to further national Common Cause goals, and advice and participation in state litigation programs).
OVERHEAD: $3,354,849* on management and general expenses and on membership development.
FUNDRAISING: $1,467,266.*
- **DEFICIT:** $413,249.
- **LITTLE-KNOWN FACTS:** Common Cause's chairman is Harvard Law School professor Archibald Cox, the Watergate special prosecutor who was fired in the "Saturday Night Massacre" of October 1973.
- **RATINGS:** No NCIB report.
- **REGISTRATION:** AR, CA, DC, FL, GA, IL, KS, MA, MD, MI, MN, NC, NJ, NY (41899), OH, OK, OR, PA, SC, TN, VA (366), WI, and WV.
- **FINANCIAL DATA:** Text and chart source was their IRS form 990 covering 1988.

*Common Cause spent $2,347,011 for informational materials that included membership or fundraising materials. Joint allocation of costs assigned $1,117,856 to membership development, $821,453 to national lobbying and communications, and $407,702 to fundraising.

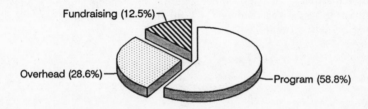

Fundraising (12.5%)

Overhead (28.6%)

Program (58.8%)

Due to deficit of 3.5%, chart is based on spending, not income.

Consumers Union of the United States
256 Washington St.
Mt. Vernon, NY 10553
(914) 667-9400

- **CONTRIBUTIONS** are tax-deductible.
- **PURPOSE:** Founded in 1936, the Consumers Union of the United States tests, rates, and reports on competing brands of appliances, cars, food products, and household equipment. They are primarily known through their monthly magazine, *Consumer Reports,* which is also the group's main source of income. Regional offices of the group represent consumer interests in the legislature, courts, and administrative agencies. In 1989 CU's purchase of a building and 18 acres of land in Yonkers, New York, doubled its work space. Following renovation, this building will become the new Consumer Reports National Testing and Research Center.
- **SIZE:** Staff of about 270.
- **INCOME:** $73,458,868 (year ending 5/31/89; accrual accounting, IRS form 990). CU does not accept corporate contributions of any kind.
- **HOW THEY USE YOUR MONEY:**
  PROGRAM: $63,352,985:
    - $62,963,536 for consumer information (publication and dissemination through magazines, books, radio, and television).
    - $389,449 for California financial services restricted fund (activities related to settlement of a class-action suit, and actions and activities undertaken to represent and protect California consumers).
  OVERHEAD: $5,492,803.
  FUNDRAISING: $2,677,000.
- **EXCESS:** $1,936,080.
- **RATINGS:** No NCIB report.
- **REGISTRATION:** CA, NY, and VA (2739).
- **FINANCIAL DATA:** Text and chart source was their IRS form 990 covering the year ending 5/31/89.

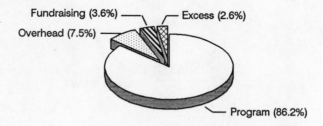

Fundraising (3.6%) — Excess (2.6%)
Overhead (7.5%)
Program (86.2%)

Council of Jewish Federations, Inc.
730 Broadway
New York, NY 10003
(212) 475-5000

- **CONTRIBUTIONS** are tax-deductible.
- **PURPOSE:** Founded in 1932 as the National Council of Jewish Federations and Welfare Funds, which merged with the Bureau of Jewish Social Research. By 1978 the present name had been adopted. Provides central services for local federations, welfare funds, and community councils raising funds for local, national, and overseas Jewish needs in approximately 800 Jewish communities throughout the United States and Canada.
- **SIZE:** There are 189 Jewish Federations throughout the country.
- **INCOME:** $14,523,416 (calendar 1988; accrual accounting, IRS form 990). During the preceding four fiscal years support had been increasing.
- **HOW THEY USE YOUR MONEY:**
  PROGRAM: $12,685,288:
  - $7,372,956 (including $164,757 in grants and allocations) for member service (developing new programs, raising funds, improving quality of Jewish education).
  - $4,441,142 for Soviet Jewish Resettlement (established in 1978 by a grant from the U.S. Department of Health and Human Services).
  - $871,190 for Operation Independence (a task force to advance economic growth and independence in Israel).
  OVERHEAD: $1,261,520.
  FUNDRAISING: $0.
- **EXCESS:** $576,608.
- **RATINGS:** No NCIB report.
- **REGISTRATION:** CA and NY (45132).
- **FINANCIAL DATA:** Text and chart source was their IRS form 990 covering 1988.

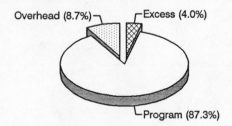

Overhead (8.7%)￢　￢Excess (4.0%)

Program (87.3%)

130

Council on Economic Priorities
30 Irving Pl.
New York, NY 10003
(212) 420-1133

- **CONTRIBUTIONS** are tax-deductible.
- **PURPOSE:** Established in 1969 to engage in impartial analyses of current national issues; especially active in investigating issues of corporate social responsibility and national security. In 1990 the council's US-USSR Project on Military Spending and Economic Priorities will employ three teams of experts from both countries to assess military spending in both nations, the impact of such spending on each country's economy, and the implications for national security.
- **SIZE:** Staff of twenty-three.
- **INCOME:** $858,461 (calendar 1988; accrual accounting, IRS form 990). Apart from a slight dip in 1986, during the preceding four fiscal years support had been increasing.
- **HOW THEY USE YOUR MONEY:**
  PROGRAM: $633,790 for preparation of studies and reports on economic, environmental, and national-security issues.
  OVERHEAD: $154,124.
  FUNDRAISING: $86,500.
- **DEFICIT:** $15,953.
- **LITTLE-KNOWN FACTS:** In the first five months after its December 1988 publication, the council's *Shopping for a Better World* sold over 290,000 copies. Its rating of the social records of 138 companies and the 1,300 products they make changed the shopping decisions of 78 percent of readers, according to a council survey.
- **RATINGS:** NCIB reported (9/7/88, using figures for calendar 1987) that the council met all nine NCIB standards.
- **REGISTRATION:** NY (44075).
- **FINANCIAL DATA:** Text and chart source was their IRS form 990 covering 1988.

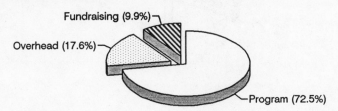

Fundraising (9.9%)
Overhead (17.6%)
Program (72.5%)

Due to deficit of 1.8%, chart is based on spending, not income.

131

Council on Foreign Relations, Inc.
58 E. 68th St.
New York, NY 10021
(212) 734-0400

- **CONTRIBUTIONS** are tax-deductible.
- **PURPOSE:** Established in 1921 to study the international aspects of American politics, economy, and strategy. These studies are conducted by staff members with the advice of study groups of statesmen, business leaders, and academic experts.
- **SIZE:** A membership of about 2,500 supports the work of ninety-five staff members and thirty-eight regional groups. The council's *Foreign Affairs* magazine has a circulation of 95,000.
- **INCOME:** $15,063,900 (year ending 6/30/89; NYS form 497).
- **HOW THEY USE YOUR MONEY:**
  PROGRAM: $7,524,900.
  OVERHEAD: $2,412,000.
  FUNDRAISING: $508,600.
- **EXCESS:** $4,618,400. According to the council's treasurer, "most [of this money] was long-term pledges," including about $2 million in an expected contribution for capital investment, and "earnings from the investment fund in excess of the annual draw for operations."
- **RATINGS:** NCIB reported (6/27/86, using figures for the year ending 6/30/84) that the council met all eight of NCIB's old evaluation standards.
- **REGISTRATION:** NY (7798).
- **FINANCIAL DATA:** Text and chart source was their NYS form 497 covering the year ending 6/30/89.

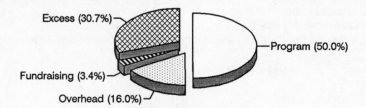

Excess (30.7%)

Program (50.0%)

Fundraising (3.4%)

Overhead (16.0%)

The Cousteau Society
930 W. 21st St.
Norfolk, VA 23517
(804) 627-1144

- **CONTRIBUTIONS** are tax-deductible.
- **PURPOSE:** Established 1973 to protect and improve the quality of life through research and programs on conservation of natural resources and protection of the environment. The society's research is disseminated through television, films, and publications. Jacques Y. Cousteau contributes his research, writing, and film production without remuneration.
- **SIZE:** In December 1988, the *Calypso Log* noted that membership had grown to 245,721, including 84,507 family members.
- **INCOME:** $13,902,988 (calendar 1988; accrual accounting, IRS form 990).
- **HOW THEY USE YOUR MONEY:**
  PROGRAM: $10,193,046:
    - $7,634,448 for research and educational films.
    - $1,414,964 for membership support (periodicals to inform members of current environmental matters and society activities).
    - $1,143,634 for public education.
  OVERHEAD: $1,463,127.
  FUNDRAISING: $3,311,501.
- **DEFICIT:** $1,064,686.
- **LITTLE-KNOWN FACTS:** The Cousteau-Pechiney Turbosail (a wind-propulsion system invented by a Cousteau Society team in France) can reduce fuel consumption by as much as 50 percent.
- **RATINGS:** NCIB reported (8/7/86, using figures for calendar 1984) that the society met standards 2 through 8, but not standard 1 of NCIB's old evaluation system.
- **REGISTRATION:** AR, CA, CT, FL, IL, KY, MA, MD, ME, MN, NC, ND, NJ, NM, NV, NY (43953), OH, OK, OR, PA, RI, SC, TN, VA (398), WA, WI, and WV.
- **FINANCIAL DATA:** Text and chart source was their IRS form 990 covering 1988.

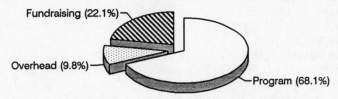

Fundraising (22.1%)

Overhead (9.8%)

Program (68.1%)

Due to deficit of 7.1%, chart is based on spending, not income.

Covenant House

346 Ninth Ave., 2nd Fl.
New York, NY 10001
(212) 727-4000 • (800) 922-6465 • Counseling Hotline: (800) 999-9999

- **CONTRIBUTIONS** are tax-deductible.
- **PURPOSE:** Bruce Ritter, a Franciscan priest, was visited one night in 1968 by a group of homeless children seeking shelter; he established Covenant House in 1972, and it has became an international agency caring for homeless children under twenty-one ("runaways and throwaways"). Provides food, shelter, clothing, and medical and legal assistance. In 1988 an AIDS-education program was initiated to treat and care for youngsters with the HIV virus or AIDS.
- **SIZE:** Covenant House, through common control, is affiliated with several U.S. and international child-care organizations: Under 21 (New York; controls Dove Services, Inc., a vocational-training corporation); Testamentum (housing for members of the Covenant House community and residential services for the Under 21 program); Covenant Houses in Texas, Florida, New Orleans, and Alaska; Covenant International Foundation; Covenant House Toronto; Casas Alianza in Guatemala, Panama, Mexico, and Honduras.
- **INCOME:** $66,107,196 (year ending 6/30/89; accrual accounting, IRS form 990). During the preceding four fiscal years support had been increasing.
- **HOW THEY USE YOUR MONEY:**
  PROGRAM: $41,636,409:
    - $5,083,875 for the Rights of Passage program (shelter for up to 18 months for adolescents, who receive counseling and help with education, housing, and employment).
    - $5,080,518* for public education (to help identify and help potential runaways and "throwaway" adolescents).
    - $2,889,710 for a toll-free phone number to provide immediate counseling.
    - $2,837,922 for shelter and crisis care (serving over 1,400 adolescents a day in the United States and Central America).
    - $1,411,301 for the outreach program (to steer youths to shelters).
    - $24,333,083 for payments to affiliates.
  OVERHEAD: $2,181,715.
  FUNDRAISING: $12,162,912.*
- **EXCESS:** $10,126,160.
- **LITTLE-KNOWN FACTS:** Beginning in December 1989, reports circulated about alleged financial and sexual improprieties involving Covenant House's founder. After being asked to step aside during the investigations, Father Ritter resigned in early March 1990. Ironically, in a message he wrote for the 1989 annual report, long before the stories first surfaced in the news, Father Ritter considered who would succeed him: "Ideally, this succession should not occur unexpectedly or in a time of crisis." He added, "Whatever Covenant House is, is not due to Bruce Ritter."
- **RATINGS:** Due to the revelations about questionable Covenant House dealings, NCIB revised its evaluation of the group three times during the first three months

---

*Informational mailings that cost $6,919,530 contained appeals for funds; $4,056,539 was allocated to public education, and the rest to fundraising.

of 1990. NCIB finally reported (3/30/90. using figures from the year ending 6/30/89) that Covenant House, Inc., did *not* meet standard 1 (specifically, 1g—on conflicts of interests involving board or staff), and there was a question about standard 8 (accountability and disclosure of relevant financial information), but that the group met the seven other NCIB standards.

■ **REGISTRATION:** CT, FL, IL, MD, MI, MN, NC, NH, NJ, NY (44346), OH, PA, TN, VA (2358), WI, and WV.

■ **FINANCIAL DATA:** Text and chart source was their IRS form 990 covering the year ending 6/30/89. Footnote source was their independently audited statement accompanying IRS form 990.

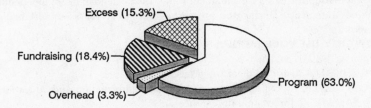

Excess (15.3%)

Fundraising (18.4%)

Overhead (3.3%)

Program (63.0%)

Cystic Fibrosis Foundation
6931 Arlington Rd. #200
Bethesda, MD 20814
(301) 951-4422 • 1-800-FIGHT-CF

- ■ **CONTRIBUTIONS** are tax-deductible.
- ■ **PURPOSE:** The National Cystic Fibrosis Research Foundation was founded in 1955; the name was shortened in 1974. CFF seeks to develop the "means to control and prevent cystic fibrosis and to improve the quality of life for people with the disease."
- ■ **SIZE:** 58 local groups and over 120 affiliated care centers providing patient services.
- ■ **INCOME:** $49,065,379 (national office and active chapters, and the Cystic Fibrosis Foundation Research Development Fund, Inc.; calendar 1988; independently audited statement). During the preceding four fiscal years support had been increasing.
- ■ **HOW THEY USE YOUR MONEY:**
  PROGRAM: $39,318,676:
  - • $20,594,138 for medical programs.
  - • $14,650,821* for public and professional information and education.
  - • $4,073,717 for community services.
  OVERHEAD: $4,370,333.
  FUNDRAISING: $5,905,026.*
- ■ **DEFICIT:** $528,656.
- ■ **RATINGS:** NCIB reported (11/14/88, using figures for the year ending 2/28/87) that the foundation met all nine NCIB standards.
- ■ **REGISTRATION:** NY (5312), TN, and VA (412).
- ■ **FINANCIAL DATA:** Text and chart source was their independently audited statement covering 1988.

*An estimated $10,208,000 for informational materials and activities that included fundraising appeals was jointly allocated thus: $3,073,000 for fundraising and $7,135,000 for public and professional information and education.

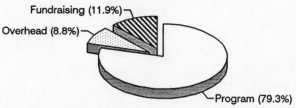

Fundraising (11.9%)
Overhead (8.8%)
Program (79.3%)

Due to deficit of 1.1%, chart is based on spending, not income.

Deafness Research Foundation
9 E. 38th St., 7th Fl.
New York, NY 10016
(212) 684-6556 • (TTY) (212) 684-6559 • (800) 535-3323

■ **CONTRIBUTIONS** are tax-deductible.
■ **PURPOSE:** Established in 1958 to further research into causes, treatments, and prevention of hearing impairment and other ear disorders.
■ **SIZE:** Maintains a National Temporal Bone Bank Program which seeks donations of the internal auditory structures fundamental to ear research and specialist training. Currently the program consists of a network of four regional centers, over a hundred hospitals, and several thousand registered future donors.
■ **INCOME:** $1,934,433 (calendar 1988; accrual accounting, IRS form 990).
■ **HOW THEY USE YOUR MONEY:**
PROGRAM: $1,690,850:
 • $1,288,721 for research grants.
 • $378,480 for public education.
 • $23,649 for a symposium to educate physicians on the progress of new research.
OVERHEAD: $265,173.
FUNDRAISING: $152,733.
■ **DEFICIT:** $174,323.
■ **RATINGS:** NCIB reported (5/24/88, using figures for the year ending 9/30/87) that the foundation met all eight of NCIB's old evaluation standards.
■ **REGISTRATION:** NY (5686) and VA (2661).
■ **FINANCIAL DATA:** Text and chart source was their IRS form 990 covering 1988.

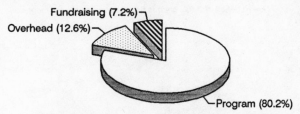

Fundraising (7.2%)
Overhead (12.6%)
Program (80.2%)

Due to deficit of 8.3%, chart is based on spending, not income.

Defenders of Wildlife, Inc.
1244 19th St., N.W.
Washington, DC 20036
(202) 659-9510

- **CONTRIBUTIONS** are tax-deductible.
- **PURPOSE:** Established in 1947 to prevent the decline of native animal and plant species, restore threatened habitat and wildlife populations, and promote wildlife appreciation and education.
- **SIZE:** 80,000 members.
- **INCOME:** $3,804,405 (calendar 1988; accrual accounting, IRS form 990).
- **HOW THEY USE YOUR MONEY:**
  PROGRAM: $2,596,406.
  OVERHEAD: $583,583.
  FUNDRAISING: $778,386.
- **DEFICIT:** $153,970.
- **RATINGS:** As of June 1,1990, NCIB was preparing a new report.
- **REGISTRATION:** NY (11825) and VA (429).
- **FINANCIAL DATA:** Text and chart source was their IRS form 990 covering 1988.

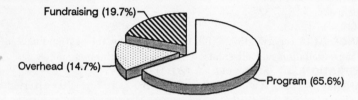

Fundraising (19.7%)
Overhead (14.7%)
Program (65.6%)

Due to deficit of 3.9%, chart is based on spending, not income.

Direct Relief International
2801-B De La Vina St.
Santa Barbara, CA 93140
(805) 687-3694

- **CONTRIBUTIONS** are tax-deductible.
- **PURPOSE:** Originally established in 1948 as the William Zimdin Foundation; was renamed Direct Relief Foundation in 1957 and adopted its present name in fiscal 1982. It donates contributed pharmaceuticals, medical supplies, and equipment to health facilities and local health projects in medically underdeveloped areas of the world, giving emergency assistance to victims of natural disasters, refugees, and others. DRI also arranges for medical, dental, and paramedical volunteer personnel to provide teaching, training, and clinical assistance in foreign locations.
- **SIZE:** Twenty-two staff members.
- **INCOME:** $9,497,278 (year ending 9/30/88; accrual accounting, IRS form 990).
- **HOW THEY USE YOUR MONEY:**
  PROGRAM: $9,208,227.
  OVERHEAD: $161,253.
  FUNDRAISING: $204,793.
- **DEFICIT:** $76,995.
- **RATINGS:** NCIB reported (11/28/89, using figures for the year ending 9/30/88) that Direct Relief International met all nine NCIB standards.
- **REGISTRATION:** CA (00045) and NY (44631).
- **FINANCIAL DATA:** Text and chart source was their IRS form 990 covering the year ending 9/30/88.

Overhead (1.7%) ⌐Fundraising (2.1%)

Program (96.2%)⌐

Due to deficit of 0.8%, chart is based on spending, not income.

Disability Rights Education and Defense Fund, Inc.
2212 Sixth St.
Berkeley, CA 94710
(415) 644-2555 • (TDD) (415) 644-2629

■ **CONTRIBUTIONS** are tax-deductible.

■ **PURPOSE:** Founded in 1979 and dedicated to the "independent-living movement and the civil rights of persons with disabilities." The fund also provides legal services and technical assistance.

■ **SIZE:** Eighteen staff members.

■ **INCOME:** $297,344 (year ending 9/30/88; accrual accounting, IRS form 990).

■ **HOW THEY USE YOUR MONEY:**
PROGRAM: $285,985:
- $183,127 for legal assistance (for disabled persons on noncriminal matters).
- $97,890 for work on laws and public policies that challenge discrimination against the disabled (in education, jobs, and community life).
- $4,968 for teaching parents and families of disabled children their rights.

OVERHEAD: $6,723.
FUNDRAISING: $21,096.

■ **DEFICIT:** $16,460.

■ **LITTLE-KNOWN FACTS:** The fund filed an *amicus curiae* brief on behalf of the National Hemophilia Foundation and several parents in *Chalk v. Orange County Department of Education,* a case involving a teacher with AIDS who had been dismissed by the school board, which felt he was a threat to the children. A district court upheld the school district's action; an appeal in the Ninth District Court reversed the decision, because medical evidence did not support the action.

■ **RATINGS:** No NCIB report.

■ **REGISTRATION:** CA (43584) and DC.

■ **FINANCIAL DATA:** Text and chart source was their IRS form 990 covering the year ending 9/30/88.

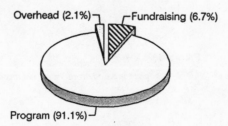

Overhead (2.1%) ⌐   ⌐Fundraising (6.7%)

Program (91.1%)⌐

Due to deficit of 5.2%, chart is based on spending, not income.

Earth Island Institute, Inc.
300 Broadway, #28
San Francisco, CA 94133
(415) 788-3666

- **CONTRIBUTIONS** are tax-deductible.
- **PURPOSE:** Founded in 1982 by David Brower and others who had split with Friends of the Earth (which Brower had founded on leaving the Sierra Club). Earth Island's aim is to promote "social welfare through education of the general public in global conservation, environmental and ecological principles," often by demonstrating the international political aspects of environmental issues. In the spring 1989 "Save Our Forests" issue of *Earth Island Journal*, the institute committed itself to planting at least one tree for every issue published.
- **SIZE:** The institute has a network of more than twenty projects.
- **INCOME:** $766,232 (calendar 1988; modified cash accounting, IRS form 990).
- **HOW THEY USE YOUR MONEY:**
  PROGRAM: $570,568:
    - $327,475 for their Dolphin Campaign (educating the public about killings of dolphins by the tuna industry).
    - $107,303 for video production (news concerning environmental problems and issues in Central America).
    - $50,972 for the Ben Linder Fund (to purchase hydroelectric equipment for rural development projects in Nicaragua).
    - $36,321 to publish *Earth Island Journal*.
    - $27,879 for the Central Coast Conservation Center (for a large conference).
    - $10,223 for David Brower's trip to the USSR (to help plan the restoration of the ecosystem of Siberia's Lake Baikal, in volume the world's largest freshwater lake).
    - $9,240 to publish a calendar of local environmental events.
    - $1,155 for the Climate Protection Network (to inform the nation of the effects of global warming).
  OVERHEAD: $126,157.
  FUNDRAISING: $24,337.
- **EXCESS:** $45,170.
- **LITTLE-KNOWN FACTS:** In early 1990, shortly before the twentieth anniversary of Earth Day, the three largest tunafish companies in the United States announced that they would no longer use fishing methods that kill dolphins. Earth Island's Dolphin Project was a key reason for this change.
- **RATINGS:** No NCIB report.
- **REGISTRATION:** CA (48928).
- **FINANCIAL DATA:** Text and chart source was their IRS form 990 covering 1988.

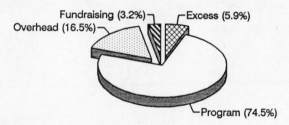

Fundraising (3.2%) — Excess (5.9%)
Overhead (16.5%) —
Program (74.5%)

Environmental Action, Inc.
1525 New Hampshire Ave., N.W.
Washington, DC 20036
(202) 745-4870

- **CONTRIBUTIONS** are *not* tax-deductible.
- **PURPOSE:** Founded in 1970 by organizers of the first Earth Day. EA works to eliminate environmental toxins and global warming, reduce solid wastes, promote recycling, and improve air quality. It pursues scientific, economic, sociological, political, and ecological research.
- **SIZE:** 20,000 members.
- **INCOME:** $425,247 (year ending 9/30/88; accrual accounting, IRS form 990).
- **HOW THEY USE YOUR MONEY:**
  PROGRAM: $247,673:
  - $124,529 for EA's bimonthly magazine.
  - $62,534 on lobbying for national legislation and federal regulations ($31,819 to promote safe, clean, and affordable energy; $30,715 to reduce the environmental impact of toxic substances).
  - $8,812 for casework.
  - $51,798 for certain expenses of the Environmental Action Political Action Committee.
  OVERHEAD: $90,937.
  FUNDRAISING: $74,057.
- **EXCESS:** $12,580.
- **LITTLE-KNOWN FACTS:** EA makes a point of using recycled paper for its stationery. During the FY88, there were a number of related-party transactions between Environmental Action (EA) and Environmental Action Foundation (EAF). EAF charged EA $115,971 and EA charged EAF $83,975, both for services rendered. Furthermore, EA received $72,000 in education grants from EAF to support *Environmental Action* magazine. (As of September 30, 1988, EAF was still owed $50,187.)
- **RATINGS:** No NCIB report.
- **REGISTRATION:** DC.
- **FINANCIAL DATA:** Text and chart source was their IRS form 990 covering the year ending 9/30/88.

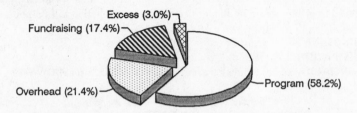

Excess (3.0%)
Fundraising (17.4%)
Overhead (21.4%)
Program (58.2%)

142

Environmental Action Foundation
1525 New Hampshire Ave., N.W.
Washington, DC 20036
(202) 745-4871

- **CONTRIBUTIONS** are tax-deductible.
- **PURPOSE:** Promotes a healthy environment through research, public education, organizing, advocacy, and legal action, and by building a data bank of environmental information (culled from other sources and self-generated, which it makes available to the general public). In April 1988, the Environmental Task Force, Inc., merged into EAF.
- **INCOME:** $588,086 (year ending 9/30/88; accrual accounting, IRS form 990). Apart from a brief dip in 1985, during the preceding four fiscal years support had been increasing.
- **HOW THEY USE YOUR MONEY:**
  PROGRAM: $449,017:
    - $73,301 for public education and legal assistance for victims of waste and toxic substances.
    - $92,342 for an energy project dealing with electric utilities and energy policy.
    - $94,177 for the Energy Conservation Coalition.
    - $50,564 for a solid-waste project.
    - $10,284 for *Power Line* (a bimonthly energy newsjournal).
    - $10,018 for a conference and materials on the relation between environmental protection and the economy.
    - $10,405 for education on biological alternatives to sprays against gypsy moths.
    - $32,983 (including $13,650 in grants and allocations) for EA's LUST project (Leaking Underground Storage Tanks).
    - $74,943 (including $72,000 in grants and allocations) for grants to *Environmental Action* magazine.
  OVERHEAD: $40,748.
  FUNDRAISING: $61,203.
- **EXCESS:** $37,118.
- **RATINGS:** No NCIB report.
- **REGISTRATION:** NY.
- **FINANCIAL DATA:** Text and chart source was their IRS form 990 covering the year ending 9/30/88.

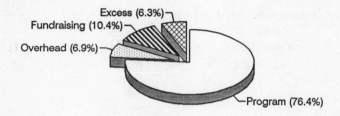

Excess (6.3%)
Fundraising (10.4%)
Overhead (6.9%)
Program (76.4%)

143

Environmental Defense Fund, Inc.
257 Park Ave. S., 16th Fl.
New York, NY 10010
(212) 505-2100

- **CONTRIBUTIONS** are tax-deductible.
- **PURPOSE:** Founded in 1967, EDF seeks to protect the environment through independent scientific research, lobbying, and public education. Recently, EDF began its biggest program ever, to address the problem of global warming. An EDF physicist was the only American environmentalist invited to brief Prime Minister Margaret Thatcher and her cabinet on global warming.
- **SIZE:** 125,000 members nationwide; seven regional offices.
- **INCOME:** $12,902,741 (year ending 9/30/89; annual report).
- **HOW THEY USE YOUR MONEY:**

PROGRAM: $9,866,457 on programs including energy and air quality (acid rain, energy conservation and planning, ozone depletion and global warming, assistance in drafting state laws to reduce SO_2 emissions); toxic chemicals (to reduce lead in gasoline, reduce dioxin pollution, maintain health-based regulation of hazardous waste, challenge EPA standards for radiation exposure); wildlife and water resources (to draft provisions for the Endangered Species Act, to protect rare wild plants and Antarctic marine mammals, to support the Marine Mammal Protection Act through legal action, and to evaluate regulatory policies governing biotechnology); and education, legislative action, and membership (to inform and educate members, and provide technical assistance on legislative issues to strengthen the protection of natural resources and the environment).

OVERHEAD: $409,913.

FUNDRAISING: $1,611,244.

MEMBERSHIP DEVELOPMENT: $197,918.

- **EXCESS:** $817,209.
- **LITTLE-KNOWN FACTS:** A 1985 EDF study was the first to detail the long-distance effects of acid rain produced by sulfur dioxide pollution from smokestacks.
- **RATINGS:** NCIB reported (9/21/89, using figures from the year ending 9/30/88) that the Environmental Defense Fund met all nine NCIB standards.
- **REGISTRATION:** CA, IL, MA, MD, MI, MN, NC, NJ, NY (41682), SC, VA (485), WI, and WV.
- **FINANCIAL DATA:** Text and chart source was their annual report covering the year ending 9/30/89.

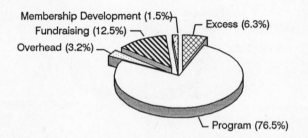

Membership Development (1.5%)
Fundraising (12.5%)
Overhead (3.2%)
Excess (6.3%)
Program (76.5%)

Epilepsy Foundation of America
4351 Garden City Dr., Suite 406
Landover, MD 20785
(301) 459-3700 • (800) EFA-1000

- **CONTRIBUTIONS** are tax-deductible.
- **PURPOSE:** The Epilepsy Foundation (founded 1954 as the Federal Association for Epilepsy) and the Epilepsy Association of America (founded 1965) merged to form EFA in 1968; the National Epilepsy League, a Chicago group, merged with EFA in 1978. Established "to promote research into the causes and treatments of epilepsy, to support educational and vocational programs for persons with epilepsy, and to provide educational information about epilepsy to the general public." The national office (considered here) coordinates national and affiliated programs and the dissemination of information.
- **SIZE:** Eighty-four affiliated organizations, "of which three had provisional status, fifty-six were full affiliates serving a local area, and twenty-five had responsibilities throughout their respective states."
- **INCOME:** $9,332,419 (national office only; calendar 1988; accrual accounting, IRS form 990). During the preceding four years support had been increasing.
- **HOW THEY USE YOUR MONEY:**
PROGRAM: $5,002,107:
  - $800,466 for research ($561,565 in grants and allocations).
  - $897,440 for public health education.
  - $465,443 for professional education ($28,500 in grants and allocations).
  - $1,238,899 for community service.
  - $1,599,859 for patient services ($15,000 in grants and allocations).

  OVERHEAD: $828,553.

  FUNDRAISING: $2,617,211. "The lowest fund-raising cost ratio for national operations in [EFA] history," according to the 1988 EFA annual report.
- **EXCESS:** $884,548.
- **LITTLE-KNOWN FACTS:** According to EFA's 1988 IRS form 990, it exchanged a mailing list valued at $547 with the Democratic Congressional Committee, while one of the foundation's six vice-presidents, Rep. Tony Coelho (D-CA), who has epilepsy, served as Democratic whip. His *Yes I Can* Foundation for the Disabled contributed $1.2 million to EFA in 1988 for long-range programs.
- **RATINGS:** NCIB reported (8/29/88, using figures for calendar 1986) that EFA met all nine NCIB standards.
- **REGISTRATION:** CA, CT, IL, MA, MD, MI, NE, NH, NJ, NY (41218), OH, OK, OR, PA, VA (489), and WV.
- **FINANCIAL DATA:** Text and chart source was their IRS form 990 (national headquarters *only*) covering 1988. *Yes I Can* Foundation information was the 1988 EFA annual report. NCIB's report examines the *entire* organization.

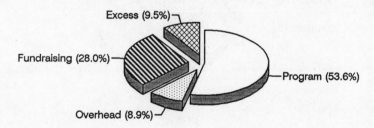

Excess (9.5%)
Fundraising (28.0%)
Overhead (8.9%)
Program (53.6%)

FAIR (Federation for American Immigration Reform)
1666 Connecticut Ave., N.W., Suite 400
Washington, DC 20009
(202) 328-7004

- **CONTRIBUTIONS** are tax-deductible.
- **PURPOSE:** Since 1979, FAIR has worked to end illegal immigration and set reasonable levels of legal immigration. Encourages "population control and economic development worldwide, especially in major [immigrant] source countries." In 1986 FAIR set up the Immigration Reform Law Institute (IRLI) to promote reasonable immigration laws and policies by educating the courts and the public on these matters.
- **SIZE:** 2,000 grass-roots activists.
- **INCOME:** $1,843,300 (calendar 1988; accrual accounting, IRS form 990). During the preceding four fiscal years support had been increasing.
- **HOW THEY USE YOUR MONEY:**
PROGRAM: $1,338,734:
  - $290,608 for membership development.
  - $261,156 for membership education and service (newsletter for members; maintenance of membership rolls).
  - $235,336 for litigation and other expenses for IRLI.
  - $204,028 for publications and information (monographs, a syndicated column, occasional articles, and an information exchange service on American immigration policy).
  - $137,168 for lobbying.
  - $128,966 for media.
  - $81,472 for public education (speeches, public appearances, and other forms of direct and indirect contact).
  OVERHEAD: $158,989.
  FUNDRAISING: $192,301.
- **EXCESS:** $153,276.
- **LITTLE-KNOWN FACTS:** FAIR believes that American immigration policy has been undermined by "ethnic activists, business and agricultural interests, and political ideologues." Accordingly, FAIR activists have repealed or defeated sanctuary resolutions in Los Angeles, Seattle, and Austin, and a series of FAIR ads in Florida generated 10,000 letters urging then-President Jimmy Carter to stop the Mariel boatlift from Cuba.
- **RATINGS:** As of June 1, 1990, NCIB was preparing a new report.
- **REGISTRATION:** DC, IL, MN, and NY (52442).
- **FINANCIAL DATA:** Text and chart source was their IRS form 990 covering 1988.

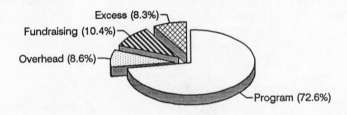

Excess (8.3%)
Fundraising (10.4%)
Overhead (8.6%)
Program (72.6%)

Food for Survival, Inc./The New York City Foodbank
Hunts Point Co-op Market, Bldg. F
Bronx, NY 10474
(212) 991-4300

- **CONTRIBUTIONS** are tax-deductible.
- **PURPOSE:** Since 1983, has solicited, collected, and stored food, distributing it to qualified tax-exempt organizations feeding the poor, ill, and needy. Food for Survival is a member of the Second Harvest network of foodbanks.
- **SIZE:** Food for Survival has collected (and distributed to 530 feeding programs) more than 21 million pounds of food since 1983.
- **INCOME:** $1,972,308 (year ending 6/30/88; accrual accounting, IRS form 990). During the preceding four fiscal years support had been increasing.
- **HOW THEY USE YOUR MONEY:**
PROGRAM: $1,053,515.
OVERHEAD: $217,962.
FUNDRAISING: $202,897.
- **EXCESS:** $497,934. According to the controller for the foodbank: "We did fundraising for renovation. We were buying a cooler for larger freezer capacity." The cooler was bought in 1989–90 and the renovation is continuing.
- **LITTLE-KNOWN FACTS:** During the year, the foodbank received a total of $758,225 in grants from New York city and state agencies.
- **RATINGS:** No NCIB report.
- **REGISTRATION:** NY (52372).
- **FINANCIAL DATA:** Text and chart source was their IRS form 990 covering the year ending 6/30/88.

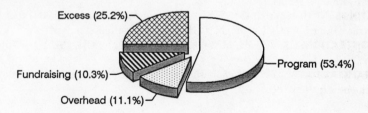

Food for the Hungry, Inc.
7729 E. Greenway Rd.
Scottsdale, AZ 85252
(609) 998-3100 • (800) 2-HUNGER

- **CONTRIBUTIONS** are tax-deductible.
- **PURPOSE:** Established 1971 as a nonprofit, nondenominational Christian organization for "providing disaster relief and long-range self-help assistance to the hungry."
- **SIZE:** Relief programs in fourteen countries and child sponsorship programs in ten (which served 6,288 children).
- **INCOME:** $20,879,407 (year ending 9/30/88; accrual accounting, IRS form 990).
- **HOW THEY USE YOUR MONEY:**
  PROGRAM: $18,851,159:
  - $18,353,125 (including $14,943,016 in grants and allocations) for direct disaster relief and developmental assistance in Africa, Asia, and Latin America.
  - $498,034 (including $69,803 in grants and allocations) to increase U.S. awareness of world hunger.

  OVERHEAD: $1,044,618.
  FUNDRAISING: $723,102.
- **EXCESS:** $260,528.
- **LITTLE-KNOWN FACTS:** FH stresses the "spiritual element" of each child sponsorship with regular Bible studies and teachings. FH says that "a careful strategy has been outlined that allows the Gospel to be proclaimed within the context of our overall programs."
- **RATINGS:** NCIB reported (3/25/86, using figures for calendar 1984) that Food for the Hungry met all eight of NCIB's old evaluation standards.
- **REGISTRATION:** CA, CT, MI, MN, NC, NJ, NY (49113), OH, PA, VA (775), and WV.
- **FINANCIAL DATA:** Text and chart source was their IRS form 990 covering the year ending 9/30/88.

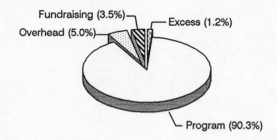

Fundraising (3.5%)

Overhead (5.0%)

Excess (1.2%)

Program (90.3%)

The Fortune Society
39 W. 19th St., 7th Fl.
New York, NY 10011
(212) 206-7070

- **CONTRIBUTIONS** are tax-deductible.
- **PURPOSE:** Organized in 1967 and incorporated as a nonprofit the following year, the society provides counseling, educational, and job-placement services to ex-offenders in the New York City area. It seeks greater public awareness of the American prison system and understanding of prisoners' problems during their incarceration and when they return to society.
- **SIZE:** About 175 adults and 35 youths visit the society's office each month seeking assistance.
- **INCOME:** $736,008 (calendar 1988; IRS form 990).
- **HOW THEY USE YOUR MONEY:**
  PROGRAM: $540,542:
  - $142,305 for adult counseling (including referrals for legal, drug, or alcohol problems).
  - $108,843 (including $19,453 in grants and allocations) for adolescent counseling (referrals for legal, drug, and alcohol problems; placement in vocational training and full-time employment).
  - $133,407 (including $124,620 in grants and allocations) for education (to test basic education and for diploma preparation of about 247 students tutored a total of 7,000 hours).
  - $100,077 for career development (e.g., preparation of résumés, operation, interviews and referrals, job orientation).
  - $55,910 for advocacy (to inform the public of inmates' and ex-offenders' problems, and of the present state of the prison system).
  OVERHEAD: $163,068.
  FUNDRAISING: $43,927.
- **DEFICIT:** $11,529.
- **RATINGS:** NCIB reported (2/13/85, using figures for calendar 1983) that the society met all eight of NCIB's old evaluation standards.
- **REGISTRATION:** NC and NY (41612).
- **FINANCIAL DATA:** Text and chart source was their IRS form 990 covering 1988.

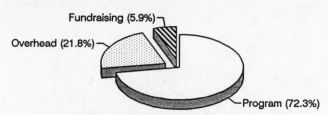

Fundraising (5.9%)
Overhead (21.8%)
Program (72.3%)

Due to deficit of 1.5%, chart is based on spending, not income.

149

The Freedom from Hunger Foundation, Inc.
1644 DaVinci Ct.
Davis, CA 95617
(916) 758-6200

- **CONTRIBUTIONS** are tax-deductible.
- **PURPOSE:** Established 1946, the American Freedom from Hunger Foundation became Meals for Millions/Freedom from Hunger Foundation in 1979, when Meals for Millions assumed the original foundation's assets. Present name was adopted in 1987. Develops solutions to world hunger problems.
- **SIZE:** Programs in eleven countries worldwide.
- **INCOME:** $3,178,358 (calendar 1988; accrual accounting, IRS form 990).
- **HOW THEY USE YOUR MONEY:**
PROGRAM: $2,940,690:
    - $2,488,549 for Aid in Food Nutrition (in Antigua, Arizona, Bolivia, Ecuador-Esmeraldas, Ghana, Honduras, Kenya, Mali, Mississippi, Nepal, Sierra Leone, Thailand, and Togo).
    - $298,809 for program information (on food and nutrition).
    - $151,292 for program support (to aid food technology).
    - $2,040 for program development (development studies and upgrade of technical facilities).
OVERHEAD: $393,177.
FUNDRAISING: $557,662.
- **DEFICIT:** $713,171.
- **LITTLE-KNOWN FACTS:** Although over 26 percent of support comes from the U.S. Agency for International Development, the foundation's 1988 independent audit discovered slight noncompliance with laws and regulations. Financial reports relating to one grant were not promptly submitted, and the total allowable federal and nonfederal shares of grant outlays in another were inaccurately reported. The audit stated that, subject to these corrections, all federal financial-assistance programs were in full compliance.
- **RATINGS:** NCIB reported (11/4/88, using figures for calendar 1987) that the foundation met all nine NCIB standards.
- **REGISTRATION:** CA (04124), NY (40449), and VA (2355).
- **FINANCIAL DATA:** Text and chart source was their IRS form 990 covering 1988. Little-Known Fact source was their independently audited statement covering 1988.

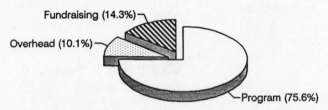

Fundraising (14.3%)
Overhead (10.1%)
Program (75.6%)

Due to deficit of 18.3%, chart is based on spending, not income.

The Fresh Air Fund
1040 Ave. of the Americas
New York, NY 10018
(212) 221-0900

■ **CONTRIBUTIONS** are tax-deductible.

■ **PURPOSE:** Since 1877, when a small group of children from New York City tenements visited host families on farms in Sherman, Pennsylvania, the fund has provided more than 1.6 million underprivileged New York City children with free summer vacations. The two main programs are Friendly Town (for 6-to-16-year-olds) and the Fresh Air Camps (for 8-to-15-year-olds).

■ **SIZE:** 7,000 children visited families in rural and suburban communities in thirteen states and Canada in 1989. Another 2,500 enjoyed Fresh Air Camps.

■ **INCOME:** $7,347,804 (year ending 9/30/88; independently audited statement).

■ **HOW THEY USE YOUR MONEY:**
PROGRAM: $3,745,686:
- $1,665,238 for Friendly Town activities.
- $1,756,131 for Fresh Air Camps' summer programs.
- $324,317 for the camps off-season.

OVERHEAD: $493,365.
FUNDRAISING: $603,042.

■ **EXCESS:** $2,505,711. The fund says that some of this money was due to gains on the sale of securities that year. Also, bequests and legacies were about half a million dollars greater than in 1987. (The fund policy is that bequests and legacies go directly into an investment fund and not be used for day-to-day expenses.)

■ **LITTLE-KNOWN FACTS:** 326 Friendly Towns are located from Maine to Virginia.

■ **RATINGS:** No NCIB report.

■ **REGISTRATION:** NY (8845).

■ **FINANCIAL DATA:** Text and chart source was their independently audited statement covering the year ending 9/30/88.

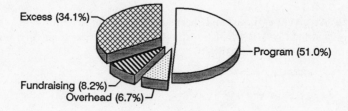

Excess (34.1%)
Program (51.0%)
Fundraising (8.2%)
Overhead (6.7%)

151

Friends of the Earth, Inc., and FOE Foundation
530 Seventh St., S.E.
Washington, DC 20003
(202) 543-4312

- **CONTRIBUTIONS** to FOE are *not* tax-deductible, but those to the FOE Foundation are.
- **PURPOSE:** The U.S. branch of FOE was founded in 1969 by David Brower (see Earth Island Institute profile). Concentrates on lobbying and organizing to have important environmental issues put on the public agenda. Issues they are concerned about include safe, clean, economical alternatives to nuclear power (FOE fought construction of Tennessee's Clinch River Breeder Reactor) and polluting fossil fuels; health risks from herbicides; and preservation and rational use of the earth (FOE helped protect Grand Canyon, Bryce and Zion Canyons, and other national parks from dams and coal developers). The FOE Foundation, founded in 1972, works toward the same ends through education, research, litigation, and publishing. Increasingly, FOEF's attention has been drawn toward global issues and strengthening the links between FOE-US and the thirty-three other member nation groups of FOE International. FOEPAC, the group's political-action committee, was established in 1981.
- **SIZE:** About 15,000 members in the United States.
- **INCOME:** $391,705 (FOE, year ending 6/30/88; NYS form 497); $379,649 (FOEF, year ending 6/30/87; NYS form 497).
- **HOW THEY USE YOUR MONEY:**
  PROGRAM: $287,104 (FOE FY88); $245,585 (FOEF FY87).
  OVERHEAD: $104,848 (FOE FY88); $108,438 (FOEF FY87).
  FUNDRAISING: $17,198 (FOE FY88); $97,270 (FOEF FY87).
- **DEFICIT:** $17,445 (FOE FY88); $71,644 (FOEF FY87).
- **LITTLE-KNOWN FACTS:** In 1990 Paul McCartney's world tour was associated with FOE. FOE's annual reports are printed on recycled paper.
- **RATINGS:** As of June 1, 1990, NCIB was preparing a new report.
- **REGISTRATION:** NY (FOE: 43136; FOEF: 43083) and VA (FOE: 2691; FOEF: 2692).
- **FINANCIAL DATA:** FOE text and chart source was their NYS form 497 covering the year ending 6/30/88. FOEF text and chart source was their NYS form 497 covering the year ending 6/30/87.

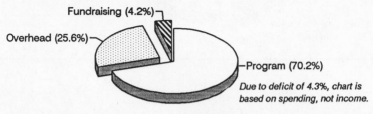

Fundraising (4.2%)

Overhead (25.6%)

Program (70.2%)

Due to deficit of 4.3%, chart is based on spending, not income.

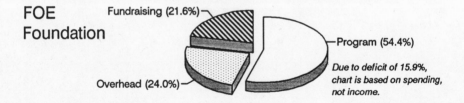

FOE Foundation

Fundraising (21.6%)

Program (54.4%)

Due to deficit of 15.9%, chart is based on spending, not income.

Overhead (24.0%)

The Fund for Animals, Inc.
200 W. 57th St., Suite 508
New York, NY 10019
(212) 246-2096

- **CONTRIBUTIONS** are tax-deductible.
- **PURPOSE:** Established 1967; works to protect wildlife and fight cruelty to animals (domestic and wild) through legal action, direct activism, public education, and lobbying. The Fund for Animals has succeeded in placing over 170 animal species on the Endangered Species list.
- **SIZE:** A staff of twenty is supported by over 200,000 members.
- **INCOME:** $1,245,386 (calendar 1988; NYS form 497).
- **HOW THEY USE YOUR MONEY:**
  PROGRAM: $749,416.
  OVERHEAD: $263,850.
  FUNDRAISING: $112,600.
- **EXCESS:** $119,520.
- **LITTLE-KNOWN FACTS:** The group owns and operates the Black Beauty Farm for homeless and abused horses (Texas) and the Animal Trust Sanctuary shelter for dogs, cats, and small feral animals (Ramona, California).
- **RATINGS:** NCIB reported (8/1/88, using figures for calendar 1987) that the Fund for Animals met all nine NCIB standards.
- **REGISTRATION:** NY (12749).
- **FINANCIAL DATA:** Text and chart source was their NYS form 497 covering 1988.

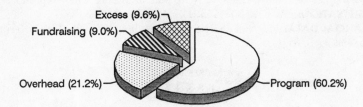

Excess (9.6%)
Fundraising (9.0%)
Overhead (21.2%)
Program (60.2%)

Fund for an Open Society
311 S. Juniper St., Suite 400
Philadelphia, PA 19107
(215) 735-6915

■ **CONTRIBUTIONS** are tax-deductible.
■ **PURPOSE:** Since 1975 the Fund for an Open Society has financed mortgages to help decrease residential segregation.
■ **SIZE:** As of July 31, 1988, Open had three full-time and four part-time employees or consultants, and had originated 138 mortgages.
■ **INCOME:** $634,464 (year ending 5/31/89; accrual accounting, IRS form 990). Support peaked in 1986.
■ **HOW THEY USE YOUR MONEY:**
 PROGRAM: $423,319:
   • $305,496 for the mortgage program.
   • $89,285 for the notes program (soliciting and sale of notes, of which proceeds are used to grant mortgages).
   • $28,538 for education.
 OVERHEAD: $93,318.
 FUNDRAISING: $115,580.
■ **EXCESS:** $2,247.
■ **LITTLE-KNOWN FACTS:** Open's Committee for Tithing in Investment (OCTI) pursues recent trends toward socially responsible investing. OCTI offers investors information about Open notes, which help fund Open's affordable mortgages for homebuyers making pro-integration moves.
■ **RATINGS:** As of August 1, 1990, NCIB was preparing a new report.
■ **REGISTRATION:** CA, GA, NY (45521), and PA.
■ **FINANCIAL DATA:** Text and chart source was their IRS form 990 covering the year ending 5/31/89.

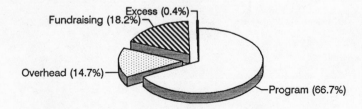

The Fund for Peace
345 East 46th St., Suite 207
New York, NY 10017
(212) 661-5900
1755 Massachusetts Ave., N.W., Suite 555
Washington, DC 20036
(202) 797-0882

- **CONTRIBUTIONS** are tax-deductible.
- **PURPOSE:** Although not formally organized until 1967, it originated in the Pierce Butler, Jr., Foundation for Education in World Law (founded 1957), which changed its name (1969) to the Fund for Education in World Order. The fund's divisions include the Center for International Policy, the Center for National Security Studies (jointly funded by the American Civil Liberties Union Foundation), the Institute for the Study of World Politics, the Indochina Project, and the National Security Archive. The Center for Defense Information and Public Interest Radio, programs originally established by the fund, became separate nonprofit groups in 1988.
- **SIZE:** Fifty staff members.
- **INCOME:** $1,942,211 (calendar 1988; NYS form 497).
- **HOW THEY USE YOUR MONEY:**
  PROGRAM: $2,085,682.
  OVERHEAD: $173,282.
  FUNDRAISING: $30,412.
- **DEFICIT:** $347,165.
- **LITTLE-KNOWN FACTS:** The National Security Archive, which collects formerly classified materials released under the Freedom of Information Act, has published a chronology of incidents relating to the Iran-contra scandal. Recently the archive won a major court ruling waiving certain FOIA processing costs for requests not made by formal news organizations (such as freelance writers).
- **RATINGS:** NCIB reported (11/23/88, using figures from calendar 1987) that the Fund for Peace met all nine NCIB standards.
- **REGISTRATION:** NY (6102).
- **FINANCIAL DATA:** Text and chart source was their NYS form 497 covering 1988.

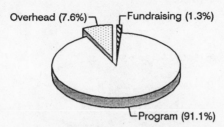

Overhead (7.6%) ─ ┌─Fundraising (1.3%)

─Program (91.1%)

Due to deficit of 15.2%, chart is based on spending, not income.

Gay Men's Health Crisis
129 W. 20th St.
New York, NY 10011
(212) 807-7035 • Hotline: (212) 807-6655 • (TDD) (212) 645-7470

- **CONTRIBUTIONS** are tax-deductible.
- **PURPOSE:** Beginning at an August 1981 fundraising party in the home of New York writer Larry Kramer, and formally incorporated in June 1982, GMHC was the world's first AIDS organization. GMHC works to maintain and improve the quality of life for persons with AIDS or AIDS-related complex and their carepartners, advocates fair and effective public policies and practices concerning HIV infection, and increases awareness through education and AIDS prevention programs. Services are usually provided by volunteers.
- **SIZE:** GMHC is the largest nongovernmental distributor of AIDS-education literature (727,600 pieces in FY89) and videos in the world. The GMHC Hotline logged 47,893 calls in FY89.
- **INCOME:** $13,624,926 (year ending 6/30/89; annual report).
- **HOW THEY USE YOUR MONEY:**
  PROGRAM: $7,173,457:
  - $4,087,203 for persons with AIDS and clinical services (including crisis intervention and counseling, direct financial aid, welfare and legal advocacy, and buddy and home-attended services).
  - $2,530,156 for public information and education (including a 24-hour information and referral hotline, a newsletter, and an AIDS information handbook).
  - $556,098 for policy development (support of fair and effective public policies and practices concerning HIV infection).
  OVERHEAD: $1,045,596.
  FUNDRAISING: $2,065,390.
- **EXCESS:** $3,340,483.
- **LITTLE-KNOWN FACTS:** Larry Kramer, founder of GMHC, now works for the AIDS Coalition to Unleash Power (ACT-UP), formed in 1987 to end the AIDS crisis through "direct, confrontational political action." (ACT-UP is not a registered nonprofit organization.)
- **RATINGS:** No NCIB report.
- **REGISTRATION:** NY (51432).
- **FINANCIAL DATA:** Text and chart source was their annual report covering the year ending 6/30/89.

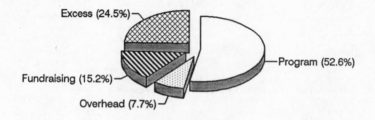

Excess (24.5%)
Program (52.6%)
Fundraising (15.2%)
Overhead (7.7%)

Girls, Inc.
30 E. 33rd St., 7th Fl.
New York, NY 10016
(212) 689-3700

- **CONTRIBUTIONS** are tax-deductible.
- **PURPOSE:** Up until April 1990, Girls Incorporated was known as Girls Clubs of America. The name change came about after the settlement of a two-and-a-half-year lawsuit against Boys Clubs of America to protect GCA's unique service mark (BCA was referring to itself as the "Boys and Girls Clubs of America"; that name was formally adopted in the fall of 1990). GCA was founded as a national organization in 1945, although local Girls Clubs had existed earlier. The slogan of Girls, Inc., "Growing up is serious business," captures the thinking behind its major current programs: AIDS education; Friendly PEERsuasion (a substance-abuse program); Operation SMART (a program sponsored by the National Science Foundation to encourage girls in sciences, math, and relevant technology); and prevention of adolescent pregnancy.
- **SIZE:** More than 200 centers in 112 cities serve more than 250,000 girls.
- **INCOME:** $2,978,374 (national headquarters only; year ending 9/30/89; accrual accounting, IRS form 990).
- **HOW THEY USE YOUR MONEY:**
  PROGRAM: $2,541,071:
  - $1,715,117 for program development.
  - $799,719 for direct services to clubs.
  - $26,235 for national leadership activities.

  OVERHEAD: $558,502.
  FUNDRAISING: $200,395.
- **DEFICIT:** $321,594.
- **RATINGS:** NCIB reported (12/9/88, on the national service center *only*, using figures from the year ending 9/30/87) that Girls Clubs of America (the previous name of Girls, Inc.) met all nine NCIB standards.
- **REGISTRATION:** NY (8984).
- **FINANCIAL DATA:** Text and chart source was the GCA IRS form 990 (for the national headquarters *only*) covering the year ending 9/30/89.

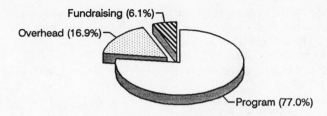

Fundraising (6.1%)
Overhead (16.9%)
Program (77.0%)

Due to deficit of 9.7%, chart is based on spending, not income.

Goodwill Industries of America, Inc.
9200 Wisconsin Ave.
Bethesda, MD 20814
(301) 530-6500

- **CONTRIBUTIONS** are tax-deductible.
- **PURPOSE:** Founded in 1902 as the Morgan Memorial Cooperative Industries and Stores; took present name in 1946. This international nonprofit organization's stated purpose is "to provide leadership and assistance to organizational members . . . to help the handicapped, disabled, and disadvantaged attain their fullest potential."
- **SIZE:** 171 member groups in the United States, 6 in Canada, and 43 affiliated members in 30 other nations.
- **INCOME:** $5,660,880 (calendar 1988; accrual accounting, IRS form 990). During the preceding four fiscal years support had been increasing. Programs and services provided by GIA are financed in part by dues from each local agency's year-end earned income.
- **HOW THEY USE YOUR MONEY:**
  PROGRAM: $4,029,767:
  - $1,991,260 for direct services to membership.
  - $1,596,810 for support services to membership (such as materials to aid implementation and development of job opportunities for the handicapped in American industry).
  - $350,758 for general counsel, governing meetings, and other services (such special projects as the Goodwill Industries Volunteer Services, International Council, and the Goodwill Archives).
  - $90,939 for international programs (serving member groups in foreign countries via technical consultations and training).
  OVERHEAD: $1,099,968.
  FUNDRAISING: $823.
- **EXCESS:** $530,322.
- **LITTLE-KNOWN FACTS:** In 1988 GIA's Projects with Industry Program (supported by grants from the U.S. departments of Education and Labor) placed more than 1,500 disabled adults in private-sector employment—far above the goal of 1,000.
- **RATINGS:** NCIB reported (11/6/87) on the Goodwill Industries of America national service center *only* (using figures from calendar 1986) that the center met all eight of NCIB's old evaluation standards.
- **REGISTRATION:** MA, MD, NJ, and NY (42908).
- **FINANCIAL DATA:** Text and chart source was their IRS form 990 covering 1988.

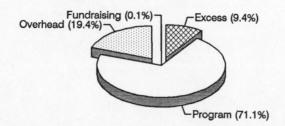

Fundraising (0.1%)
Overhead (19.4%)
Excess (9.4%)
Program (71.1%)

158

Billy Graham Evangelistic Association
1300 Harmon Place
Minneapolis, MN 55403
(612) 338-0500

- **CONTRIBUTIONS** are tax-deductible.
- **PURPOSE:** Established in 1950; conducts evangelical crusades and fundraising activities worldwide, promotes Bible study, and sponsors schools of evangelism and writing.
- **SIZE:** 450 staff members.
- **INCOME:** $89,178,246 (association and affiliates; calendar 1988; annual report).
- **HOW THEY USE YOUR MONEY:**
  PROGRAM: $59,273,450.
  OVERHEAD: $5,103,605.
  FUNDRAISING: $4,406,642.
- **EXCESS:** $20,394,549.
- **LITTLE-KNOWN FACTS:** *Decision,* the association's monthly publication, is printed in English, French, German, and Spanish, and in braille editions.
- **RATINGS:** No NCIB report.
- **REGISTRATION:** Although registered to raise money in Virginia, the association is considered a religious organization and is not required to file any financial information.
- **FINANCIAL DATA:** Text and chart source was their annual report covering 1988.

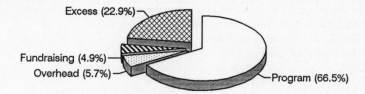

Excess (22.9%)
Fundraising (4.9%)
Overhead (5.7%)
Program (66.5%)

Greenpeace USA, Inc.
1436 U St., N.W.
Washington, DC 20009
(202) 462-1177

- **CONTRIBUTIONS** are tax-deductible.
- **PURPOSE:** Founded in 1971 in British Columbia, Canada, by a group opposed to nuclear testing on Amchitka Island, Alaska. Works for ocean ecology and wildlife preservation, and against nuclear proliferation (and nuclear power) and toxics. In addition to lobbying and electoral work, has also engaged in high-profile direct action. In 1985, a Greenpeace vessel, the *Rainbow Warrior*, was sunk by a French naval vessel during a protest against nuclear testing.
- **SIZE:** 1,200,000 U.S. supporters; part of an organization of over 3 million that has offices in twenty-three countries.
- **INCOME:** $33,390,747 (calendar 1988; 1988 annual report).
- **HOW THEY USE YOUR MONEY:**
PROGRAM: $21,329,521:
  - $5,372,739 for grants to affiliates ($5,350,500 went to Greenpeace International).
  - $4,224,527 for ocean ecology programs.
  - $3,949,065 for toxics programs.
  - $1,949,581 for public information.
  - $1,901,338 for nuclear disarmament programs.
  - $1,274,528 for operation of the Greenpeace merchandise program (which produced $2,225,494 in revenues for the group).
  - $1,125,835 for *Greenpeace* magazine.
  - $478,681 for the Action Team.
  - $460,051 for media.
  - $327,046 for prevention of development of Antarctica.
  - $244,914 for Pacific programs.
  - $21,216 for Latin America/Caribbean programs.
OVERHEAD: $1,747,807.
FUNDRAISING: $8,024,971.
- **EXCESS:** $2,828,448.
- **LITTLE-KNOWN FACTS:** In December 1989 the 887-ton Greenpeace flagship was damaged when it was "shouldered" by a U.S. Navy vessel while protesting the launching of a Trident 2 missile off the coast of Florida. The Navy called the shouldering, which left a gash in the Greenpeace ship, a reaction to its proximity to the test site. The Navy went on to explain that it had broadcast notification of the test four times a day for four days prior, urging people to protest no less than 5,000 yards from the launching.
- **RATINGS:** As of June 1, 1990, NCIB had requested but not received sufficient information for a report.
- **REGISTRATION:** CA, DC, GA, IL, MA, MD, MI, MN, MO, NC, NY (49832), OH, OR, PA, SC, TN, TX, VA (880), WA, and WI.
- **FINANCIAL DATA:** Text and chart source was their annual report covering 1988.

160

Greenpeace Action
1436 U St., N.W., Suite 201-A
Washington, DC 20009
(202) 462-1177

- **CONTRIBUTIONS** are *not* tax-deductible.
- **PURPOSE:** Greenpeace Action was formed in 1987 to lobby for and support Greenpeace's work in the United States. GA's agenda is set each year by the board of directors in association with Greenpeace USA and other Greenpeace organizations worldwide.
- **INCOME:** $2,585,698 (calendar 1988; accrual accounting, IRS form 990).
- **HOW THEY USE YOUR MONEY:**
  PROGRAM: $1,569,659:
  - $524,584 for ocean ecology (to promote biological integrity and genetic diversity in marine ecosystems).
  - $517,690 for reducing toxic wastes through peaceful action and education.
  - $517,310 for nuclear disarmament.
  - $10,075 for *Greenpeace* magazine.
  OVERHEAD: $215,842.
  FUNDRAISING: $787,333.
- **EXCESS:** $12,864.
- **LITTLE-KNOWN FACTS:** In keeping with its environmentalist policies GA uses recycled paper for its brochures and stationery. Under a sublicense agreement, Greenpeace Action must pay a royalty fee, based on a percentage of gross revenues, for the right and license to use the trademarked name "Greenpeace."
- **RATINGS:** No NCIB report.
- **REGISTRATION:** CA, DC, GA, IL, MA, MD, MI, MN, MO, NC, NY, OH, OR, PA, SC, TN, TX, VA (2719), WA, and WI.
- **FINANCIAL DATA:** Text and chart source was their IRS form 990 covering 1988.

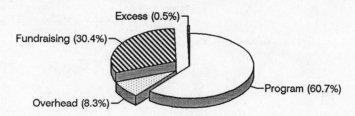

Excess (0.5%)
Fundraising (30.4%)
Overhead (8.3%)
Program (60.7%)

Greenpeace USA

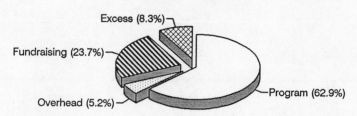

Excess (8.3%)
Fundraising (23.7%)
Overhead (5.2%)
Program (62.9%)

Gray Panthers Project Fund
311 S. Juniper St., Suite 601
Philadelphia, PA 19107
(215) 382-3300 • (215) 545-6555

- **CONTRIBUTIONS** are tax-deductible.
- **PURPOSE:** Founded in 1971, the Gray Panthers seek to combat discrimination against people on the basis of age. In 1974 the group absorbed the Retired Professional Action Group.
- **SIZE:** Six staff members supported by 100 local groups.
- **INCOME:** $724,139 (calendar 1988; IRS form 990).
- **HOW THEY USE YOUR MONEY:**
  PROGRAM: $644,925:
  - $478,882 for public education.
  - $100,131 for network development.
  - $36,622 for their convention.
  - $29,290 for the "Mahler Grantee."

  OVERHEAD: $77,524.
  FUNDRAISING: $61,861.
- **DEFICIT:** $60,171.
- **RATINGS:** As of June 1,1990, NCIB was preparing a new report.
- **REGISTRATION:** MA, MI, NJ, NY (47231), PA, and TN.
- **FINANCIAL DATA:** Text and chart source was their IRS form 990 covering 1988.

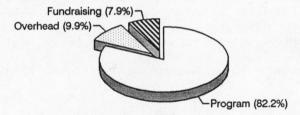

Fundraising (7.9%)
Overhead (9.9%)
Program (82.2%)

Due to deficit of 7.7%, chart is based on spending, not income.

162

Guide Dog Foundation for the Blind, Inc.
371 E. Jericho Tpke.
Smithtown, NY 11787
(516) 265-2121 • (800) 548-4337

- **CONTRIBUTIONS** are tax-deductible.
- **PURPOSE:** Founded in 1946; also known as the Second Sight Guiding Eyes–Guide Dog Foundation; gives qualified blind applicants trained guide dogs, which have been raised in volunteer homes for one year, trained for four to six months, and then participated in a four-week residential training program with their new owners at the foundation's Smithtown location.
- **SIZE:** The staff of 29 is supported by 450 members.
- **INCOME:** $1,182,229 (year ending 6/30/88; accrual accounting, independently audited statement).
- **HOW THEY USE YOUR MONEY:**
  PROGRAM: $767,369.
  OVERHEAD: $143,968.
  FUNDRAISING: $95,241.
- **EXCESS:** $175,651.
- **RATINGS:** NCIB reported (6/4/87, using figures from the year ending 6/30/86) that the group met all eight of NCIB's old evaluation standards.
- **REGISTRATION:** NY (4888) and VA (2611).
- **FINANCIAL DATA:** Text and chart source was their independently audited statement covering the year ending 6/30/88.

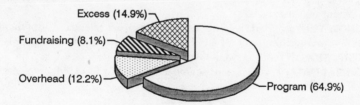

Excess (14.9%)
Fundraising (8.1%)
Overhead (12.2%)
Program (64.9%)

163

Guiding Eyes for the Blind, Inc.
611 Granite Springs Rd.
Yorktown Heights, NY 10598
(914) 245-4024

- **CONTRIBUTIONS** are tax-deductible.
- **PURPOSE:** Founded in 1956; provides trained guide dogs for deserving blind persons. Instructors must undergo a three-year course, and dogs and their new owners must participate in a four-week training program in Yorktown Heights.
- **SIZE:** About fifty-two staff members; 3,500 guide-dog teams taught since the group's founding.
- **INCOME:** $4,597,137 (calendar 1988; accrual accounting, IRS form 990).
- **HOW THEY USE YOUR MONEY:**
PROGRAM: $1,849,686:
  - $1,236,784 for guide dog training.
  - $51,820 for public education (educating both blind and sighted people about guide dogs and their use).
  - $401,960 for a breeding program for dogs.
  - $159,122 for graduate services (to make sure graduates are "functioning properly").
OVERHEAD: $510,148.
FUNDRAISING: $678,648.
- **EXCESS:** $1,558,655. A spokesman for the group says that this figure is "entirely bequests, put into . . . an endowment fund. Eventually [interest on this money will] cover half of our operation costs." Only $100,000 in bequests is allocated to program expenses.
- **RATINGS:** NCIB reported (2/8/88, using figures from calendar 1986) that Guiding Eyes for the Blind met all eight of NCIB's old evaluation standards.
- **REGISTRATION:** NY (8951) and VA (2310).
- **FINANCIAL DATA:** Text and chart source was their IRS form 990 covering 1988.

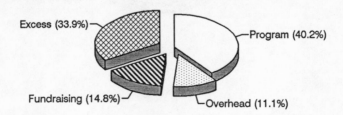

Excess (33.9%)　Program (40.2%)　Fundraising (14.8%)　Overhead (11.1%)

Habitat for Humanity International, Inc.
419 W. Church St.
Americus, GA 31709
(912) 924-6935

- **CONTRIBUTIONS** are tax-deductible.
- **PURPOSE:** Founded in 1976 by restless millionaire Millard Fuller as an ecumenical Christian housing ministry (with a "theology of the hammer") to eliminate poverty housing, make decent shelter "a matter of conscience and action," and witness to the Gospel. Donated money, materials, and labor are used to construct housing for selected individuals who receive no-profit, no-interest mortgages, must make payments over a fixed period (typically 20 years), and contribute "sweat equity" by participating in the construction of their own and other Habitat homes. In late 1989 the owners of a house constructed by Habitat's predecessor, the Koinonia Partners' Fund for Humanity, held the program's first mortgage-burning, six months early.
- **SIZE:** 445 local affiliates in the United States, Australia, Canada, and South Africa, plus sponsored projects in twenty-six countries.
- **INCOME:** $10,204,695 (calendar 1988; IRS form 990). Habitat does not accept state or federal funds because it sees its projects as supplements to, rather than replacements for, public housing.
- **HOW THEY USE YOUR MONEY:**
PROGRAM: $5,659,770,* of which $2,754,066 was grants and allocations—$1,771,167 to sponsored projects abroad, and $982,899 to affiliated projects in the United States.
OVERHEAD: $687,998.
FUNDRAISING: $2,396,646.*
- **EXCESS:** $1,460,281.
- **LITTLE-KNOWN FACTS:** While no longer a board member, former President Jimmy Carter supports Habitat and has pledged to volunteer for one week a year. Carter and his wife, Rosalynn, who serves on the international board of advisors, have contributed their carpentry skills on at least eight work projects.
- **RATINGS:** NCIB reported (8/8/90, using figures from calendar 1989), that Habitat for Humanity met all nine NCIB standards.
- **REGISTRATION:** GA and VA (2651).
- **FINANCIAL DATA:** Text and chart source was their IRS form 990 covering 1988. Footnote source was their independently audited statement covering 1988.

*Costs of $1,949,737 in direct-mail activities were allocated in Habitat's 1988 audited statement between fundraising ($1,380,530) and "public awareness and education" ($569,207).

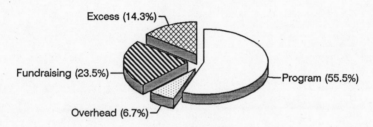

Excess (14.3%)
Fundraising (23.5%)
Overhead (6.7%)
Program (55.5%)

HALT—An Organization of Americans for Legal Reform
1319 F St., N.W., Suite 300
Washington, DC 20004
(202) 347-9600

- **CONTRIBUTIONS** are tax-deductible.
- **PURPOSE:** Founded in 1977 and formerly known as HALT—Help Abolish Legal Tyranny; seeks to reform the legal system, simplifying the language and procedures of the law to enable people to handle their own legal affairs. HALT also works to improve the quality of available legal services and reduce their cost, supports no-fault accident insurance to reduce unnecessary litigation, and publishes citizens' legal manuals.
- **SIZE:** The work of twenty staff members at four local groups is supported by 140,000 members.
- **INCOME:** $2,290,367 (calendar 1988; accrual accounting, IRS form 990).
- **HOW THEY USE YOUR MONEY:**
  PROGRAM: $1,931,630.
  OVERHEAD: $276,176.
  FUNDRAISING: $295,258.
- **DEFICIT:** $212,697.
- **RATINGS:** NCIB reported (5/21/90, using figures from calendar 1988) that HALT did not meet standard 6a, and there was a question about standard 8, but HALT met all other new NCIB standards.
- **REGISTRATION:** NY (50794) and VA (2743).
- **FINANCIAL DATA:** Text and chart source was their IRS form 990 covering 1988.

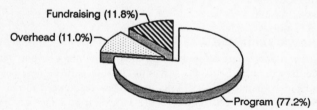

Fundraising (11.8%)
Overhead (11.0%)
Program (77.2%)

Due to deficit of 8.5%, chart is based on spending, not income.

Handgun Control, Inc.
1225 Eye St., N.W., Suite 1100
Washington, DC 20005
(202) 898-0792

- **CONTRIBUTIONS** are *not* tax-deductible.
- **PURPOSE:** A membership organization incorporated in 1974 to work for the adoption of reasonable and practical measures for the control of handguns.
- **SIZE:** Staff of twenty-eight; 180,000 members.
- **INCOME:** $5,506,411 (calendar 1988; accrual accounting, IRS form 990).
- **HOW THEY USE YOUR MONEY:**
  PROGRAM: $4,637,771*:
  - $2,017,113 for legislation and adjudication (lobbying, formulation of policy, and legal work).
  - $1,512,973* for membership development.
  - $888,519 for education and public relations (direct mail, articles development, press releases, press conferences).
  - $201,844 for member services.
  - $17,322 for fundraising and administration for Handgun Control's Political Action Committee.
  OVERHEAD: $373,214.
  FUNDRAISING: $720,697.*
- **DEFICIT:** $225,271.
- **LITTLE-KNOWN FACTS:** Handgun Control's Political Action Committee is a separate fund which accepts contributions to influence the selection and nomination of office seekers to further the group's goals.
- **RATINGS:** No NCIB report.
- **REGISTRATION:** CA, DC, NY (45370), and VA (895).
- **FINANCIAL DATA:** Text and chart source was their IRS form 990 covering 1988. Footnote source was their independently audited statement covering 1988.

*Costs for $2,651,541 worth of informational materials and activities that included fundraising appeals were allocated thus: $483,077 to fundraising, $1,043,011 to membership development, and the remainder split among other program expenses.

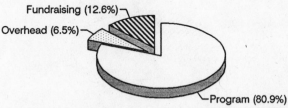

Fundraising (12.6%)
Overhead (6.5%)
Program (80.9%)

Due to deficit of 3.9%, chart is based on spending, not income.

Help Hospitalized Veterans, Inc.
2065 Kurtz St.
San Diego, CA 92110
(619) 291-5846

- **CONTRIBUTIONS** are tax-deductible.
- **PURPOSE:** Distributes arts-and-crafts kits to occupational-therapy departments and wards of U.S. military and VA hospitals. Also, HHV examines the causes and effects of drug and alcohol abuse in the United States, especially within the military and veteran populations, and seeks solutions to the problems.
- **SIZE:** In its nineteen-year history, HHV has distributed 10 million kits (retail value over $60 million) to 260 hospitals in fifty states.
- **INCOME:** $11,009,327 (year ending 7/31/89; accrual accounting, IRS form 990).
- **HOW THEY USE YOUR MONEY:**
  PROGRAM: $6,538,074:
  - $5,513,313 to distribute arts-and-crafts kits.
  - $1,024,761 to Citizens for a Drug Free America (an affiliated nonprofit group).
  OVERHEAD: $925,590.
  FUNDRAISING: $3,846,933, including $934,733 to Richard A. Viguerie, the New Right direct-mail fundraiser.
- **DEFICIT:** $301,270.
- **LITTLE-KNOWN FACTS:** Since September 1, 1988, HHV has donated 10 percent of its contribution income to Citizens for a Drug Free America and Citizens for a Drug Free America Foundation, which were established in April 1988 "for the purpose of mobilizing America's citizenry in an all-out effort to win the war on drugs."
- **RATINGS:** NCIB reported (6/30/88, using figures from year ending 8/31/87) that Help Hospitalized Veterans met standards 1, 2, 3, 5, 6, 7, and 8, but that it did not meet standard 4.
- **REGISTRATION:** CA (13082).
- **FINANCIAL DATA:** Text and chart source was their IRS form 990 covering the year ending 7/31/89.

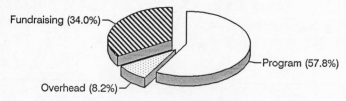

Fundraising (34.0%)

Program (57.8%)

Overhead (8.2%)

Due to deficit of 2.7%, chart is based on spending, not income.

The Heritage Foundation
214 Massachusetts Ave., N.E.
Washington, DC 20002
(202) 546-4400

- **CONTRIBUTIONS** are tax-deductible.
- **PURPOSE:** Founded in 1973 with a $250,000 grant from Joseph Coors, the Heritage Foundation has striven "not merely to understand the way the world works, but to change it." It advocates principles of free competitive enterprise, limited government, individual liberty, and a strong national defense. Its greatest accomplishment has been its three "Mandate for Leadership" studies of how conservative ideas and ideals could be incorporated into the federal government.
- **SIZE:** Over 130,000 supporters.
- **INCOME:** $14,968,286 (calendar 1988; accrual accounting, IRS form 990). Except for a dip in 1987, during the preceding four fiscal years support had been increasing.
- **HOW THEY USE YOUR MONEY:**
  PROGRAM: $9,722,343:
  - $3,732,473 (including $373,322 in grants and allocations) for research (on domestic and foreign matters).
  - $1,905,784 for public information (a syndicated newspaper column, radio and TV appearances, etc.).
  - $1,447,139 for the Resource Bank (a networking operation for conservative groups and ideas).
  - $1,346,347 for policy studies (e.g., publication of *Policy Review* quarterly, monographs, scholarly books, proceedings of lectures and seminars).
  - $1,290,600 for legislative and government information (conferences, briefings, seminars, and studies of the federal government).
  OVERHEAD: $797,162.
  FUNDRAISING: $1,877,190.
- **EXCESS:** $2,571,591.
- **LITTLE-KNOWN FACTS:** A 1982 Heritage-supported study, "High Frontier," was the impetus for development of the Strategic Defense Initiative (Star Wars).
- **RATINGS:** NCIB reported (2/2/87, using figures from calendar 1985) that the Heritage Foundation met all eight of NCIB's old evaluation standards.
- **REGISTRATION:** CA, CT, IL, MA, MD, MN, NC, NJ, NY (46906), OH, OK, OR, PA, TN, VA (918), and WV.
- **FINANCIAL DATA:** Text and chart source was their IRS form 990 covering 1988.

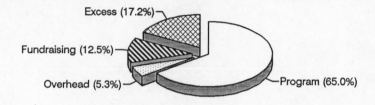

169

The Hole in the Wall Gang Camp Fund, Inc.
555 Long Wharf Drive
New Haven, CT 06511
(203) 772-0522

■ **CONTRIBUTIONS** are tax-deductible.

■ **PURPOSE:** Formed in 1988 "to establish and maintain a camp in Connecticut for children (aged 7 to 17) who are . . . physically incapacitated or suffering from severe illnesses" such as cancer (leukemia or tumors), genetic blood diseases (thalassemia, sickle cell anemia, hemophilia), and the HIV virus, and "whose medical attention would preclude attendance at regular summer camps."

■ **SIZE:** 456 "camperships" granted for the 1989 sessions.

■ **INCOME:** $4,342,524 (year ending 11/30/89; accrual accounting, IRS form 990).

■ **HOW THEY USE YOUR MONEY:**

PROGRAM: $1,655,736 to provide four 11-day and one 5-day summer camping sessions at the fund's facility in Ashford/Eastford, CT.

OVERHEAD: $376,351.

FUNDRAISING: $182,061.

■ **EXCESS:** $2,128,370. Patricia Montgomery, the group's bookkeeper, says that $350,000 of these funds was donated property (in Maine) held for resale, and $1,432,138 was applied toward building and improvement of the campground facilities, to be used over the next twenty years.

■ **LITTLE-KNOWN FACTS:** Paul Newman, a founder of the camp (named after Butch Cassidy's hideaway), contributed a total of $2,492,355 during the year ending 11/30/88.

■ **RATINGS:** No NCIB report.

■ **REGISTRATION:** All fifty states, including CT (2670) and VA (2737).

■ **FINANCIAL DATA:** Text and chart source was their IRS form 990 covering the year ending 11/30/89. Little-Known Fact source was their IRS form 990 covering the year ending 11/30/88.

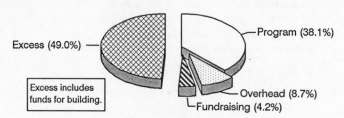

Excess (49.0%) —

Excess includes funds for building.

Program (38.1%)

Overhead (8.7%)

Fundraising (4.2%)

The Humane Society of the United States, Inc.
2100 L St., N.W.
Washington, DC 20037
(202) 452-1100

- **CONTRIBUTIONS** are tax-deductible.
- **PURPOSE:** Founded in 1954, to promote "the humane treatment of animals and to instill compassion in mankind." It engages in broad activities to reduce overbreeding of cats and dogs, promote responsible pet care, end cruelty and abuse of animals, and protect marine mammals and endangered species. Affiliated with the World Society for the Protection of Animals.
- **SIZE:** 800,000 members in eight regional groups.
- **INCOME:** $11,912,719 (calendar 1988; accrual accounting, IRS form 990).
- **HOW THEY USE YOUR MONEY:**
PROGRAM: $8,665,387:
  - $5,963,746 for humane education, membership, and program services.
  - $956,828 for cruelty investigation and litigation.
  - $1,799,448 for membership development.
OVERHEAD: $1,369,287.
FUNDRAISING: $698,668.
- **EXCESS:** $1,179,377.
- **LITTLE-KNOWN FACTS:** The society shares a common governing board with: the National Humane Education Center, the National Association for the Advancement of Humane Education, the Boulder County Humane Society Fund, the Elsa Horne Voss Animal Welfare Foundation, the Alice Morgan Wright–Edith Goode Fund, and the Sussman Fund.
- **RATINGS:** NCIB reported (8/30/89, using figures from calendar 1988) that "there is a question with regard to the Humane Society of the United States meeting NCIB standards 1 and 8. It meets the other standards of the NCIB."
- **REGISTRATION:** CA, CT, FL, IL, MD, MI, MN, NC, NJ, NY (11833), OH, PA, and VA (2435).
- **FINANCIAL DATA:** Text and chart source was their IRS form 990 covering 1988.

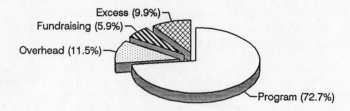

Excess (9.9%)
Fundraising (5.9%)
Overhead (11.5%)
Program (72.7%)

Human Rights Watch
485 Fifth Ave.
New York, NY 10017
(212) 972-8400

■ **CONTRIBUTIONS** are tax-deductible.
■ **PURPOSE:** Human Rights Watch embraces Americas Watch (founded 1981), Helsinki Watch (1978), Asia Watch (1985), Africa Watch and Middle East Watch (both 1988), and the Fund for Free Expression (incorporated 1975). The latter is the parent organization of the "Watch Committees" that form Human Rights Watch. Each committee monitors the human-rights practices of governments within its own geographical sphere of concern and lends support to individuals and groups who monitor and defend human rights in their own countries. Staff members and consultants travel to conduct on-site investigations of trouble spots, and violations of human rights are widely publicized and protested. In addition to defending local monitors worldwide, Human Rights Watch has monitored violations of the laws of war by both sides in a dozen military conflicts. The organization makes a major effort to persuade the U.S. government to use its influence to promote human rights around the world.
■ **SIZE:** By late 1989, staff numbered seventy, and the Human Rights Watch committees worked in some fifty countries. There are offices in New York, Washington, Los Angeles, London, El Salvador, and Hong Kong.
■ **INCOME:** $4,201,386* for the Fund for Free Expression, Inc. (calendar 1988; amended IRS form 990); $602,912* for Helsinki Watch (calendar 1988; cash accounting, IRS form 990-PF).
■ **HOW THEY USE YOUR MONEY:**
PROGRAM (FFE): $2,398,238,† including:
  • $860,049 for the Americas Watch Committee.
  • $329,840 for the Asia Watch Committee.

   Out of the *entire* amount FFE spent on program expenses, $1,307,303 was in the form of grants and allocations for special human-rights projects that affect or serve one or more of the regional Watch committees, in addition to projects promoting free expression in the United States and abroad. This figure includes some money within the total amounts given above for the Americas Watch and Asia Watch committees, in addition to $110,661 in start-up costs for Africa Watch and Middle East Watch.

*Human Rights Watch was established in 1988. Up to that time, the Fund for Free Expression, Inc. (including all the Watch Committees), and Helsinki Watch filed separate IRS forms 990.
†World events and activation of new Watch Committees altered the distribution of expenses in 1989 and (projected) in 1990. Unaudited figures for 1989 indicate total income of $4,400,251 for Human Rights Watch. Proposed budget allocations for each Watch Committee in 1989 and 1990 was:

	1989	1990
Africa Watch	10%	15%
Americas Watch	30%	20%
Asia Watch	20%	20%
Fund/Human Rights Watch	10%	10%
Helsinki Watch	25%	20%
Middle East Watch	5%	15%

PROGRAM (HW): $730,307:
- $650,190 for the Helsinki Watch program.
- $74,198 for the International Helsinki Federation.
- $5,919 for miscellaneous other expenses.

OVERHEAD: $312,877 (FFE; this figure increased in mid-1989 due to a move to larger quarters and the formation of new Watch Committees); $7,613 (HW).

FUNDRAISING: $419,062 (FFE only), including $221,637 for development ($216,522 for direct mail), and $155,295 for Tenth Anniversary expenses.

■ **EXCESS:** $1,071,209 (FFE).

■ **DEFICIT:** $135,008 (HW).

■ **LITTLE-KNOWN FACTS:** Human-rights activist Vaclav Havel, who became president of Czechoslovakia in 1989, was among those arrested by police just before the November 11, 1988, opening of an unofficial Prague symposium jointly organized by Helsinki Watch and Havel's own Charter 77 group. Havel and other Charter 77 leaders were released a few days later and Helsinki Watch Executive Director Jeri Laber went to Prague to inform them of a Vienna press conference organized by the International Helsinki Federation to publicize the arrests, and of statements by delegates to the Helsinki Review Conference in Vienna.

■ **RATINGS:** No NCIB report on either group.

■ **REGISTRATION:** NY (49148) (FFE); NY (49063) (HW).

■ **FINANCIAL DATA:** HW text and chart source was their IRS form 990-PF covering 1988. FFE text and chart source was their amended IRS form 990 covering 1988. Human Rights Watch unaudited 1989 income source was their 1989 annual report. Budget data for 1989 and 1990 came from Human Rights Watch.

Fund for Free Expression

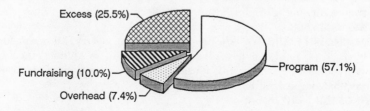

Excess (25.5%)
Fundraising (10.0%)
Overhead (7.4%)
Program (57.1%)

Helsinki Watch

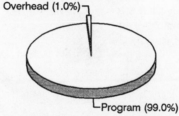

Overhead (1.0%)
Program (99.0%)

Due to deficit of 18.3%, chart is based on spending, not income.

Human Resources Center
I. U. Willets Rd.
Albertson, NY 11507
(516) 747-5400

- **CONTRIBUTIONS** are tax-deductible.
- **PURPOSE:** Founded in 1952 to provide comprehensive education, training, and employment programs to help people with disabilities (from infancy through adulthood) to achieve their maximum potential with dignity and independence. The center has five main components: the Industry-Labor Council; Vocational Rehabilitative Services; Abilities, Inc.; the Research and Training Institute; and the Human Resources School. The National Center on Employment, an outgrowth of the White House Conference on Handicapped Individuals, was formed in 1977 to conduct national studies on job placement and career education of the disabled and employer attitudes toward them.
- **SIZE:** About 4,500 persons a year are served by the center. The school serves over 200 children from forty-seven Long Island school districts.
- **INCOME:** $12,717,339 (year ending 6/30/89; combined independently audited statement of the Human Resources Center, Human Resources School, and Abilities, Inc.).
- **HOW THEY USE YOUR MONEY:**
PROGRAM: $10,123,738:
  - $5,943,081 for education and recreation programs.
  - $2,477,628 for vocational rehabilitation.
  - $1,022,577 for work-demonstration programs.
  - $680,452 for research and utilization programs.
OVERHEAD: $656,570.
FUNDRAISING: $904,960, including public relations and the building fund campaign.
LOSS FROM PHASE-OUT: $186,763 from discontinuance and liquidation of the electronics division of Abilities, Inc. (1/1/89 to 3/31/90).
- **EXCESS:** $845,308
- **LITTLE-KNOWN FACTS:** Western Electric, Grumman, Sperry, European American Bank, IBM, and Litton have all subcontracted work to Abilities, Inc., which also worked on the wire assembly for the F-2 fighter plane until it was disqualified by changing federal law.
- **RATINGS:** No NCIB report.
- **REGISTRATION:** NY (10703).
- **FINANCIAL DATA:** Text and chart source was the combined independently audited statement of the Human Resources Center, Human Resources School, and Abilities, Inc., covering the year ending 6/30/89.

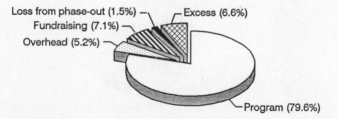

Loss from phase-out (1.5%) — Excess (6.6%)
Fundraising (7.1%) —
Overhead (5.2%) —
Program (79.6%)

174

The Hunger Project
1388 Sutter St.
San Francisco, CA 94109
(415) 928-8700

The Global Hunger Project
One Madison Ave.
New York, NY 10010
(212) 532-4255

- **CONTRIBUTIONS** are tax-deductible.
- **PURPOSE:** Begun in 1977 by John Denver, Robert Fuller, and Werner Erhard (founder of est) to "mobilize a strategic international effort to end chronic hunger by the end of the century. The Hunger Project does not engage in direct relief efforts. Instead, through programs of communication and education; high-level, internationally visible events; strategically designed and targeted global initiatives; participation in national and international conferences; and support of on-the-ground projects," it works to make *ending* hunger a priority around the world.
- **SIZE:** The Global Hunger Project has activities in more than thirty countries; domestic U.S. operations are handled by the Hunger Project office in San Francisco.
- **INCOME:** $10,205,968 (calendar 1989; Global Hunger Project's independently audited statement).
- **HOW THEY USE YOUR MONEY:**
  PROGRAM: $7,704,235:
  - $4,074,100 for educational programs, grants, and strategic initiatives.
  - $2,508,189 for global operations and U.S. volunteer activities.
  - $1,121,946 for publications.
  OVERHEAD: $1,267,550.
  FUNDRAISING: $1,209,183.
- **EXCESS:** $25,000.
- **LITTLE-KNOWN FACTS:** The project draws a distinction between "famine" (which it considers an emergency condition accounting for only 10 percent of the hunger-related deaths in the world) and "hunger" (which it considers a chronic problem due to the "lack, over a long period of time, of a diet sufficient to sustain healthy, productive life"). Following U.N. agencies and nongovernmental organizations, the project defines the end of hunger as "a society-wide issue" as the point at which the infant mortality rate drops below 50 deaths (of infants under one year of age) per 1,000 live births.
- **RATINGS:** NCIB reported (4/21/89, using figures from calendar 1987) that the Global Hunger Project met all nine NCIB standards.
- **REGISTRATION:** CA (22003), CT (1727), GA, IL, MA, NJ, NY (47629), SC, and VA (1014).
- **FINANCIAL DATA:** Text and chart source was their independently audited statement for calendar 1989.

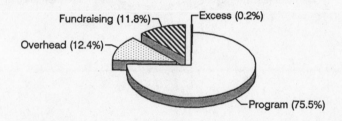

Fundraising (11.8%)
Excess (0.2%)
Overhead (12.4%)
Program (75.5%)

Huntington's Disease Society of America
140 West 22nd St., 6th Fl.
New York, NY 10011
(212) 242-1968 • Hotline: (800) 345-HDSA

- **CONTRIBUTIONS** are tax-deductible.
- **PURPOSE:** Huntington's disease is a hereditary brain disorder producing gradual loss of control over body and mind for ten to fifteen years, until death. Founded in 1967, the society is dedicated to the eradication of Huntington's disease, care of patients, assistance for families, and education of the public.
- **SIZE:** Forty-three chapters and branches.
- **INCOME:** $935,462 (national office, year ending 9/30/88; accrual accounting, IRS form 990).
- **HOW THEY USE YOUR MONEY:**
  PROGRAM: $601,761:
  - $250,251 (including $204,426 in grants and allocations) for research.
  - $110,475 for public education (e.g., newsletters, brochures, and science updates).
  - $106,824 for patient services (counseling and referral of patients and their families).
  - $134,211 for community development (workshops and seminars on Huntington's through nationwide chapter affiliates and branches).

  OVERHEAD: $85,903.
  FUNDRAISING: $121,501.
- **EXCESS:** $126,297.
- **LITTLE-KNOWN FACTS:** The logo of the society shows two adult and two child figures, one each with the double helix emblem of DNA to reflect the 50 percent chance a child of a Huntington's parent has of inheriting the disorder, which usually appears between the ages of thirty and fifty, after most people have married, had children, and passed on the gene.
- **RATINGS:** NCIB reported (5/23/88, using figures from the year ending 9/30/87) that the Huntington's Disease Society of America met all eight of NCIB's old evaluation standards.
- **REGISTRATION:** NY (55734).
- **FINANCIAL DATA:** Text and chart source was their IRS form 990 (for the national headquarters *only*) covering the year ending 9/30/88.

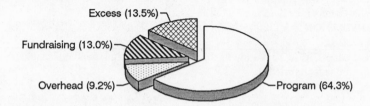

Excess (13.5%)
Fundraising (13.0%)
Overhead (9.2%)
Program (64.3%)

Institute of Noetic Sciences
475 Gate 5 Rd., Suite 300
Sausalito, CA 94965
(415) 331-5650 • (800) 525-7985

- **CONTRIBUTIONS** are tax-deductible.
- **PURPOSE:** The institute was founded in 1972 to use research and education, on the nature and potentials of consciousness and the mind, for the benefit of humankind and the planet. The word *noetic* comes from the Greek *nous,* meaning "mind," "intelligence," and "understanding."
- **SIZE:** 20,145 members (1988).
- **INCOME:** $2,375,227 (calendar 1988; accrual accounting, IRS form 990). During the preceding four fiscal years support had been increasing.
- **HOW THEY USE YOUR MONEY:**
  PROGRAM: $1,751,133:
  - $291,450 for inner mechanisms of the healing response (including research into mind-body functions in immunology, also known as psychoneuroimmunology) and bio-energy medicine (including research on electromagnetism and the healing process).
  - $280,064 for studies of exceptional abilities (mental and physical prodigies, meditation, outstanding professional achievement, and "nonordinary states of awareness") and altruistic spirit (creative altruism and the altruistic personality).
  - $97,504 for Global Mind Change (including Citizens' Summits held between Washington and Moscow, and the First Planetary Congress of the Association of Space Explorers).

       Dollar breakdowns were available for only three programs; the remaining money was spent on various education functions.
  OVERHEAD: $183,117.
  FUNDRAISING: $368,252. Rather than consider this category to be fundraising in the conventional sense of seeking charitable contributions, the institute prefers the term "membership solicitation." Members are solicited for contributions, and they receive publications, including the *Noetic Sciences Journal.*
- **EXCESS:** $72,725.
- **LITTLE-KNOWN FACTS:** Edgar Mitchell, founder of the institute, conducted an experiment in extrasensory perception (ESP) during his mission in space as the lunar module pilot of Apollo 14.
- **RATINGS:** No NCIB report.
- **REGISTRATION:** CA (15899).
- **FINANCIAL DATA:** Text and chart source was their IRS form 990 covering 1988.

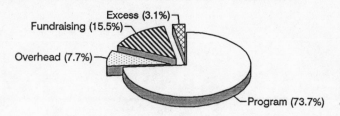

Excess (3.1%)
Fundraising (15.5%)
Overhead (7.7%)
Program (73.7%)

International Peace Academy
777 U.N. Plaza, 4th Fl.
New York, NY 10017
(212) 949-8480

- **CONTRIBUTIONS** are tax-deductible.
- **PURPOSE:** Works with the United Nations, regional organizations, and governments worldwide to conduct international training seminars, off-the-record workshops, and consultations on peacekeeping, multilateral negotiations, and mediation for military and diplomatic officials.
- **SIZE:** In twenty years, the academy "has built an influential, global network of over 4,000 diplomats, peacekeeping officers, and policy-makers from 150 nations."
- **INCOME:** $1,166,729 (calendar 1988; accrual accounting, IRS form 990).
- **HOW THEY USE YOUR MONEY:**
  PROGRAM: $587,132 on seminars, conferences, and workshops on peacekeeping, peacemaking, and multilateral negotiations.
  OVERHEAD: $519,086.
  FUNDRAISING: $102,181.
- **DEFICIT:** $41,670.
- **LITTLE-KNOWN FACTS:** In 1988 an off-the-record workshop was held near Moscow, co-sponsored by the Soviet Institute of World Economy and International Relations, on "Soviet and American Perceptions of Third World Regional Conflicts: Their Origins and Resolution." Conclusions noted the declining usefulness of superpower force in the Third World; the indivisibility of security in an interdependent world; and the potential utility of the U.N. and ad-hoc regional mechanisms in fostering international peace and security.
- **RATINGS:** NCIB reported (9/9/88, using figures from calendar 1987) that the academy met all nine NCIB standards.
- **REGISTRATION:** NY (42137).
- **FINANCIAL DATA:** Text and chart source was their IRS form 990 covering 1988.

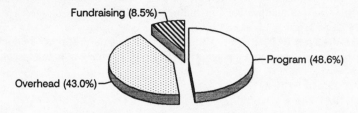

Due to deficit of 3.4%, chart is based on spending, not income.

178

International Physicians for the Prevention of Nuclear War
126 Rogers St.
Cambridge, MA 02142
(617) 868-5050

- **CONTRIBUTIONS** are tax-deductible.
- **PURPOSE:** Formed in December 1980 by American and Soviet physicians meeting in Geneva. IPPNW, winner of the 1985 Nobel Peace Prize, aims to focus international attention on the medical and environmental consequences of nuclear war; it favors complete abolition of nuclear weapons, with "prudent interim measures designed to slow the arms race or engender the trust needed for its cessation." (The American affiliate, Physicians for Social Responsibility, is profiled elsewhere in this book.)
- **SIZE:** More than 200,000 members in sixty-one countries.
- **INCOME:** $2,066,075 (year ending 6/30/88; cash accounting, IRS form 990). During the preceding four fiscal years support had been increasing. (From 7/1/83 to 6/30/87 the group received $233,042 in award money from the Nobel Foundation.)
- **HOW THEY USE YOUR MONEY:**
PROGRAM: $947,503:
  - $779,697 for education, meetings, speakers, publications, etc.
  - $167,806 for its international congresses.
OVERHEAD: $93,279.
FUNDRAISING: $787,077.
- **EXCESS:** $238,216.
- **LITTLE-KNOWN FACTS:** IPPNW, the first U.S.-based organization asked by Soviet health authorities to supply aid after the 1988 Armenian earthquake, has been working for the past three years (with consultants from World Health Organization, UNICEF, and the Red Cross) to use satellite communications to aid disaster relief and deliver health-care information to the developing world. SatelLife, an independent organization established by IPPNW, is working with the Annenberg Center for the Health Sciences in California and the Soviet Academy of Sciences to accomplish this task.
- **RATINGS:** No NCIB report.
- **REGISTRATION:** MA and NY (54217).
- **FINANCIAL DATA:** Text and chart source was their IRS form 990 covering the year ending 6/30/88.

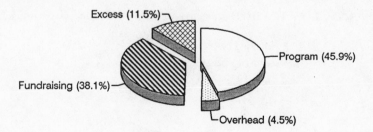

Excess (11.5%)
Fundraising (38.1%)
Program (45.9%)
Overhead (4.5%)

International Rescue Committee
386 Park Ave. S., 10th Fl.
New York, NY 10016
(212) 679-0010

- **CONTRIBUTIONS** are tax-deductible.
- **PURPOSE:** A private, nonprofit organization devoted to assisting refugees worldwide, founded in 1933 at the urging of Albert Einstein to assist people fleeing Hitler. Provides relief to refugees in countries of first asylum abroad, and resettlement of refugees admitted to the United States or other free countries. In 1988 and 1989 Nobel laureate Elie Wiesel, a vice-president of the IRC, nominated it for the Nobel Peace Prize.
- **SIZE:** As of December 31, 1988, the IRC had active relief programs mainly in Thailand (refugees from Indochina), Pakistan (Afghanistan), Sudan (Ethiopia), Malawi (Mozambique), Hong Kong (China), El Salvador, and Costa Rica. There were also offices and programs in Geneva, Madrid, Munich, Paris, Poland, Rome, and Vienna.
- **INCOME:** $29,131,838 (calendar 1988; accrual accounting, IRS form 990). During the preceding four fiscal years support had been increasing.
- **HOW THEY USE YOUR MONEY:**
PROGRAM: $26,982,500:
  - $7,225,768 for refugee resettlement in the United States.
  - $12,555,630 for Asia and Near East (assistance, rehabilitation, medical, and educational programs for victims of totalitarian oppression and persecution).
  - $2,076,748 for Latin America.
  - $2,560,904 for Europe.
  - $2,563,450 for other program services.
OVERHEAD: $1,036,746.
FUNDRAISING: $855,106.
- **EXCESS:** $257,486.
- **LITTLE-KNOWN FACTS:** During 1988 IRC was still assisting more than 250 refugees who had fled to France from Franco during the Spanish Civil War in 1939.
- **RATINGS:** NCIB reported (8/3/89, using figures from calendar 1988) that the IRC met all nine NCIB standards.
- **REGISTRATION:** CA, CT, IL, MA, ME, NJ, NY (6996), OH, OR, PA, and VA (1035).
- **FINANCIAL DATA:** Text and chart source was their IRS form 990 covering 1988.

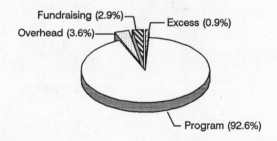

Fundraising (2.9%)
Overhead (3.6%)
Excess (0.9%)
Program (92.6%)

International Social Service, American Branch
95 Madison Ave.
New York, NY 10016
(212) 532-5858

- **CONTRIBUTIONS** are tax-deductible.
- **PURPOSE:** Founded in 1921, the ISS is an international social-work agency aiding adults and children with problems relating to family separation or migration across national boundaries. The intercountry casework staff administers direct client service in such areas as custody and care of children, family reunification, health, adoptions, migration, rights to benefits and pensions, and socio-legal problems. The ISS also undertakes studies and research of related issues, and serves as an advocate for "mobile" people.
- **INCOME:** $141,606 (calendar 1988; independently audited statement).
- **HOW THEY USE YOUR MONEY:**
  PROGRAM: $179,199.
  OVERHEAD: $30,357.
  FUNDRAISING: $6,288.
- **DEFICIT:** $74,238.
- **RATINGS:** No NCIB report.
- **REGISTRATION:** NY (12387) and VA (2328 or 3320).
- **FINANCIAL DATA:** Text and chart source was their independently audited statement covering 1988.

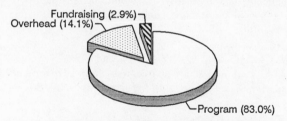

Fundraising (2.9%)
Overhead (14.1%)
Program (83.0%)

Due to deficit of 34.4%, chart is based on spending, not income.

181

Jewish National Fund
42 E. 69th St.
New York, NY 10021
(212) 879-9300 • (800) 542-TREE

- **CONTRIBUTIONS** are tax-deductible.
- **PURPOSE:** Founded in 1901 at the Fifth Zionist Congress in Basel, Switzerland, to buy land for the Jewish people's return to their ancient homeland. In 1961 the Jewish National Fund of America, Inc., appointed Keren Kayemeth LeIsrael, Ltd., as its sole agent in Israel. The fund buys land and is responsible for afforestation and land reclamation in Israel. Along with sponsoring and planting trees in Israel, it is best known for its little blue fundraising coinboxes.
- **SIZE:** The fund has planted over 195 million trees.
- **INCOME:** $10,613,323 (national office; year ending 9/30/88; IRS form 990).
- **HOW THEY USE YOUR MONEY:**
PROGRAM: $8,501,491:
  - $6,383,035 to buy and plant trees on land, and develop it for the absorption of refugees.
  - $2,118,456 for education and public information.
OVERHEAD: $1,530,326.
FUNDRAISING: $1,900,510.
- **DEFICIT:** $1,319,004.
- **LITTLE-KNOWN FACTS:** In 1987 and 1988, forest fires (at least 30 percent attributed to malicious arson) destroyed 1.2 million trees planted by the fund. In 1989, after a special fundraising effort to buy firefighting equipment, only 410,000 trees were lost to fire.
- **RATINGS:** No NCIB report.
- **REGISTRATION:** CT, MI, MN, NJ, NY (8503), and TN.
- **FINANCIAL DATA:** Text and chart source was their IRS form 990 (for the national headquarters *only*) covering the year ending 9/30/88.

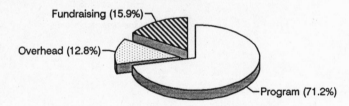

Fundraising (15.9%)
Overhead (12.8%)
Program (71.2%)

Due to deficit of 11.1%, chart is based on spending, not income.

Jobs with Peace Campaign
76 Summer St.
Boston, MA 02110
(617) 338-5783

- **CONTRIBUTIONS** are tax-deductible.
- **PURPOSE:** Established in 1982 as a nationwide grassroots effort to reduce military spending and invest the money in housing, health, child care, education, mass transit, and the environment. Since 1983 the Jobs with Peace Educational Fund, Inc., has distributed educational materials and publications about effects of federal budget policies and spending.
- **SIZE:** Eleven local campaigns, a base office in Boston, and a program office in Washington.
- **INCOME:** $600,912 (Jobs with Peace Educational Fund, Inc., calendar 1988; accrual accounting, IRS form 990).
- **HOW THEY USE YOUR MONEY:**
  PROGRAM: $475,756:
    - $326,549 for analyses (of the effects of federal budget and income-tax policies on state and local economies) and public education.
    - $149,207 for technical assistance to other groups researching similar issues.
  OVERHEAD: $89,805.
  FUNDRAISING: $31,830.
- **EXCESS:** $3,521.
- **RATINGS:** No NCIB report.
- **REGISTRATION:** MA.
- **FINANCIAL DATA:** Text and chart source was the IRS form 990 for the Jobs with Peace Educational Fund, Inc., covering 1988.

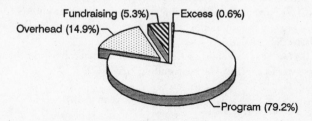

Fundraising (5.3%) — Excess (0.6%)
Overhead (14.9%) —
Program (79.2%)

183

Junior Achievement, Inc.
45 E. Clubhouse Dr.
Colorado Springs, CO 80906
(719) 540-8000

- **CONTRIBUTIONS** are tax-deductible.
- **PURPOSE:** Created in 1919 to provide "high-quality, experience-based economic education" to young people and the changing work force. After "franchises" are issued to local boards of directors (who raise local funds, hire local staff, and pay a "franchise fee" to help fund the national organization), headquarters provides local groups with products to sell.
- **SIZE:** There are about 225 local Junior Achievement areas, each separately incorporated.
- **INCOME:** $7,564,327 (national headquarters only; year ending 6/30/89; annual report).
- **HOW THEY USE YOUR MONEY:**
  PROGRAM: $6,026,172:
  - $2,680,791 for field services.
  - $1,160,354 for communications and marketing.
  - $1,089,564 for research and development.
  - $1,095,463 for human resources.
  OVERHEAD: $931,112.
  FUNDRAISING: $523,156 for national office only.
  DEPRECIATION: $502,401.
- **DEFICIT:** $418,514.
- **LITTLE-KNOWN FACTS:** Annually 1,200,000 students in grades 4 through 12 participate in four economic education programs, which are organized by 100,000 volunteers (including 40,000 business executives). More than 100,000 students in seventeen foreign countries are also involved.
- **RATINGS:** NCIB reported (6/9/89, using figures from the year ending 6/30/88) that Junior Achievement's national service center met all nine NCIB standards.
- **REGISTRATION:** NY (4016).
- **FINANCIAL DATA:** Text and chart source was their annual report (for the national headquarters *only*) covering the year ending 6/30/89.

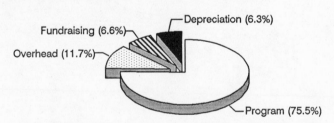

Due to deficit of 5.2%, chart is based on spending, not income.

184

Just Say No International
1777 N. California Blvd., Suite 210
Walnut Creek, CA 94596
(415) 939-6666 • (800) 258-2766

- **CONTRIBUTIONS** are tax-deductible.
- **PURPOSE:** Founded in 1986 to assist and educate the public in preventing drug abuse (including alcohol and tobacco), and support "Just Say No" clubs nationwide. Since such clubs now exist in other countries, the group's name was changed on January 1, 1989, from the Just Say No Foundation to Just Say No International. Soon after, the Pacific Institute for Research and Evaluation, Inc., filed a suit concerning the foundation's establishment and expenses, alleging breach of an oral contract and trademark infringement and seeking damages.
- **SIZE:** 15,000 "Just Say No" clubs at the end of 1988.
- **INCOME:** $1,296,270 (six months ending 12/31/88; accrual accounting, IRS form 990). (Collected $313,557 in pledge receivables on 1/30/89 from a MasterCard affinity program.)
- **HOW THEY USE YOUR MONEY:**
  PROGRAM: $359,032 for program services including information, consultation, training, a national directory of registered clubs, books, periodicals, and brochures.
  OVERHEAD: $150,650.
  FUNDRAISING: $0.
- **EXCESS:** $786,588.
- **LITTLE-KNOWN FACTS:** In August 1988 former top officials of the Just Say No Foundation charged that then-First Lady Nancy Reagan was being exploited by Procter and Gamble's efforts to tie the anti-drug campaign to its products with its "Just Say No" Back-to-School Pledge Drive. Mailings included a message from Mrs. Reagan, coupons for P&G products, and a sweepstakes entry. At the time of the mailing, a P&G vice-president was chairman of the foundation, and a former employee was executive director.
- **RATINGS:** As of June 1, 1990, NCIB had requested but not received sufficient information for a report.
- **REGISTRATION:** CA (64581).
- **FINANCIAL DATA:** Text and chart source was their IRS form 990 covering the last six months of 1988. MasterCard income source was the group's financial statement covering the last six months of 1988.

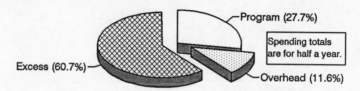

Program (27.7%)

Spending totals
are for half a year.

Excess (60.7%)

Overhead (11.6%)

Juvenile Diabetes Foundation International
432 Park Ave. S.
New York, NY 10016
(212) 889-7575 • (800) 223-1138

- **CONTRIBUTIONS** are tax-deductible.
- **PURPOSE:** Founded in 1970 by a group of parents of diabetic children who felt that, through research, diabetes could be cured, JDF gives more money directly to diabetes research than any other nongovernmental health agency in the world.
- **SIZE:** Over 150 chapters in the United States and Canada.
- **INCOME:** $17,855,468 (national office, but no affiliated chapters; year ending 6/30/88; accrual accounting, IRS form 990). During the preceding four fiscal years support had been increasing.
- **HOW THEY USE YOUR MONEY:**
  PROGRAM: $14,518,938:
  - $10,762,821 (including $9,148,096 in grants and allocations) for research support (about 327 grants to seek a cure, plus costs for workshop conferences).
  - $3,756,117 for public education.
  OVERHEAD: $792,264.
  FUNDRAISING: $2,956,125.
- **DEFICIT:** $411,859.
- **RATINGS:** NCIB reported (12/12/89, using figures from the year ending 6/30/88) that JDF met all nine NCIB standards.
- **REGISTRATION:** NY (44140) and TN.
- **FINANCIAL DATA:** Text and chart source was their IRS form 990 (for the national office *only*) covering the year ending 6/30/88.

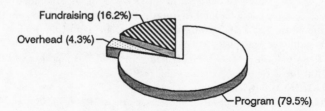

Fundraising (16.2%)
Overhead (4.3%)
Program (79.5%)

Due to deficit of 2.3%, chart is based on spending, not income.

Helen Keller International
15 W. 16th St.
New York, NY 10011
(212) 807-5800

- **CONTRIBUTIONS** are tax-deductible.
- **PURPOSE:** Established in 1919, and known successively as the Permanent Blind Relief War Fund (1925), American Braille Press for War and Civilian Blind (1946), and the American Foundation for Overseas Blind (1977), HKI absorbed the Association for the Chinese Blind in 1952. HKI seeks to prevent avoidable blindness and to provide services to the incurably blind in developing countries, where HKI feels the need is greatest.
- **SIZE:** Staff of about fifty.
- **INCOME:** $5,987,356 (year ending 6/30/89; cash accounting, IRS form 990).
- **HOW THEY USE YOUR MONEY:**
  PROGRAM: $5,350,314:
  - $4,976,917 for technical assistance.
  - $373,397 for public and development education.
  OVERHEAD: $1,251,671.
  FUNDRAISING: $608,059.
- **DEFICIT:** $1,222,688.
- **RATINGS:** NCIB reported (8/3/87, using figures for the year ending 6/30/86) that Helen Keller International met all eight of NCIB's old evaluation standards.
- **REGISTRATION:** CA, CT, GA, IL, MA, MD, MI, MN, NC, NJ, NM, NY (7218), OH, PA, TN, VA (912), and WV.
- **FINANCIAL DATA:** Text and chart source was their IRS form 990 covering the year ending 6/30/89.

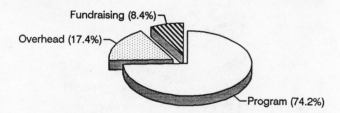

Fundraising (8.4%)
Overhead (17.4%)
Program (74.2%)

Due to deficit of 17.0%, chart is based on spending, not income.

187

Martin Luther King, Jr., Center
for Nonviolent Social Change, Inc.
449 Auburn Ave., N.E.
Atlanta, GA 30312
(404) 524-1956

- **CONTRIBUTIONS** are tax-deductible.
- **PURPOSE:** Founded in 1968 as a permanent, living memorial to Dr. Martin Luther King, Jr., whose tomb is located on the center's 23.5-acre site (a National Historic Site). The center seeks nonviolent solutions to poverty, racism, and violence through study, education, training, research, and constructive action.
- **INCOME:** $3,526,236 (year ending 6/30/88; accrual accounting, IRS form 990).
- **HOW THEY USE YOUR MONEY:**
  PROGRAM: $3,215,039:
  - $2,360,483 for community services.
  - $636,872 for education and training.
  - $217,684 for research.
  OVERHEAD: $480,983.
  FUNDRAISING: $114,787.
- **DEFICIT:** $284,573.
- **RATINGS:** NCIB reported (6/26/87, using figures from the year ending 6/30/86) that the center met all eight of NCIB's old evaluation standards.
- **REGISTRATION:** NY (46299) and VA (1192).
- **FINANCIAL DATA:** Text and chart source was their IRS form 990 covering the year ending 6/30/88.

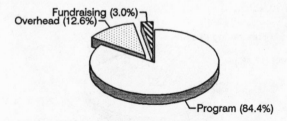

Fundraising (3.0%)
Overhead (12.6%)
Program (84.4%)

Due to deficit of 7.5%, chart is based on spending, not income.

LWV Education Fund

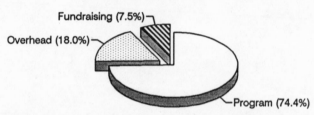

Fundraising (7.5%)
Overhead (18.0%)
Program (74.4%)

Due to deficit of 6.9%, chart is based on spending, not income.

League of Women Voters of the United States and the League of Women Voters Education Fund

1730 M St., N.W.
Washington, DC 20036
(202) 429-1965

■ **CONTRIBUTIONS** to the league are *not* tax-deductible; contributions to its education fund are.

■ **PURPOSE:** Founded in 1920, at the culmination of the women's suffrage movement, the league is a nonpartisan, grass-roots political-advocacy and membership organization. It encourages informed and active citizen participation in government, and influences public policy through education and advocacy. Its education fund, founded in 1957, works to increase public understanding of major public-policy issues and to promote involvement of citizens in government decision-making. The fund's most visible activity has been the sponsorship of presidential debates in 1976, 1980, and 1984.

■ **SIZE:** More than 100,000 members nationwide.

■ **INCOME:** $2,878,712 (league); $4,117,694 (fund; both year ending 3/31/88; accrual accounting, IRS form 990).

■ **HOW THEY USE YOUR MONEY:**
PROGRAM: $2,123,534 (league); $3,292,481 (fund).
PAYMENTS TO AFFILIATES: $20,000 (league) contribution to the fund.
OVERHEAD: $990,799 (league); $798,360 (fund).
FUNDRAISING: $224,702 (league); $333,007 (fund).

■ **DEFICIT:** $480,323 (league); $306,154 (fund).

■ **LITTLE-KNOWN FACTS:** Although the league began its life helping to educate 20 million women on how to exercise their newly won right to vote, membership is now open to anyone of either sex who is eighteen or older.

■ **RATINGS:** NCIB reported (9/21/89, using figures from the year ending 3/31/88), that the Education Fund met all nine NCIB standards, but made no conclusion about the parent organization, LWVUS.

■ **REGISTRATION:** League: NY (47457) and VA (1115); fund: NY (47456) and VA (1111).

■ **FINANCIAL DATA:** Text and chart sources (league and fund) were their IRS forms 990 covering the year ending 3/31/88.

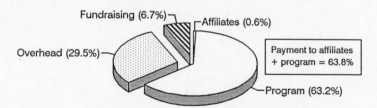

Fundraising (6.7%)
Affiliates (0.6%)
Overhead (29.5%)
Payment to affiliates + program = 63.8%
Program (63.2%)

Due to deficit of 14.3%, chart is based on spending, not income.

Lambda Legal Defense and Education Fund, Inc.
666 Broadway
New York, NY 10012
(212) 995-8585

- **CONTRIBUTIONS** are tax-deductible.
- **PURPOSE:** Founded in 1973 to litigate nationwide to counter discrimination against gay men and lesbians. Develops educational programs to raise public awareness of gay legal rights.
- **SIZE:** 15,000 members.
- **INCOME:** $897,814 (calendar 1988; accrual accounting, IRS form 990).
- **HOW THEY USE YOUR MONEY:**
  PROGRAM: $655,540 for litigation (an active docket of about fifty cases); referrals and intake (about 100 to 120 calls a week); written materials (a quarterly, *The AIDS Update;* a regularly updated legal reference, *The AIDS Legal Guide;* and a quarterly membership newsletter, *Lambda Update*); educational programs, workshops and conferences; and speakers bureau.
  OVERHEAD: $244,507.
  FUNDRAISING: $197,421.
- **DEFICIT:** $199,654.
- **LITTLE-KNOWN FACTS:** In 1983 Lambda won the nation's first AIDS discrimination case, *Sonnabend and Callen v. 49 West 12th Street.*
- **RATINGS:** No NCIB report.
- **REGISTRATION:** NY (44911) and VA (2959).
- **FINANCIAL DATA:** Text and chart source was their IRS form 990 covering 1988.

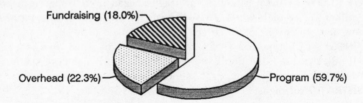

Fundraising (18.0%)

Overhead (22.3%)

Program (59.7%)

Due to deficit of 18.2%, chart is based on spending, not income.

Leukemia Society of America
733 Third Ave.
New York, NY 10017
(212) 573-8484

- **CONTRIBUTIONS** are tax-deductible.
- **PURPOSE:** Supports research into the cause, treatment, and cure of leukemia and related diseases; provides educational information; financially assists patients suffering from leukemia and related diseases.
- **SIZE:** Fifty-seven chapters nationwide.
- **INCOME:** $29,208,832 (year ending 6/30/88; consolidated annual report for headquarters, 57 chapters, and a subsidiary, Leukemia Society Research Program, Inc.).
- **HOW THEY USE YOUR MONEY:**
PROGRAM: $21,515,167:
  - $6,420,408 (including $6,063,218 in grants and allocations) for research.
  - $5,247,721 for public health education.*
  - $4,624,121 for patient services.
  - $3,699,136 for community services.
  - $1,523,781 for professional education.
OVERHEAD: $3,759,634.*
FUNDRAISING: $3,343,214.*
- **EXCESS:** $590,817.
- **LITTLE-KNOWN FACTS:** Barbara Bush serves as National Honorary Chair. In 1952 the Bushes' daughter Robin died of leukemia.
- **RATINGS:** NCIB reported (6/30/88, using figures from the year ending 6/30/87) that the Leukemia Society of America met all eight of NCIB's old evaluation standards.
- **REGISTRATION:** CA, CT, DC, FL, GA, IL, KY, MA, MN, NC, NJ, NY (7074), OH, PA, RI, SC, TN, VA, WA, and WI.
- **FINANCIAL DATA:** Text and chart source was their consolidated annual report (for headquarters, 57 chapters, and a subsidiary, Leukemia Society Research, Inc.) covering the year ending 6/30/88 .

*$2,849,887 spent on information materials and fundraising appeals was allocated thus: $1,256,202 for fundraising, $32,842 for overhead, $300,604 for patient services, $808,718 for public health education, $13,342 for professional education, and $438,179 for community service.

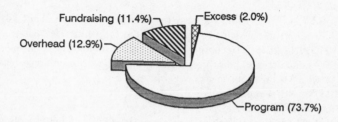

Fundraising (11.4%)
Excess (2.0%)
Overhead (12.9%)
Program (73.7%)

The Lighthouse, Inc.
111 E. 59th St.
New York, NY 10022
(212) 355-2200 • (800) 334-5497

■ **CONTRIBUTIONS** are tax-deductible.
■ **PURPOSE:** Since 1906 the Lighthouse, formerly known as the New York Association for the Blind, has been serving the needs of blind and visually impaired people through direct services, public education about vision impairment, and research into vision loss. With over 100 programs and services offered (including the first program in the Northeast tailored specifically to meet the needs of people blinded by AIDS), it is the largest such nonprofit organization in the nation. The group operates primarily in the New York metropolitan area.
■ **SIZE:** In 1988, 500 employees and 1,800 volunteers; more than 5,000 individuals benefited from the Lighthouse's services.
■ **INCOME:** $25,181,811 (year ending 6/30/89; independently audited statement). During the preceding four fiscal years support had been increasing.
■ **HOW THEY USE YOUR MONEY:**
PROGRAM: $20,022,654:
  • $6,655,152 for Lighthouse Industries and Sheltered Workshops (which employ blind people in the manufacturing and sales of products).
  • $3,214,027 for rehabilitative services.
  • $2,233,922 for individual family services.
  • $2,079,118 for recreational and cultural activities (including a summer day camp).
  • $1,235,554 for low-vision services.
  • $1,114,373 for the Child Development Center.
  • $1,016,906 for housing for blind individuals;
  • $672,875 for information analysis, research, education, and training (including research into cataract sensitivity).
  • $626,102 for communications and public education.
  • $559,419 for the National Center for Vision and Aging.
  • $183,063 for intake and medical counseling.
  • $432,143 for other expenses (e.g., music school, record room, restaurant, volunteer reading).
OVERHEAD: $1,823,398.
FUNDRAISING: $1,301,370. The Lighthouse makes *no* joint allocation of costs for direct-mail materials.
■ **EXCESS:** $2,034,389. During the year the Lighthouse gained about $6 million on sales of securities, which was applied to the following fiscal year.
■ **LITTLE-KNOWN FACTS:** "To conform with Lighthouse policy," major portions of their 1988 annual report were presented in large type "to enhance readability for those with vision problems."
■ **RATINGS:** No NCIB report.
■ **REGISTRATION:** CT, NJ, and NY.
■ **FINANCIAL DATA:** Text and chart source was their independently audited statement covering the year ending 6/30/89.

Literacy Volunteers of America
5795 S. Widewaters Pkwy.
Syracuse, NY 13214
(315) 445-8000

- **CONTRIBUTIONS** are tax-deductible.
- **PURPOSE:** Through volunteer tutoring and other educational services, LVA helps people to achieve personal goals through increased literacy skills, including English as a second language.
- **SIZE:** In FY89, 38,339 learners were served by 39,685 volunteers.
- **INCOME:** $1,602,315 (year ending 6/30/89; accrual accounting, annual report).
- **HOW THEY USE YOUR MONEY:**
  PROGRAM: $1,429,772:
  - $1,021,219 for field services.
  - $408,553 for publishing and marketing.
  OVERHEAD: $220,650.
  FUNDRAISING: $119,308.
- **DEFICIT:** $167,415.
- **LITTLE-KNOWN FACTS:** In FY89, the LVA program included 27,580 beginning readers and 10,759 other students learning English as a second language. Student achievements included getting jobs and library cards and starting further education or training.
- **RATINGS:** NCIB reported (4/6/88, on the national service center *only,* using figures from the year ending 6/30/87) that the center met all eight of NCIB's old evaluation standards.
- **REGISTRATION:** NY (41739).
- **FINANCIAL DATA:** Text and chart source was their annual report covering the year ending 6/30/89.

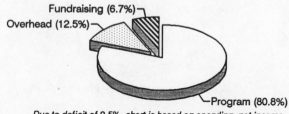

Fundraising (6.7%)
Overhead (12.5%)
Program (80.8%)

Due to deficit of 9.5%, chart is based on spending, not income.

The Lighthouse

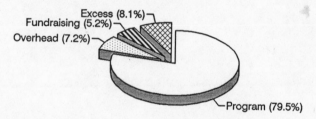

Excess (8.1%)
Fundraising (5.2%)
Overhead (7.2%)
Program (79.5%)

LULAC National Educational Service Centers, Inc.
400 First St., N.W., Suite 716
Washington, DC 20001
(202) 628-0717

- **CONTRIBUTIONS** are tax-deductible.
- **PURPOSE:** Founded by the League of United Latin American Citizens in 1973 as an educational, nonprofit corporation to increase the number of educationally disadvantaged persons, particularly Hispanic students, attending American colleges.
- **SIZE:** About 18,100 students are in the counseling and research program, and about 900 in the scholarship program.
- **INCOME:** $2,755,782 (year ending 9/30/88; accrual accounting, IRS form 990).
- **HOW THEY USE YOUR MONEY:**
  PROGRAM: $2,551,658:
  - $2,020,091 for counseling and research (counseling and other services to minority and economically disadvantaged high-school and college students).
  - $531,567 on the scholarship program (distributing college scholarships, funded by local affiliates and the general public).
  OVERHEAD: $159,886.
  FUNDRAISING: $8,416.
- **EXCESS:** $35,822.
- **RATINGS:** No NCIB report.
- **REGISTRATION:** CA, DC, IL, and NY (52507).
- **FINANCIAL DATA:** Text and chart source was their IRS form 990 covering the year ending 9/30/88.

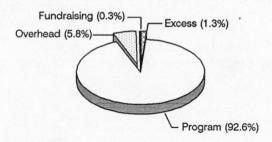

Fundraising (0.3%)
Overhead (5.8%)
Excess (1.3%)
Program (92.6%)

194

Mainstream, Inc.
1030 15th St., N.W., Suite 1010
Washington, DC 20005
(202) 898-1400

- **CONTRIBUTIONS** are tax-deductible.
- **PURPOSE:** Organized in 1975; works to "bring disabled people into the mainstream of American society" through aiding individuals and businesses in their compliance with federal antidiscrimination laws regarding the handicapped, particularly the Rehabilitation Act of 1973.
- **INCOME:** $586,098 (calendar 1988; IRS form 990). During the preceding four fiscal years support had been increasing.
- **HOW THEY USE YOUR MONEY:**
  PROGRAM: $352,022:
  - $268,784 for Project LINK (a model employment program for handicapped people).
  - $79,636 for Mainstream information programs (training and information, including newsletters and seminars, to employers of handicapped people).
  - $3,602 for the Dallas JTPA Program (a job placement service for people with disabilities).

  OVERHEAD: $242,920.
  FUNDRAISING: $11,977.
- **DEFICIT:** $20,821.
- **RATINGS:** NCIB reported (1/20/87, using figures from calendar 1986) that Mainstream met all eight of NCIB's old evaluation standards.
- **REGISTRATION:** DC and NY (46322).
- **FINANCIAL DATA:** Text and chart source was their IRS form 990 covering 1988.

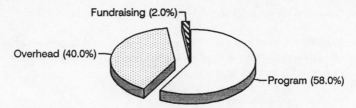

Fundraising (2.0%)
Overhead (40.0%)
Program (58.0%)

Due to deficit of 3.4%, chart is based on spending, not income.

195

Make-a-Wish Foundation of America
4601 N. 16th St., Suite 205
Phoenix, AZ 85016
(602) 240-6600 • (800) 722-WISH

- **CONTRIBUTIONS** are tax-deductible.
- **PURPOSE:** Inspired by a single wish granted in Phoenix in 1980, the Make-a-Wish Foundation was formed in 1983. to grant wishes to children under eighteen who are terminally ill or are likely not to survive beyond the age of eighteen.
- **SIZE:** During the year, the foundation fulfilled the wishes of 2,239 children with life-threatening illnesses.
- **INCOME:** $366,254 (national office, year ending 8/31/88; accrual accounting, IRS form 990); $9,493,517 (68 chapters; 1988 annual report).
- **HOW THEY USE YOUR MONEY:**
  PROGRAM: $472,903 (national office); $6,457,712 (chapters).
  OVERHEAD: $67,557 (national office); $1,776,911 (chapters).
  FUNDRAISING: $57,394 (national office); $742,857 (chapters). Discover Card Services, Inc., donated $100,000 to the foundation from a promotion to use its credit card at toy stores during November 1987. Steve's Homemade Ice Cream developed the Steve's Make-a-Wish Bar, and beginning in 1989 a percentage of the sales was to go to the foundation.
- **DEFICIT:** $231,600 (national office).
- **EXCESS:** $516,037 (chapters).
- **LITTLE-KNOWN FACTS:** Of the wishes granted, 40 percent involved a place the child wanted to visit, 30 percent involved a celebrity, 20 percent were for special gifts, 5 percent let a child work in an occupation, and 5 percent were for other reasons.
- **RATINGS:** No NCIB report.
- **REGISTRATION:** Check relevant state offices for registration of individual chapters.
- **FINANCIAL DATA:** Text and chart (for national office *only*) source was their IRS form 990 covering the year ending 8/31/88. Source of text for chapters was the foundation's 1988 annual report.

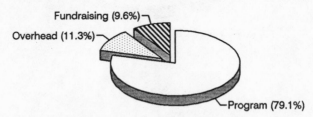

Fundraising (9.6%)
Overhead (11.3%)
Program (79.1%)

Due to deficit of 38.7%, chart is based on spending, not income.

March of Dimes Birth Defects Foundation
1275 Mamaroneck Ave.
White Plains, NY 10605
(914) 428-7100

- **CONTRIBUTIONS** are tax-deductible.
- **PURPOSE:** Founded in 1938 by President Franklin D. Roosevelt, who envisioned a "march of dimes" donated to fight polio, the National Foundation for Infantile Paralysis achieved its goal in 1955 with the development of the Salk vaccine. Having become the first national health agency to defeat the disease it set out to conquer, the March of Dimes Birth Defects Foundation now provides leadership in the prevention and treatment of birth defects and related health problems (low birthweight, prematurity, and drug abuse during pregnancy).
- **SIZE:** 133 chapters.
- **INCOME:** $119,655,000 (calendar 1988; consolidated annual report for national office and 133 chapters).
- **HOW THEY USE YOUR MONEY:**
  PROGRAM: $85,828,000:
  - $14,764,562 (including $13,899,421 in grants and allocations, $1,200,000 of it to the Salk Institute for Biological Studies) for research support.
  - $29,884,000 for public health education.
  - $28,127,000 for community services.
  - $6,345,000 for medical services.
  - $6,707,000 for professional health education.
  OVERHEAD: $11,522,000.
  FUNDRAISING: $22,651,000.
- **DEFICIT:** $346,000.
- **LITTLE-KNOWN FACTS:** Although polio has been essentially eliminated, the disease's effects are still with us. The foundation maintains a respirator-equipment pool, and chapters provide some financial assistance for braces and other appliances for post-polio patients.
- **RATINGS:** NCIB reported (2/19/88, using figures from the year ending 6/30/86) that the March of Dimes Birth Defects Foundation met all eight of NCIB's old evaluation standards.
- **REGISTRATION:** CA, CT, IL, IN, MA, MD, ME, MI, NC, NE, NJ, NY (7248), OH, OK, PA, SC, TN, VA (1186), WI, and WV.
- **FINANCIAL DATA:** Text and chart source was their consolidated annual report (for national office and 133 chapters) covering 1988.

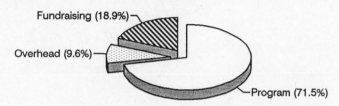

Fundraising (18.9%)
Overhead (9.6%)
Program (71.5%)

Due to deficit of 0.3%, chart is based on spending, not income.

197

Medic Alert Foundation, International
Box 1009
Turlock, CA 95381
(209) 668-3333 • (800) ID-ALERT

- **CONTRIBUTIONS** are tax-deductible.
- **PURPOSE:** Founded in 1956 by Dr. Marion Collins, whose daughter nearly died from a reaction to a common tetanus-sensitivity test. For a $25 lifetime membership fee, Medic Alert members get a personalized bracelet or necklace identifying any medical conditions relevant in an emergency. A collect call from anywhere in the world will provide medical data, name of personal physician, and emergency contacts.
- **SIZE:** 1.7 million registrants in the United States; affiliates in thirty-four foreign countries.
- **INCOME:** $8,480,740 (year ending 9/30/88; accrual accounting, IRS form 990).
- **HOW THEY USE YOUR MONEY:**
  PROGRAM: $6,849,988:
  - $3,765,776 for new members.
  - $1,231,854 for update letters.
  - $1,059,701 for reorders.
  - $248,801 for international development.
  - $238,702 for the volunteer program and public information.
  - $235,801 for professional education and training.
  - $69,353 for the emergency answering service.
  OVERHEAD: $648,199.
  FUNDRAISING: $676,225.
- **EXCESS:** $306,328.
- **LITTLE-KNOWN FACTS:** In 1988 Medic Alert's International Implant Registry began to alert physicians of registered patients of recalls of implant devices.
- **RATINGS:** NCIB reported (10/26/87, using figures from the year ending 9/30/86) that the Medic Alert Foundation International met all eight of NCIB's old evaluation standards.
- **REGISTRATION:** CA (3137), NY (42563), TN, and VA (1220).
- **FINANCIAL DATA:** Text and chart source was their IRS form 990 covering the year ending 9/30/88.

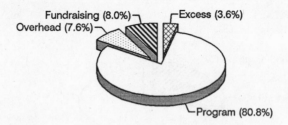

Fundraising (8.0%)
Overhead (7.6%)
Excess (3.6%)
Program (80.8%)

Mexican American Legal Defense and Education Fund
634 S. Spring St., 11th Fl.
Los Angeles, CA 90014
(213) 629-2512

- **CONTRIBUTIONS** are tax-deductible.
- **PURPOSE:** Founded 1968 in San Antonio, now headquartered in Los Angeles, the largest Hispanic population center in the nation. MALDEF promotes and protects the civil rights of Hispanics living in the United States through litigation, advocacy, educational outreach, and law-school scholarships. Portions of the MALDEF annual report are in Spanish.
- **SIZE:** MALDEF maintains regional offices in Chicago, San Antonio, San Francisco, and Washington.
- **INCOME:** $3,317,571 (year ending 4/30/88; accrual accounting, IRS form 990).
- **HOW THEY USE YOUR MONEY:**
PROGRAM: $2,576,066:
  - $1,864,504 for litigation (protecting the civil rights of Hispanics nationwide, including class-action litigation in education, employment, voting rights, and immigration).
  - $448,775 for community education and services (leadership training and development programs in four cities and the awarding of scholarships to Hispanic law students).
  - $201,954 for public policy and research (undertaken to assist litigation and community education; major topics have included employment, voting rights, and immigration).
  - $60,833 for trust fund expenditures.
OVERHEAD: $274,056.
FUNDRAISING: $266,759.
- **EXCESS:** $200,690.
- **LITTLE-KNOWN FACTS:** MALDEF has a parent leadership program to provide parents with skills and confidence for involvment with their children's education.
- **RATINGS:** NCIB reported (10/28/86, using figures from the year ending 4/30/85) that MALDEF met all eight of NCIB's old evaluation methods standards.
- **REGISTRATION:** CA and NY (48045).
- **FINANCIAL DATA:** Text and chart source was their IRS form 990 covering the year ending 4/30/88.

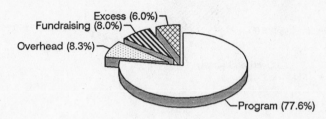

199

Mothers Against Drunk Driving (MADD)
669 Airport Freeway, Suite 310
Hurst, TX 76053
(817) 268-6233 • (800) GET-MADD

■ **CONTRIBUTIONS** are tax-deductible.

■ **PURPOSE:** Founded in 1980 by Candy Lightner shortly after her daughter was killed by a drunk driver, MADD's purpose is to mobilize "victims and their allies to establish the public conviction that impaired driving is unacceptable and criminal, in order to promote corresponding public policies, programs, and personal accountability." Founded as Mothers Against Drunk *Drivers*, MADD changed its name in 1984.

■ **SIZE:** MADD, which has 50 state groups and about 400 local groups, claims 1,000,000 members.

■ **INCOME:** $32,936,164 (year ending 6/30/88; independently audited statement).

■ **HOW THEY USE YOUR MONEY:**
PROGRAM: $18,160,197:
- $14,501,881* for public awareness.
- $2,089,158* for chapter development.
- $1,569,158 for victim service.

OVERHEAD: $1,457,971.*
FUNDRAISING: $7,849,843.*

■ **EXCESS:** $5,468,153.

■ **RATINGS:** NCIB reported (12/7/89, using figures from the year ending 6/30/88) that MADD did not meet standards 4 and 6a, and there was a question about standard 8. It met all other new NCIB standards.

■ **REGISTRATION:** NY (50543), TN, and VA (1275).

■ **FINANCIAL DATA:** Text and chart source was their independently audited statement covering the year ending 6/30/88.

*$18,985,995 spent on certain educational materials were allocated thus: $10,699,132 to public awareness; $7,596,345 to fundraising; $629,661 to chapter development; and $60,857 to management and general expenses.

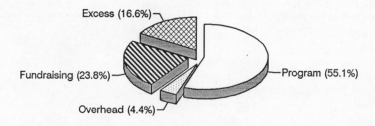

Excess (16.6%)
Fundraising (23.8%)
Overhead (4.4%)
Program (55.1%)

Ms. Foundation for Women, Inc.
141 Fifth Ave., Suite 6-S
New York, NY 10010
(212) 353-8580

- **CONTRIBUTIONS** are tax-deductible.
- **PURPOSE:** Founded in 1973 by some of the same women who began *Ms.* magazine (the foundation has always been a separate entity), the foundation is a national, multi-issue public women's fund devoted to helping women and girls "govern their own lives and influence the world around them." Resources are directed to "activities that break down racial, class, age, sexual orientation, and cultural barriers."
- **INCOME:** $1,955,782 (year ending 6/30/89; accrual accounting, IRS form 990).
- **HOW THEY USE YOUR MONEY:**

PROGRAM: $1,173,190:
- $548,245 (including $373,600 in grants and allocations) for women's educational and self-help projects.
- $327,762 (including $235,400 in grants and allocations) for "reproductive grants" and technical assistance to national, state, and local groups working to preserve every woman's right to choose abortion.
- $232,004 (including $16,848 in grants and allocations) for economic development projects and technical assistance.
- $32,500 (all in grants and allocations) for Women and AIDS Initiative (a matching grant pool with the New York Community Trust).
- $31,722 for Women Managing Wealth.
- $957 for RCRHC (a committee of funders interested in reproductive health care).

OVERHEAD: $524,271.
FUNDRAISING: $130,299.
- **EXCESS:** $128,022.
- **LITTLE-KNOWN FACTS:** According to a 1988 Ms. Foundation for Women report, less than 4 percent of total funding from *all* foundations goes to programs geared toward women and girls. Readers interested in reversing this trend can contact the Ms. Foundation for more information about groups mentioned in this book, local women's funds, and other organizations, such as the National Black Women's Health Project, the National Committee on Pay Equity, and the National Women's Political Caucus.
- **RATINGS:** No NCIB report.
- **REGISTRATION:** NY (46316).
- **FINANCIAL DATA:** Text and chart source was their IRS form 990 covering the year ending 6/30/89.

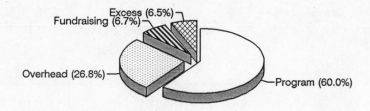

Excess (6.5%)
Fundraising (6.7%)
Overhead (26.8%)
Program (60.0%)

Muscular Dystrophy Association, Inc.
810 Seventh Ave.
New York, NY 10019
(212) 586-0808

■ **CONTRIBUTIONS** are tax-deductible.
■ **PURPOSE:** Founded in 1950, MDA performs research into the causes and cures of nine different categories of neuromuscular disease, including muscular dystrophies, motor neuron diseases, inflammatory myopathies, and six others. Patient services rendered through local MDA chapters include diagnostic exams, follow-up medical evaluations, orthopedic appliances, and physical therapy.
■ **SIZE:** MDA's 28,000 members and 163 local groups support the work of a staff of 1,000.
■ **INCOME:** $111,397,675 (calendar 1988; independently audited statement).
■ **HOW THEY USE YOUR MONEY:**
PROGRAM: $77,625,465:
  • $42,676,283 for patient and community services.
  • $20,184,260 for research.
  • $14,764,922* for professional and public health education.
OVERHEAD: $6,728,563.*
FUNDRAISING: $20,095,613.*
■ **EXCESS:** $6,948,034.
■ **LITTLE-KNOWN FACTS:** Jerry Lewis revealed in a 1984 *Parade* magazine interview that he had written MDA a letter to be opened after his death. "I wrote, 'Turn my death into pay dirt.' Anybody who's honest and cares can replace Jerry Lewis, but beg the people to give in his memory. Look at how much he gave; it probably killed him. Turn me into a theatrical martyr. Use my death positively." He advised MDA, "Don't waste it. Use it."
■ **RATINGS:** NCIB reported (10/28/88, using figures from calendar 1987) that the Muscular Dystrophy Association met all nine NCIB standards.
■ **REGISTRATION:** NY (7719), TN, and VA (1289).
■ **FINANCIAL DATA:** Text and chart source was their independently audited statement covering 1988.

*MDA's Jerry Lewis Labor Day Telethon costs of $6,045,000 were jointly allocated between fundraising ($4,594,000) and public health education ($1,451,000). Direct-mail costs of $8,245,000 were allocated to fundraising ($4,617,000), public-health education ($3,298,000), and overhead ($330,000).

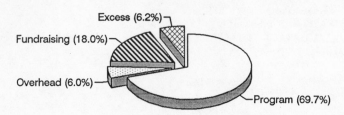

Excess (6.2%)
Fundraising (18.0%)
Overhead (6.0%)
Program (69.7%)

National Abortion Rights Action League
1101 14th St., N.W.
Washington, DC 20005
(202) 408-4600

- **CONTRIBUTIONS** are *not* tax-deductible.
- **PURPOSE:** Founded in 1969 (four years before the Supreme Court legalized abortion), NARAL works to develop and sustain a prochoice political constituency in order to maintain the right to a legal abortion for all women.
- **SIZE:** Thirty-four national affiliates.
- **INCOME:** $3,348,790 (year ending 3/31/88; accrual accounting, IRS form 990).
- **HOW THEY USE YOUR MONEY:**
PROGRAM: $2,187,631:
  - $1,237,811 for membership development.
  - $352,169 (including $203,077 in grants and allocations) for affiliate development.
  - $270,973 for communications.
  - $214,404 for legislative and political programs (lobbying).
  - $88,574 for their annual conference.
  - $23,700 for research.
OVERHEAD: $702,862.
FUNDRAISING: $593,707.
- **DEFICIT:** $135,410.
- **LITTLE-KNOWN FACTS:** NARAL, which maintains a lobbyist, has its own political action committee, NARAL-PAC.
- **RATINGS:** No NCIB report.
- **REGISTRATION:** DC, IL, MA, MD, MN, NC, NY (42528), OH, PA, VA (1297), and WI.
- **FINANCIAL DATA:** Text and chart source was their IRS form 990 covering the year ending 3/31/88.

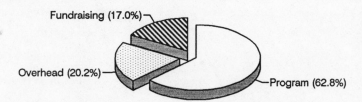

Fundraising (17.0%)
Overhead (20.2%)
Program (62.8%)

Due to deficit of 3.9%, chart is based on spending, not income.

National Alliance for the Mentally Ill
2101 Wilson Blvd., Suite 302
Arlington, VA 22201
(703) 524-7600

- **CONTRIBUTIONS** are tax-deductible.
- **PURPOSE:** Began operations 1979; incorporated 1980. Its purpose is to eradicate mental illness and improve the quality of life for seriously mentally ill people and their families.
- **SIZE:** 900 affiliates and more than 60,000 members (June 1988).
- **INCOME:** $1,797,923 (year ending 6/30/89; accrual accounting, independently audited statement).
- **HOW THEY USE YOUR MONEY:**
  PROGRAM: $1,339,283:
  - $425,438 for public education.
  - $386,406 for self-help and member support.
  - $280,355 for annual convention.
  - $247,084 for policy development and advocacy.
  OVERHEAD: $277,200.
  FUNDRAISING: $148,031.
- **EXCESS:** $33,409.
- **RATINGS:** No NCIB report.
- **REGISTRATION:** VA (2893).
- **FINANCIAL DATA:** Text and chart sources was their independently audited statement covering the year ending 6/30/89.

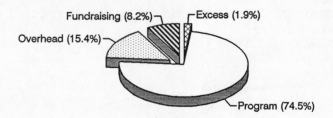

Fundraising (8.2%) Excess (1.9%)
Overhead (15.4%)
Program (74.5%)

National Alliance to End Homelessness, Inc.
1518 K St., N.W., Suite 206
Washington, DC 20005
(202) 638-1526

- **CONTRIBUTIONS** are tax-deductible.
- **PURPOSE:** Formed in 1983; present name adopted in 1988 to reflect its primary purpose: find ways to end homelessness. Includes research, advocacy, project operations, education, and assistance in providing public and private resources to private voluntary organizations serving the homeless.
- **SIZE:** A Food Stamp Information Campaign conducted by the alliance between 1985 and 1988 distributed over 2.5 million brochures; a toll-free number logged nearly 350,000 calls.
- **INCOME:** $249,585 (calendar 1988; accrual accounting, IRS form 990). Support peaked in 1986 and went down over the next two years.
- **HOW THEY USE YOUR MONEY:**
  PROGRAM: $173,963:
    - $68,815 for technical assistance (to organizations seeking to improve their services to the hungry and homeless).
    - $60,855 for council programs (the four councils—Housing and Health, Public Awareness, Employment and Training, and Education—develop programs for long-term solutions to the problems of the homeless).
    - $44,293 for the food stamp program (providing information about the nation's food assistance program).
  OVERHEAD: $60,357.
  FUNDRAISING: $42,744.
- **DEFICIT:** $27,479.
- **LITTLE-KNOWN FACTS:** Susan G. Baker, chairman of the alliance, is the wife of Secretary of State James A. Baker III. Robert A. Mosbacher, Jr., secretary of commerce in the Bush administration, has served on the alliance's board.
- **RATINGS:** No NCIB report.
- **REGISTRATION:** DC.
- **FINANCIAL DATA:** Text and chart source was their IRS form 990 covering 1988.

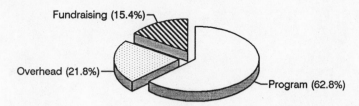

Fundraising (15.4%)
Overhead (21.8%)
Program (62.8%)

Due to deficit of 9.9%, chart is based on spending, not income.

National Association for the Advancement of Colored People
4805 Mt. Hope Dr.
Baltimore, MD 21215
(301) 358-8900

- **CONTRIBUTIONS** are tax-deductible.
- **PURPOSE:** Founded in 1909 to achieve equal rights through the democratic process, and to eliminate racial prejudice by removing racial discrimination in all aspects of life.
- **SIZE:** About 400,000 members, supporting the work of 132 staff people and 1,802 local groups.
- **INCOME:** $7,363,333 (calendar 1986; latest NYS form 497 made available).
- **HOW THEY USE YOUR MONEY:**
  PROGRAM: $3,803,783.
  OVERHEAD: $2,262,478.
  FUNDRAISING: $122,709.
- **EXCESS:** $1,174,363.
- **RATINGS:** No NCIB report.
- **REGISTRATION:** NY (8891) and VA (1292).
- **FINANCIAL DATA:** Text and chart source was their NYS form 497 covering 1986 (latest available).

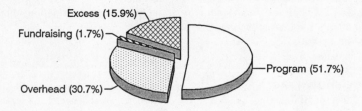

Excess (15.9%)
Fundraising (1.7%)
Overhead (30.7%)
Program (51.7%)

NAACP Special Contributions Fund
4805 Mt. Hope Dr.
Baltimore, MD 21215
(301) 358-8900

■ **CONTRIBUTIONS** are tax-deductible.

■ **PURPOSE:** The Special Contributions Fund was established in 1964 as a tax-deductible arm of the NAACP (at that time, contributions to the NAACP were not tax-deductible, but since 1981 they have been). The fund aids the NAACP's efforts in civil-rights and legal-defense litigation, voter registration, and non-political and community-action portions of housing, employment, and school-desegregation programs.

■ **INCOME:** $6,318,348 (calendar 1988; IRS form 990).

■ **HOW THEY USE YOUR MONEY:**

PROGRAM: $5,068,088:

- $1,857,455 for legal programs.
- $641,921 for economic development.
- $610,752 for youth programs.
- $455,821 for research and public information.
- $419,296 for voter registration.
- $401,130 for education.
- $228,238 for special programs.
- $211,591 for labor programs.
- $87,750 for religious affairs.
- $87,699 for prison programs.
- $66,435 for urban programs.

OVERHEAD: $511,769.

FUNDRAISING: $816,131.

■ **DEFICIT:** $77,640.

■ **RATINGS:** NCIB reported (4/14/89, using figures from calendar 1987) that the NAACP Special Contribution Fund met all nine NCIB standards.

■ **REGISTRATION:** NY (11878) and VA (1294).

■ **FINANCIAL DATA:** Text and chart source was their IRS form 990 covering 1988.

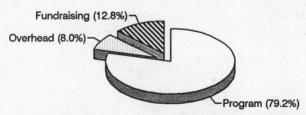

Due to deficit of 1.2%, chart is based on spending, not income.

NAACP Legal Defense and Education Fund, Inc.
99 Hudson St., Suite 1600
New York, NY 10013
(212) 219-1900 • except NY: (800) 221-7822

- **CONTRIBUTIONS** are tax-deductible.
- **PURPOSE:** Founded in 1939, the fund, which represents civil rights groups as well as individuals, serves as the legal arm of the civil rights movement. It provides and supports litigation on behalf of African Americans, other racial minorities, and women defending their legal and constitutional rights against discrimination in employment, education, housing, and other areas. It has also worked for prison reform and the abolition of capital punishment.
- **SIZE:** About sixty-eight staff members.
- **INCOME:** $9,886,606 (calendar 1988; accrual accounting, IRS form 990). During the preceding four fiscal years support had been increasing.
- **HOW THEY USE YOUR MONEY:**
  PROGRAM: $6,328,650:
  - $5,078,025 for legal programs (over 500 cases on docket, concerned with civil and human rights).
  - $607,173 for public information.
  - $550,640 for the Herbert Lehman Education Fund ($327,600 in grants and allocations—$181,200 for 175 undergraduate scholarships and $146,400 for 122 law-school scholarships handled by the Earl Warren Legal Training Program, Inc.).
  - $92,812 for community service.
  OVERHEAD: $214,443.
  FUNDRAISING: $1,592,979.
- **EXCESS:** $1,750,534.
- **LITTLE-KNOWN FACTS:** Although the NAACP LDEF was founded by the NAACP and shares its commitment to equal rights, it is *not* part of the NAACP; for over thirty years it has had a separate board, program, staff, office, and budget.
- **RATINGS:** NCIB reported (5/1/90, using figures from calendar 1988) that the fund met all nine NCIB standards.
- **REGISTRATION:** NY (43999) and VA (1293).
- **FINANCIAL DATA:** Text and chart source was their IRS form 990 covering 1988.

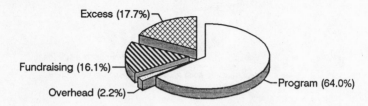

Excess (17.7%)
Fundraising (16.1%)
Overhead (2.2%)
Program (64.0%)

National Association for Sickle Cell Disease
4221 Wilshire Blvd., Suite 360
Los Angeles, CA 90010
(213) 936-7205 • (800) 421-8453

- **CONTRIBUTIONS** are tax-deductible.
- **PURPOSE:** Founded in 1971, the association is actively engaged in public education to increase awareness of the effect of sickle cell anemia on the health and economic, social, and educational well-being of the individual and his or her family. It provides technical assistance (to interested groups), screening and testing, and vocational rehabilitation, as well as camps for children with sickle cell disease.
- **SIZE:** About nine staff members and 86 local groups.
- **INCOME:** $567,977 (calendar 1988; NYS form 497).
- **HOW THEY USE YOUR MONEY:**
  PROGRAM: $563,102.
  OVERHEAD: $52,563.
  FUNDRAISING: $96,123.
- **DEFICIT:** $143,811.
- **LITTLE-KNOWN FACTS:** As sickle cell disease is a blood disorder, the association maintains its own blood banks.
- **RATINGS:** No NCIB report.
- **REGISTRATION:** NY (43877) and VA (2934).
- **FINANCIAL DATA:** Text and chart source was their NYS form 497 covering 1988.

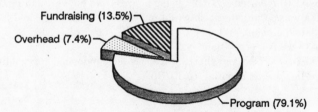

Fundraising (13.5%)
Overhead (7.4%)
Program (79.1%)

Due to deficit of 20.2%, chart is based on spending, not income.

National Audubon Society, Inc.
950 Third Ave.
New York, NY 10022
(212) 832-3200
(Legislative issues hotline: (202) 547-9017
Rare bird alert: (212) 832-6523)

- **CONTRIBUTIONS** are tax-deductible.
- **PURPOSE:** Founded in 1905 as an organization of people interested in ecology, energy, conservation, and restoration of natural resources. Emphasis is on wild-life, wildlife habitats, soil, water, and forests. The society supports thirty-five wardens, who patrol wildlife sanctuaries.
- **SIZE:** Maintains a quarter of a million acres of wildlife sanctuary, and has over half a million members.
- **INCOME:** $32,573,730 (year ending 6/30/88; accrual accounting, independently audited statement).
- **HOW THEY USE YOUR MONEY:**
  PROGRAM: $21,759,384.
  OVERHEAD: $3,055,129.
  FUNDRAISING: $2,346,354.
  MEMBERSHIP DEVELOPMENT: $3,817,858.
- **EXCESS:** $1,595,005.
- **LITTLE-KNOWN FACTS:** The society conducts research programs to aid such endangered species as the bald eagle, whooping crane, eastern timber wolf, and bog turtle.
- **RATINGS:** NCIB reported (7/6/89, using figures from the year ending 6/30/88) that the National Audubon Society (not including "the activities and finances of its 510 affiliated chapters") met all nine NCIB standards.
- **REGISTRATION:** NY (7888) and VA (1303).
- **FINANCIAL DATA:** Text and chart source was their independently audited statement covering the year ending 6/30/88.

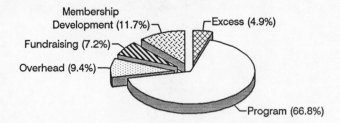

Membership Development (11.7%)
Excess (4.9%)
Fundraising (7.2%)
Overhead (9.4%)
Program (66.8%)

National Center for Missing and Exploited Children
1835 K St., N.W., Suite 600
Washington, DC 20006
(703) 235-3900 • Hotlines: (800) 843-5678 and (TDD) (800) 826-7653

- **CONTRIBUTIONS** are tax-deductible.
- **PURPOSE:** NCMEC was born out of the Missing Children's Assistance Act of 1984, which mandated that the Office of Juvenile Justice and Delinquency Prevention of the U.S. Justice Department "establish and operate a national resource center and clearinghouse." NCMEC operates a toll-free hotline for reporting information on any missing child thirteen years old or younger. It also provides technical assistance in locating and recovering missing children; in prevention, investigation, and prosecution; and in treatment of exploited children. In April 1990, NCMEC merged with the Adam Walsh Child Resource Center.
- **SIZE:** Since 1984, more than 250,000 calls have come in and over 9,700 children have been recovered. Special assistance was provided in more than 1,200 cases of sexual exploitation.
- **INCOME:** $2,992,230 (calendar 1988; accrual accounting, IRS form 990). Over $2 million of this money was in the form of a grant from the U.S. Justice Department.
- **HOW THEY USE YOUR MONEY:**
  PROGRAM: $2,220,857, spent entirely on ascertaining the causes for separation of children from their families and the ensuing exploitation of these children, and on attempts to reunite children with their families.
  OVERHEAD: $459,774.
  FUNDRAISING: $311,599.
- **DEFICIT:** $0.
- **LITTLE-KNOWN FACTS:** Fines from convictions in a nationwide postal investigation of child pornography were turned over to the center in 1988.
- **RATINGS:** No NCIB report.
- **REGISTRATION:** AR, CA, CO, CT, DC, FL, GA, HI, IA, IL, KS, KY, MA, MD, ME, MI, MN, NC, ND, NE, NH, NM, NY, OH, OK, OR, PA, RI, SC, SD, TN, VA (2623), WA, WI, and WV.
- **FINANCIAL DATA:** Text and chart source was their IRS form 990 covering 1988.

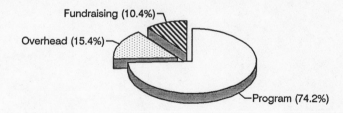

Fundraising (10.4%)
Overhead (15.4%)
Program (74.2%)

National Coalition Against Domestic Violence
Box 34103
Washington, DC 20043
(202) 638-6388 • (800) 333-SAFE

- **CONTRIBUTIONS** are tax-deductible.
- **PURPOSE:** Formed in 1978 to develop "feminist models for programs working to improve services" to battered women, to form a national communication and resource network, and to provide a national voice on issues affecting battered women and other women.
- **SIZE:** 50 state and 1,250 local groups.
- **INCOME:** $815,439 (calendar 1988; accrual accounting, independently audited statement).
- **HOW THEY USE YOUR MONEY:**
  PROGRAM: $739,756 on hotline and shelter aid, an annual conference, the Child Advocacy Task Force, HHS-Technical Assistance, Lesbian Task Force, Women of Color Task Force, Battered Women Task Force, and the Rural Women Task Force.
  OVERHEAD: $58,376.
  FUNDRAISING: $15,599.
- **EXCESS:** $1,708.
- **RATINGS:** No NCIB report.
- **REGISTRATION:** IRS.
- **FINANCIAL DATA:** Text and chart source was their independently audited statement covering 1988.

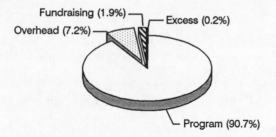

Fundraising (1.9%)
Overhead (7.2%)
Excess (0.2%)
Program (90.7%)

National Committee for Prevention of Child Abuse
332 S. Michigan Ave., Suite 950
Chicago, IL 60604
(312) 663-3520

- **CONTRIBUTIONS** are tax-deductible.
- **PURPOSE:** Established in 1972 for the "prevention of child abuse in all of its forms." In 1986 NCPCA established the National Center on Child Abuse Prevention Research, which collects and conducts research on child-abuse-prevention programs and helps NCPCA monitor the reduction of child abuse.
- **SIZE:** Sixty-seven volunteer-based chapters.
- **INCOME:** $2,816,460 (year ending 11/30/88; accrual accounting, IRS form 990), of which $201,300 came through a MasterCard affinity program. (NCPCA also reports that during 1987 it received nearly $74,000,000 of public-service advertising time and space through in-kind services from the Ad Council, Inc., and public-service ads; these contributions were not included as income.)
- **HOW THEY USE YOUR MONEY:**
PROGRAM: $2,009,639:
  - $477,284 for chapter activities.
  - $431,424 for payments to affiliates.
  - $384,325 (including $40,000 in grants and allocations) for research and demonstration (for prevention programs across the country).
  - $285,512 for publications and education (more than forty-five publications).
  - $268,654 for public awareness and relations (campaign on the problem of child abuse and its prevention, using broadcast and print media, billboards, and transit cards).
  - $91,146 for trust-fund networking (training and assistance to the forty-six states with children's trusts or prevention funds, and sponsorship of a national conference).
  - $71,294 for advocacy work.
OVERHEAD: $128,239.
FUNDRAISING: $239,668.
- **EXCESS:** $438,914.
- **LITTLE-KNOWN FACTS:** Robert J. Keeshan, better known as Captain Kangaroo, serves as a member of the board.
- **RATINGS:** NCIB reported (8/10/89) on the National Committee for Prevention of Child Abuse, national service center only (using figures from the year ending 11/30/88), that the center met all nine NCIB standards.
- **REGISTRATION:** IL and NY (50961).
- **FINANCIAL DATA:** Text and chart source was their IRS form 990 covering the year ending 11/30/88.

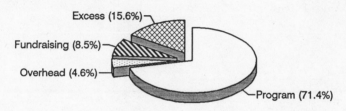

Excess (15.6%)
Fundraising (8.5%)
Overhead (4.6%)
Program (71.4%)

213

National Conference of Christians and Jews
71 Fifth Ave., Suite 1100
New York, NY 10003
(212) 206-0006

- **CONTRIBUTIONS** are tax-deductible.
- **PURPOSE:** Founded in 1927 as a nonsectarian educational and human-relations organization, the conference promotes religious, racial, and ethnic inclusiveness in American society.
- **SIZE:** More than seventy offices nationwide.
- **INCOME:** $14,047,950 (year ending 8/31/89; independently audited statement). During the preceding four fiscal years support had been increasing.
- **HOW THEY USE YOUR MONEY:**
  PROGRAM: $10,146,260 for programs including those on children and young adults, and on interreligious and community activities.
  OVERHEAD: $465,479.
  FUNDRAISING: $1,559,942.
- **EXCESS:** $1,876,269.
- **LITTLE-KNOWN FACTS:** In 1988, the NCCJ began programs with and on behalf of Native Americans. The year marked the tenth anniversary of the American Indian Religious Freedom Act, which has failed in every attempt to invoke its protection, against development or encroachment, for Indian sacred sites on public land.
- **RATINGS:** NCIB reported (1/20/89, using figures from the year ending 8/31/87), that the National Conference of Christians and Jews met all nine NCIB standards.
- **REGISTRATION:** AL, AR, AZ, CA, CO, CT, DC, DE, FL, GA, IA, IL, KS, KY, LA, MA, MD, MI, MN, MO, NC, NE, NJ, NV, NY (8416), OH, OK, PA, RI, TN, TX, UT, VA, and WI.
- **FINANCIAL DATA:** Text and chart source was their independently audited statement covering the year ending 8/31/89.

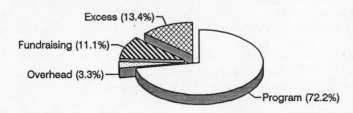

Excess (13.4%)
Fundraising (11.1%)
Overhead (3.3%)
Program (72.2%)

National Council of La Raza
810 First St., N.E., Suite 300
Washington, DC 20002
(202) 289-1380

- **CONTRIBUTIONS** are tax-deductible.
- **PURPOSE:** Founded in 1968, the council is actually an umbrella group working for civil rights and economic opportunities for Hispanics. It provides technical assistance to Hispanic community-based organizations in the fields of comprehensive community development (including economic development), housing, employment and training, business assistance, and health. It also provides policy analysis and advocates on behalf of Hispanics.
- **SIZE:** About eighty members.
- **INCOME:** $2,074,199 (year ending 9/30/86; accrual accounting, latest IRS form 990 filed in California in late 1989).
- **HOW THEY USE YOUR MONEY:**
  PROGRAM: $841,972:
  - $614,631 for nonfederal programs.
  - $227,341 for conventions.
  OVERHEAD: $855,172.
  FUNDRAISING: $52,533.
- **EXCESS:** $324,522.
- **RATINGS:** No NCIB report.
- **REGISTRATION:** CA.
- **FINANCIAL DATA:** Text and chart source was their IRS form 990 covering the year ending 9/30/86 (latest filing in California in late 1989).

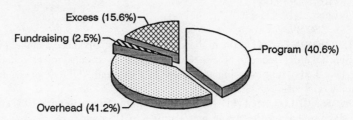

Excess (15.6%)
Fundraising (2.5%)
Program (40.6%)
Overhead (41.2%)

215

National Council on the Aging
600 Maryland Ave., S.W., West Wing 100
Washington, DC 20024
(202) 479-1200

- **CONTRIBUTIONS** are tax-deductible.
- **PURPOSE:** Founded in 1950; works to improve the lives and well-being of older Americans, and serves as a resource for information, training, technical assistance, advocacy, and research on every aspect of aging. One of NCOA's largest assignments is training and placement of older workers. Has eight special-membership units—the National Association of Older Worker Employment Services; the National Center on Rural Aging; the National Health Promotion Institute; the National Institute of Senior Centers; the National Institute of Senior Housing; the National Institute on Adult Daycare; the National Institute on Community-Based Long-Term Care; and the National Voluntary Organizations for Independent Living for the Aging.
- **SIZE:** Staff of more than 100.
- **INCOME:** $40,411,346 (calendar 1988; accrual accounting, IRS form 990), including $19,310,330 from the U.S. Department of Labor.
- **HOW THEY USE YOUR MONEY:**
  PROGRAM: $38,237,608:
  - $36,247,064 for programs in employment, work, and retirement.
  - $659,289 for community-health and social-services programs.
  - $585,986 for member services.
  - $449,292 for conference and professional training.
  - $295,977 for life-enrichment programs.
  OVERHEAD: $1,980,684.
  FUNDRAISING: $133,156.
- **EXCESS:** $59,898.
- **LITTLE-KNOWN FACTS:** In the mid-sixties NCOA first advanced a model program for linking older helpers in one-to-one service to youngsters at schools and hospitals. Today that experiment endures in a national ACTION program called Foster Grandparents.
- **RATINGS:** NCIB reported (11/14/88, using figures from calendar 1987) that the National Council on the Aging met all nine NCIB standards.
- **REGISTRATION:** DC, NJ, and NY (9384).
- **FINANCIAL DATA:** Text and chart source was their IRS form 990 covering 1988.

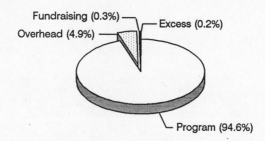

Fundraising (0.3%) — Excess (0.2%)
Overhead (4.9%)
Program (94.6%)

National Crime Prevention Council
1700 K St., N.W., 2nd Fl.
Washington, DC 20006
(202) 466-6272

- **CONTRIBUTIONS** are tax-deductible.
- **PURPOSE:** Since 1982 NCPC has worked to help people prevent crime and create safer, more caring neighborhoods. It provides original materials (and demonstrations) to teach crime prevention at all levels, and sustains a network of people actively engaged in preventing crime.
- **SIZE:** NCPC's monthly newsletter is mailed to over 21,000 readers. The council itself serves as secretariat for 126 member organizations.
- **INCOME:** $4,143,634 (year ending 9/30/88; accrual accounting, IRS form 990). The U.S. Justice Department is the largest funder of NCPC. During the preceding four fiscal years support from all sources had been increasing.
- **HOW THEY USE YOUR MONEY:**
  PROGRAM: $3,564,066:
  - $2,897,815 for a Justice Department grant to continue the National Citizens Crime Prevention Campaign and fund various other crime-prevention initiatives, and to educate children in the prevention of crime and drug abuse.
  - $293,207 for a three-year Lilly Foundation program for three Indiana community boards' projects in which teens have responsible roles in solving community problems.
  - $181,367 from a Justice Department Office of Juvenile Justice and Delinquency Prevention grant for Teens, Crime, and the Community (to reduce teen victimization, use teens as crime-prevention and community resources, and expand the teen crime-prevention curriculum unit to ten additional high schools).
  - Eleven other much smaller programs were also run by the council.

  OVERHEAD: $402,214.
  FUNDRAISING: $148,893.
- **EXCESS:** $28,461.
- **LITTLE-KNOWN FACTS:** The U.S. Justice Department funds the public-service announcements featuring McGruff and his motto "Take a Bite Out of Crime"; according to NCPC, every taxpayer dollar spent yields nearly $100 worth of donated advertising (a total of $40–50 million worth of airtime and print space).
- **RATINGS:** NCIB reported (12/13/88, using figures from the year ending 9/30/87) that the National Crime Prevention Council met all nine NCIB standards.
- **REGISTRATION:** DC and NY.
- **FINANCIAL DATA:** Text and chart source was their IRS form 990 covering the year ending 9/30/88.

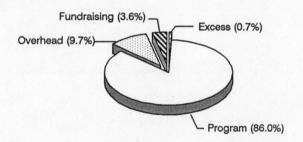

Fundraising (3.6%)
Excess (0.7%)
Overhead (9.7%)
Program (86.0%)

National Down Syndrome Society, Inc.
666 Broadway
New York, NY 10012
(212) 460-9330 • (800) 221-4602

- **CONTRIBUTIONS** are tax-deductible.
- **PURPOSE:** Founded in 1979, the society is devoted to researching the causes and treatment of Down syndrome and raises funds to support all areas of DS research.
- **SIZE:** Four staff members.
- **INCOME:** $525,316 (year ending 3/31/89; accrual accounting, IRS form 990). Support had been increasing during the preceding four fiscal years.
- **HOW THEY USE YOUR MONEY:**
  PROGRAM: $324,253:
  - $124,381 for public health information (developing a film available on free loan, preparation of educational pamphlets and materials, and maintenance of a 24-hour hotline).
  - $149,676 (including grants and allocations totaling $75,000) for research on Down syndrome (sponsorship of symposia on genetic and brain research, granting of scholarship stipends).
  - $50,196 for respite (a program enabling young children with Down syndrome to visit with volunteer families, helping the children become more independent, and giving their parents a break).
  OVERHEAD: $38,851.
  FUNDRAISING: $45,819.
- **EXCESS:** $116,393.
- **LITTLE-KNOWN FACTS:** The society publishes (and offers on computer) a directory of parent support groups and early intervention programs.
- **RATINGS:** NCIB reported (3/24/87, using figures from the year ending 3/31/86) that the National Down Syndrome Society met all eight of NCIB's old evaluation standards.
- **REGISTRATION:** NY (48739).
- **FINANCIAL DATA:** Text and chart source was their IRS form 990 covering the year ending 3/31/89.

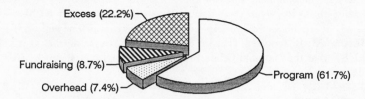

Excess (22.2%)
Fundraising (8.7%)
Overhead (7.4%)
Program (61.7%)

National Easter Seal Society
70 E. Lake St.
Chicago, IL 60601
(312) 726-6200 • (312) 726-4258 (TDD) • (800) 221-6877

- **CONTRIBUTIONS** are tax-deductible.
- **PURPOSE:** Founded in 1919 to identify the needs of people with disabilities and provide appropriate rehabilitation. Seventy years later, it has initiated Computer Assisted Technology Services (CATS) to promote greater independence and productivity for disabled people, through the use of appropriate technology. The national society is a service organization for fifty-eight affiliates, providing such services as a telethon, group insurance, pensions, accounting, etc.
- **SIZE:** In FY88, served 1,070,408 people.
- **INCOME:** $6,857,359 (national headquarters, exclusive of affiliates; year ending 8/31/89; accrual accounting, independently audited statement). During the preceding four fiscal years support had been increasing.
- **HOW THEY USE YOUR MONEY:**
PROGRAM: $5,739,756:
  - $5,043,427 for services to affiliates.
  - $2,290,056 for fundraising services (such as the national telethon).
  - $837,024 for program development.
  - $823,566 for advocacy for persons with disabilities.
  - $809,962 for management advisory services for affiliates.
  - $282,819 for professional education and training.
  - $390,842 for research.
  - $305,487 for public health education.
  OVERHEAD: $701,782.
  FUNDRAISING: $283,089.
- **EXCESS:** $132,732.
- **LITTLE-KNOWN FACTS:** Easter Seals' 1989 telethon garnered $37,002,000 in contributions. This money was distributed to affiliate societies based upon the geographic sources of the gifts. In addition to the fundraising, just over two hours of national airtime was devoted to advocacy and public education about persons with disabilities, and the issues affecting them. Thanks to $1,456,582 in corporate sponsorships and an assessment paid by affiliates with their membership fees, net production costs of the entire telethon were only $683,039.
- **RATINGS:** NCIB reported (10/23/86, using figures from the year ending 8/31/85) that the National Easter Seal Society, "national service center *only*," met all eight of NCIB's old evaluation standards.
- **REGISTRATION:** CA, IL, NY (8110), and PA.
- **FINANCIAL DATA:** Text and chart source was their independently audited statement (for the national headquarters *only*) covering the year ending 8/31/89.

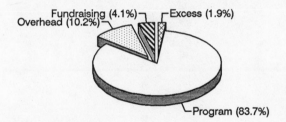

Fundraising (4.1%)
Overhead (10.2%)
Excess (1.9%)
Program (83.7%)

National Emergency Civil Liberties Committee
175 Fifth Ave.
New York, NY 10010
(212) 673-2040

- **CONTRIBUTIONS** to the NECLC are *not* tax-deductible, though contributions to its foundations are.
- **PURPOSE:** Founded in 1951 (it became the *National* Committee in 1968) and dedicated to reestablishing in full the traditional freedoms granted under the Constitution and the Bill of Rights, including every variety of dissent. The legal staff handles test cases in courts *without* charge to clients.
- **SIZE:** Although the work of the five-person staff is supported by only 160 members, the committee's thrice-yearly newsletter, *Rights,* has a circulation of 8,500.
- **INCOME:** $291,702 (year ending 11/30/88; NYS form 497).
- **HOW THEY USE YOUR MONEY:**
  PROGRAM: $116,941.
  OVERHEAD: $113,228.
  FUNDRAISING: $75,309.
- **DEFICIT:** $13,776.
- **RATINGS:** No NCIB report.
- **REGISTRATION:** NY (3935).
- **FINANCIAL DATA:** Text and chart source was their NYS form 497 covering the year ending 11/30/88.

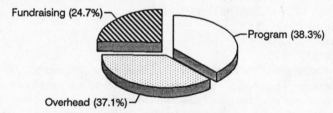

Fundraising (24.7%)

Program (38.3%)

Overhead (37.1%)

Due to deficit of 4.5%, chart is based on spending, not income.

National Emergency Medicine Association
306 W. Joppa Rd.
Baltimore, MD 21204
(301) 494-0300 • (800) 332-6362

- **CONTRIBUTIONS** are tax-deductible.
- **PURPOSE:** Formed in 1982 to foster development and delivery of quality emergency services. One special project, National Heart Research, concerns itself with cardiac emergencies.
- **SIZE:** About 5,000 members.
- **INCOME:** $8,425,745 (calendar 1988; accrual accounting, IRS form 990). During the preceding four fiscal years support had been increasing.
- **HOW THEY USE YOUR MONEY:**
  PROGRAM: $2,586,278:
  - $2,383,965* for public health education.
  - $202,313* (including $191,000 in grants and allocations) for research.
  OVERHEAD: $676,556.*
  FUNDRAISING: $4,854,628.*
- **EXCESS:** $308,283.
- **LITTLE-KNOWN FACTS:** The association's educational radio program, "The Heart of the Matter," is provided to over 250 stations nationwide. A direct-mail fundraising program also focuses on heart disease prevention. A single direct-mail marketing organization raised 99 percent of NEMA's public support during 1988, and 58 percent of income was spent on fundraising. On March 3, 1989, NEMA says, it "entered into a revised contract with this organization which will decrease the Association's direct-mail consulting rates by approximately 50 percent."
- **RATINGS:** NCIB reported (8/11/89, using figures from calendar 1988) that NEMA did not meet standards 6a and 7, and there was a question with regard to standards 3 and 4, but it met all other new NCIB standards.
- **REGISTRATION:** CA, CT, IL, IN, MA, MD, MI, MN, NC, NJ, NM, NY (52232), OH, PA, RI, SC, TN, VA (2241), and WI.
- **FINANCIAL DATA:** Text and chart source was their IRS form 990 covering 1988. Footnote and Little-Known Facts source was their independently audited statement covering 1988.

*Based on a total of $7,472,029 spent on informational materials and activities that included fundraising appeals, joint allocation of costs are listed as: less than 1 percent for grant programs; 1 percent for radio education (alerting the American audience to emergency medical care and heart trauma); 9 percent for management and general expenses (overhead); 27 percent for mail education; 63 percent for fundraising.

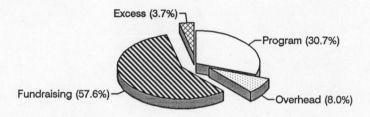

National Foundation for Cancer Research, Inc.
7315 Wisconsin Ave., Suite 332W
Bethesda, MD 20814
(301) 654-1250 • (800) 227-8713

- **CONTRIBUTIONS** are tax-deductible.
- **PURPOSE:** Founded in 1974 "to support basic science cancer research projects, including the theories of Dr. Albert Szent-Gyorgyi, who discovered Vitamin C." (These theories seem to involve the belief that cancer is a disturbance of normal cellular function at the submolecular level.) The foundation operates laboratories and research and clinical facilities, and it awards scholarships and assistance for other medical problems (e.g., kidney disease, sight or hearing failure, and drug and alcohol abuse).
- **SIZE:** Funds forty laboratories in the United States and eight other countries.
- **INCOME:** $13,897,328 (year ending 9/30/88; accrual accounting, independently audited statement).
- **HOW THEY USE YOUR MONEY:**
  PROGRAM: $9,796,968*:
  - $8,166,877 for research.
  - $1,630,091 for public education.
  OVERHEAD: $647,587.
  FUNDRAISING: $3,051,974.*
- **EXCESS:** $400,799.
- **RATINGS:** As of June 1, 1990, NCIB was preparing a new report.
- **REGISTRATION:** TN.
- **FINANCIAL DATA:** Text and chart source was their independently audited statement covering the year ending 9/30/88.

*Costs of about $2,900,000 for informational materials and activities that included fundraising appeals were allocated thus: about $1,800,000 to fundraising and about $1,100,000 to program.

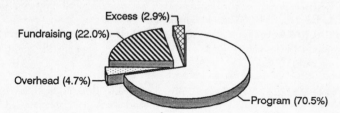

Excess (2.9%)
Fundraising (22.0%)
Overhead (4.7%)
Program (70.5%)

National Health Council, Inc.
350 Fifth Ave., Suite 1118
New York, NY 10118
(212) 268-8900

- **CONTRIBUTIONS** are tax-deductible.
- **PURPOSE:** Founded in 1920, the council, which seeks to improve the health of the nation, is a national membership association of voluntary and professional societies in the health field; federal government agencies concerned with health; and national organizations and business groups with strong health interests.
- **SIZE:** Ninety-four members and a staff of thirteen.
- **INCOME:** $1,003,882 (calendar 1988; NYS form 497).
- **HOW THEY USE YOUR MONEY:**
  PROGRAM: $820,669.
  OVERHEAD: $64,775.
  FUNDRAISING: $15,485.
- **EXCESS:** $102,953.
- **LITTLE-KNOWN FACTS:** The council promotes standardized financial reporting of health groups through its publication of "The Black Book" *(Standards of Accounting and Reporting for Voluntary Health and Welfare Organizations).*
- **RATINGS:** NCIB reported (9/4/87, using figures from calendar 1986) that the group met all eight of NCIB's old evaluation standards.
- **REGISTRATION:** NY (7022).
- **FINANCIAL DATA:** Text and chart source was their NYS form 497 covering 1988.

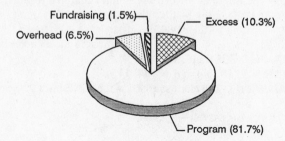

Fundraising (1.5%)
Overhead (6.5%)
Excess (10.3%)
Program (81.7%)

National Hispanic Scholarship Fund
Box 748
San Francisco, CA 94101
(415) 892-9971

- **CONTRIBUTIONS** are tax-deductible.
- **PURPOSE:** Founded in 1975 on a $5,000 mortgage taken out by Ernest Z. Robles. Awards are granted to college and graduate students of Hispanic background who are American citizens or permanent residents and who attend a college in one of the fifty states or Puerto Rico. Applications are accepted from June 5 to October 5 every year.
- **SIZE:** Since its beginning, the fund has awarded over 9,600 scholarships worth $6.4 million.
- **INCOME:** $2,509,183 (calendar 1988; accrual accounting, IRS form 990). More than half of this money came from the Anheuser-Busch Companies (Jesse Aguirre, vice-president of corporate relations for the companies, serves on the fund's board of directors). During the preceding four fiscal years support had been increasing.
- **HOW THEY USE YOUR MONEY:**
  PROGRAM: $1,600,900 for scholarships.
  OVERHEAD: $340,472.
  FUNDRAISING: $48,614.
- **EXCESS:** $519,197.
- **LITTLE-KNOWN FACTS:** Scholars are selected on the basis of academic achievement, personal strengths, leadership, and financial need. To assure national representation, the fund has divided the country into five regions, apportioning scholarship funds among the regions proportionate to the size of their Hispanic populations (according to the 1980 census).
- **RATINGS:** NCIB reported (7/12/89, using figures from calendar 1987) that the fund met all nine NCIB standards.
- **REGISTRATION:** CA (18386) and NY (49115).
- **FINANCIAL DATA:** Text and chart source was their IRS form 990 covering 1988.

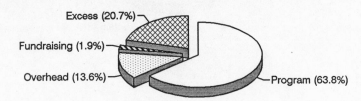

Excess (20.7%)
Fundraising (1.9%)
Overhead (13.6%)
Program (63.8%)

National Hospice Organization, Inc.
1901 N. Moore St., Suite 901
Arlington, VA 22209
(703) 243-5900

- **CONTRIBUTIONS** are tax-deductible.
- **PURPOSE:** Founded in 1978 to provide skilled and compassionate care for people with terminal illnesses and their families. It has established standards for such care, and works to make it available to every terminally ill American in need of such services.
- **SIZE:** More than 1,680 hospices located nationwide; however, budget problems trimmed NHO staff down to only ten people by the end of 1988.
- **INCOME:** $1,523,171 (calendar 1988; accrual accounting, IRS form 990).
- **HOW THEY USE YOUR MONEY:**
  PROGRAM: $1,209,080:
    - $567,690 for education, training, and publications (including newsletters, directories, and brochures).
    - $451,440 for the annual meeting, conferences, and symposia.
    - $58,031 for committee activity (to promote the services and standards of hospices to the membership and public).
    - $49,088 for governance (policy direction, etc.).
    - $82,831 for the Combined Federal Campaign (the government's annual charity drive).
  OVERHEAD: $262,285.
  FUNDRAISING: $33,213.
- **EXCESS:** $18,593.
- **LITTLE-KNOWN FACTS:** Of approximately 483,000 cancer deaths in 1987, according to the 1988 NHO annual report, about 34.9 percent were served by hospice programs. Public Health Service estimates show that 13,971 people with AIDS died in 1987, and "NHO estimates that hospice programs served 38.6 percent of these people."
- **RATINGS:** NCIB reported (2/29/88, using figures from calendar 1986) that the organization met all eight of NCIB's old evaluation standards.
- **REGISTRATION:** NY (52829).
- **FINANCIAL DATA:** Text and chart source was their IRS form 990 covering 1988.

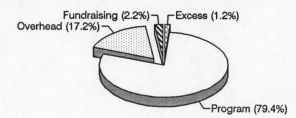

Fundraising (2.2%) Excess (1.2%)
Overhead (17.2%)
Program (79.4%)

National Humane Education Society, Inc.
211 Gibson St., N.W., Suite 104
Leesburg, VA 22075
(703) 777-8319

- **CONTRIBUTIONS** are tax-deductible.
- **PURPOSE:** Founded in 1948 to educate both children and adults in the humane care of animals. The society engages in animal rescue and relief efforts, and direct-mail education programs, throughout the country.
- **SIZE:** The society's Peace Plantation Animal Sanctuary in Walton, New York, takes care of 600 cats and 50 dogs.
- **INCOME:** $1,998,197 (year ending 6/30/88; NYS form 497).
- **HOW THEY USE YOUR MONEY:**
  PROGRAM: $1,821,586.
  OVERHEAD: $132,657.
  FUNDRAISING: $204,159.
- **DEFICIT:** $160,205.
- **RATINGS:** No NCIB report.
- **REGISTRATION:** NY (49121) and VA (1331).
- **FINANCIAL DATA:** Text and chart source was their NYS form 497 covering the year ending 6/30/88.

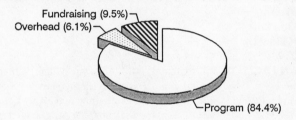

Fundraising (9.5%)
Overhead (6.1%)
Program (84.4%)

Due to deficit of 7.4%, chart is based on spending, not income.

226

National Kidney Foundation
30 E. 33rd St.
New York, NY 10016
(212) 889-2210 • (800) 622-9010

- **CONTRIBUTIONS** are tax-deductible.
- **PURPOSE:** Established in 1950 as the National Nephrosis Foundation, renamed in 1964; seeks to eradicate diseases of the kidney and urinary tract. It does no research of its own, but makes grants to researchers of kidney and urological diseases, and hypertension and diabetes (the leading causes of kidney failure). Participating member of the American Council on Transplantation.
- **SIZE:** 50 affiliates with more than 200 chapters nationwide.
- **INCOME:** $18,705,522 (year ending 6/30/89; combined statement of national office and affiliates, 1989 annual report).
- **HOW THEY USE YOUR MONEY:**
  PROGRAM: $12,891,142:
  - $3,616,119 for patient services.
  - $2,622,744 for public health education.
  - $2,506,244 for research.
  - $2,343,446 for community services.
  - $1,802,589 for professional education.
  OVERHEAD: $1,700,029.
  FUNDRAISING: $1,693,125.
- **EXCESS:** $2,421,226.
- **LITTLE-KNOWN FACTS:** NKF's Organ Donor Program has distributed over 50 million donor cards. A Task Force on Organ Donation began educational programs in 1989 aimed at critical-care nurses (those who usually ask families to donate a loved one's organs) and high school driver's-education classes.
- **RATINGS:** NCIB reported (10/18/89, using figures from the year ending 6/30/88) that the National Kidney Foundation met all nine NCIB standards.
- **REGISTRATION:** NY (6431).
- **FINANCIAL DATA:** Text and chart source was their annual report (combined statement for national office and affiliates) covering the year ending 6/30/89.

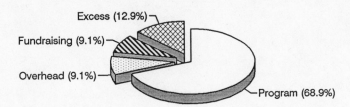

Excess (12.9%)
Fundraising (9.1%)
Overhead (9.1%)
Program (68.9%)

National League of Families of
American Prisoners and Missing in Southeast Asia
1001 Connecticut Ave., N.W., Suite 219
Washington, DC 20036
(202) 223-6846

- **CONTRIBUTIONS** are tax-deductible.
- **PURPOSE:** Founded in 1970 as a nonpartisan organization dedicated to collecting and disseminating pertinent information, continuing efforts to account for missing men, and pressing for the release of U.S. prisoners "still in the hands of the enemy."
- **INCOME:** $1,343,643 (calendar 1988; accrual accounting, IRS form 990).
- **HOW THEY USE YOUR MONEY:**
  PROGRAM: $918,711.
  OVERHEAD: $79,996.
  FUNDRAISING: $302,982.
- **EXCESS:** $41,954.
- **LITTLE-KNOWN FACTS:** Until November 1, 1988, the American Legion provided office space free of charge. The league now leases separate offices.
- **RATINGS:** As of June 1, 1990, NCIB was preparing a new report.
- **REGISTRATION:** NY (52098), TN, and VA (1337).
- **FINANCIAL DATA:** Text and chart source was their IRS form 990 covering 1988.

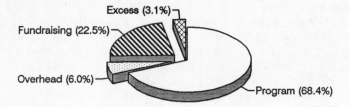

Excess (3.1%)
Fundraising (22.5%)
Overhead (6.0%)
Program (68.4%)

228

National Legal Aid and Defenders Association
1625 K St., N.W., 8th Fl.
Washington, DC 20006
(202) 452-0620

- **CONTRIBUTIONS** are tax-deductible.
- **PURPOSE:** Organized in 1911 (but not incorporated until 1949), the association is a central organization for the promotion, development, and assistance of legal aid ("any type of civil legal services" provided to persons or organizations unable to employ legal counsel) and defender work (counsel for the defense in criminal matters, in vacating or modifying previous convictions or commitments, or in release from confinement).
- **INCOME:** $1,592,555 (calendar 1988; NYS form 497).
- **HOW THEY USE YOUR MONEY:**
  PROGRAM: $1,103,176.
  OVERHEAD: $414,130.
  FUNDRAISING: $7,636.
- **EXCESS:** $67,613.
- **RATINGS:** NCIB reported (10/3/86, using figures from calendar 1985) that the group met all eight of NCIB's old evaluation standards.
- **REGISTRATION:** NY (4791).
- **FINANCIAL DATA:** Text and chart source was their NYS form 497 covering 1988.

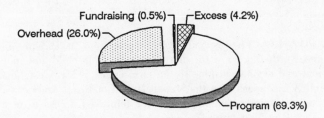

Fundraising (0.5%) Excess (4.2%)
Overhead (26.0%)
Program (69.3%)

The National Mental Health Association, Inc.
1021 Prince St.
Alexandria, VA 22314
(703) 684-7722

■ **CONTRIBUTIONS** are tax-deductible.

■ **PURPOSE:** Traces its origins back much further than its organization in 1950, to the founding of the Connecticut Society for Mental Hygiene in 1908. NMHA works for better care and treatment for the mentally ill, promotion of mental health, and prevention of mental illnesses through research. Lately this has encompassed advocacy for the homeless, for children, and for Americans living in rural areas.

■ **SIZE:** More than 600 affiliates nationwide.

■ **INCOME:** $2,084,879 (national headquarters only; calendar 1988; accrual accounting, IRS form 990). During the preceding four fiscal years support had been increasing.

■ **HOW THEY USE YOUR MONEY:**
PROGRAM: $1,930,019:
- $730,641 for public health education.
- $581,996 for community services.
- $421,306 for professional education and training.
- $119,308 for research (awards and grants).
- $76,768 for patient services.
OVERHEAD: $148,213.
FUNDRAISING: $89,973.

■ **DEFICIT:** $83,326.

■ **LITTLE-KNOWN FACTS:** Responding to reports from its affiliates in Indiana, Texas, and North Dakota of the alarming increase in child and spouse abuse, depression, and alcoholism (due to the farm crisis), NMHA established a National Action Commission on the Mental Health of Rural Americans. Its 1988 report gave eighteen recommendations for improved access to mental-health services for 60 million rural Americans.

■ **RATINGS:** NCIB reported (6/15/89, using figures from calendar 1987) that the group met all nine NCIB standards.

■ **REGISTRATION:** NY (42227) and VA (2379).

■ **FINANCIAL DATA:** Text and chart source was their IRS form 990 (for the national headquarters *only*) covering 1988. NCIB report covers the *entire* organization.

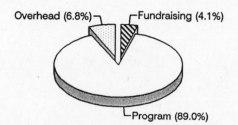

Overhead (6.8%) ⌐Fundraising (4.1%)

⌐Program (89.0%)

Due to deficit of 3.8%, chart is based on spending, not income.

230

National Multiple Sclerosis Society
205 East 42nd St.
New York, NY 10017
(212) 986-3240 • (800) 624-8236

■ **CONTRIBUTIONS** are tax-deductible.

■ **PURPOSE:** Multiple sclerosis is a chronic disease of the central nervous system that affects an estimated quarter of a million Americans. Symptoms include tingling sensations, numbness, slurred speech, blurred or double vision, bladder problems, and, sometimes, paralysis. Both cause and cure remain elusive. The society was established in 1946 to prevent, treat, and cure the disease, and to improve the quality of life of affected individuals and their families.

■ **SIZE:** Ninety-five chapters and about 386,000 members as of September 30, 1988.

■ **INCOME:** $58,667,891 (year ending 9/30/88; accrual accounting, 1988 combined annual report).

■ **HOW THEY USE YOUR MONEY:**
PROGRAM: $37,623,146:
- $12,515,850 for patient services.
- $8,380,213 (including $7,627,852 in grants) for research and research fellowships.
- $7,499,227 for public education.
- $5,966,831 for community services.
- $3,261,025 for professional education and training.

OVERHEAD: $5,087,189.

FUNDRAISING: $8,995,494.

■ **EXCESS:** $6,962,062.

■ **LITTLE-KNOWN FACTS:** The society does not endorse products, services, or manufacturers, but its 1988 annual report featured sixteen pages of ads for such products as electric wheelchairs, walking shoes, a remote telephone extension, and a "personal bowel system" that imitates natural peristaltic action.

■ **RATINGS:** NCIB reported (6/30/88, using figures from the year ending 9/30/87) that the group met all eight of NCIB's old evaluation standards.

■ **REGISTRATION:** NY (7134), TN, and VA (1339).

■ **FINANCIAL DATA:** Text and chart source was their combined annual report, for headquarters and chapters, covering the year ending 9/30/88.

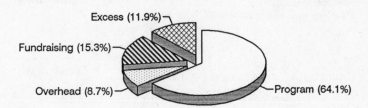

Excess (11.9%)
Fundraising (15.3%)
Overhead (8.7%)
Program (64.1%)

National Organization for Women, Inc.
1000 16th St., N.W., Suite 700
Washington, DC 20036
(202) 331-0066

- **CONTRIBUTIONS** are *not* tax-deductible.
- **PURPOSE:** Founded in 1966, NOW is a group of men and women dedicated to "full equality for women in truly equal partnership with men." It seeks an end to prejudice and discrimination against women in every important field of American society. Political activities include lobbying and litigation, efforts to increase the number of women elected to public office, and two political action committees, NOW-PAC and NOW-EQUALITY-PAC.
- **SIZE:** 9 regional, 50 state, and 800 local groups.
- **INCOME:** $5,487,264 (calendar 1988; independently audited statement).
- **HOW THEY USE YOUR MONEY:**

PROGRAM: $1,707,331:
- $685,521 for regions, states, and chapters.
- $451,610 for communications.
- $434,152 for general issues.
- $70,672 for political development projects.
- $65,376 for conference expenses.

OVERHEAD: $1,027,370:
- $603,098 for general and administrative expenses.
- $424,272 for membership maintenance.

FUNDRAISING: $492,891.

MEMBERSHIP DEVELOPMENT: $1,987,259.

OTHER: $305,388.

- **LITTLE-KNOWN FACTS:** NOW's first president was Betty Friedan, author of *The Feminine Mystique.*
- **RATINGS:** No NCIB report.
- **REGISTRATION:** NY (47685) and VA (1342).
- **FINANCIAL DATA:** Text and chart source was their independently audited statement covering 1988.

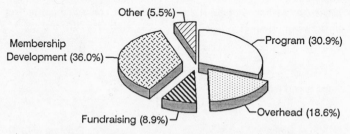

Other (5.5%)

Membership Development (36.0%)

Program (30.9%)

Fundraising (8.9%)

Overhead (18.6%)

Due to deficit of 0.6%, chart is based on spending, not income.

NOW Legal Defense and Education Fund, Inc.
99 Hudson St.
New York, NY 10013
(212) 925-6635

- **CONTRIBUTIONS** are tax-deductible.
- **PURPOSE:** Founded in 1970; recent cases have dealt with discrimination, employment, family law and domestic violence, reproductive rights, and sexual harassment.
- **SIZE:** Four attorneys. During 1988 the Legal Program lost two of its former staff of six.
- **INCOME:** $1,245,801 (calendar 1988; accrual accounting, IRS form 990).
- **HOW THEY USE YOUR MONEY:**
PROGRAM: $1,034,252:
    - $591,097 for legal research and education (not including $207,019 worth of donated services).
    - $133,151 for public information and education.
    - $310,004 for their Project on Equal Education Rights, which includes Project SISTER (a way to keep girls from dropping out of school) and programs on adolescent sexual harassment in schools, vocational education, and technological careers for girls and women.
OVERHEAD: $358,517.
FUNDRAISING: $230,412.
- **DEFICIT:** $377,380.
- **LITTLE-KNOWN FACTS:** Two board members are shared with the National Organization of Women.
- **RATINGS:** NCIB reported (5/16/88, using figures from calendar 1986) that the NOW Legal Defense Fund met all eight of NCIB's old standards.
- **REGISTRATION:** MA, MD, MI, NY (44886), PA, and WI.
- **FINANCIAL DATA:** Text and chart source was their IRS form 990 covering 1988.

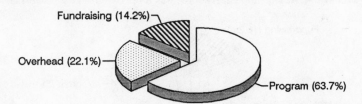

Fundraising (14.2%)
Overhead (22.1%)
Program (63.7%)

Due to deficit of 23.2%, chart is based on spending, not income.

233

National Peace Institute Foundation
110 Maryland Ave., N.E., Suite 409
Washington, DC 20002
(202) 546-9500 • (800) 23PEACE

- **CONTRIBUTIONS** are tax-deductible.
- **PURPOSE:** Formed in 1982 to help develop the field of conflict analysis and resolution in international and domestic disputes, as the educational arm of the National Peace Academy Campaign, which led the citizen effort to create the U.S. Institute of Peace. (The foundation is not affiliated with, nor does it accept funds from, the institute.) In 1987 the foundation was approved for association with the United Nations.
- **SIZE:** 15,000 members in 1988.
- **INCOME:** $480,625 (calendar 1988; accrual accounting, IRS form 990). During the preceding four fiscal years support had been increasing.
- **HOW THEY USE YOUR MONEY:**
  PROGRAM: $265,313:
  - $259,340 (including $20,000 in grants and allocations) for public education.
  - $5,973 for government relations (consultation with Congress and other government bodies on the U.S. Institute of Peace, peace education, and conflict resolution).
  OVERHEAD: $170,983.
  FUNDRAISING: $84,170.
- **DEFICIT:** $39,841.
- **LITTLE-KNOWN FACTS:** The board of directors includes a retired vice-admiral, and its advisory board includes a U.S. Army major general and a lieutenant general, both retired.
- **RATINGS:** No NCIB report.
- **REGISTRATION:** VA (1346).
- **FINANCIAL DATA:** Text and chart source was their IRS form 990 covering 1988.

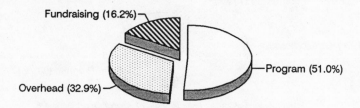

Fundraising (16.2%)

Overhead (32.9%)

Program (51.0%)

Due to deficit of 7.7%, chart is based on spending, not income.

234

National Rifle Association of America
1600 Rhode Island Ave., N.W.
Washington, DC 20005
(202) 828-6000 • (800) 368-5714

■ **CONTRIBUTIONS** are *not* tax-deductible.

■ **PURPOSE:** Established in 1871 to train marksmen, the NRA has grown to encompass (in the late 1940s) hunter education and (in the 1970s) political activities involving the Second Amendment. In 1988 the NRA, which mails political-preference charts to its members, endorsed 1,360 candidates for state office; 84 percent won. Once thought to be a practically invincible foe, the NRA has suffered recent defeats in Congress (a 1986 ban on Teflon-coated "cop-killer" bullets), Maryland (a ban on the sale and manufacture of Saturday-night spe-cials), and California (an assembly vote making the manufacture and sale of assault weapons a felony).

■ **SIZE:** 2,818,981 paid members.

■ **INCOME:** $76,279,887 (calendar 1988; accrual accounting, IRS form 990).

■ **HOW THEY USE YOUR MONEY:**

PROGRAM: $67,057,513*:

- • $26,226,852 for member services.
- • $17,725,922 for publications.
- • $13,712,696 for the Institute for Legislative Action (legislative liaison).
- • $3,664,087 for competitions (NRA competitive-shooting events).
- • $2,112,291 for field services.
- • $1,643,211 for education and training.
- • $1,020,181 for police activities.
- • $867,441 for hunter services.
- • $84,832 for other expenses.

OVERHEAD: $10,492,636.

FUNDRAISING: $4,506,648. The NRA offers an affinity card through Signet Bank, but no breakdown of funds received through the program was included in their tax return.

■ **DEFICIT:** $5,776,910.

■ **LITTLE-KNOWN FACTS:** In 1988 the NRA published its first preschool-age publi-cation: a coloring book entitled *David's First Hunt.*

■ **RATINGS:** No NCIB report.

■ **REGISTRATION:** DC and NY (45899).

■ **FINANCIAL DATA:** Text, chart, and footnote source was their IRS form 990 covering 1988.

*From various program expenses, $2,069,465 was allocated for NRA's political action committee, the NRA Political Victory Fund.

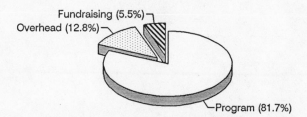

Due to deficit of 7.0%, chart is based on spending, not income.

National Right to Life Committee
419 Seventh St., N.W., Suite 402
Washington, DC 20004
(202) 626-8800

- **CONTRIBUTIONS** are *not* tax-deductible.
- **PURPOSE:** Founded in 1973 (the year of the Supreme Court's decision legalizing abortion), the committee not only works against abortion but also opposes euthanasia and infanticide. It supports abortion alternative programs such as adoption. Political activities include lobbying Congress; encouraging the passage and ratification of a constitutional amendment to protect all human life; and maintaining two political action committees: Federal PAC and the National Right to Life Political Action Committee.
- **SIZE:** The committee, which claims 7,000,000 members, has 50 state and 2,500 local groups.
- **INCOME:** $6,261,916 (year ending 4/30/89; accrual accounting, IRS form 990).
- **HOW THEY USE YOUR MONEY:**
  PROGRAM: $3,689,453:
  - $1,073,994 for a public-awareness program.
  - $806,954 for organization, membership and educational development, general communications, and annual convention expenses.
  - $729,803 for a biweekly newspaper.
  - $413,245 for PAC program administrative expenses.
  - $347,854 for the legislative program.
  - $250,332 for public relations.
  - $67,271 for voter identification.
  OVERHEAD: $751,042.
  FUNDRAISING: $2,168,553.
- **DEFICIT:** $347,132.
- **RATINGS:** No NCIB report.
- **REGISTRATION:** VA (3109).
- **FINANCIAL DATA:** Text and chart source was their IRS form 990 covering the year ending 4/30/89.

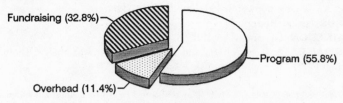

Fundraising (32.8%)

Program (55.8%)

Overhead (11.4%)

Due to deficit of 5.3%, chart is based on spending, not income.

National Right to Work Legal Defense and Education Foundation, Inc.
8001 Braddock Rd., Suite 600
Springfield, VA 22160
(703) 321-8510

- **CONTRIBUTIONS** are tax-deductible.
- **PURPOSE:** Founded in 1968 to defend workers against the "injustices of compulsory unionism" by providing free legal aid to "victimized employees" who request its assistance. A parent organization, the National Right to Work Committee, is active in Congress and state legislatures, advocating elimination of compulsory unionism.
- **SIZE:** The foundation's 1988 annual report acknowledges "the help of tens of thousands of dedicated, pro-freedom supporters [and] more than three hundred cases."
- **INCOME:** $3,945,086 (including $193,282 in court-awarded fees and expenses; calendar 1988; accrual accounting, IRS form 990). During the preceding four fiscal years support had been decreasing.
- **HOW THEY USE YOUR MONEY:**
PROGRAM: $3,459,232:
  - $2,123,975 for litigation activities.
  - $1,335,257* for legal-defense information services and reports.
OVERHEAD: $282,812.
FUNDRAISING: $223,607.*
- **DEFICIT:** $20,565.
- **LITTLE-KNOWN FACTS:** Two libel suits were filed against the foundation in 1987 for comments to the press by a staff attorney and for a foundation press release. Both arose out of legal aid provided to William H. Hinote, a union member who was "ambushed and shot five times in 1982" after crossing a union picket line at his place of work. (Hinote was eventually awarded $1.2 million in damages over the shooting, in a separate suit handled by the foundation.) The foundation believes it will prevail in the libel suits, with no liability, but that the legal defense will be a financial drain on its resources.
- **RATINGS:** As of June 1, 1990, NCIB had requested but not received sufficient information for a report.
- **REGISTRATION:** IL, NJ, NY (45579), OH, and VA (1348).
- **FINANCIAL DATA:** Text and chart source was their IRS form 990 covering 1988. Program expense details and footnote source was their independently audited statement covering 1988.

*Informational materials and activities that included fundraising appeals, worth $1,341,938, were allocated thus: $188,451 to fundraising and $1,153,487 to legal-defense information services and reports.

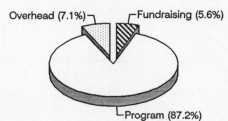

Overhead (7.1%) Fundraising (5.6%)

Program (87.2%)

Due to deficit of 0.3%, chart is based on spending, not income.

National Sudden Infant Death Syndrome Foundation
10500 Little Patuxent Parkway, Suite 420
Columbia, MD 21044
(301) 964-8000 • (800) 221-SIDS

- **CONTRIBUTIONS** are tax-deductible.
- **PURPOSE:** The National SIDS Foundation was founded in 1962 and reorganized in 1976. Its two major purposes are to provide support (education and direct contact) to families following the loss of a child to SIDS, and to support research into diagnosis, treatment, and prevention of SIDS.
- **SIZE:** In 1989, seventy-six active chapters, which transfer a percentage of the funds they raise to the national office.
- **INCOME:** $1,062,540 (year ending 6/30/89; modified accrual accounting, IRS form 990).
- **HOW THEY USE YOUR MONEY:**
  PROGRAM: $688,332:
  - $579,755 for education and services to families.
  - $108,577 for grants and allocations for research and fellowships.
  OVERHEAD: $106,884.
  FUNDRAISING: $56,702.
- **EXCESS:** $210,622.
- **LITTLE-KNOWN FACTS:** In 1989 the national office and the SIDS Alliance agreed to jointly conduct a single eighteen-month national advertising and fundraising campaign. A committee representing both the SIDS Alliance and the national office was to evaluate the success of the campaign by May 1990, and make a recommendation on merging the two groups.
- **RATINGS:** NCIB reported (12/1/87, using figures from the year ending 6/30/86) that the group met all eight of NCIB's old evaluation standards.
- **REGISTRATION:** CA, IL, MA, MD, MI, NC, NY (42524), OH, OR, PA, SC, and VA (1352).
- **FINANCIAL DATA:** Text and chart source was their IRS form 990 covering the year ending 6/30/89.

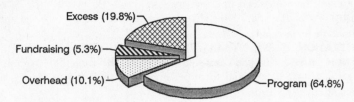

Excess (19.8%)
Fundraising (5.3%)
Overhead (10.1%)
Program (64.8%)

National Trust for Historic Preservation in the United States

1785 Massachusetts Ave., N.W.
Washington, DC 20036
(202) 673-4000 • (800) 672-4183

- **CONTRIBUTIONS** are tax-deductible.
- **PURPOSE:** Chartered by Congress in 1949 as a private nonprofit membership organization "to encourage the public to participate in the preservation of America's history and culture, and to own historic properties."
- **SIZE:** 3,809 members in 1963; more than 220,000 members in 1988.
- **INCOME:** $24,237,296 (year ending 9/30/88; independently audited statement).
- **HOW THEY USE YOUR MONEY:**
  PROGRAM: $16,572,290:
  - $6,292,559 for preservation services.
  - $5,660,626 for historic properties.
  - $2,848,045 for publications.
  - $1,771,060 for education.

  OVERHEAD: $1,926,914.
  FUNDRAISING: $1,999,379.
  MEMBERSHIP DEVELOPMENT: $2,411,602.
- **EXCESS:** $1,327,111.
- **LITTLE-KNOWN FACTS:** Trust properties include the Frank Lloyd Wright Home and Studio; Montpelier, the home of James Madison; and the Woodrow Wilson House.
- **RATINGS:** NCIB reported (6/26/86, using figures from the year ending 9/30/85) that the trust met all eight of NCIB's old evaluation standards.
- **REGISTRATION:** NY (42255), TN, and VA (1356).
- **FINANCIAL DATA:** Text and chart source was their independently audited statement covering the year ending 9/30/88.

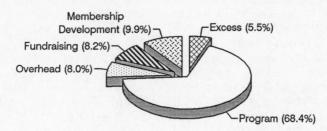

Membership Development (9.9%)
Excess (5.5%)
Fundraising (8.2%)
Overhead (8.0%)
Program (68.4%)

239

National Wildlife Federation and NWF Endowment
1400 16th St., N.W.
Washington, DC 20036
(202) 797-6800

- **CONTRIBUTIONS** are tax-deductible.
- **PURPOSE:** Adopted its present name two years after its creation in 1936. Works to educate the public about conservation and the symptoms of and solutions to environmental abuse and neglect. The NWF Endowment was established in 1957 to accept and manage substantial gifts and bequests to the NWF; a seven-member board manages its portfolio, and investment income supports the NWF's work.
- **SIZE:** Fifty state and territorial affiliates, with 5.1 million members or supporters.
- **INCOME:** $60,067,324 (NWF, including $389,279 in royalties from VISA affinity cards and $1,424,486 from the NWF Endowment); $4,712,170 (NWF Endowment; all figures for the year ending 8/31/88; accrual accounting, IRS form 990). During the preceding four fiscal years support had been increasing.
- **HOW THEY USE YOUR MONEY:**
  PROGRAM: $48,498,314 (NWF):
  - $12,433,260 for associate member programs (distribution of *National Wildlife* and *International Wildlife* magazines).
  - $11,325,651 for nature-education materials (books, games, records, and cards with nature and conservation themes).
  - $8,616,085 for Ranger Rick membership program (827,900 children aged 6 to 12 received *Ranger Rick* magazine).
  - $2,586,507 for *Your Big Backyard* magazine.
  - $13,536,811 for other programs, including $1,632,736 for resource-conservation programs and $975,107 for conservation research programs.
  PAYMENTS TO AFFILIATES: $2,595,063 (NWF to the NWF Endowment); $1,424,486 (NWF Endowment to NWF).
  OVERHEAD: $2,383,579 (NWF); $777,316 (NWF Endowment).
  FUNDRAISING: $3,828,832 (NWF; none for the NWF Endowment).
- **EXCESS:** $2,761,536 (NWF); $2,510,368 (NWF Endowment).
- **LITTLE-KNOWN FACTS:** In 1988 NWF continued to support federal legislation encouraging debt-for-nature swaps.
- **RATINGS:** NCIB reported (2/13/89) on the NWF and the NWF Endowment (using figures from the year ending 8/31/87), stating that the NWF met all nine NCIB standards. (No separate conclusion about the endowment alone.)
- **REGISTRATION:** CA, CT, GA, HI, IL, MA, MD, MN, NC, ND, NH, NJ, NM, NY (7118), OH, OK, OR, TN, VA (1357), WI, and WV.
- **FINANCIAL DATA:** Text and chart sources (NWF and NWF Endowment) were their IRS forms 990 covering the year ending 8/31/88.

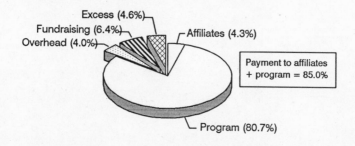

Excess (4.6%)
Fundraising (6.4%)
Overhead (4.0%)
Affiliates (4.3%)

Payment to affiliates
+ program = 85.0%

Program (80.7%)

Native American Rights Fund
1506 Broadway
Boulder, CO 80302
(303) 447-8760

- **CONTRIBUTIONS** are tax-deductible.
- **PURPOSE:** Established in 1970, "to protect the most important rights of the Indian peoples." Has five priorities: (1) preservation of tribal existence; (2) protection of tribal natural resources; (3) promotion of human rights; (4) development of Indian law; and (5) accountability of governments to Native Americans.
- **SIZE:** During this reporting period, NARF says it processed about 400 requests from tribes, individuals, and organizations.
- **INCOME:** $4,363,522 (year ending 9/30/88; accrual accounting, IRS form 990). During the preceding four fiscal years support had been increasing.
- **HOW THEY USE YOUR MONEY:**
  PROGRAM: $3,255,079:
  - $3,015,855 in grants and allocations for litigation and client services (an average annual caseload of 200 in the areas of tribal existence, natural-resources protection, Indian law development, and human rights).
  - $239,224 in grants and allocations for the National Indian Law Library (for materials in the field of Indian law).
  OVERHEAD: $417,789.
  FUNDRAISING: $501,802.
- **EXCESS:** $188,852.
- **LITTLE-KNOWN FACTS:** Works on behalf of Alaskan Natives and Hawaiian Natives, as well as American Indians.
- **RATINGS:** NCIB reported (10/16/87, using figures from the year ending 9/30/86) that the group met all eight of NCIB's old evaluation standards.
- **REGISTRATION:** MA, MD, MN, NC, NY (45278), OH, TN, VA (2380), WI, WV.
- **FINANCIAL DATA:** Text and chart source was their IRS form 990 covering the year ending 9/30/88.

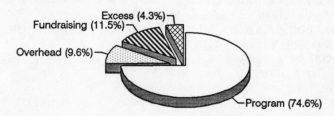

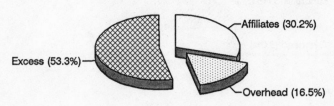

NWF Endowment

Natural Resources Defense Council
40 W. 20th St.
New York, NY 10011
(212) 727-2700

- **CONTRIBUTIONS** are tax-deductible.
- **PURPOSE:** Formed in 1970 to protect the environment by collecting and making available information relating to environmental protection and by taking appropriate legal steps to assure that the environment is protected.
- **SIZE:** Membership goal of 100,000 for FY89.
- **INCOME:** $13,475,075 (year ending 3/31/89; accrual accounting, IRS form 990). During the preceding four fiscal years support had been increasing.
- **HOW THEY USE YOUR MONEY:**
  PROGRAM: $9,146,805:
  - $4,371,174 (including $25,600 in grants and allocations) for environmental programs, including litigation and public policy.
  - $2,292,473 for scientific support and research.
  - $1,772,926* for public education.
  - $226,051 (including $15,000 in grants and allocations) for legislative activities and internships.
  - $484,181* for membership services.

  OVERHEAD: $1,214,728.
  FUNDRAISING: $2,022,413.*
- **EXCESS:** $1,091,129.
- **LITTLE-KNOWN FACTS:** In April 1988, NRDC and the Soviet Academy of Sciences set off three underground chemical explosions in the Black Rock Desert in Nevada to simulate very small nuclear explosions and demonstrate the capabilities of seismic monitoring equipment. The project continued testing in Nevada and in Kazakhstan in August and September 1988 to show that seismic estimation of explosion yields was superior to the hydrodynamic method favored by the Reagan administration.
- **RATINGS:** NCIB reported (5/25/90, using figures from the year ending 3/31/89) that NRDC met all nine NCIB standards.
- **REGISTRATION:** CA, IL, MA, MI, MO, NC, NH, NJ, NY (41686), OH, PA, RI, TN, VA (1358), WI, and WV.
- **FINANCIAL DATA:** Text and chart source was their IRS form 990 covering the year ending 3/31/89.

*The NRDC adopted AICPA ruling SOP 87-2 on joint allocation of costs on April 1, 1988, and has accordingly divided costs thus: public education: $727,927; membership services: $458,965; and fundraising: $1,048,769.

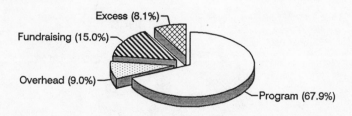

Excess (8.1%)

Fundraising (15.0%)

Overhead (9.0%)

Program (67.9%)

The Nature Conservancy
1815 N. Lynn St.
Arlington, VA 22209
(703) 841-5300

- **CONTRIBUTIONS** are tax-deductible.
- **PURPOSE:** Established in 1951; "places the highest priority on the preservation of rare and endangered species through the systematic protection of critical habitats." "Living resources" are protected in the United States and abroad through: (1) identification of the types, locations, and survival needs of rare species and lands; (2) protection of lands and species by obtaining land as a gift or purchase, or by assisting the government, individual owner, or other conservation group in their preservation efforts; (3) management of those preserves using both paid and volunteer land stewards.
- **SIZE:** The Conservancy manages the world's largest privately owned sanctuary system: 1,100 preserves totaling 3,994,766 acres in fifty states, Canada, Latin America, and the Caribbean.
- **INCOME:** $168,554,000 (year ending 6/30/89; independently audited statement).
- **HOW THEY USE YOUR MONEY:**
  PROGRAM: $125,395,000:
    - $96,130,000 for land protected until such a time that the government could take over stewardship.
    - $11,053,000 for protection (operations).
    - $9,106,000 for stewardship expenses.
    - $6,728,000 for identification.
    - $2,378,000 for supported membership services.
  OVERHEAD: $12,255,000.
  FUNDRAISING: $12,528,000.
  MEMBERSHIP DEVELOPMENT: $5,278,000.
  LOSS ON SALE: $649,000 for loss on sale of trade lands.
- **EXCESS:** $12,449,000, to be used to buy future land when available.
- **LITTLE-KNOWN FACTS:** In 1989 the Conservancy worked with American Express Bank to complete two debt-for-nature swaps in Latin America totaling $9.2 million: one will conserve rain forests in Costa Rica, and the other will support protection efforts in Ecuador, the Andes, the Amazon, and the Galápagos Islands.
- **RATINGS:** NCIB reported (3/24/89, using figures from the year ending 6/30/88) that the Nature Conservancy met all nine NCIB standards.
- **REGISTRATION:** CT, NC, NJ, NY (8219), OR, VA (1359), and WI.
- **FINANCIAL DATA:** Text and chart source was their independently audited statement covering the year ending 6/30/89.

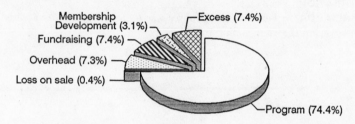

Membership Development (3.1%) — Excess (7.4%)
Fundraising (7.4%)
Overhead (7.3%)
Loss on sale (0.4%)
Program (74.4%)

New Israel Fund
111 W. 40th St., Suite 2300
New York, NY 10018
(212) 302-0066

- **CONTRIBUTIONS** are tax-deductible.
- **PURPOSE:** The New Israel Fund was begun in 1979 in the belief that Diaspora Jews living in democratic societies could be a great resource for Israelis. The fund supports projects that strengthen democracy, advance social justice, and promote pluralism; many such projects deal with problems in Israeli society before they become headlines. In 1988 the fund, which has long supported projects on Jewish-Arab coexistence, set up a special fund for projects that respond constructively and effectively to the intifada.
- **SIZE:** 12,000 donors in 1989 (up from only 80 in 1980).
- **INCOME:** $4,906,215 (year ending 6/30/89; accrual accounting, independently audited statement). During the preceding four fiscal years support had been increasing.
- **HOW THEY USE YOUR MONEY:**
PROGRAM: $4,438,618:
  - $1,578,243 for donor-advised grants.
  - $1,523,312 for grants to Israeli nonprofit groups.
  - $531,281 for New Israel Fund projects.
  - $462,369 for educational activities.
  - $343,413 for grant management.
    Sponsored projects deal with women's rights, the rights of Ethiopian Jewish immigrants, civil rights and liberties, and even secular humanism. The Israel section of Amnesty International received $5,429 and the Peace Now Education Fund received $92,063.
OVERHEAD: $547,808.
FUNDRAISING: $563,249:
  - $545,061 for fundraising
  - $18,188 for direct mail.
- **DEFICIT:** $643,460.
- **LITTLE-KNOWN FACTS:** Since 1982 the fund has supported Neve Shalom/Wahat al-Salam, an integrated community of Israeli Jews, Moslems, and Christians living together by choice in the Judean Hills between Jerusalem and Tel Aviv. NS/WAS is best known for its School for Peace, which brings together groups of twenty Arab and twenty Jewish teenagers in three-day seminars on coexistence. Over 9,500 adolescents and 3,000 adults have participated so far. In FY89 NS/WAS received $221,926 in grants from the New Israel Fund.
- **RATINGS:** No NCIB report.
- **REGISTRATION:** NY.
- **FINANCIAL DATA:** Text and chart source was their independently audited statement covering the year ending 6/30/89.

Overseas Development Council
1717 Massachusetts Ave., N.W.
Washington, DC 20036
(202) 234-8701

- **CONTRIBUTIONS** are tax-deductible.
- **PURPOSE:** Formed in 1969, ODC aims to increase American understanding of the economic and social problems facing the developing countries and the importance of these countries to the United States in an increasingly interdependent world. Through an extensive outreach program consisting of policy publications, congressional testimony, meetings, seminars, and conferences, ODC seeks to illuminate the public debate on these issues for representatives of the executive branch and Congress, corporations and financial institutions, the private voluntary community, the multilateral financial institutions, academia, and the media.
- **SIZE:** ODC has a permanent staff of 23. The council also has a two-part membership structure: a board of directors and the much larger ODC Council. All 30 board directors are part of this larger council. The ODC Council currently has 243 individual members.
- **INCOME:** $1,915,338 (calendar 1989; independently audited statement).
- **HOW THEY USE YOUR MONEY:**
PROGRAM: $1,091,623.
OVERHEAD: $538,872.
FUNDRAISING: $108,317.
- **EXCESS:** $176,526.
- **RATINGS:** NCIB reported (4/27/89, using figures from calendar 1987) that the Overseas Development Council met all nine NCIB standards.
- **REGISTRATION:** NY (45115).
- **FINANCIAL DATA:** Text and chart source was their independently audited statement covering 1989.

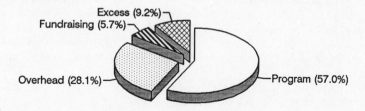

Excess (9.2%)
Fundraising (5.7%)
Overhead (28.1%)
Program (57.0%)

New Israel Fund

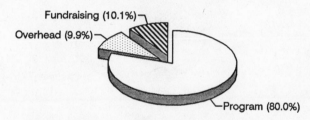

Fundraising (10.1%)
Overhead (9.9%)
Program (80.0%)

Due to deficit of 11.6%, chart is based on spending, not income.

Oxfam-America, Inc.
115 Broadway
Boston, MA 02116
(617) 482-1211

■ **CONTRIBUTIONS** are tax-deductible.

■ **PURPOSE:** Oxfam-America (established in 1970) is one of seven autonomous units of Oxfam, an international disaster-relief and self-help development organization founded in 1942 as the Oxford Committee for Famine Relief. Oxfam-America promotes long-term, self-sustaining development among low-income people throughout the world, and educates people on the basic needs of the world's poor, such as hunger relief and development.

■ **SIZE:** 343 grants to fund projects in thirty-four countries.

■ **INCOME:** $10,615,831 (year ending 10/31/88; accrual accounting, independently audited statement). The group neither seeks nor accepts U.S. government funds.

■ **HOW THEY USE YOUR MONEY:**
PROGRAM: $7,892,185:
   • $6,763,676 for overseas grants (including $2,168,040 for projects in Africa; $1,236,925 for projects in Asia; and $2,064,213 for projects in Latin America and the Caribbean).
   • $1,128,509 (including $10,200 in grants and allocations) for education.
OVERHEAD: $638,478.
FUNDRAISING: $1,841,301.

■ **EXCESS:** $243,867.

■ **LITTLE-KNOWN FACTS:** In 1989 Oxfam-America began "Turn Aid Around," a three-year policy campaign to critique the uses and abuses of U.S. foreign aid, and to highlight alternative "empowering" approaches to relief and development. Minimally, "empowerment" as defined by Oxfam means the provision of basic survival needs; personal growth (including access to information, such as the many Oxfam literacy programs); economic development; and political access.

■ **RATINGS:** NCIB reported (9/3/87, using figures from the year ending 10/31/86) that Oxfam-America met all eight of NCIB's old evaluation standards. By October 1989 NCIB reported that Oxfam-America met all nine new NCIB standards.

■ **REGISTRATION:** CA, CT, GA, IL, MA, MD, MI, MN, NC, NH, NJ, NM, NY (42386), OH, TN, and VA (1436).

■ **FINANCIAL DATA:** Text and chart source was their independently audited statement covering the year ending 10/31/88.

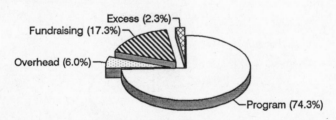

Excess (2.3%)
Fundraising (17.3%)
Overhead (6.0%)
Program (74.3%)

Paralyzed Veterans of America
801 18th St., N.W.
Washington, DC 20006
(202) USA-1300

- **CONTRIBUTIONS** Although PVA is a 501(c)(4) group, they say contributions are tax-deductible.
- **PURPOSE:** Established in 1946 and chartered by Congress in 1971, Paralyzed Veterans of America works for appropriate health care and other benefits for veterans and other persons who have suffered injuries or diseases of the spinal cord; supports research into treatment; and educates the public on the problems of spinal-cord dysfunctions. PVA controls several organizations whose accounts are included in the financial information that follows: PVA Spinal Cord Research Foundation; Paralysis Society of America of the PVA; 801-18th Street Associates (owners and operators of PVA's national headquarters building); and the PVA Spinal Cord Injury Education and Training Foundation.
- **SIZE:** Thirty-two chapters and fifteen subchapters.
- **INCOME:** $41,759,605 (year ending 9/30/89; independently audited statement). PVA neither seeks nor receives government funds.
- **HOW THEY USE YOUR MONEY:**
PROGRAM: $24,634,796:
  - $11,236,925 for membership and benefit programs.
  - $10,356,311 for public-affairs programs.
  - $3,041,560 for research.
OVERHEAD: $4,830,483.
FUNDRAISING: $12,717,171, including $11,921,141 for mail programs.
- **DEFICIT:** $422,845.
- **LITTLE-KNOWN FACTS:** PVA's principal fundraising activities are performed on a contract basis through PVA-EPVA, Inc., a 50 percent-owned company which manufactures and mails greeting cards with contribution requests to prospective contributors. Recipients of the cards have no legal obligation to contribute or return the cards. During the PVA-EPVA, Inc., fiscal year ending April 30, 1989, sales of $18,609,366, after expenses, resulted in a net loss after income taxes of $863,847.
- **RATINGS:** NCIB reported (5/4/89, using figures from the year ending 9/30/87) that PVA did not meet standard 6a, but that it met all other new NCIB standards.
- **REGISTRATION:** FL, IL, MA, MD, MN, NH, NY (44556), OH, OK, OR, and VA (1442).
- **FINANCIAL DATA:** Text and chart source was their independently audited statement covering the year ending 9/30/89.

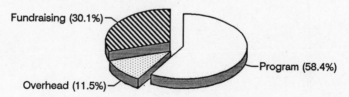

Fundraising (30.1%)
Program (58.4%)
Overhead (11.5%)

Due to deficit of 1.0%, chart is based on spending, not income.

Parents Without Partners, Inc.
8087 Colesville Rd.
Silver Spring, MD 20910
(301) 588-9354 • (800) 637-7974

- **CONTRIBUTIONS** are tax-deductible.
- **PURPOSE:** Founded in 1957 as a group of custodial and noncustodial parents who are single due to widowhood, divorce, separation, or other reasons. PWP researches single-parent topics, including public acceptance of such parents and their children, and alleviation of problems surrounding the welfare and upbringing of their children.
- **SIZE:** Over 115,000 members support 90 regional and 700 local groups.
- **INCOME:** $2,351,525 (year ending 6/30/89; accrual accounting, IRS form 990).
- **HOW THEY USE YOUR MONEY:**
  PROGRAM: $1,411,338:
  - $798,308 for membership services and processing.
  - $363,363 for chapter support.
  - $126,458 for volunteer support.
  - $123,209 for conventions and meetings.
  OVERHEAD: $545,554.
  FUNDRAISING: $0.
- **EXCESS:** $394,633.
- **LITTLE-KNOWN FACTS:** PWP's toll-free number provides referrals to assistance sources for nonmember single parents.
- **RATINGS:** No NCIB report.
- **REGISTRATION:** CA, NY (45298), and SC.
- **FINANCIAL DATA:** Text and chart source was their IRS form 990 covering the year ending 6/30/89.

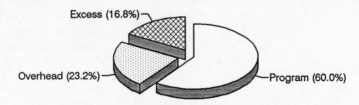

Parkinson's Disease Foundation
640-650 W. 168th St.
New York, NY 10032
(212) 923-4700 • (800) 457-6676

- **CONTRIBUTIONS** are tax-deductible.
- **PURPOSE:** Founded in 1957 by William Black's gift of $5 million (at that time, the largest gift by a living donor), the Parkinson's Disease Foundation seeks, through research, the cause and cure of Parkinsonism and related disorders.
- **SIZE:** In 1988, 169 published papers resulting from the Parkinson's Disease Foundation laboratories and investigators.
- **INCOME:** $2,691,358 (year ending 6/30/89; accrual accounting, independently audited statement).
- **HOW THEY USE YOUR MONEY:**
  PROGRAM: $1,465,227:
    - $1,242,727 for research (including $35,000 in fellowship money and $74,917 in research grants for the California Parkinson's Disease Foundation).
    - $222,500 for public and patient information, and referral services (including $25,000 for the Michigan Parkinson Foundation).
  OVERHEAD: $218,567.
  FUNDRAISING: $72,156.
- **EXCESS:** $935,408. According to Dinah Orr of the foundation, most of this was due to an unexpected increase of over $600,000 in bequests during the year, money which is applied to research and to increase the foundation's endowment.
- **LITTLE-KNOWN FACTS:** In 1988 visiting Italian scientist Dr. Gianni Pezzoli played a major part in establishing an important new finding: that a Parkinsonian state in rats *can* be reversed through the transplantation of tissue plus the infusion of nerve-growth factor into the cerebral ventricle.
- **RATINGS:** NCIB reported (2/14/90, using figures from the year ending 6/30/89) that "there is a question with respect to standard 1g, on material conflict of interest involving a board member," but that the foundation met all other new NCIB standards.
- **REGISTRATION:** NJ, NY (5191), and VA (2706).
- **FINANCIAL DATA:** Text and chart source was their independently audited statement covering the year ending 6/30/89.

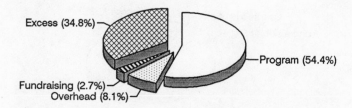

Excess (34.8%)
Program (54.4%)
Fundraising (2.7%)
Overhead (8.1%)

The Pathfinder Fund
9 Galen St., Suite 217
Watertown, MA 02172
(617) 731-1700

■ **CONTRIBUTIONS** are tax-deductible.
■ **PURPOSE:** Founded 1957 to find, demonstrate, and promote new and more efficient family planning programs in developing countries. The fund's efforts to aid such countries in their implementation of population policies favorable to national development take into account upholding human rights; enhancing the status and role of women; and respecting the views of family planning clients.
■ **SIZE:** About 115 staff members.
■ **INCOME:** $20,162,686 (year ending 6/30/89; IRS form 990). During the preceding four fiscal years support had been increasing.
■ **HOW THEY USE YOUR MONEY:**
PROGRAM: $17,019,895:
  • $13,657,318 (including $8,635,342 in grants and allocations) for family planning (to help deliver effective fertility-control services to those in need).
  • $2,041,440 (including $1,288,144 in grants and allocations) paid for training programs (to develop materials for teachers of family planning in less developed countries).
  • $814,107 (including $500,233 in grants and allocations) for population policy (to help form national population policies). .
  • $507,030 (including $318,706 in grants and allocations) for other expenses (e.g., to identify and support those people in Third World countries who are instrumental in advancing family planning in their nations and to increase women's rights and choices).
OVERHEAD: $2,983,778.
FUNDRAISING: $96,989.
■ **EXCESS:** $62,024.
■ **RATINGS:** NCIB reported (7/25/86, using figures from the year ending 6/30/85) that the Pathfinder Fund met NCIB's old evaluation standards 2 through 8, but did not meet NCIB standard 1.
■ **REGISTRATION:** MA, MN, and NY (47615).
■ **FINANCIAL DATA:** Text and chart source was their IRS form 990 covering the year ending 6/30/89.

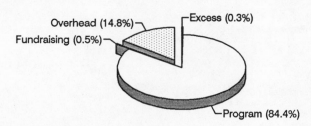

Overhead (14.8%)
Excess (0.3%)
Fundraising (0.5%)
Program (84.4%)

People for the American Way, Inc.
2000 M St., N.W., Suite 400
Washington, DC 20036
(202) 467-4999

- **CONTRIBUTIONS** are tax-deductible.
- **PURPOSE:** Founded in 1980, when the religious right and other conservative organizations were gaining greater prominence, PFAW is a nonpartisan constitutional-liberties organization that seeks to popularize American democratic values in "public debates that define the nature of American society."
- **SIZE:** Headquarters in Washington and offices in New York, North Carolina, and Texas.
- **INCOME:** $3,546,387 (calendar 1988; accrual accounting, IRS form 990).
- **HOW THEY USE YOUR MONEY:**
  PROGRAM: $2,663,031:
  - $589,757 for state operations.
  - $523,999 for issues development.
  - $464,015 for communications (press conferences, press releases, and distribution of op-ed pieces and editorial memoranda).
  - $432,853* for membership and public information.
  - $352,275 for program management and development.
  - $206,822 for legal costs (research and the employment of various legal procedures to further PFAW's aims).
  - $93,310 for public-policy programs (research, analysis, and educational support).

  OVERHEAD: $564,721.
  FUNDRAISING: $599,637.*
- **DEFICIT:** $281,002.
- **RATINGS:** NCIB reported (11/20/87, using figures from 1986) that PFAW and the PFAW Action Fund (see following profile) met NCIB's old evaluation standards 2, 3, 5, 6, and 8; they did not meet standards 1 and 4; and "there is a question with regard to standard 7."
- **REGISTRATION:** DC, NY (50734), and VA (342).
- **FINANCIAL DATA:** Text and chart source was their IRS form 990 covering 1988. Footnote source was their independently audited statement covering 1988.

*Costs of $104,835 worth of informational materials that included fundraising appeals were allocated thus: $67,836 to membership and public information, and $36,999 to fundraising.

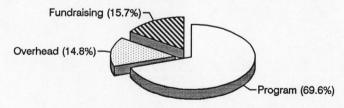

Fundraising (15.7%)

Overhead (14.8%)

Program (69.6%)

Due to deficit of 7.3%, chart is based on spending, not income.

People for the American Way Action Fund
2000 M St., N.W., Suite 400
Washington, DC 20036
(202) 467-4999

- **CONTRIBUTIONS** are *not* tax-deductible.
- **PURPOSE:** Incorporated in 1984 to obtain, develop, and provide educational information on issues affecting human and civil rights secured by the Constitution.
- **SIZE:** More than 275,000 members.
- **INCOME:** $2,958,694 (calendar 1988; accrual accounting, IRS form 990).
- **HOW THEY USE YOUR MONEY:**
  PROGRAM: $1,920,081:
    - $1,481,365* for membership and public information.
    - $342,281 for the public-policy program.
    - $96,435 for program management and development.
  OVERHEAD: $408,875.
  FUNDRAISING: $506,530.*
- **EXCESS:** $123,208.
- **RATINGS:** (See preceding profile.)
- **REGISTRATION:** DC and VA (1468).
- **FINANCIAL DATA:** Text and chart source was their IRS form 990 covering 1988. Footnote source was their independently audited statement covering 1988.

*Costs of $1,400,950 for informational materials that included fundraising appeals were allocated thus: $1,133,319 to membership and public information, and $267,631 to fundraising.

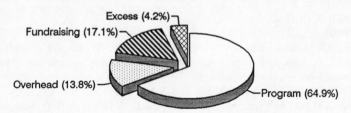

Excess (4.2%)
Fundraising (17.1%)
Overhead (13.8%)
Program (64.9%)

People for the Ethical Treatment of Animals, Inc.
Box 42516
Washington, DC 20015
(202) 726-0156 • (301) 770-7444

■ **CONTRIBUTIONS** are tax-deductible.

■ **PURPOSE:** Formed in 1980 "to cultivate, promote, and disseminate knowledge and information concerning animal rights, abuse, and related subjects."

■ **INCOME:** $6,793,809 (year ending 7/31/89; accrual accounting, independently audited statement).

■ **HOW THEY USE YOUR MONEY:**
PROGRAM: $4,918,571:
- $1,327,700 for research and cruelty investigations (visiting labs and examining microfiches at the National Library of Medicine).
- $1,427,393 for public outreach, training, and organizing (including public-service announcements by actors Mike Farrell and Rue McClanahan).
- $2,163,478 for campaigns and educational programs (such as PETA's cruelty-free products and "recommended toy company" lists).

OVERHEAD: $493,408.
MEMBERSHIP DEVELOPMENT: $1,110,478.

■ **EXCESS:** $271,352.

■ **LITTLE-KNOWN FACTS:** Known mostly for work on behalf of mammals, including chimpanzees used in AIDS research, PETA also intervened when a Maryland teacher "was planning to pull the wings and legs off of live insects during a science class." After PETA's protest, "the lesson in wanton cruelty was stopped."

■ **RATINGS:** NCIB reported (7/20/90, using figures from the year ending 7/31/89) that PETA did not meet standard 1a, and that there was insufficient information to determine if it met standard 6a, but that PETA did meet all other new NCIB standards.

■ **REGISTRATION:** NY (52904) and VA (2526).

■ **FINANCIAL DATA:** Text and chart source was their independently audited statement covering the year ending 7/31/89.

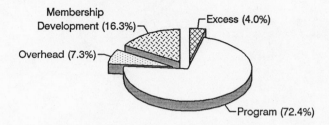

Membership Development (16.3%) — Excess (4.0%) — Overhead (7.3%) — Program (72.4%)

The People-to-People Health Foundation, Inc.
Project HOPE Health Sciences Education Center
Millwood, VA 22646
(703) 837-2100

- **CONTRIBUTIONS** are tax-deductible.
- **PURPOSE:** The foundation was begun in 1958. Project HOPE (Health Opportunity for People Everywhere), its principal activity, teaches modern medical techniques to health-care workers in developing countries worldwide. From 1960 until 1974, activities were directed from the S.S. *Hope;* since 1974, programs have been land-based. HOPE's Center for Health Affairs was established in 1981 and conducts research and policy analysis to help solve health-care-system problems throughout the world.
- **SIZE:** Programs of education and training, textbook distribution, and medical relief have reached fifty-eight countries.
- **INCOME:** $53,200,000 (year ending 6/30/89; independently audited statement).
- **HOW THEY USE YOUR MONEY:**
  PROGRAM: $48,462,000.
  OVERHEAD: $1,862,000.
  FUNDRAISING: $2,161,000.
  INFORMATION SERVICES: $295,000.
- **EXCESS:** $420,000.
- **LITTLE-KNOWN FACTS:** The maiden voyage of the S.S. *Hope,* in 1960, was to Indonesia and Vietnam.
- **RATINGS:** NCIB reported (9/6/89, using figures from the year ending 6/30/88) that the group met all nine NCIB standards.
- **REGISTRATION:** NY (9440) and VA (1472).
- **FINANCIAL DATA:** Text and chart source was their independently audited statement covering the year ending 6/30/89.

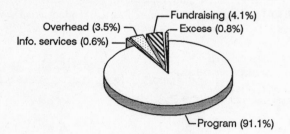

Fundraising (4.1%)
Overhead (3.5%)
Excess (0.8%)
Info. services (0.6%)
Program (91.1%)

Phoenix House Foundation, Inc.
164 West 74th St.
New York, NY 10023
(212) 595-5810

- **CONTRIBUTIONS** are tax-deductible.
- **PURPOSE:** Founded in 1967, Phoenix House provides drug-abuse treatment through individual, group, and family counseling and through vocational rehabilitation. Among its programs are Phoenix Academy (a special residential school), Step One (a day school at Phoenix House), residential treatment (a live-in drug-abuse program), Riverside Center (a short-term treatment unit), IMPACT (Intervention Moves Parents and Children Together, a program involving both adolescents and their families), and the Drug Education and Prevention Unit (a national adolescent drug-prevention program in public and private schools for students, parents, and faculty).
- **SIZE:** Six different related organizations: Oxford Project, Inc.; Phoenix House Orange County, Inc.; Phoenix Programs of New York, Inc.; Tuum Est, Inc.; Phoenix House of San Diego, Inc.; and Phoenix House of California, Inc.
- **INCOME:** $5,407,895 (year ending 6/30/88; accrual accounting, IRS form 990).
- **HOW THEY USE YOUR MONEY:**
  PROGRAM: $2,494,490:
    - $1,162,280 (including $587,264 in grants and allocations) for house operating expenditures (providing direct care and treatment to residents).
    - $1,097,855 for other direct program expenditures (costs associated with departments providing direct services to residents, e.g., purchasing resident goods and supplies, providing information services).
    - $156,926 for program support services (departments providing indirect support to residents, e.g., warehousing residents' supplies).
    - $77,429 for research (preparing and maintaining data regarding the results of programs).
  OVERHEAD: $2,321,079.
  PLANT COSTS: $351,244 for repair, maintenance, and alterations.
  FUNDRAISING: $0.
- **EXCESS:** $241,082.
- **RATINGS:** No NCIB report.
- **REGISTRATION:** NY (41464).
- **FINANCIAL DATA:** Text and chart source was their IRS form 990 covering the year ending 6/30/88.

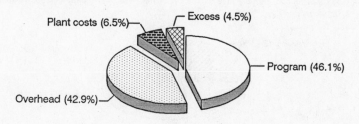

Plant costs (6.5%) — Excess (4.5%) — Program (46.1%) — Overhead (42.9%)

Physicians for Social Responsibility, Inc.
1000 16th St., N.W., Suite 810
Washington, DC 20036
(202) 785-3777

- **CONTRIBUTIONS** are tax-deductible.
- **PURPOSE:** The U.S. affiliate of International Physicians for the Prevention of Nuclear War (see profile), which received the 1985 Nobel Peace Prize. PSR's purpose is "to educate the medical community and the general public on the implications of the nuclear-arms race." It has calculated the direct cost of the nuclear-arms race in tax dollars and has publicized the dangers of aging nuclear-weapons-production facilities such as Rocky Flats, Hanford, and Savannah River. In December 1988, the PSR board voted to expand its concerns to include biological and chemical weapons.
- **SIZE:** 155 affiliated chapters nationwide.
- **INCOME:** $2,413,081 (calendar 1988; accrual accounting, IRS form 990). According to their 1988 independently audited statement, PSR received fees from an affinity-card program totaling $35,584. The IRS has determined that "fees, net of related expenses, are considered unrelated business taxable income" and so the group paid $3,214 in taxes.
- **HOW THEY USE YOUR MONEY:**
  PROGRAM: $1,478,036*:
    - $960,723 for public and medical education.
    - $147,804 for media and public affairs.
    - $369,509 for chapter development.
  OVERHEAD: $447,909.
  FUNDRAISING: $636,980.*
- **DEFICIT:** $149,844.
- **LITTLE-KNOWN FACTS:** In 1988, PSR decided to offer full membership (and voting rights) to nonphysicians, including such health-care professionals as nurses, psychologists, veterinarians, pharmacists, and others with the equivalent of a doctorate.
- **RATINGS:** No NCIB report.
- **REGISTRATION:** NY (50197).
- **FINANCIAL DATA:** Text and chart source was their IRS form 990 covering 1988. Footnote and affinity-card income source was their independently audited statement covering 1988.

*Costs of $321,724 for dual-purpose materials and activities were allocated thus: $293,506 to fundraising and $28,218 to program.

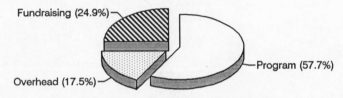

Fundraising (24.9%)
Program (57.7%)
Overhead (17.5%)

Due to deficit of 5.8%, chart is based on spending, not income.

Plan International USA
155 Plan Way
Warwick, RI 02886
(401) 738-5600 • (800) 556-7918

■ **CONTRIBUTIONS** are tax-deductible.
■ **PURPOSE:** Known from its establishment in 1937 (during the Spanish Civil War) until June 1990 as Foster Parents Plan. The plan is organized for and dedicated to providing sponsorship of needy children, providing guidance and practical assistance in strengthening and reinforcing their families, gaining the interest and support of persons of good will, enhancing our abilities to understand the causes and conditions of Third World poverty, providing the means for transmission of funds, providing a nonsectarian organization purely humanitarian in character, and cooperating and exchanging information with similar groups.
■ **SIZE:** There are related national organizations in Australia, Belgium, Canada, Japan, the Netherlands, the United Kingdom, and West Germany. The international headquarters administers programs in twenty-four countries. An average 92,559 children are assigned each year to sponsors.
■ **INCOME:** $28,494,020 (year ending 6/30/89; accrual accounting, IRS form 990). During the preceding four fiscal years support had been increasing.
■ **HOW THEY USE YOUR MONEY:**
PROGRAM: $21,354,111:
  • $18,720,338 in grants and allocations for program and management support.
  • $1,663,000 in grants and allocations for development education.
  • $423,851 for the Intercultural Communication Program (letters and information exchanged through sponsorship).
  • $546,922 in the form of gifts from sponsors to children.
OVERHEAD: $2,537,531.
FUNDRAISING: $3,721,807.
■ **EXCESS:** $880,571.
■ **RATINGS:** NCIB reported (12/31/87, using figures for the year ending 6/30/86) that Foster Parents Plan, Inc., met all eight of NCIB's old evaluation standards.
■ **REGISTRATION:** NY (4638) and all other states *except* AZ, DE, IA, ID, IN, MS, MT, VT, and WY.
■ **FINANCIAL DATA:** Text and chart source was their IRS form 990 covering the year ending 6/30/89.

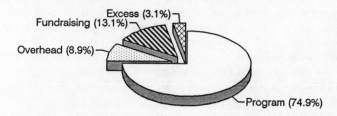

Excess (3.1%)
Fundraising (13.1%)
Overhead (8.9%)
Program (74.9%)

Planned Parenthood Federation of America, Inc.
810 Seventh Ave.
New York, NY 10019
(212) 541-7800

■ **CONTRIBUTIONS** are tax-deductible.

■ **PURPOSE:** The nation's oldest and largest voluntary family planning organization, PPFA traces its origins to the first birth control clinic in America (founded in 1916 by Margaret Sanger). Its international division, Family Planning International Assistance (FPIA), works in developing countries. The Alan Guttmacher Institute, an independent corporation for research, policy analysis, and public education on reproductive health, is a special affiliate of PPFA. By the end of 1988, 62 of PPFA's 177 affiliates were offering testing and counseling for HIV.

■ **SIZE:** From 1980 to 1988 PPFA's client roster rose 65 percent to 3.8 million American women, men, and teens served in 850 clinics (150 more than in 1980); its donor base rose 400 percent, to 250,000.

■ **INCOME:** $40,781,967 (calendar 1988; accrual accounting, IRS form 990).

■ **HOW THEY USE YOUR MONEY:**
PROGRAM: $36,852,302:
  • $4,611,500 (including $512,763 in grants and allocations) for services to American affiliates.
  • $4,466,379 (including $393,621 in grants and allocations) for "service to the field of family planning."
  • $27,774,423 (including $4,425,291 in grants and allocations) for international assistance in family planning. FPIA distributed more than 232 million condoms and almost 29 million cycles of oral contraceptives to 270 organizations in seventy-six countries.
PAYMENTS TO AFFILIATES: $1,314,894 (including membership dues paid to the International Planned Parenthood Federation in London and support of research and analysis at the Alan Guttmacher Institute in New York and Washington).
OVERHEAD: $5,656,403.
FUNDRAISING: $3,608,898.

■ **DEFICIT:** $6,650,530.

■ **LITTLE-KNOWN FACTS:** The primary source for FPIA funds, a cooperative agreement with the U.S. Agency for International Development (AID), was threatened in 1985 by the Reagan administration's intention to deny funding to any group that performed, advocated, or counseled for abortions. In February 1988, PPFA obtained a court order to continue AID funding pending the outcome of their suit challenging the constitutionality of the new policy. In April 1990, abortion was once again given as the reason behind a funding cut when AT&T announced it would no longer make grants to the group.

■ **RATINGS:** NCIB reported (9/25/87, using figures from calendar 1985) that PPFA met all eight of NCIB's old evaluation standards.

■ **REGISTRATION:** CA, CT, IL, KY, MA, MD, MN, NE, NH, NJ, NM, NY (6692), OH, OK, OR, PA, VA (1482), and WV.

■ **FINANCIAL DATA:** Text and chart source was their IRS form 990 (for the national headquarters *only*) covering 1988. NCIB's report examines the *entire* organization.

Population Institute
110 Maryland Ave., N.E., Suite 207
Washington, DC 20002
(202) 544-3300

- **CONTRIBUTIONS** are tax-deductible.
- **PURPOSE:** A fundraising organization founded in 1969 to assist "institutions, communications media, policy leaders, and the public in their understanding of population-related problems and the development of appropriate responses."
- **SIZE:** Over 30,000 community leaders.
- **INCOME:** $1,818,510 (for calendar 1987; accrual accounting, 1987 annual report).
- **HOW THEY USE YOUR MONEY:**
PROGRAM: $1,302,027:
  - $561,883 for information and education.
  - $297,631 for community leaders.
  - $193,963 for public education.
  - $153,866 for international programs.
  - $94,684 for public policy.
OVERHEAD: $365,084 for administration.
FUNDRAISING: $207,961.
- **DEFICIT:** $56,562.
- **RATINGS:** NCIB reported (12/11/89, using figures from calendar 1988) that the Population Institute met all nine NCIB standards.
- **REGISTRATION:** NY (46877) and VA (1501).
- **FINANCIAL DATA:** Text and chart source was their annual report covering 1987.

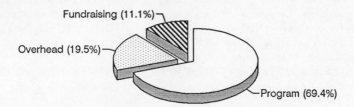

Due to deficit of 3.0%, chart is based on spending, not income.

Planned Parenthood

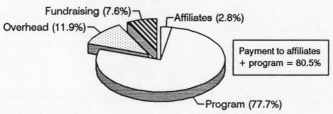

Due to deficit of 14.0%, chart is based on spending, not income.

259

Prison Fellowship Ministries
1856 Old Reston Ave.
Reston, VA 22090
(703) 478-0100

- **CONTRIBUTIONS** are tax-deductible.
- **PURPOSE:** PFM was founded in 1976 by Charles W. Colson, who became a born-again Christian while serving time for obstruction of justice in the Watergate scandal. It aims "to minister to the needs of inmates confined in prison communities and to their families" and to "promote biblical standards of justice in the criminal-justice system."
- **SIZE:** Programs in thirty-four countries around the world; more than 22,000 volunteers served inmates in 550 prisons in the United States alone.
- **INCOME:** $13,473,326 (calendar 1988; accrual accounting, IRS form 990).
- **HOW THEY USE YOUR MONEY:**
PROGRAM: $9,856,819:
  - $6,878,527 for ministries to prisoners, ex-prisoners, and their families.
  - $1,745,102 for public education.
  - $628,924 for Prison Fellowship International (assisting in the development of prison ministries at the request of other nations).
  - $604,266 for criminal justice advocacy.
OVERHEAD: $1,168,154.
FUNDRAISING: $1,668,783.
- **EXCESS:** $779,570.
- **LITTLE-KNOWN FACTS:** During the year PFM gave a 1987 Chrysler (bluebook value $11,150) to former president Gordon D. Loux as part of his compensation. Mr. Loux has served as chairman of the Evangelical Council for Financial Accountability. Charles W. Colson, chairman of PFM, had an apartment provided for him during the same period in lieu of hotel accommodations for his traveling on behalf of PFM.
- **RATINGS:** No NCIB report.
- **REGISTRATION:** AZ, CA, KS, NM, PA, TN, VA (1529), and WI.
- **FINANCIAL DATA:** Text and chart source was their IRS form 990 covering 1988.

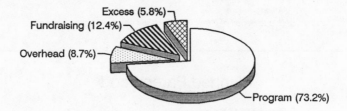

Excess (5.8%)
Fundraising (12.4%)
Overhead (8.7%)
Program (73.2%)

Project CURE, Inc.
140 N. Foster St.
Dothan, AL 36302
(205) 793-6555 • (800) 552-CURE

- ■ **CONTRIBUTIONS** are *not* tax-deductible.
- ■ **PURPOSE:** Founded 1979 by a cancer patient who had used nonconventional treatments for the disease, Project CURE lobbies Congress and the medical community for acceptance of effective and humane cancer treatments, which it believes have been suppressed by the organized medical community. The Center for Alternate Cancer Research, an educational program, was launched in 1986 and provides information about alternative cancer therapies and practitioners of such treatments.
- ■ **SIZE:** More than 100,000 supporters.
- ■ **INCOME:** $11,146,723 (calendar 1988; accrual accounting, IRS form 990).
- ■ **HOW THEY USE YOUR MONEY:**
  PROGRAM: $7,995,803*:
    - • Precisely half of this money went toward lobbying the U.S. Congress on alternative health issues (through encouraging citizens to contact their representatives, and by meeting with members of Congress and their aides).
    - • The other half was spent on educating the public and health professionals on cancer, cancer research, and alternative cancer therapies.
  OVERHEAD: $595,175.*
  FUNDRAISING: $2,718,162.*
- ■ **DEFICIT:** $162,417.
- ■ **RATINGS:** As of June 1, 1990, NCIB had requested but not received sufficient information for a report.
- ■ **REGISTRATION:** AZ, AR, CA, CO, DC, FL, GA, HI, ID, IL, IN, KS, MA, MD, ME, MI, MN, MO, MS, MT, NC, ND, NH, NJ, NM, NV, NY (51731), OH, OK, OR, PA, RI, SC, SD, TN, UT, VA (1535), VT, WA, WI, and WV.
- ■ **FINANCIAL DATA:** Text and chart source was their IRS form 990 covering 1988. Footnote source was their NYS form 497 covering 1988.

*Although the Project's NYS form 497 agrees with its federal tax return figures for total revenues and the size of the group's deficit, there are significant differences in fund distribution. The New York State form indicates $5,078,165 spent on program, $354,204 spent on overhead, and $5,876,771 spent on fundraising.

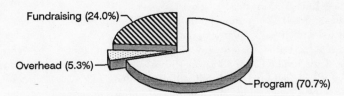

Fundraising (24.0%)
Overhead (5.3%)
Program (70.7%)

Due to deficit of 1.4%, chart is based on spending, not income.

Public Citizen, Inc., and Public Citizen Foundation
2000 P St., N.W., Suite 605
Washington, DC 20036
(202) 293-9142

■ **CONTRIBUTIONS** to Public Citizen are *not* tax-deductible, but contributions to the foundation are.

■ **PURPOSE:** Public Citizen is a consumer-activist group founded by Ralph Nader in 1971. It is concerned with consumer advocacy (lobbying for strong consumer-protection laws), a healthy environment (including safe and clean energy sources) and workplace, and for corporate and government accountability. Contributions to lobbying groups are not tax-deductible, so the Public Citizen Foundation which supports the educational, research, and public information activities of Public Citizen, Inc., was set up for tax-deductible donations.

■ **SIZE:** About 100,000 supporters.

■ **INCOME:** $7,661,851 (parent group); $1,129,482 (foundation; both calendar 1988; accrual accounting, IRS form 990).

■ **HOW THEY USE YOUR MONEY:**
PROGRAM (PARENT GROUP): $4,728,864, including:
- $2,590,696 for publications (including the book *Worst Pills, Best Pills* and the monthly *Health Letter,* which was transferred on 6/1/88 to the foundation).
- $623,322 for litigation.
- $501,310 for health research (monitoring federal agencies having jurisdiction over health products and care, workplace safety, and the environment).
- $411,232 for Buyers Up (a consumer purchasing group for home heating oil, etc.).
- $264,499 for organizing (to educate citizens and mobilize support for Public Citizen efforts).
- $210,632 for Congress Watch (a lobbying group).
- $127,173 for Critical Mass Energy Project (study of the cost, efficiency, and safety of nuclear power).

PROGRAM (FOUNDATION): $1,095,532, including:
- $642,305 in grants to Public Citizen, Inc.
- $369,079 for health research and *Health Letter.*
- $62,138 for production and publications.
- $9,482 for Public Citizen Foundation Development Group; $920 for Critical Mass Energy Projects.

OVERHEAD: $448,426 (parent group); $8,265 (foundation).
FUNDRAISING: $266,497 (parent group only).

■ **EXCESS:** $2,218,064 (parent group); $25,685 (foundation). The large excess recorded for Public Citizen was due to unanticipated earnings from *Best Pills, Worst Pills,* a self-published and self-distributed book which, according to a Public Citizen spokesman, "became almost an instant best-seller, selling half a million copies . . . in 1988. We earned several million dollars on the sale of this book, and paid off some debts with it, and put some money in the bank."

■ **LITTLE-KNOWN FACTS:** Public Citizen makes available a list of toll-free hotline numbers for various government and nongovernmental organizations.

- **RATINGS:** As of June 1, 1990, NCIB had requested but not received sufficient information for a report.
- **REGISTRATION:** NY (46206) and VA (1540).
- **FINANCIAL DATA:** Text and chart sources (parent and foundation) were their IRS forms 990 covering 1988.

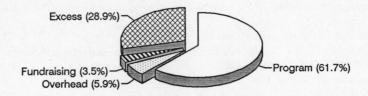

Excess (28.9%)

Fundraising (3.5%)
Overhead (5.9%)

Program (61.7%)

Public Citizen Foundation

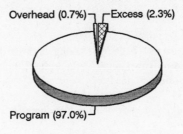

Overhead (0.7%) — Excess (2.3%)

Program (97.0%)

263

Puerto Rican Legal Defense and Education Fund, Inc.
99 Hudson St., 14th Fl.
New York, NY 10013
(212) 219-3360 • (800) 328-2322

- **CONTRIBUTIONS** are tax-deductible.
- **PURPOSE:** Founded in 1972; works to protect and promote the civil rights of Puerto Rican and Hispanic communities, and increase Puerto Rican representation in the legal profession. The fund also engages in class-action litigation in federal courts on important community issues such as housing discrimination, education, and employment.
- **SIZE:** About sixteen staff members.
- **INCOME:** $1,070,119 (year ending 6/30/89; accrual accounting, IRS form 990).
- **HOW THEY USE YOUR MONEY:**
  PROGRAM: $788,158:
    - $648,060 for litigation (to secure protection under the law for Puerto Ricans).
    - $140,098 for education (scholarships for law students and a rights-education program for the Puerto Rican community; a total of $5,000 went toward scholarships).
  OVERHEAD: $43,367.
  FUNDRAISING: $49,054.
- **EXCESS:** $189,540.
- **RATINGS:** NCIB reported (7/26/85, using figures from the year ending 6/30/84) that the Puerto Rican Legal Defense and Education Fund met all eight of NCIB's old evaluation standards.
- **REGISTRATION:** NY (43157).
- **FINANCIAL DATA:** Text and chart source was their IRS form 990 covering the year ending 6/30/89.

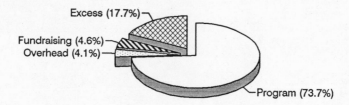

Excess (17.7%)
Fundraising (4.6%)
Overhead (4.1%)
Program (73.7%)

Reading Is Fundamental, Inc.
Smithsonian Institution
600 Maryland Ave., S.W., Suite 500
Washington, DC 20560
(202) 287-3220

- **CONTRIBUTIONS** are tax-deductible.
- **PURPOSE:** First Lady Barbara Bush's favorite good cause was founded in 1966 by Mrs. Robert S. McNamara to put books (more than 93 million since its founding) in the hands of children in schools, libraries, community centers, migrant-labor camps, shelters, hospitals, etc., to motivate children to learn to read.
- **SIZE:** 7,502,624 books distributed to 2,338,252 children in 1988. Three-quarters of the children were aged six to eleven; 11 percent were younger, the rest older.
- **INCOME:** $8,686,449 (year ending 9/30/88; accrual accounting, IRS form 990).
- **HOW THEY USE YOUR MONEY:**
  PROGRAM: $7,887,368:
    - $7,208,331 to distribute books and provide technical assistance.
    - $679,037 for national projects undertaken to provide local programs with materials.
  OVERHEAD: $119,912.
  FUNDRAISING: $63,746.
- **EXCESS:** $615,423.
- **LITTLE-KNOWN FACTS:** The Smithsonian Institution acts as RIF's fiscal agent, providing accounting services, some administrative services, and telephones, for which it charged $115,000 in FY88. In FY88, the Smithsonian was to pay RIF interest of $138,315 on nonfederal contract funds it held as fiscal agent.
- **RATINGS:** NCIB reported (8/7/87, using figures from the year ending 9/30/86) that RIF met all eight of NCIB's old evaluation standards.
- **REGISTRATION:** IL, MN, NJ, NY (49037), and OH.
- **FINANCIAL DATA:** Text and chart source was their IRS form 990 covering the year ending 9/30/88.

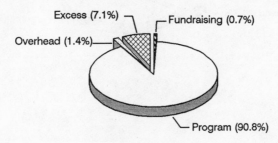

Excess (7.1%) — Fundraising (0.7%)
Overhead (1.4%)
Program (90.8%)

Recording for the Blind
20 Roszel Rd.
Princeton, NJ 08540
(609) 452-0606 • (800) 221-4792

- **CONTRIBUTIONS** are tax-deductible.
- **PURPOSE:** Established in 1948 to serve veterans blinded in World War II. It provides "print-handicapped people with the reading tools to educate themselves in competition with their sighted peers. This objective is accomplished by providing, free of charge, textbooks and educational material recorded by volunteers with specialized knowledge of the subject matter." RFB's annual report is available on cassette tape.
- **SIZE:** In 1988–89 thirty-one recording studios around the country recorded 2,778 new books; a total of 139,554 books were circulated to 23,983 borrowers.
- **INCOME:** $7,718,032 (year ending 6/30/89; annual report).
- **HOW THEY USE YOUR MONEY:**
  PROGRAM: $4,975,290.
  OVERHEAD: $901,611.
  FUNDRAISING: $1,154,257.
  PUBLIC AFFAIRS: $222,131.
- **EXCESS:** $464,743.
- **LITTLE-KNOWN FACTS:** In 1983 former President Richard M. Nixon visited RFB headquarters and recorded his latest book, *Real Peace.*
- **RATINGS:** NCIB reported (4/24/89, using figures from the year ending 6/30/88) that RFB met all nine NCIB standards.
- **REGISTRATION:** CA, MA, MI, MN, NC, NJ, NY (7244), PA, and WI.
- **FINANCIAL DATA:** Text and chart source was their annual report covering the year ending 6/30/89.

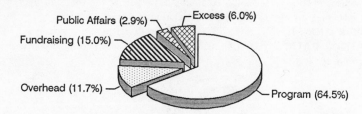

Public Affairs (2.9%)
Excess (6.0%)
Fundraising (15.0%)
Overhead (11.7%)
Program (64.5%)

Religious Coalition for Abortion Rights, Inc.
100 Maryland Avenue, N.E.
Washington, DC 20002
(202) 543-7032

- **CONTRIBUTIONS** are *not* tax-deductible.
- **PURPOSE:** Founded in 1973, the coalition is a group of religious organizations working within religious communities to encourage and coordinate support for safeguarding the legal option of abortion and for all aspects of abortion rights. The coalition also monitors developments in Congress and state legislatures, and alerts members and individuals on both state and national levels accordingly.
- **SIZE:** In 1987, twenty-two affiliates throughout the nation. The quarterly newsletter *Religious Coalition for Abortion Rights—Options* has a circulation of 50,000.
- **INCOME:** $528,771 (calendar 1988; accrual accounting, independently audited statement).
- **HOW THEY USE YOUR MONEY:**
  PROGRAM: $374,421:
  - $196,902 for public outreach.
  - $118,223 (including $85,200 in grants) for state organizing.
  - $59,296 for national legislative program.
  OVERHEAD: $55,164.
  FUNDRAISING: $101,432.
- **DEFICIT:** $2,246.
- **RATINGS:** No NCIB report.
- **REGISTRATION:** MA, NC, NY (52551), and PA.
- **FINANCIAL DATA:** Text and chart source was their independently audited statement covering 1988.

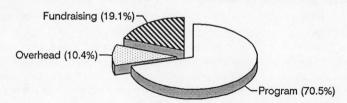

Fundraising (19.1%)
Overhead (10.4%)
Program (70.5%)

Due to deficit of 0.4%, chart is based on spending, not income.

267

Will Rogers Memorial Fund
785 Mamaroneck Ave.
White Plains, NY 10605
(914) 761-5550

■ **CONTRIBUTIONS** are tax-deductible.

■ **PURPOSE:** Founded in 1927 (incorporated in 1936) to raise funds for a sanatorium at Saranac Lake, New York, for entertainers with tuberculosis, which was closed in 1975 as obsolete. The fund still offers medical care (through affiliated hospitals) for entertainment-industry patients with pulmonary diseases, and also funds research (primarily pulmonary but also AIDS research), produces and distributes health-education materials, and studies the effect of nutrition on Alzheimer's disease.

■ **INCOME:** $2,841,075 (year ending 3/31/89; accrual accounting, IRS form 990).

■ **HOW THEY USE YOUR MONEY:**
PROGRAM: $1,581,503:
- $569,341 for health education (messages on TV and 6,000 radio stations).
- $237,225 for medical care (for entertainment and communication employees by pulmonary specialists in sixty-four cities nationwide).
- $774,937 for research (for pulmonary and nutritional research, and fellowships in the fields of AIDS and pulmonary disease).

OVERHEAD: $105,981.
FUNDRAISING: $289,277.

■ **EXCESS:** $864,314. During the year considered, there was an unanticipated increase in money coming from movie audiences. A fund spokeswoman also noted: "Our expenses were down a little that year. Any money [left over after operating expenses] is then put aside so we can keep the grants and research going across the country."

■ **LITTLE-KNOWN FACTS:** Movie-theater ushers often collect audience donations by passing contribution cans after a short film is shown on the fund's work. Because of this practice, the fund's independent auditor notes "it was not practical to extend our audits beyond accounting for the receipts as recorded on the books and records maintained at the office of the fund." In other words, there's no guarantee that all of the money collected at theaters ultimately reaches the Will Rogers Memorial Fund's White Plains office. The NCIB report expressed similar concerns.

■ **RATINGS:** NCIB reported (1/13/89, using figures from the year ending 3/31/88) that the fund did not meet standards 1d and 6b, but it did meet all other NCIB standards.

■ **REGISTRATION:** CT, NJ, NY (4079), PA, and VA (2091).

■ **FINANCIAL DATA:** Text and chart source was their IRS form 990 covering the year ending 3/31/89.

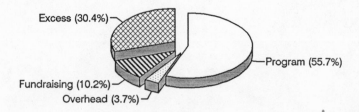

Excess (30.4%)
Program (55.7%)
Fundraising (10.2%)
Overhead (3.7%)

Rural Advancement Fund
(National Sharecroppers Fund)
2128 Commonwealth Ave.
Charlotte, NC 28205
(704) 334-3051

- **CONTRIBUTIONS** to the Rural Advancement Fund are tax-deductible, but contributions to the National Sharecroppers Fund are *not*.
- **PURPOSE:** Founded in 1966 to provide a tax-deductible arm of the NSF, the Rural Advancement Fund seeks "to ensure equal rights for all rural people, and to promote a just, sustainable system of agriculture based on family farms and the wise stewardship of human and environmental resources." This is achieved through technical assistance, financial aid, and educational programs to and for the benefit of rural communities and areas throughout the country.
- **INCOME:** $1,130,859 (year ending 8/31/88; NYS form 497).
- **HOW THEY USE YOUR MONEY:**
  PROGRAM: $569,467. Programs include the Farm Survival Project, the Rural Advancement Fund International, the Rural Justice Project, and the Community Empowerment Project.
  OVERHEAD: $140,447.
  FUNDRAISING: $67,039.
- **EXCESS:** $353,906. According to a fund accountant, most of this figure is a gain on the sale of property: "We had property down in Wadesboro [North Carolina], and we sold it. The money was later used to keep projects going in 1989."
- **RATINGS:** NCIB reported (7/26/89, using figures from the year ending 8/31/88) that the fund met all nine NCIB standards.
- **REGISTRATION:** NY (12873).
- **FINANCIAL DATA:** Text and chart source was their NYS form 497 covering the year ending 8/31/88.

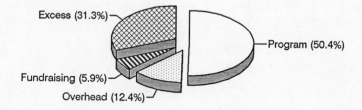

269

Salk Institute for Biological Studies
Box 85800
San Diego, CA 92138
(619) 453-4100

- **CONTRIBUTIONS** are tax-deductible.
- **PURPOSE:** Founded in 1960. Research and advanced instruction are carried out in biology; in the cause, prevention, and cure of disease; and in "the factors and circumstances conducive to the fulfillment of man's biological potential." Work is carried out in six research centers, dealing with cancer, human heredity, brain research, molecular medicine, plant biology, and AIDS research.
- **SIZE:** The staff of more than 500 includes more than 200 doctoral-level scientists and four Nobel laureates.
- **INCOME:** $41,508,646 (year ending 6/30/88; accrual accounting, IRS form 990). The largest grants received (nearly $28 million) came from U.S. government agencies.
- **HOW THEY USE YOUR MONEY:**
  PROGRAM: $31,441,314.
  OVERHEAD: $7,611,694.
  FUNDRAISING: $1,324,065.
- **EXCESS:** $1,131,573.
- **LITTLE-KNOWN FACTS:** Francis Crick, codiscoverer of the structure of DNA (for which he won a Nobel Prize), serves as a Distinguished Research Professor for the institute.
- **RATINGS:** No NCIB report.
- **REGISTRATION:** CA (4214), CT, DC, GA, HI, IL, MA, MD, MI, MN, NC, ND, NE, NJ, NY (10201), OH, OK, OR, PA, RI, SC, TN, VA (1708), and WV.
- **FINANCIAL DATA:** Text and chart source was their IRS form 990 covering the year ending 6/30/88.

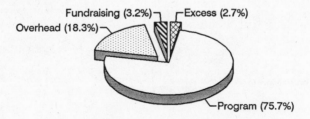

Fundraising (3.2%) — Excess (2.7%)
Overhead (18.3%)
Program (75.7%)

Save the Children Federation

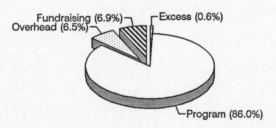

Fundraising (6.9%) — Excess (0.6%)
Overhead (6.5%)
Program (86.0%)

Save the Children Federation, Inc.
54 Wilton Rd.
PO Box 950
Westport, CT 06881
(203) 221-4000 • Sponsor Information: (800) 243-5075

- **CONTRIBUTIONS** are tax-deductible.
- **PURPOSE:** Founded in 1932 to aid Appalachian victims of the Great Depression. In 1939 operations were expanded to include European war refugees. STCF's stated purpose, to address "the critical needs of children and their families around the world through community development," is served in forty-three countries, including the United States. Programs include refugee and disaster relief, human resources development, education and training, health and nutrition, small-scale industry and crafts, community improvement, and agriculture.
- **SIZE:** Over 160,000 sponsors and contributors.
- **INCOME:** $84,301,087 (year ending 6/30/88; accrual accounting, IRS form 990). Apart from a dip in FY86, during the preceding four fiscal years support had been increasing.
- **HOW THEY USE YOUR MONEY:**
PROGRAM: $72,480,940:
  - $35,732,825 (including $28,606,241 in grants and allocations) for refugee and disaster relief (sometimes direct relief; more often long-term development).
  - $13,974,998 (including $4,898,372 in grants and allocations) for education and human development.
  - $7,789,820 (including $2,706,379 in grants and allocations) for health and nutrition.
  - $4,856,501 (including $1,648,480 in grants and allocations) for community and home infrastructure.
  - $4,531,047 (including $1,563,995 in grants and allocations) for food production and agriculture.
  - $4,503,141 (including $1,755,498 in grants and allocations) for enterprise (support of crafts, cooperatives, credit unions, and savings-and-loan groups).
  - $1,092,608 (including $370,855 in grants and allocations) for resource conservation.

OVERHEAD: $5,511,436.
FUNDRAISING: $5,787,195.
- **EXCESS:** $521,516.
- **LITTLE-KNOWN FACTS:** In the wake of the Ethiopian famine of 1984–85, STCF has given special attention to the needs of more than 150,000 orphaned children. The federation has a network of group homes in local villages. Each home accommodates no more than six children and is run by a resident housemother— often a local widow who lost her own family in the famine. According to the 1988 STCF annual report, "the group homes are now being replicated nationwide."
- **RATINGS:** NCIB reported (8/16/88, using figures from the year ending 6/30/87), that the group met all nine NCIB standards.
- **REGISTRATION:** NY (11226) and VA (1719).
- **FINANCIAL DATA:** Text and chart source was their IRS form 990 covering the year ending 6/30/88.

The Salvation Army
National Headquarters
799 Bloomfield Ave.
Verona, NJ 07044
(201) 239-0606

- **CONTRIBUTIONS** are tax-deductible.
- **PURPOSE:** Founded in England in 1865, first came to the United States in 1880, and was incorporated in New York in 1899. It is an international religious and charitable movement organized and operated on a "quasi-military" pattern, in which clergy are officers and adherents are soldiers. The Salvation Army works with the homeless, drug addicts, unwed mothers, prisoners, poor children, and senior citizens; preaches the Gospel; supplies basic human necessities; provides personal counseling; and undertakes the spiritual, moral, and physical regeneration of anyone in need who comes within its sphere.
- **SIZE:** Nationwide, 12,061,990 hours of service from 1,132,360 volunteers.
- **INCOME:** $4,611,857 (national headquarters; year ending 9/30/89; annual report).
- **HOW THEY USE YOUR MONEY:**
  PROGRAM: $3,032,185:
  - $2,549,395 for national publications.
  - $281,792 for national communications.
  - $144,926 for national public affairs.
  - $56,072 for the Asbury, New Jersey, Student Center.

  OVERHEAD: $1,407,787.

  FUNDRAISING: The annual report lists no specific amount for fundraising.
- **EXCESS:** $171,885.
- **LITTLE-KNOWN FACTS:** During the year the Salvation Army lodged 5,055,904 homeless people, helped 6,052,336 individuals during Thanksgiving and Christmas, and served a total of 49,746,288 meals.
- **RATINGS:** No NCIB report.
- **REGISTRATION:** VA (1709).
- **FINANCIAL DATA:** Text and chart source was their annual report (for the national headquarters *only*) covering the year ending 9/30/89.

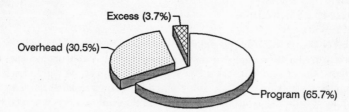

Excess (3.7%)

Overhead (30.5%)

Program (65.7%)

Second Harvest, the National Food Bank Network
116 S. Michigan Ave., Suite 4
Chicago, IL 60603
(312) 263-2303

- **CONTRIBUTIONS** are tax-deductible.
- **PURPOSE:** Begun in 1979 as an outgrowth of a local agency in Phoenix, Arizona, that solicited and distributed food; now grown to a nationwide network of certified food banks. The food banks distribute food to day-care and senior centers, soup kitchens, drug and alcohol treatment centers, shelters, after-school programs, and church groups with meal programs. Recently Second Harvest has repackaged some of its bulk food donations into smaller, more manageable packages.
- **SIZE:** In 1989 Second Harvest distributed its two-billionth pound of food to its 185 member food banks in forty-five states.
- **INCOME:** $2,290,028 (calendar 1989; independently audited statement). Second Harvest receives no government funding.
- **HOW THEY USE YOUR MONEY:**
  PROGRAM: $1,854,569:
    - $845,656 for network services, including the training and technical services (e.g., annual monitoring, compliance verification) given to the food bank network.
    - $464,679 for distribution of donated products.
    - $293,049 for product solicitation.
    - $251,185 for public education on hunger, food banking, etc.
  OVERHEAD: $230,402.
  FUNDRAISING: $146,525.
- **EXCESS:** $58,532.
- **LITTLE-KNOWN FACTS:** Second Harvest does not take title to any donated food (it only serves as a conduit for the food's distribution), so the value of the food is not noted in financial statements. However, according to unaudited totals given in the 1989 Second Harvest annual report, the group solicited 153 million (unaudited) pounds of product from 244 national companies, and member food banks received an additional 266 million (inaudited) pounds in donations from local companies. The market value of one pound of food in 1989 was $2.02.
- **RATINGS:** NCIB reported (2/11/87, based on figures from calendar 1985) that Second Harvest met all eight of NCIB's old evaluation standards.
- **REGISTRATION:** IL, NY (53975), and VA (3071).
- **FINANCIAL DATA:** Text and chart source was their independently audited statement covering 1989.

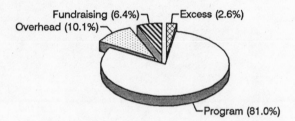

Fundraising (6.4%)
Overhead (10.1%)
Excess (2.6%)
Program (81.0%)

Sex Information and Education Council
of the United States
32 Washington Pl.
New York, NY 10003
(212) 673-3850

- **CONTRIBUTIONS** are tax-deductible.
- **PURPOSE:** Founded in 1964, SIECUS is a group of educators, social workers, physicians, clergy, youth organizations, and parents' groups interested in human-sexuality education and sexual health care. SIECUS supports scientific research into human sexuality; promotes social policies that foster positive attitudes, values, and practices related to human sexuality; and encourages development of responsible, nonexploitative sexual behavior. The bimonthly *SIECUS Report* covers sex education, human sexuality, and AIDS.
- **SIZE:** About 3,600 members.
- **INCOME:** $333,015 (year ending 9/30/88; NYS form 497).
- **HOW THEY USE YOUR MONEY:**
  PROGRAM: $192,659.
  OVERHEAD: $97,440.
  FUNDRAISING: $18,572.
- **EXCESS:** $24,344.
- **RATINGS:** No NCIB report.
- **REGISTRATION:** NY (11895).
- **FINANCIAL DATA:** Text and chart source was their NYS form 497 covering the year ending 9/30/88.

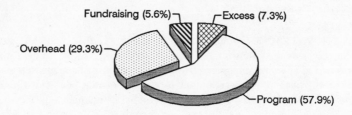

Fundraising (5.6%) — Excess (7.3%)
Overhead (29.3%) —
Program (57.9%)

Shriners' Hospitals for Crippled Children
PO Box 31356
Tampa, FL 33631
(813) 281-0300 • (800) 237-5055

- **CONTRIBUTIONS** are tax-deductible.
- **PURPOSE:** A network of twenty-two hospitals supported by members of the Shrine of North America, which offer free special medical care to children (regardless of race, religion, or relationship to a Shriner) up to their eighteenth birthday. Nineteen hospitals treat children with orthopedic problems, and three Shriners' burn institutes give medical, surgical, and rehabilitative care to severely burned children.
- **SIZE:** 1,546 pediatric burn victims and 15,004 orthopedic pediatric patients were admitted to hospitals during 1988; 6,523 burn victims and 140,874 orthopedic patients visited outpatient clinics.
- **INCOME:** $339,265,930 (calendar 1988; accrual accounting, IRS form 990).
- **HOW THEY USE YOUR MONEY:**
  PROGRAM: $142,820,532:
  - $116,508,217 for treatment of orthopedic pediatric patients.
  - $26,312,315 for treatment of pediatric burn victims.
  OVERHEAD: $8,961,502.
  FUNDRAISING: $2,037,964.
- **EXCESS:** $185,445,932. Lewis Molnar, executive vice-president of the hospitals, points out that, because nearly all of the hospitals' income comes from earnings on their endowment fund, excess moneys are "retained for investment purposes to generate additional revenues to support our operations in future years."
- **LITTLE-KNOWN FACTS:** The Philadelphia hospital pursues clinical research on computer-controlled neuromuscular stimulation of paralyzed muscles. The long-term goal is to enable children to stand and walk; so far two patients have achieved standing.
- **RATINGS:** As of June 1, 1990, NCIB had requested but not received sufficient information for a report.
- **REGISTRATION:** CA and PA.
- **FINANCIAL DATA:** Text and chart source was their IRS form 990 covering 1988.

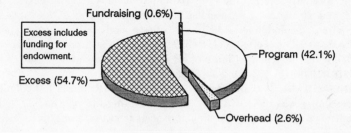

Fundraising (0.6%)

Excess includes funding for endowment.

Excess (54.7%)

Program (42.1%)

Overhead (2.6%)

Sierra Club
730 Polk St.
San Francisco, CA 94109
(415) 776-2211

- **CONTRIBUTIONS** are *not* tax-deductible.
- **PURPOSE:** Founded in 1892 by naturalist John Muir to explore, enjoy, and protect the earth's wilderness areas, the Sierra Club has always sponsored nature-appreciation outings. In 1976 it organized SCCOPE (Sierra Club Committee on Political Education), a political-action committee. In 1988 club members identified global warming as one of the top three priorities to be addressed in a national conservation campaign during 1989–91.
- **SIZE:** Fifty-seven volunteer chapters, more than 350 volunteer groups, over 490,000 members.
- **INCOME:** $28,359,498 (year ending 9/30/88; accrual accounting, IRS form 990), including $331,680 in royalty payments from the Sierra Club affinity card.
- **HOW THEY USE YOUR MONEY:**
  PROGRAM: $19,041,995:
    - $6,765,740 (including grants and allocations totaling $33,964) for studying and influencing public policy (this included received donated legal services of $3,309,800).
    - $4,672,504 for membership.
    - $4,327,600 for information and education (such as Sierra Club Books and *Sierra* magazine).
    - $3,206,154 for outdoor activities (national and international outing programs).
    - $69,997 for affiliates.
  OVERHEAD: $5,586,832.
  FUNDRAISING: $3,430,243.
- **EXCESS:** $300,428.
- **LITTLE-KNOWN FACTS:** Sierra Club maintains a complicated financial arrangement with the Sierra Club Foundation and the Sierra Club Legal Defense Fund. In 1988, the foundation contributed $1,481,700 and the fund contributed $3,309,800 in legal services to the Sierra Club. In addition, the club's wholly owned subsidiary, Sierra Club Property Management, Inc., is the general partner of National Headquarters Associates (a limited partnership), which was formed to acquire and rehabilitate a building to house both club and foundation.
- **RATINGS:** NCIB reported (11/9/89, using figures from the year ending 9/30/88) that the Sierra Club met all nine NCIB standards.
- **REGISTRATION:** CA (4332), NY (12554), VA (2383), and WI.
- **FINANCIAL DATA:** Text and chart source was their IRS form 990 (affinity-card income source was their IRS form 990-T) covering the year ending 9/30/88. Little-Known Facts source was their financial report covering the same year.

Sierra Club Foundation
730 Polk St.
San Francisco, CA 94109
(415) 923-5679

- **CONTRIBUTIONS** are tax-deductible.
- **PURPOSE:** Founded in 1960, the Sierra Club Foundation receives, administers, and distributes funds for charitable, scientific, literary, and educational programs. It has the status of lobbying charity, and can, on a limited basis, support and carry out legislative programs.
- **INCOME:** $3,981,829 (year ending 9/30/88; accrual accounting, IRS form 990).
- **HOW THEY USE YOUR MONEY:**
  PROGRAM: $1,990,290 (distributed in the form of grants and allocations*):
  - $909,809 for general conservation.
  - $810,977 for educational and research programs.
  - $186,435 for legal aid lobbying.
  - $83,069 for land preservation.
  OVERHEAD: $374,004.
  FUNDRAISING: $1,002,924. Fundraising is under contract and in conjunction with the Sierra Club, and no other organization.
- **EXCESS:** $614,611.
- **LITTLE-KNOWN FACTS:** Gifts to the Sierra Club *Foundation* which are distributed as grants or allocations to the Sierra Club are the sole source of tax-deductible support to that group.
- **RATINGS:** NCIB reported (8/28/87, using figures from the year ending 9/30/86) that the foundation met all eight of NCIB's old evaluation standards.
- **REGISTRATION:** CA (02363) and NY (43182).
- **FINANCIAL DATA:** Text and chart source was their IRS form 990 covering the year ending 9/30/88. Footnote source: their annual report for the same year.

*Applications for grants are carefully screened to be sure the projects are nonpolitical. Among the grants was $45,000 to the Sierra Club Legal Defense Fund to pay a portion of administrative expenses associated with fundraising.

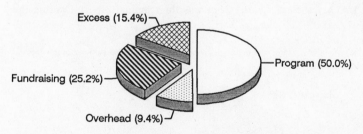

Excess (15.4%)
Fundraising (25.2%)
Overhead (9.4%)
Program (50.0%)

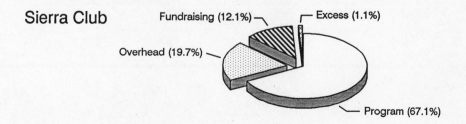

Sierra Club

Fundraising (12.1%)
Excess (1.1%)
Overhead (19.7%)
Program (67.1%)

Sierra Club Legal Defense Fund, Inc.
2044 Fillmore St.
San Francisco, CA 94115
(415) 567-6100

- **CONTRIBUTIONS** are tax-deductible.
- **PURPOSE:** Founded in 1970 as a public-interest environmental law firm, it provides attorneys and limited financial resources to the Sierra Club, other citizen groups, and individuals. Although it works closely with the Sierra Club, it is independent and not part of it.
- **SIZE:** More than 120,000 members.
- **INCOME:** $8,295,344 (year ending 7/31/89; annual report). During the preceding four fiscal years support had been increasing.
- **HOW THEY USE YOUR MONEY:**
  PROGRAM: $4,748,452* for public information and litigation. Among the organizations represented by the fund in litigation were the American Lung Association (Hawaii); Defenders of Wildlife; the Environmental Defense Fund; Friends of the Earth; Greenpeace USA; the Humane Society of the United States; the Natural Resources Defense Council; the Sierra Club; the Wilderness Society; and various local offices of the Audubon Society.
  OVERHEAD: $499,339.
  FUNDRAISING: $1,490,965.*
- **EXCESS:** $1,556,558, earmarked for long, expensive litigation already in progress, including a suit which would force Exxon to remain in Alaska as long as necessary to clean up the *Exxon Valdez* spill, restore (as much as possible) the Prince William Sound ecosystem, and pay civil penalties to the government.
- **LITTLE-KNOWN FACTS:** The fund acted internationally in 1988, petitioning a United Nations agency for a group of Ecuadorian Indians whose rain-forest homeland was threatened by an American oil company.
- **RATINGS:** NCIB reported (8/28/86, using figures from the year ending 7/31/85) that the Sierra Club Legal Defense Fund met all eight of NCIB's old evaluation standards.
- **REGISTRATION:** CA (13012), IL, MI, NJ, NY (49314), WA, WI, and WV.
- **FINANCIAL DATA:** Text and chart source was their annual report covering the year ending 7/31/89.

*Costs for $554,000 worth of dual-purpose mailings were allocated thus: $441,000 to fundraising and $113,000 to public information.

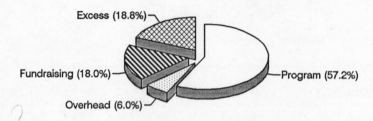

Excess (18.8%)
Fundraising (18.0%)
Overhead (6.0%)
Program (57.2%)

Southern Christian Leadership Conference
334 Auburn Ave., N.E.
Atlanta, GA 30303
(404) 522-1420

- **CONTRIBUTIONS** are *not* tax-deductible.
- **PURPOSE:** Founded in 1957 (the first president was Dr. Martin Luther King, Jr.), SCLC is a nonsectarian coordinating and service agency for local groups seeking full citizenship rights, equality, and the integration of African Americans in all aspects of life in the United States. SCLC subscribes to the Gandhian philosophy of nonviolence.
- **SIZE:** SCLC's eighty chapters work primarily in sixteen southern and border states.
- **INCOME:** $638,801 (year ending 6/30/85—the latest NYS form 497 filing available).
- **HOW THEY USE YOUR MONEY:**
  PROGRAM: $513,205.
  OVERHEAD: $186,397.
  FUNDRAISING: $20,338.
- **DEFICIT:** $81,139.
- **RATINGS:** As of June 1, 1990, NCIB had requested but not received sufficient information for a report.
- **REGISTRATION:** NY (42805).
- **FINANCIAL DATA:** Text and chart source was their NYS form 497 covering the year ending 6/30/85 (latest available).

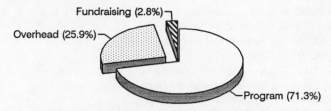

Fundraising (2.8%)
Overhead (25.9%)
Program (71.3%)

Due to deficit of 11.3%, chart is based on spending, not income.

Special Olympics International Headquarters
1350 New York Ave., N.W., Suite 500
Washington, DC 20005
(202) 628-3630

- **CONTRIBUTIONS** are tax-deductible.
- **PURPOSE:** Incorporated in 1968, provides year-round sports training and athletic competition in a variety of Olympic-type sports for children and adults with mental retardation.
- **SIZE:** Chapters in all fifty states, the District of Columbia, Guam, American Samoa, and the U.S. Virgin Islands, and seventy-eight national programs abroad.
- **INCOME:** $26,419,000 (year ending 6/30/89; combined independently audited statement for Special Olympics International and supporting organization). Nike's donation of 48,611 pairs of shoes was not recorded as support. In FY89 sales of *A Very Special Christmas,* a benefit album created with donated artist and producer time, earned $6,000,000 in net proceeds after A & M Records deducted production and distribution costs. In FY88 the album earned $5,000,000.
- **HOW THEY USE YOUR MONEY:**
PROGRAM: $16,010,562, including:
  - $4,371,086 for distributions to U.S. chapters.
  - $2,841,915 for public affairs and education.
  - $2,569,667 for sports and training programs.
  - $2,338,565 for distributions to international games.
  - $1,989,905 for international programs.
  - $1,657,284 for U.S. chapter programs.
  - $184,607 for International Games programs.

  OVERHEAD: $2,036,894, including:
  - $1,145,868 for executive services.
  - $864,917 for finance and administration.

  FUNDRAISING: $3,209,391:
  - $1,827,693 for direct-mail campaigns.
  - $797,199 for marketing and development.
  - $507,943 for telemarketing campaigns.
  - $76,556 for Combined Federal Campaign-domestic.
- **EXCESS:** $5,162,153.
- **LITTLE-KNOWN FACTS:** The Special Olympics were begun by the Joseph P. Kennedy, Jr., Foundation (which has several board members in common with SOI) and maintain ties to the Kennedy family—five family members or in-laws sit on the board and others are sizable donors, and vice-president Rafer Johnson was an aide to Robert F. Kennedy when the latter was assassinated in 1968. According to SOI's independently audited statement, "the Joseph P. Kennedy Family Fund is a restricted fund of SOI held for purposes to be designated by the Kennedy Family." The family's interest is probably explained by the fact that Rosemary Kennedy, a sister of the late president, is mentally retarded.
- **RATINGS:** As of June 1, 1990, NCIB was preparing a new report.
- **REGISTRATION:** CA, DC, NY (46238), and VA (2488).
- **FINANCIAL DATA:** Text and chart source was the combined independently audited statement (for Special Olympics International, Inc., and supporting organization; no state and national affiliates) covering the year ending 6/30/89.

Statue of Liberty–Ellis Island Foundation, Inc.
52 Vanderbilt Ave.
New York, NY 10017
(212) 883-1986

- **CONTRIBUTIONS** are tax-deductible.
- **PURPOSE:** Incorporated in 1981 to raise funds to preserve and restore the two national landmarks and to plan for their centennial celebrations (the statue's in 1986, Ellis Island's in 1992).
- **INCOME:** $21,927,883 (year ending 3/31/89; accrual accounting, IRS form 990).
- **HOW THEY USE YOUR MONEY:**
  PROGRAM: $35,326,637:
    - $34,883,794 (including $8,362,924 in grants and allocations to the National Park Service) went toward restoration and preservation of the Statue of Liberty National Monument.
    - $442,843 was spent on public awareness and education.
  OVERHEAD: $1,255,367.
  FUNDRAISING: $2,593,513. Unusual fundraising efforts have included one of the first affinity cards (donations from American Express); commemorative coins minted by the U.S. Treasury ($773,834 received in FY89); and the American Immigrant Wall of Honor (a $100 contribution ensures one name on the Ellis Island wall; $8,131,362 received in FY89).
- **DEFICIT:** $17,247,634.
- **LITTLE-KNOWN FACTS:** The foundation's NYC office lease expires in May 1992, the year of the Ellis Island celebration.
- **RATINGS:** NCIB reported (7/22/88, using figures from the year ending 3/31/87) that the foundation met all nine NCIB standards.
- **REGISTRATION:** AR, CA (51650), CT (2175), DC, FL (186596), GA, HI (015-0192-01), IL (13774), KS (12SC F20758), MA (018594), MD, ME (747), MI (MICS 9675), MN, NC, ND (11, 572FNP), NE (01383), NH, NJ (2684-02797), NM, NY (51229), OH (0785-19), OK, OR (125-12804), PA (3440), RI, SC (306), TN (471), VA (1806), WA, WI, and WV.
- **FINANCIAL DATA:** Text and chart source was their IRS form 990 covering the year ending 3/31/89.

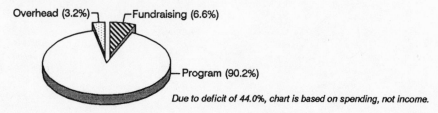

Overhead (3.2%) — Fundraising (6.6%)

— Program (90.2%)

Due to deficit of 44.0%, chart is based on spending, not income.

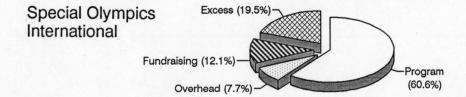

Special Olympics International

Excess (19.5%) —

Fundraising (12.1%) —

Overhead (7.7%) —

— Program (60.6%)

Straight, Inc.
3001 Gandy Blvd.
St. Petersburg, FL 33702
(813) 576-8929 • Hotline: (800) 9-FRIEND

- **CONTRIBUTIONS** are tax-deductible.
- **PURPOSE:** Founded in 1985 by the Straight Foundation (established in 1976), a voluntary, family-oriented drug-treatment program for youths, based on peer support (kids helping kids, parents helping parents, and families helping families) under the supervision of trained professionals.
- **SIZE:** Twenty-five facilities, mainly in East Coast states, and in Michigan, Texas, California, and Washington, have treated over 35,000 family members since 1976.
- **INCOME:** $12,112,698 (year ending 9/30/88; independently audited statement).
- **HOW THEY USE YOUR MONEY:**
  PROGRAM: $8,693,990.
  OVERHEAD: $1,214,226.
  FUNDRAISING: $570,857.
- **EXCESS:** $1,633,625.
- **LITTLE-KNOWN FACTS:** 70 percent of the graduates from Straight's five-phase program remain drug-free.
- **RATINGS:** No NCIB report.
- **REGISTRATION:** VA (2593).
- **FINANCIAL DATA:** Text and chart source was their independently audited statement covering the year ending 9/30/88.

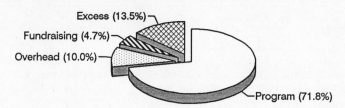

282

Sunshine Foundation
4010 Levick St.
Philadelphia, PA 19135
(215) 335-2622

- **CONTRIBUTIONS** are tax-deductible.
- **PURPOSE:** Founded in 1976, the Sunshine Foundation is a group of volunteers who fulfill the wishes of chronically or terminally ill children, most of whom suffer from kidney disease, leukemia, or cancer.
- **SIZE:** Over 10,000 requests granted since 1976.
- **INCOME:** $1,440,764 (year ending 6/30/89; accrual accounting, IRS form 990).
- **HOW THEY USE YOUR MONEY:**
  PROGRAM: $1,017,952.
  OVERHEAD: $303,619.
  FUNDRAISING: $365,092.
- **DEFICIT:** $245,899.
- **LITTLE-KNOWN FACTS:** The foundation runs a travel agency that grossed $185,455 in the year considered.
- **RATINGS:** NCIB reported (1/26/90, using figures from the year ending 6/30/88) that the group met all nine NCIB standards.
- **REGISTRATION:** NY (52177), VA (1829), and forty-three other states.
- **FINANCIAL DATA:** Text and chart source was their IRS form 990 covering the year ending 6/30/89.

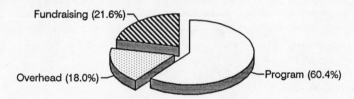

Fundraising (21.6%)

Overhead (18.0%)

Program (60.4%)

Due to deficit of 14.6%, chart is based on spending, not income.

TechnoServe, Inc.
148 East Ave.
Norwalk, CT 06851
(203) 852-0377 • (800) 99-WORKS

■ **CONTRIBUTIONS** are tax-deductible.

■ **PURPOSE:** A private, nonsectarian international development organization founded in 1968, "a working solution to world hunger." By providing technical and management assistance to community-based enterprises owned by rural groups in Africa and Latin America, TechnoServe seeks to increase food production and improve local conditions (health, nutrition, education, living conditions, and economies) from the bottom up, avoiding long-term dependence on outside aid.

■ **SIZE:** Ninety-six major activities assisting agricultural enterprises and institutions directly benefited 534,000 people and helped produce, process, and bring to market 100 million pounds of food and fiber in 1988.

■ **INCOME:** $6,661,237 (calendar 1988; accrual accounting, IRS form 990).

■ **HOW THEY USE YOUR MONEY:**
PROGRAM: $5,371,361:
  • $2,622,527 for over thirty enterprises in Africa (Ghana, Kenya, Zaire, Rwanda, and the Sudan).
  • $2,294,138 for fifty-four enterprises in Latin America (Costa Rica, El Salvador, Panama, and Peru).
  • $62,746 for the Belize Enterprise for Sustained Technology.
  • $140,311 for working visits to several potential host countries.
  • $251,639 to explain TechnoServe's methods to other nonprofits and similar development institutions.
OVERHEAD: $918,124.
FUNDRAISING: $463,738.

■ **DEFICIT:** $91,986.

■ **LITTLE-KNOWN FACTS:** An example of how TechnoServe works: Their Sudanese staff realized that knowledge of current national market prices would help poor farmers, who are often at the mercy of unscrupulous buyers. Research showed that nearly half of the farmers in the Sudan's El Obeid district listened to the radio between 3 and 6 P.M. This information was brought to the Agricultural Bank of Sudan, the auction-market administration, and the Kordofan Radio Broadcast Service. Beginning in 1988, auction-market prices became a regular part of the five-o'clock news report, and village dealers had to raise their buying prices. "Initial figures show an average increase in small farmers' net margin on sesame of 31 percent."

■ **RATINGS:** NCIB reported (7/27/90, using figures from calendar 1989) that TechnoServe met all nine NCIB standards.

■ **REGISTRATION:** CA, CT, IL, IN, MA, MD, ME, MI, MN, ND, NE, NY (41389), OH, OK, VA (1838), and WI.

■ **FINANCIAL DATA:** Text and chart source was their IRS form 990 covering 1988.

284

Union of Concerned Scientists, Inc.
26 Church St.
Cambridge, MA 02238
(617) 547-5552

- **CONTRIBUTIONS** are tax-deductible.
- **PURPOSE:** Established in 1969 as an informal Boston area faculty group, UCS is now "an independent, nonprofit organization of scientists and other citizens concerned about the impact of advanced technology on society." It advocates national-security policies that reduce the threat of nuclear war, and it works for an environmentally sound energy policy and for nuclear-power safety.
- **SIZE:** 100,000 sponsors nationwide.
- **INCOME:** $3,128,248 (year ending 9/30/88; accrual accounting, IRS form 990).
- **HOW THEY USE YOUR MONEY:**
  PROGRAM: $2,434,201:
    - $1,479,153 for the nuclear-arms program (research by scientists, engineers, and other professionals on effects of nuclear arms and public education).
    - $741,026 for the energy program (independent research on nuclear-plant safety, disseminating the results to the public).
    - $214,022 to the legislative program (congressional committee appearances and meetings with individual congressmen; writing, printing, and mailing legislative alerts to UCS sponsors).
  OVERHEAD: $109,277.
  FUNDRAISING: $620,014.
- **DEFICIT:** $35,244.
- **LITTLE-KNOWN FACTS:** UCS's energy-policy research and public-education efforts have expanded to include global warming and the greenhouse effect.
- **RATINGS:** NCIB reported (12/21/88, using figures from the year ending 9/30/87) that UCS met all nine NCIB standards.
- **REGISTRATION:** CA, DC, IL, MA, MD, MI, MN, NC, NJ, NY (47828), OR, and WI.
- **FINANCIAL DATA:** Text and chart source was their IRS form 990 covering the year ending 9/30/88.

Fundraising (19.6%)

Overhead (3.5%)

Program (76.9%)

Due to deficit of 1.1%, chart is based on spending, not income.

TechnoServe, Inc.

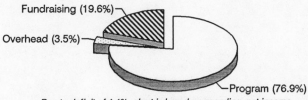

Fundraising (6.9%)

Overhead (13.6%)

Program (79.5%)

Due to deficit of 1.4%, chart is based on spending, not income.

United Cerebral Palsy Association, Inc.
370 Seventh Ave.
New York, NY 10001
(212) 268-6655

- **CONTRIBUTIONS** are tax-deductible.
- **PURPOSE:** Founded in 1948, UCPA is a national grouping of state and local affiliates working to help persons with cerebral palsy and their families. UCPA seeks to prevent cerebral palsy, minimize the disease's effects, and mainstream affected individuals. Programs include support of research; medical, therapeutic, and social services for people with cerebral palsy; and vocational training and special education.
- **SIZE:** Nearly 200 member groups.
- **INCOME:** $5,132,034 (year ending 9/30/88; National Office of the United Cerebral Palsy Association, NYS form 497).
- **HOW THEY USE YOUR MONEY:**
  PROGRAM: $2,871,480.
  OVERHEAD: $1,639,476.
  FUNDRAISING: $949,847.
- **DEFICIT:** $328,769.
- **RATINGS:** As of June 1, 1990, NCIB was preparing a new report.
- **REGISTRATION:** NY (8415) and VA (1886).
- **FINANCIAL DATA:** Text and chart source was their NYS form 497 (for the national headquarters *only*) covering the year ending 9/30/88.

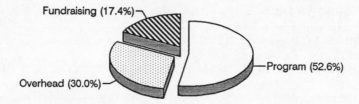

Fundraising (17.4%)

Program (52.6%)

Overhead (30.0%)

Due to deficit of 6.0%, chart is based on spending, not income.

United Jewish Appeal
99 Park Ave.
New York, NY 10016
(212) 818-9100

- **CONTRIBUTIONS** are tax-deductible.
- **PURPOSE:** Founded just over fifty years ago to raise funds for the United Israel Appeal, Inc. (UIA), which distributes them in Israel through the Jewish Agency. Contributions also support the American Jewish Joint Distribution Committee, Inc. (JDC, which aids Jews in thirty-four countries, including Israel), the New York Association for New Americans, Inc. (NYANA, a program to help immigrants), the Israel Education Fund (which has built about 700 cultural and educational facilities in Israel since 1964), and Project Renewal (since 1977, has paired U.S. communities with disadvantaged Israeli neighborhoods to help modernize them).
- **SIZE:** The UJA/Federation Campaign comprises 168 Jewish federations and 377 nonfederated campaigns in the United States.
- **INCOME:** $377,720,000 (year ending 6/30/89; annual report).
- **HOW THEY USE YOUR MONEY:**
PROGRAM: $343,305,000:
  - $270,261,000 for UIA (including $6,827,000 for the Israel Education Fund and $13,320,000 for Project Renewal).
  - $60,125,000 for JDC.
  - $12,217,000 for NYANA.
  - $702,000 for the Council of Jewish Federations, Inc.
OVERHEAD: $2,735,000.
FUNDRAISING: $19,205,000 (including campaign expenses of $16,828,000 and missions expenses of $2,377,000).
- **EXCESS:** $12,475,000.
- **RATINGS:** No NCIB report.
- **REGISTRATION:** NY.
- **FINANCIAL DATA:** Text and chart source was their annual report covering the year ending 6/30/89.

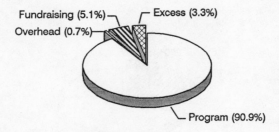

287

United Negro College Fund
500 E. 62nd St.
New York, NY 10021
(212) 326-1100 • (212) 644-9600 • (800) 331-2244

- **CONTRIBUTIONS** are tax-deductible.
- **PURPOSE:** The largest black fundraising organization in the nation, formed in 1944 to assist historically black colleges and universities to raise funds from the public.
- **SIZE:** Forty-one member institutions (Clark College and Atlanta University merged in July 1989, *after* the profile period).
- **INCOME:** $45,844,100 (year ending 3/31/89; accrual accounting, IRS form 990). During the preceding four fiscal years support had been increasing.
- **HOW THEY USE YOUR MONEY:**
  PROGRAM: $31,293,617:
  - $28,601,377 distributed to member and nonmember institutions.
  - $2,692,240 for services to forty-two member institutions ($737,796 for institutional services, $954,889 for special projects, $664,779* for public education and information, $34,585 for UNCF health and human services, and $300,191 for workshop training).
  OVERHEAD: $2,731,090.
  FUNDRAISING: $8,168,644.*
- **EXCESS:** $3,650,749.
- **LITTLE-KNOWN FACTS:** President George Bush served as a UNCF volunteer in 1948. Vice-President Dan Quayle, on the other hand, had difficulty remembering the exact phrasing of UNCF's famous slogan, "A Mind Is a Terrible Thing to Waste," during a speech to the group in 1989.
- **RATINGS:** NCIB reported (2/11/88, using figures from the year ending 3/31/87) that the UNCF met all eight of NCIB's old evaluation standards.
- **REGISTRATION:** NY (7086) and VA (1907).
- **FINANCIAL DATA:** Text and chart source was their IRS form 990 covering the year ending 3/31/89. Footnote and member institutions' program expenses source was their independently audited statement covering the same year.

*The fund's national telethon (for fundraising and education) spent $3,642,855 and raised $9,327,210. Of the costs, $533,046 was allocated to public education and information, the rest to fundraising.

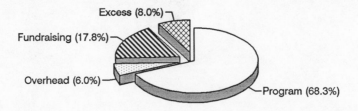

Excess (8.0%)
Fundraising (17.8%)
Overhead (6.0%)
Program (68.3%)

United Neighborhood Centers of America, Inc.
1319 F St., N.W., Suite 603
Washington, DC 20004
(202) 393-3929

- **CONTRIBUTIONS** are tax-deductible.
- **PURPOSE:** Founded in 1911 (in 1959 became the National Federation of Settlements and, in 1979, the National Federation of Settlements and Neighborhood Centers), UNCA promotes "the welfare of settlements and of the neighborhoods in which they are located" and helps them to "act on public matters of interest." A settlement helps neighbors, and motivates them to make their needs known and to join forces in meeting their own specific problems.
- **INCOME:** $298,753 (calendar 1988; NYS form 497).
- **HOW THEY USE YOUR MONEY:**
  PROGRAM: $260,245.
  OVERHEAD: $45,470.
  FUNDRAISING: $11,432.
- **DEFICIT:** $18,394.
- **RATINGS:** NCIB reported (10/3/86, using figures from calendar 1985) that United Neighborhood Centers of America met all eight of NCIB's old evaluation standards.
- **REGISTRATION:** NY (11901).
- **FINANCIAL DATA:** Text and chart source was their NYS form 497 covering 1988.

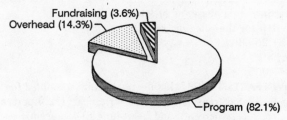

Fundraising (3.6%)
Overhead (14.3%)
Program (82.1%)

Due to deficit of 5.8%, chart is based on spending, not income.

289

United Network for Organ Sharing
1100 Boulders Parkway, Suite 500
PO Box 13770
Richmond, VA 23225
(804) 330-8517 • (800) 24-DONOR

■ **CONTRIBUTIONS** are tax-deductible.
■ **PURPOSE:** Originally established in 1977 as part of the South-Eastern Organ Procurement Foundation; incorporated separately in 1984 to operate the national network for organ procurement and transplantation called for by the passage of the federal Organ Transplantation Act that year. Under contract to the U.S. Department of Health and Human Services to be the sole national organ network, and to establish a fair and equitable distribution system, UNOS operates two computerized databases: one lists potential transplant recipients (to ensure swift matching of available organs); the other is a scientific registry of relevant data for ongoing evaluation of the clinical and scientific status of organ transplants in the United States.
■ **SIZE:** UNOS matched 10,953 organs and recipients in 1988.
■ **INCOME:** $5,877,690, of which $3,459,675 was received from $200 fees from patients registering for inclusion in the database (calendar 1988; accrual accounting, IRS form 990). During the preceding three fiscal years support had been increasing.
■ **HOW THEY USE YOUR MONEY:**
PROGRAM: $4,164,743:
  • $2,965,933 for matching donated organs with recipients (16,067 potential recipients in the database, as of late 1988).
  • $1,198,810 for the scientific registry.
OVERHEAD: $1,265,882.
FUNDRAISING: $0.
■ **EXCESS:** $447,065.
■ **LITTLE-KNOWN FACTS:** In 1987, kidney transplants accounted for 78.3 percent of all UNOS-facilitated transplants; others were heart (12.0 percent), liver (8.1 percent), pancreas (1.2 percent), and heart-lung (0.4 percent).
■ **RATINGS:** No NCIB report.
■ **REGISTRATION:** VA (1908).
■ **FINANCIAL DATA:** Text and chart source was their IRS form 990 covering 1988.

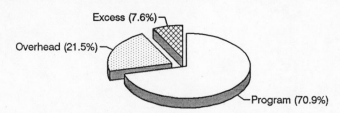

Excess (7.6%)
Overhead (21.5%)
Program (70.9%)

United Service Organizations, Inc.
601 Indiana Ave., N.W.
Washington, DC 20004
(202) 783-8121

- **CONTRIBUTIONS** are tax-deductible.
- **PURPOSE:** Founded in 1941 by the National Board of the YMCA, the National Board of the YWCA, the National Catholic Community Service, the Salvation Army, the National Jewish Welfare Board, and Travelers Aid–International Social Service of America; chartered by Congress in 1979. The USO is a voluntary civilian agency contributing (in peace or war) to the morale of men and women in the U.S. armed forces throughout the world and seeing to their religious, spiritual, social, educational, and entertainment needs.
- **SIZE:** Estimated 1.5 million people (members of the armed services and their families) were served by some 20,000 USO volunteers in 1988.
- **INCOME:** $13,795,451 (domestic headquarters; calendar 1988; accrual accounting, IRS form 990). During the preceding four fiscal years support had been increasing.
- **HOW THEY USE YOUR MONEY:**
  PROGRAM: $8,426,609:
  - $6,596,282 for services to military personnel (including intercultural understanding, community outreach, informal education, community-involvement recreation, religious understanding, social development, snack bars, and gift shops).
  - $712,348 for celebrity entertainment for overseas shows.
  - $1,004,615 for public information.
  - $113,364 for program and council relations (training and coordinating USO volunteers).
  OVERHEAD: $1,789,267.
  FUNDRAISING: $1,749,787.
- **EXCESS:** $1,829,788.
- **LITTLE-KNOWN FACTS:** Bob Hope is "Ambassador of Good Will" on the 1988–89 list of officers of the USO World Board of Governors.
- **RATINGS:** NCIB reported (7/18/88, using figures from calendar 1986) that the USO met all nine NCIB standards.
- **REGISTRATION:** CT, DC, NJ, NY, and VA (2574).
- **FINANCIAL DATA:** Text and chart source was their IRS form 990 covering 1988.

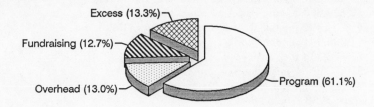

Excess (13.3%)
Fundraising (12.7%)
Overhead (13.0%)
Program (61.1%)

United States Olympic Committee
1750 E. Boulder St.
Colorado Springs, CO 80909
(719) 632-5551

- **CONTRIBUTIONS** are tax-deductible.
- **PURPOSE:** Traces its origins to 1896 and the first American Olympic team, but was not formally organized until 1921, and did not receive a federal charter until 1950. USOC took its present name in 1961, and was recognized in 1978, through Public Law 95-606, as the coordinating body for U.S. amateur athletic activity directly related to international Olympic competition and the Pan-American Games.
- **SIZE:** Training centers in Colorado Springs, at Lake Placid, and at Northern Michigan University, which accept a maximum of 1,000 athletes each year: 839 for U.S. teams for the winter and summer games, plus 161 other athletes.
- **INCOME 1988:** $79,702,301 (calendar 1988; independently audited statement).
- **INCOME 1985–88:** However, one must note USOC's quadrennial schedule. For the four-year period ending 12/31/88 (which included the 1988 Olympic Games), USOC recorded *net* total revenues of $181,609,961 after a transfer of $82,110,474 to the U.S. Olympic Foundation. (Expense breakdowns below are given for 1988 *alone* and then for 1985–88; USOC considers the four-year figures more relevant than those for a single year.)
- **HOW THEY USE YOUR MONEY:**

PROGRAM 1988: $41,359,937.

PROGRAM 1985–88: $113,434,025:
  - $17,712,662 for sports development.
  - $16,354,717 for the Colorado Springs training center.
  - $14,900,720 for games preparation.
  - $12,192,194 for sports medicine.
  - $9,199,171 for National Governing Bodies support.
  - $7,794,834 for the U.S. Olympic Festival.
  - $6,965,546 for the Summer Olympic Games (1988).
  - $6,386,151 for public information and *Olympian.* magazine.
  - $4,212,469 for the Lake Placid training center.
  - $3,267,176 for operations.
  - $3,192,816 for the USOC gift shop.
  - $3,066,095 for Friendship Fund grants (begun 1986, terminated 1988; to aid National Olympic Committees around the world).
  - $2,129,880 for the Pan-American Games.
  - $1,934,392 for the Winter Olympic Games (1988).
  - $1,830,991 for the World University Games.
  - $1,658,438 for substance-abuse programs.
  - $506,309 for miscellaneous programs.
  - $129,464 for the Northern Michigan University training center.

OVERHEAD 1988: $6,283,349.

OVERHEAD 1985–88: $20,577,922.

FUNDRAISING 1988: $11,951,651.

FUNDRAISING 1985–88: $23,654,217.

Unrelated Losses 1988: $1,623,308.
Unrelated Losses 1985–88: $2,712,788.
- **EXCESS 1988:** $18,484,056.
- **EXCESS 1985–88:** $21,231,009.
- **LITTLE-KNOWN FACTS:** Selected companies are granted the right to use U.S. Olympic symbols and terminology on retail products, in return for a royalty on each sale. Thirty-two licensing agreements produced $15 million for USOC during 1985–88. *USOC does not directly endorse these products.* In 1988 alone, multiyear television licensing agreements with the International Olympic Committee and games organizing committees yielded $5,000,000 for the 1988 games and $3,645,000 for the 1992 games, and a separate TV agreement yielded $2,697,373 for the rights to broadcast the Olympic trials.
- **RATINGS:** NCIB reported (11/14/88, using figures from calendar 1987 and for the three-year period ending December 31, 1987) that USOC met all nine NCIB standards.
- **REGISTRATION:** All states that accept form 990, including NY (7076) and VA (2746).
- **FINANCIAL DATA:** 1988 text and chart source was their independently audited statement covering that year. 1985–88 text and chart source was the same audit, covering the four-year period ending 12/31/88.

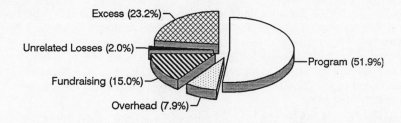

U.S. Olympic Cmte. '85-'88

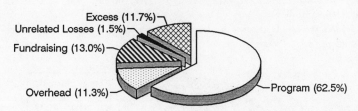

U.S. Committee for UNICEF
333 East 38th St.
New York, NY 10016
(212) 686-5522

■ **CONTRIBUTIONS** are tax-deductible.

■ **PURPOSE:** Founded in 1947. Works to inform Americans of the needs of children throughout the world and support child relief and rehabilitation in foreign countries by raising funds in the United States for UNICEF-assisted projects. Recent projects include water, health (including pediatric AIDS), education, and emergency assistance in Africa, Asia, and Latin America.

■ **SIZE:** National headquarters in New York, plus seven field offices and a congressional-relations office in Washington, D.C.

■ **INCOME:** $26,822,000 (year ending 3/31/89; accrual accounting, IRS form 990).

■ **HOW THEY USE YOUR MONEY:**
PROGRAM: $18,965,000 (foreign and domestic):
  • $15,774,000 for UNICEF. The committee's board of directors authorized grants totaling $12,002,000 to UNICEF-assisted projects to improve health, education, and welfare of children.
  • $3,191,000 for domestic programs:
     $221,000 for public education.
     $816,000 for public information (e.g., newsletter, TV, radio spots, speaking engagements).
     $2,154,000 for state and local representation (a program by which the national committee assists local volunteer groups).
OVERHEAD: $3,617,000.
FUNDRAISING: $4,372,000. UNICEF greeting cards generated $8,079,000. After expenses, the net available for programs was $1,749,000, *plus* grants totaling $280,000 of the $353,000 in contributions received through the program.

■ **DEFICIT:** $132,000.

■ **LITTLE-KNOWN FACTS:** The UNICEF Change for Good program raises funds by collecting spare foreign currency from returning international travelers.

■ **RATINGS:** NCIB reported (5/31/90, using figures from the year ending 3/31/89) that the U.S. Committee for UNICEF met all nine NCIB standards.

■ **REGISTRATION:** CA, CT, IL, MA, MD, MI, NC, NJ, NY (7268), OH, OK, PA, VA (1910), and WV.

■ **FINANCIAL DATA:** Text and chart source was their IRS form 990 covering the year ending 3/31/89.

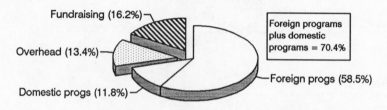

Fundraising (16.2%)
Overhead (13.4%)
Domestic progs (11.8%)
Foreign programs plus domestic programs = 70.4%
Foreign progs (58.5%)

Due to deficit of 0.5%, chart is based on spending, not income

Veterans of the Vietnam War, Inc.
2090 Bald Mountain Rd.
Wilkes-Barre, PA 18702
(717) 825-7215 • (800) VIETNAM • (800) NAM-9090 in PA

- **CONTRIBUTIONS** are tax-deductible, since VVW has been classified as a 501(c)(19) organization.
- **PURPOSE:** Provides information to veterans and the general public regarding U.S. military personnel who participated in the Vietnam War.
- **SIZE:** During 1987 an estimated "one million plus" individuals were reached through VVW programs.
- **INCOME:** $1,945,422 (calendar 1987; cash accounting, IRS form 990).
- **HOW THEY USE YOUR MONEY:**
  PROGRAM: $1,332,374 for advocacy, direct aid, employment, rehabilitation, public information, and counseling over a toll-free hotline.
  OVERHEAD: $64,742.
  FUNDRAISING: $547,690.
- **EXCESS:** $616.
- **RATINGS:** As of June 1, 1990, NCIB had requested but not received sufficient information for a report.
- **REGISTRATION:** VA (2829).
- **FINANCIAL DATA:** Text and chart source was their IRS form 990 covering 1987.

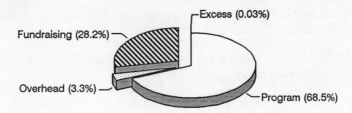

Excess (0.03%)

Fundraising (28.2%)

Overhead (3.3%)

Program (68.5%)

Vietnam Veterans of America, Inc.
1224 M St., N.W.
Washington, DC 20005
(202) 628-2700 • (800) 424-7275

- **CONTRIBUTIONS** are tax-deductible.
- **PURPOSE:** Founded in 1978 as a New York City veterans' advocacy group, VVA is now a nationwide membership group, the only congressionally chartered Vietnam veterans' organization. VVA works to help, foster, promote, and develop the improvement of the condition of veterans from the Vietnam era (1964–75).
- **INCOME:** $2,237,309 (group; year ending 2/28/89; accrual accounting, IRS form 990).
- **HOW THEY USE YOUR MONEY:**
  PROGRAM: $1,809,721 (including $929,978 in grants and allocations).
  OVERHEAD: $199,701.
  FUNDRAISING: $31,853.
- **EXCESS:** $196,034.
- **LITTLE-KNOWN FACTS:** National President Mary Stout (first elected in 1987 and overwhelmingly reelected in 1989) is the first woman to head a veterans' organization.
- **RATINGS:** No NCIB report.
- **REGISTRATION:** NY (48757) and TN.
- **FINANCIAL DATA:** Text and chart source was their IRS form 990 covering the year ending 2/29/89.

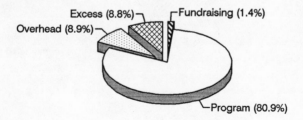

Excess (8.8%)
Overhead (8.9%)
Fundraising (1.4%)
Program (80.9%)

Vietnam Veterans of America Foundation
2100 M St., N.W., Suite 407
Washington, DC 20039
(202) 828-2630

- **CONTRIBUTIONS** are tax-deductible.
- **PURPOSE:** Incorporated in 1980 as a national clearinghouse for information on Vietnam veterans and their concerns, particularly as they relate to the Vietnam war experience. Also sponsors studies and research on the socioeconomic welfare and readjustment of Vietnam-era veterans, and works through education to eliminate prejudice and discrimination against them.
- **INCOME:** $3,550,833 (year ending 4/30/89; accrual accounting, IRS form 990). During the preceding four fiscal years support had been increasing.
- **HOW THEY USE YOUR MONEY:**
  PROGRAM: $2,661,013, including $1,178,074 in grants and allocations, such as $25,000 for a Department of Veterans Affairs–sponsored trip to Vietnam for PTSD (post-traumatic stress disease) treatment for Vietnam vets; two separate grants totaling $20,576 for trips to the Soviet Union to exchange information on PTSD (presumably as it related to Soviet veterans of Afghanistan); $1,000 for the American Legion Home for the Homeless; $1,000 for repair of vandalism at the Vietnam Veterans Memorial in Washington.
  OVERHEAD: $233,746.
  FUNDRAISING: $487,663.
- **EXCESS:** $168,411.
- **LITTLE-KNOWN FACTS:** The foundation made a grant of $800,000 to a related organization, Vietnam Veterans of America, Inc., to support national programs of health, legal, and administrative services.
- **RATINGS:** No NCIB report.
- **REGISTRATION:** NY (49816) and VA (2442).
- **FINANCIAL DATA:** Text and chart source was their IRS form 990 covering the year ending 4/30/89.

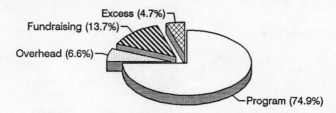

Excess (4.7%)
Fundraising (13.7%)
Overhead (6.6%)
Program (74.9%)

297

Adam Walsh Child Resource Center, Inc.
3111 S. Dixie Highway
West Palm Beach, FL 33405
(305) 833-9080 • (800) FOR-ADAM

- **CONTRIBUTIONS** are tax-deductible.
- **PURPOSE:** Founded by John Walsh in 1982 and named for his missing son, the center was organized "to promote the welfare of children and advocate children's rights." In April 1990, the center merged with the National Center for Missing and Exploited Children.
- **SIZE:** Seven offices around the country.
- **INCOME:** $444,812 (year ending 6/30/87; accrual accounting, IRS form 990), including $50,000 from Bristol-Myers for a "Safe 'n' Fun" promotion.
- **HOW THEY USE YOUR MONEY:**
PROGRAM: $421,605:
  - $108,428 for public awareness.
  - $106,450 for community education.
  - $49,633 for family support.
  - $47,255 for information and referral.
  - $43,465 for safety programs.
  - $35,840 for research and data collection.
  - $30,534 for legislation.
OVERHEAD: $105,690.
FUNDRAISING: $66,975.
- **DEFICIT:** $149,458.
- **RATINGS:** No NCIB report.
- **REGISTRATION:** AZ, CA, DC, FL, IA, IL, KS, KY, MA, MD, ME, MN, NC, NH. NY (52567), OH, SC, TN, VA (2201), VT, WI, and WV.
- **FINANCIAL DATA:** Text and chart source was their IRS form 990 covering the year ending 6/30/87.

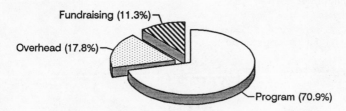

Fundraising (11.3%)
Overhead (17.8%)
Program (70.9%)

Due to deficit of 25.1%, chart is based on spending, not income.

Simon Wiesenthal Center
9760 W. Pico Blvd.
Los Angeles, CA 90035
(213) 553-9036

- **CONTRIBUTIONS** are tax-deductible.
- **PURPOSE:** Established in 1977 as North America's first National Holocaust Center, an institution dedicated to the study of the Holocaust, its contemporary implications, and related human-rights issues.
- **SIZE:** Internationally, over 375,000 member families; headquarters in Los Angeles; offices in New York, Chicago, Miami, Toronto, Jerusalem, and Paris.
- **INCOME:** $15,018,997 (year ending 6/30/89; accrual accounting, IRS form 990).
- **HOW THEY USE YOUR MONEY:**
  PROGRAM: $8,804,686:
  - $5,637,996 to develop programs in Holocaust Studies and research, media, educational outreach to schools and other organizations, and international social action.
  - $3,166,690 in restricted funds for construction of the new Beit Hashoah–Museum of Tolerance in Los Angeles.

  OVERHEAD: $2,731,483.
  FUNDRAISING: $1,718,171.
- **EXCESS:** $1,764,657 (for increased operating costs in the center's new museum).
- **LITTLE-KNOWN FACTS:** The center has embarked upon a capital campaign to finish building and to endow a new 165,000-square-foot complex to house a multimedia learning center, archival area, auditorium, operational and administrative offices, and the new Beit Hashoah–Museum of Tolerance. Besides installations on the Holocaust, this new museum will confront the social dynamics of prejudice, bigotry, and racism using American history and culture as its text. Interactive exhibits will encourage self-awareness and an understanding of human-rights issues.
- **RATINGS:** No NCIB report.
- **REGISTRATION:** AZ, CA (59137), CO, DE, FL, HI, IA, ID, IL, KS, KY, LA, MD, MI, MO, NE, NM, NV, NY (54944), OR, SD, TN, UT, VA (2323), VT, WA, and WY.
- **FINANCIAL DATA:** Text and chart source was their IRS form 990 covering the year ending 6/30/89.

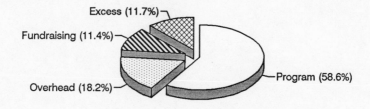

Excess (11.7%)
Fundraising (11.4%)
Overhead (18.2%)
Program (58.6%)

The Wilderness Society
1400 I St., N.W., 10th Fl.
Washington, DC 20005
(202) 842-3400

- **CONTRIBUTIONS** are tax-deductible.
- **PURPOSE:** Founded in 1935, the society is the only national organization devoted exclusively to issues relating to the preservation and proper management of America's wilderness and public lands.
- **SIZE:** Over 225,000 members.
- **INCOME:** $10,928,494 (year ending 9/30/88; accrual accounting, IRS form 990). During the preceding four fiscal years support had been increasing.
- **HOW THEY USE YOUR MONEY:**
PROGRAM: $7,845,339:
  - $2,809,641 (including $3,950 in grants and allocations) for conservation.
  - $2,894,329 (including $3,300 in grants and allocations) for public education.
  - $2,141,369 for informing the membership of specific issues.
  - $2,500 to the Sierra Club Legal Defense Fund.
OVERHEAD: $1,108,402.
FUNDRAISING: $616,010.
MEMBERSHIP RECRUITMENT: $1,362,697.
- **DEFICIT:** $3,954.
- **RATINGS:** As of June 1, 1990, NCIB was preparing a new report.
- **REGISTRATION:** DC, NY (11962), TN, and VA (2089).
- **FINANCIAL DATA:** Text and chart source was their IRS form 990 covering the year ending 9/30/88.

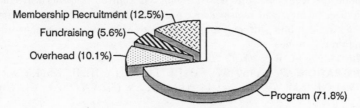

Membership Recruitment (12.5%)
Fundraising (5.6%)
Overhead (10.1%)
Program (71.8%)

Due to deficit of 0.04%, chart is based on spending, not income.

Witness for Peace
Box 567
Durham, NC 27702
(919) 688-5049

- **CONTRIBUTIONS** are tax-deductible.
- **PURPOSE:** Since 1983 Witness for Peace has held a faith-based commitment to nonviolent action and a change in U.S. policy toward Nicaragua. Work has centered around on-site reports of the effects of U.S. policy there. In 1988 the group expanded its interests to include all of Central America. The 1989 schedule included seven delegations to Guatemala, two to El Salvador, and two to Honduras.
- **SIZE:** National office in Durham, plus three program offices, ten regional offices, and an office in Nicaragua; their nationwide newsletter has a circulation of about 45,000.
- **INCOME:** $1,154,490 (calendar 1988; accrual accounting, IRS form 990). During the preceding four fiscal years support had been increasing.
- **HOW THEY USE YOUR MONEY:**
PROGRAM: $615,068; the largest of many programs were:
  - $265,480 to gather affidavits from Nicaraguan civilians documenting the effects of U.S. policy on the Nicaraguan population and society, particularly in Managua and in the Atlantic coast town of Bluefields.
  - $126,240 for media and liaison programs operating out of the Washington office.
OVERHEAD: $130,273.
FUNDRAISING: $476,558.
- **DEFICIT:** $67,409.
- **LITTLE-KNOWN FACTS:** WFP developed a booklet entitled *Black Nicaragua* to "increase the interest of African Americans regarding Nicaragua and Central America." The group reported that this project did increase the number of African Americans challenging U.S. policy in Nicaragua, but no figures or other details were given.
- **RATINGS:** No NCIB report.
- **REGISTRATION:** NY (54959).
- **FINANCIAL DATA:** Text and chart source was their IRS form 990 covering 1988.

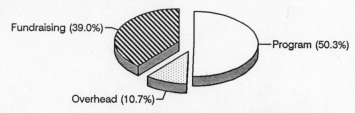

Fundraising (39.0%) Program (50.3%) Overhead (10.7%)

Due to deficit of 5.5%, chart is based on spending, not income.

301

Women's Liberation Writing Collective, Inc.
321 W. 47th St.
New York, NY 10036
(212) 307-5055

■ **CONTRIBUTIONS** are tax-deductible.

■ **PURPOSE:** Founded in 1970 to support women's groups that seek to promote equality for women. One of the collective's special projects is Women Against Pornography, which educates the public "to the dangers inherent in pornography." Among its programs are slide shows, public forums, a newsletter, and guided tours of New York City's Times Square sex shops.

■ **INCOME:** $35,158 (year ending 6/30/88; cash accounting, IRS form 990).

■ **HOW THEY USE YOUR MONEY:**
PROGRAM: $29,202:
- $13,897 for literature (including production and mailing of a newsletter and educational material, and a free lending library).
- $4,090 for slide shows (to disseminate information).
- $6,760 for conferences and workshops.
- $4,455 for speaking engagements with the distribution of literature.

OVERHEAD: $2,054.
FUNDRAISING: $3,736.

■ **EXCESS:** $166.

■ **LITTLE-KNOWN FACTS:** The collective was formed by a group of feminist writers who staged a sit-in at the offices of the *Ladies' Home Journal* seeking coverage of the women's movement. They were given a multipage section in an issue of the magazine, and decided to use the money they were paid for the section to support other underfinanced feminist projects.

■ **RATINGS:** No NCIB report.

■ **REGISTRATION:** NY (48553).

■ **FINANCIAL DATA:** Text and chart source was their IRS form 990 covering the year ending 6/30/88.

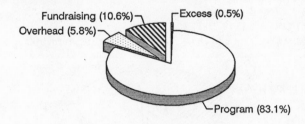

Fundraising (10.6%)
Overhead (5.8%)
Excess (0.5%)
Program (83.1%)

World Hunger Year, Inc.
261 W. 35th St., Rm. 1402
New York, NY 10001
(212) 629-8850

■ **CONTRIBUTIONS** are tax-deductible.
■ **PURPOSE:** Founded in 1975 by singer-songwriter Harry Chapin and radio talk-show host Bill Ayres "to inform the general public, the media, and policy-makers on the extent and causes of hunger in the United States and abroad; to initiate, organize, and participate in targeted programs promoting more effective government and private-sector policies directed towards the elimination of hunger, homelessness, and poverty."
■ **INCOME:** $401,804 (calendar 1988; accrual accounting, IRS form 990).
■ **HOW THEY USE YOUR MONEY:**
PROGRAM: $296,742:
  • $73,707 for special events.
  • $72,732 for *Food Monitor* (also known as *WHY* magazine).
  • $19,026 for media awards.
  • $50,393 for Hungerline (a media-resource service for hunger-related issues).
  • $64,064 for the Campaign to End Hunger and Homelessness (an educational campaign that included $25,000 in grants and allocations).
  • $3,537 for the Harry Chapin Food Self-Reliance Award (to local groups for their promotion of food self-reliance).
  • $13,285* for the Hungerthon (a twenty-four-hour live radio broadcast from the United Nations featuring musical performances and authorities on domestic and world hunger issues; it benefits both WHY and the U.S. Committee for UNICEF).
OVERHEAD: $38,285.
FUNDRAISING: $56,725.*
■ **EXCESS:** $10,051.
■ **LITTLE-KNOWN FACTS:** A decade before most of the world heard of Bob Geldof, Harry Chapin used his concerts as a forum for his concern about hunger. In recognition of Chapin's groundwork, during the 1985 Live Aid Philadelphia concert, his widow addressed the crowd.
■ **RATINGS:** No NCIB report.
■ **REGISTRATION:** NY (45384).
■ **FINANCIAL DATA:** Text and chart source was their IRS form 990 covering 1988.

*Hungerthon fundraising costs have *not* been separately determined.

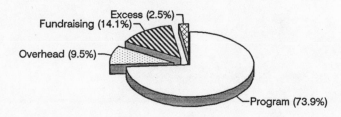

Excess (2.5%)
Fundraising (14.1%)
Overhead (9.5%)
Program (73.9%)

World Jewish Congress (American Section), Inc.
501 Madison Ave.
New York, NY 10022
(212) 755-5770

- **CONTRIBUTIONS** are tax-deductible.
- **PURPOSE:** Founded in 1936, WJC is an international organization of representative bodies seeking to secure and safeguard the rights, status, and interests of Jews and Jewish communities worldwide. WJC is committed to the support of national and international protection of human rights, regardless of race or religion.
- **SIZE:** The American section of WJC comprises over twenty national Jewish organizations, including the American Jewish Congress (founded 1918).
- **INCOME:** $4,543,133 (calendar 1988; accrual accounting, IRS form 990).
- **HOW THEY USE YOUR MONEY:**
  PROGRAM: $3,540,230:
  - $2,837,877 (including $1,959,745 in grants and allocations to the World Jewish Congress's headquarters) for international affairs.
  - $346,277 (including $2,500 in grants and allocations) for disseminating information to the Jewish community.
  - $290,432 for integration and interaction of Jewish organizations.
  - $65,644 for academic, cultural, and youth programs.

  OVERHEAD: $483,044.

  FUNDRAISING: $1,024,937.
- **DEFICIT:** $505,078.
- **LITTLE-KNOWN FACTS:** The WJC has consultative status at the United Nations, UNICEF, the Organization of American States, and various other intergovernmental and governmental authorities.
- **RATINGS:** No NCIB report.
- **REGISTRATION:** MA, MI, and NY (49454).
- **FINANCIAL DATA:** Text and chart source was their IRS form 990 covering 1988.

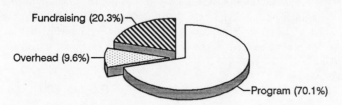

Fundraising (20.3%)

Overhead (9.6%)

Program (70.1%)

Due to deficit of 10.0%, chart is based on spending, not income.

304

World Mercy Fund, Inc.
121 S. St. Asaph St.
Alexandria, VA 22314
(703) 548-4646

- **CONTRIBUTIONS** are tax-deductible.
- **PURPOSE:** Works to "alleviate the suffering of people throughout the world, but with particular emphasis in the Third World, especially Africa."
- **SIZE:** Headquarters in Alexandria, Virginia; affiliates in Austria, Switzerland, Germany, and Ireland.
- **INCOME:** $4,397,279 (year ending 5/31/89; accrual accounting, IRS form 990). During the preceding four fiscal years support had been increasing.
- **HOW THEY USE YOUR MONEY:**
  PROGRAM: $3,508,050, of which $2,211,650 went to Third World countries for aid in food, transportation, education, agriculture (projects such as irrigation, hospitals, transportation, health care, and medication).
  OVERHEAD: $133,657.
  FUNDRAISING: $1,320,034.
- **DEFICIT:** $564,462.
- **LITTLE-KNOWN FACTS:** The largest projects for the American, Austrian, and German offices were in Nigeria; the largest project of the Swiss office was in Sierra Leone; and of the Irish office, in Jerusalem.
- **RATINGS:** As of June 1, 1990, NCIB was preparing a new report.
- **REGISTRATION:** VA (2777).
- **FINANCIAL DATA:** Text and chart source was their IRS form 990 covering the year ending 5/31/89.

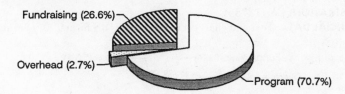

Fundraising (26.6%)

Overhead (2.7%)

Program (70.7%)

Due to deficit of 11.4%, chart is based on spending, not income.

World Research, Inc.
11722 Sorrento Valley Rd.
San Diego, CA 92121
(619) 566-3456

- **CONTRIBUTIONS** are tax-deductible.
- **PURPOSE:** Founded in 1969, World Research, Inc., researches student attitudes and opinion changes to create multimedia educational programs to provide information on the conflict between the individual and the state (the problems resulting from excessive government regulation in a society). WRI maintains a library on economics, history, and philosophy.
- **INCOME:** $321,909 (calendar 1988; accrual accounting, IRS form 990).
- **HOW THEY USE YOUR MONEY:**
  PROGRAM: $277,098:
  - $110,072 (including $55,000 in grants and allocations) to produce *Crisis Points* (classroom video and teacher materials dealing with social and economic problems facing young people).
  - $103,661 for a circulation film/video library and other distribution of WRI educational materials.
  - $63,365 for the production and distribution of *Reach Out, Can't You See Me?* and *Come in from the Storm,* classroom programs dealing with alcohol abuse, rape, and child abuse, respectively.
  OVERHEAD: $8,457.
  FUNDRAISING: $19,400.
- **EXCESS:** $16,954.
- **RATINGS:** As of June 1, 1990, NCIB had requested but not received sufficient information for a report.
- **REGISTRATION:** CA (12755).
- **FINANCIAL DATA:** Text and chart source was their IRS form 990 covering 1988.

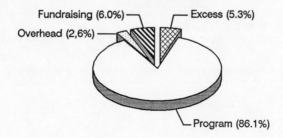

Fundraising (6.0%) — Excess (5.3%)
Overhead (2,6%) —
Program (86.1%)

World Wildlife Fund and the Conservation Foundation
1250 24th St., N.W., Suite 500
Washington, DC 20037
(202) 293-4800

■ **CONTRIBUTIONS** are tax-deductible.
■ **PURPOSE:** Founded in 1961, part of the twenty-four-member international WWF network. Protects endangered wildlife and tropical forest habitats (primarily in Latin America, Africa, and Asia) through field activities and "practical, rigorously planned, scientifically based conservation projects." It is a leader in "debt-for-nature" swaps (see below). In 1985 WWF-US affiliated with the Conservation Foundation, Inc., a nonprofit research organization known for its expertise in social-science and policy analysis. The former president of WWF-US, William Reilly, now serves as head of the U.S. Environmental Protection Agency.
■ **SIZE:** More than 100 staff members and 462,000 supporting members. WWF-US has carried out more than 1,350 conservation projects in 103 countries.
■ **INCOME:** $35,594,727 (year ending 6/30/89; accrual accounting, independently audited statement). During the preceding four fiscal years support had been increasing.
■ **HOW THEY USE YOUR MONEY:**
PROGRAM: $26,656,903:
  - $7,482,396* for public education.
  - $5,748,638 for programs in Latin America/Caribbean/Brazil.
  - $4,154,668* for membership development.
  - $2,053,642 for programs in Africa/Madagascar.
  - $1,714,839 for programs in Asia/Pacific.
  - $1,425,506 for science programs.
  - $1,422,476 for sustainable development.
  - $1,253,366 for public policy programs.
  - $1,052,072 for the general program.
  - $349,300 for TRAFFIC (an international program to end trade in endangered species).
OVERHEAD: $1,117,998.
FUNDRAISING: $3,534,566.*
DEFERRED RENT: $405,828.
■ **EXCESS:** $3,879,432.
■ **LITTLE-KNOWN FACTS:** In 1988 WWF-US made three debt-for-nature swaps: in Ecuador ($1 million for management of seven parks and other protected areas, plus an endowment to support the local WWF associate), Costa Rica ($3 million, over three years, for the nation's park system), and the Philippines (up to $2 million to manage parks, provide conservation training, and carry out other conservation measures). U.S. banks allowed WWF to buy $1 million in Ecuadorian debt for only $335,000, tripling the value of the investment.
■ **RATINGS:** As of June 1, 1990, NCIB was preparing a new report.

*A joint allocation of costs totaling $8,053,768 for dual-purpose activities split expenses thus: $2,293,594 for fundraising; $1,747,335 for membership development; and $4,012,839 for public information.

- ■ **REGISTRATION:** CA, DC, FL, GA, IL, KS, MA, MD, MI, MN, MO, NC, ND, NJ, NM, NY (10193), OH, OK, OR, PA, SC, TN, VA (2120), WA, WI, and WV.
- ■ **FINANCIAL DATA:** Text and chart source was their independently audited statement covering the year ending 6/30/89.

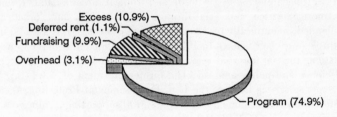

Excess (10.9%)
Deferred rent (1.1%)
Fundraising (9.9%)
Overhead (3.1%)
Program (74.9%)

Young Adult Institute and Workshop, Inc.
460 W. 34th St.
New York, NY 10001
(212) 563-7474

- **CONTRIBUTIONS** are tax-deductible.
- **PURPOSE:** YAI serves the needs of mentally retarded and developmentally disabled children and adults in the New York metropolitan area.
- **SIZE:** More than fifty programs.
- **INCOME:** $21,451,959 (year ending 6/30/88; accrual accounting, IRS form 990). During the preceding four fiscal years support had been increasing.
- **HOW THEY USE YOUR MONEY:**
  PROGRAM: $16,752,848:
    - $7,008,725 for clinical programs (to enhance communication, learning, and adult behavior skills).
    - $8,541,010 for residences (hostels for young adults with multiple handicaps).
    - $1,203,113 for community services (supportive services to clients living in a family setting).
  OVERHEAD: $4,040,787.
  FUNDRAISING: $0.
- **EXCESS:** $658,324.
- **RATINGS:** No NCIB report.
- **REGISTRATION:** NY (42749).
- **FINANCIAL DATA:** Text and chart source was their IRS form 990 covering the year ending 6/30/88.

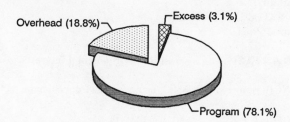

309

Zero Population Growth, Inc.
1400 16th St., N.W.
Washington, DC 20036
(202) 332-2200

- **CONTRIBUTIONS** are tax-deductible.
- **PURPOSE:** Founded in 1968 to "achieve a sustainable balance of the earth's population, resources, and the environment—both in the United States and worldwide. ZPG supports voluntary family planning and the right of each individual to freely and responsibly determine family size."
- **SIZE:** 25,000. In 1988 membership grew by 33 percent over 1987. Local chapters active in Florida, Minnesota, Oregon, Washington, Utah, and California (San Luis Obispo, Los Angeles, San Jose, and the Bay area).
- **INCOME:** $901,132 (calendar 1988; accrual accounting, IRS form 990). During the preceding four fiscal years support had been increasing.
- **HOW THEY USE YOUR MONEY:**
  PROGRAM: $865,778:
    - $276,727 for membership services (such as newsletters and other publications "designed to keep members informed about population-related issues and events and to involve members in ZPG programs").
    - $318,271 for public education (including mailings to the general public about population issues and ZPG projects).
    - $113,555 for population education (related training aids and curriculum materials for teachers of grades K–12).
    - $84,686 for field services ("information, services, materials, and support to ZPG chapters, federations, and other activists" to strengthen effectiveness and visibility).
  OVERHEAD: $121,801.
  FUNDRAISING: $59,310.
- **DEFICIT:** $145,757.
- **LITTLE-KNOWN FACTS:** In line with its environmental interests, ZPG uses recycled paper.
- **RATINGS:** NCIB reported (12/4/89, using figures from calendar 1988) that ZPG met all nine NCIB standards.
- **REGISTRATION:** NY (50212) and VA (2165).
- **FINANCIAL DATA:** Text and chart source was their IRS form 990 covering 1988.

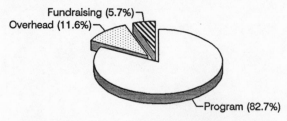

Fundraising (5.7%)
Overhead (11.6%)
Program (82.7%)

Due to deficit of 13.9%, chart is based on spending, not income.

310

The Giver's Guide

☐ Appendix A ☐

INDEX OF PROFILES BY CATEGORY

■ S O M E   R E A D E R S   M A Y be interested in a particular cause—cancer research, civil rights, environmentalism, or famine relief, to name a few—rather than a single favorite group. This subject index was created for those readers.

Before skimming the subject headings and looking back at the profiles, however, be aware of some important restrictions on the usefulness of this index.

First of all, the 250 organizations profiled in this book are only a small portion of the universe of charities and nonprofit groups operating in this country. Inclusion of a group does not imply endorsement; exclusion has no significance either.

Second, a particular group *may not* be listed under all of the causes for which it has programs (Oxfam-America, for instance, has programs in Africa, but it is not listed under "African Americans, Africa"). Examine several related subject headings if you suspect a group runs programs in your field of interest, or contact the organization directly. Remember that as time goes by, some groups may introduce new programs or de-emphasize old ones.

Third, and this is most important, direct comparison of two or more groups listed under the same subject heading could lead to misunderstandings. Often different fiscal years, source materials, or accounting methods were used to prepare the profiles you may wish to compare. Even if profiles and pie charts of Group A and Group B *both* feature financial data for 1988, taken from the IRS form 990 and using accrual accounting, there may be other differences you're not considering. It could be like comparing the amount of money spent in 1988 on hurricane preparation in South Carolina with the money spent in Maine; they're both Atlantic coast states, and you're looking at the same year, but other factors prevent a meaningful comparison.

The best way to use this subject index is as a means of finding groups or causes that will be new to you. There are plenty of causes that could use your help.

AFRICAN AMERICANS, AFRICA

The Africa Fund
Africare
Fund for an Open Society
National Association for the Advancement of Colored People
NAACP Legal Defense and Education Fund
NAACP Special Contributions Fund
National Association for Sickle Cell Disease
Southern Christian Leadership Conference
United Negro College Fund

AIDS

AIDS Project Los Angeles
American Foundation for AIDS Research
Gay Men's Health Crisis
Lambda Legal Defense and Education Fund

ANIMALS

American Society for the Prevention of Cruelty to Animals (ASPCA)
Animal Welfare Institute
Defenders of Wildlife
The Fund for Animals
The Humane Society of the United States
National Audubon Society
National Humane Education Society
National Wildlife Federation
People for the Ethical Treatment of Animals
World Wildlife Fund

BLINDNESS

American Foundation for the Blind
Braille Institute of America
Guide Dog Foundation for the Blind

Guiding Eyes for the Blind
Helen Keller International (under K)
The Lighthouse
Recording for the Blind

CANCER

ALSAC–St. Jude Children's Research Hospital
AMC Cancer Research Center
American Cancer Society
American Institute for Cancer Research
Cancer Care/The National Cancer Care Foundation
City of Hope
Leukemia Society of America
National Foundation for Cancer Research
Project CURE

CHILDREN

Child Welfare League of America
Children's Defense Fund
The Fresh Air Fund
Just Say No International
Parents Without Partners
U.S. Committee for UNICEF

CHILDREN, MISSING AND RUNAWAYS

Adam Walsh Child Resource Center (under W)
Child Find of America
Covenant House
National Center for Missing and Exploited Children

CHILD SPONSORSHIP

Children's Aid International
Christian Children's Fund
Food for the Hungry
Pearl S. Buck Foundation (under B)
Plan International USA
Save the Children Federation

CHRISTIAN

Billy Graham Evangelistic Association (under G)

Bread for the World
Bread for the World Institute on Hunger and Development
Catholic Relief Services
Christian Anti-Communism Crusade
Christian Children's Fund
Food for the Hungry
Prison Fellowship Ministries
The Salvation Army
Southern Christian Leadership Conference

CIVIL RIGHTS, SOCIAL ACTION, ADVOCACY

Accuracy in Media
ACLU Foundation
American Civil Liberties Union
American Cultural Traditions
Americans United for Separation of Church and State
Center for Community Change
Center for Constitutional Rights
Center for Democratic Renewal
Christian Anti-Communism Crusade
Council on Economic Priorities
FAIR (Federation for American Immigration Reform)
The Fund for Peace
Gray Panthers Project Fund
The Hunger Project
League of Women Voters Education Fund
League of Women Voters of the United States
Mainstream
Martin Luther King, Jr., Center for Nonviolent Social Change (under K)
Mexican American Legal Defense and Education Fund
Ms. Foundation for Women
National Association for the Advancement of Colored People
NAACP Legal Defense and Education Fund
NAACP Special Contributions Fund
National Conference of Christians and Jews
National Emergency Civil Liberties Committee
National Organization for Women
NOW Legal Defense and Education Fund
National Right to Work Legal Defense and Education Foundation

Native American Rights Fund
The Pathfinder Fund
People for the American Way
People for the American Way Action Fund
Population Institute
Public Citizen
Public Citizen Foundation
Puerto Rican Legal Defense and Education Fund
Southern Christian Leadership Conference
Zero Population Growth

CONSUMER PROTECTION, LEGAL AID

Bankcard Holders of America
Center for Auto Safety
Center for Science in the Public Interest
Consumers Union of the United States
HALT–An Organization of Americans for Legal Reform
National Legal Aid and Defender Association
Public Citizen
Public Citizen Foundation

CRIME, DELINQUENCY, PRISONERS

The Fortune Society
Mothers Against Drunk Driving (MADD)
National Coalition Against Domestic Violence
National Committee for Prevention of Child Abuse
National Crime Prevention Council
Prison Fellowship Ministries

DEAFNESS

Alexander Graham Bell Association for the Deaf (under B)
Deafness Research Foundation

DISABLED

Disability Rights Education and Defense Fund
Goodwill Industries of America
Human Resources Center
Mainstream

DRUGS

Help Hospitalized Veterans

Just Say No International
Phoenix House Foundation
Straight, Inc.

ENVIRONMENT
The Cousteau Society
Earth Island Institute
Environmental Action
Environmental Action Foundation
Environmental Defense Fund
Friends of the Earth
Friends of the Earth Foundation
Greenpeace USA
Greenpeace Action
Natural Resources Defense Council
The Nature Conservancy
Sierra Club
Sierra Club Foundation
Sierra Club Legal Defense Fund
The Wilderness Society

FAMILY PLANNING (including abortion pro and con)
American Cultural Traditions
National Abortion Rights Action League
National Right to Life Committee
Planned Parenthood Federation of America
Population Institute
Religious Coalition for Abortion Rights
Zero Population Growth

FOOD BANKS, AGRICULTURE
City Harvest, Inc.
Food for Survival/The New York City Foodbank
Rural Advancement Fund (National Sharecroppers Fund)
Second Harvest, the National Food Bank Network

GOOD GOVERNMENT
Common Cause
Council on Economic Priorities

League of Women Voters Education Fund
League of Women Voters of the United States

GUN LAWS
Coalition to Stop Gun Violence
Handgun Control
National Rifle Association of America

HEALTH
ALS Association
American Heart Association
American Lung Association
Cystic Fibrosis Foundation
Direct Relief International
Epilepsy Foundation of America
Huntington's Disease Society of America
Juvenile Diabetes Foundation International
March of Dimes Birth Defects Foundation
Medic Alert Foundation, International
Muscular Dystrophy Association
National Association for Sickle Cell Disease
National Easter Seal Society
National Emergency Medicine Association
National Health Council
National Kidney Foundation
National Multiple Sclerosis Society
National Sudden Infant Death Syndrome Foundation
Parkinson's Disease Foundation
The People-to-People Health Foundation (Project HOPE)
Sex Information and Education Council of the United States
United Cerebral Palsy Association
Will Rogers Memorial Fund (under R)

HISPANICS
LULAC National Educational Service Centers
Mexican American Legal Defense and Education Fund
National Council of La Raza
National Hispanic Scholarship Fund
Puerto Rican Legal Defense and Education Fund

HOMELESSNESS
Bowery Residents' Committee Human Services Corporation
Center for Community Change
Coalition for the Homeless
Comic Relief
National Alliance to End Homelessness
The Salvation Army

HOSPITALS, MEDICAL RESEARCH INSTITUTIONS
ALSAC–St. Jude Children's Research Hospital
City of Hope
Institute of Noetic Sciences
Salk Institute for Biological Studies
Shriners' Hospitals for Crippled Children

HOUSING, NEIGHBORHOODS
Fund for an Open Society
Habitat for Humanity International
United Neighborhood Centers of America

HUMAN RIGHTS
Amnesty International of the U.S.A.
Human Rights Watch

HUNGER
Bread for the World
Bread for the World Institute on Hunger and Development
Food for the Hungry
The Freedom from Hunger Foundation
The Hunger Project
Oxfam-America
Save the Children Federation
World Hunger Year

IMMIGRATION
American Refugee Committee
FAIR (Federation for American Immigration Reform)
International Rescue Committee
United Jewish Appeal

JEWS, ISRAEL
American Jewish Committee
American Jewish World Service
Americans for Peace Now
Anti-Defamation League of B'nai B'rith
Council of Jewish Federations
Jewish National Fund
New Israel Fund
Simon Wiesenthal Center (under W)
United Jewish Appeal
World Jewish Congress (American Section)

LITERACY, EDUCATION
Junior Achievement
Literacy Volunteers of America
LULAC National Educational Service Centers
National Hispanic Scholarship Fund
Reading Is Fundamental
United Jewish Appeal
United Negro College Fund

LONG-TERM DEVELOPMENT
Africare
American Friends Service Committee
American Jewish World Service
CARE USA
The Hunger Project
Overseas Development Council
Oxfam-America
TechnoServe

MENTAL HEALTH
Alzheimer's Association
American Health Assistance Foundation
American Mental Health Fund
Bowery Residents' Committee Human Services Corporation
National Alliance for the Mentally Ill
The National Mental Health Association

MENTAL RETARDATION
Association for Retarded Citizens of the United States
National Down Syndrome Society
Special Olympics International Headquarters
Young Adult Institute and Workshop

NUCLEAR WAR
The Fund for Peace
International Physicians for the Prevention of Nuclear War
Physicians for Social Responsibility
Union of Concerned Scientists

PEACE, INTERNATIONAL RELATIONS
American Friends Service Committee
Americans for Peace Now
Central Committee for Conscientious Objectors
Council on Foreign Relations
The Fund for Peace
International Peace Academy
International Social Service, American Branch
Jobs with Peace Campaign
National Peace Institute Foundation
New Israel Fund
Overseas Development Council
Witness for Peace

PRESERVATION
National Trust for Historic Preservation in the United States
Statue of Liberty–Ellis Island Foundation

PUBLIC INTEREST LAW FIRMS
American Civil Liberties Union
Americans United for Separation of Church and State
Asian American Legal Defense and Education Fund
Center for Constitutional Rights
Christic Institute
Coalition for the Homeless
Disability Rights Education and Defense Fund
Environmental Defense Fund
Lambda Legal Defense and Education Fund

Mexican American Legal Defense and Education Fund
NAACP Legal Defense and Education Fund
National Emergency Civil Liberties Committee
NOW Legal Defense and Education Fund
National Right to Work Legal Defense and Education Foundation
Native American Rights Fund
Natural Resources Defense Council
Puerto Rican Legal Defense and Education Fund
Sierra Club Legal Defense Fund

PUBLIC POLICY RESEARCH, PLANNING
American Enterprise Institute for Public Policy Research
Brookings Institution
Council on Economic Priorities
Council on Foreign Relations
The Fund for Peace
The Heritage Foundation

RELIEF ORGANIZATIONS
American Friends Service Committee
American National Red Cross
AmeriCares Foundation
Bread for the World
Bread for the World Institute on Hunger and Development
CARE USA
Catholic Relief Services
Direct Relief International
Food for the Hungry
The Freedom from Hunger Foundation
Overseas Development Council
Oxfam-America
World Mercy Fund

SENIOR CITIZENS
Gray Panthers Project Fund
National Council on the Aging

SPORTS
Special Olympics International Headquarters
United States Olympic Committee

TERMINALLY ILL CHILDREN AND ADULTS
The Hole in the Wall Gang Camp Fund
Make-a-Wish Foundation of America
National Hospice Organization
Sunshine Foundation

TRANSPLANTS
National Kidney Foundation
United Network for Organ Sharing

VETERANS, ACTIVE-SERVICE PERSONNEL, PRISONERS OF WAR
Account for POW/MIAs
AMVETS National Service Foundation
Help Hospitalized Veterans
National League of Families of American Prisoners & Missing in Southeast Asia
Paralyzed Veterans of America
United Service Organizations
Veterans of the Vietnam War
Vietnam Veterans of America
Vietnam Veterans of America Foundation

WOMEN'S RIGHTS (see also Family Planning)
Ms. Foundation for Women
National Coalition Against Domestic Violence
National Organization for Women
NOW Legal Defense and Education Fund
Women's Liberation Writing Collective (parent of Women Against Pornography)

YOUTH DEVELOPMENT
Big Brothers/Big Sisters of America
Boys and Girls Clubs of America
Boys Town/Father Flanagan's Boys' Home
The Fresh Air Fund
Girls, Inc.
Straight, Inc.

□ Appendix B □

GUIDELINES OF THE NATIONAL CHARITIES INFORMATION BUREAU

■ OVER THE LAST few years the National Charities Information Bureau has been revising and refining its standards. Changes in the field of philanthropy, and the fact that this task had not been done essentially since NCIB was formed in 1918, prompted these undertakings. Some of the changes are discussed in earlier sections of this book.

For the purposes of this book, readers should only concern themselves with two sets of standards: new (or revised) and old.

Since July 1, 1988, groups have been judged on a set of *nine* (new) standards covering internal operations and external reporting of those operations. The most detailed standard is the first. Some of the eight lettered subsections (or portions of them) appear in brackets. These brackets mark standards that are at present optional. Reports summarized in this book *did not require* groups to follow the standards listed in brackets. The bracketed standards take effect on January 1, 1991; after that date, groups will be held to the expanded set of new standards.

The 1991 changes (along with further subdivisions of some sections) will make NCIB's future reports more specific, especially when one wants to isolate the particular reason why a group might not meet all nine standards. Standard 8, for instance, deals with the issue of "accountability." Under the present version of the nine NCIB standards, even if a group adheres to *all but one* of the requirements of Standard 8, it will still fail the *entire* accountability standard. After January 1, 1991, NCIB will be able to tell donors exactly which part of the standard wasn't met.

Compare that specificity with the old set of standards, which was in effect prior to July 1, 1988. NCIB judged groups based on *eight* standards (reprinted at the end of this appendix, and refered to in the profiles as the "old evaluation standards"). For example, Standard 1 (Board Governance) in the old set of standards does not make nearly as many demands of a group as Standard 1 in the new set.

As in any transition period, the rules in effect during the change from old to new may be confusing. Readers who see a report cited in a profile may wish to contact NCIB at the address listed in Chapter 1. Reports requested from NCIB clearly indicate which set of standards was applied when the group was evaluated.

NCIB STANDARDS IN PHILANTHROPY
(revised)

The support of philanthropic organizations soliciting funds from the general public is based on public trust. The most reliable evaluation of an organization is a detailed review.

Yet the organization's compliance with a basic set of standards can indicate whether it is fulfilling its obligations to contributors, to those who benefit from its programs, and to the general public.

Responsibility for ensuring sound policy guidance and governance and for meeting these basic standards rests with the governing boards, which are answerable to the public.

The National Charities Information Bureau recommends and applies the following nine standards as common measures of governance and management.

GOVERNANCE, POLICY, AND PROGRAM FUNDAMENTALS

1. Board Governance: The board should be an independent, volunteer body. It is responsible for policy setting, fiscal guidance, and ongoing governance, and should regularly review the organization's policies, programs, and operations. The board should have
   a. a minimum of 5 voting members;
   b. [an individual attendance policy];
   c. [specific terms of office for its officers and members];
   d. in-person, face-to-face meetings, at least twice a year, with a majority of voting members in attendance at each meeting;
   e. no fees to members for board service, but payments may be made for costs incurred as a result of board participation;

    f. no more than one paid staff member [usually the chief staff officer, who shall not chair the board or serve as treasurer];

    g. no material conflicts of interest involving board or staff, and [policy guidelines to avoid such conflicts];

    h. [a policy promoting pluralism and diversity within the organization's board, staff, and constituencies].

2. Purpose: The organization's purpose, approved by the board, should be formally and specifically stated.

3. Programs: The organization's activities should be consistent with its statement of purpose.

4. Information: Promotion, fund raising, and public information should describe accurately the organization's identity, purpose, programs, and financial needs.

5. Financial Support and Related Activities: The board is accountable for all authorized activities generating financial support on the organization's behalf.

    a. Fund-raising practices should encourage voluntary giving and should not be intimidating.

    b. Descriptive and financial information for all substantial income and all revenue-generating activities conducted by the organization should be disclosed on request.

    c. Basic descriptive and financial information for income derived from authorized commercial activities, involving the organization's name, which are conducted by for-profit organizations, should be available. All public promotion of such commercial activity should either include this information or indicate that it is available from the organization.

6. Use of Funds: The organization's use of funds should reflect

    a. reasonable annual program, management/general, and fund-raising expenses, with at least 60 percent of annual expenses applied to program;

    b. consideration of current and future needs and resources in planning for program continuity.

        Usually, the organization's net assets available for the following fiscal year should not be more than twice the higher of the current year's expenses or the next year's budget. There should not be a persistent or increasing deficit in the unrestricted fund balance.

REPORTING AND FISCAL FUNDAMENTALS

7. Annual Reporting: An annual report, or equivalent package of documentation, should be available on request, and should include

 a. an explicit narrative description of the organization's major activities, presented in the same major categories and covering the same fiscal period as the audited financial statements;
 b. a list of board members;
 c. audited financial statements or, at a minimum, a comprehensive financial summary that (1) reflects all revenues, (2) reports expenses in the same program, management/general, and fundraising categories as in the audited financial statements, and (3) reports all ending balances. (When the annual report does not include the full audited financial statements, it should indicate that they are available on request.)

8. Accountability: Complete financial statements should be prepared in conformity with generally accepted accounting principles (GAAP), accompanied by a report of an independent certified public accountant, and reviewed by the board.

A statement of functional allocation of expenses should be available on request, if this is not required by generally accepted accounting principles to be included among the financial statements.

Combined financial statements for a national organization operating with affiliates should be prepared in the foregoing manner.

9. Budget: The organization should prepare a detailed annual budget consistent with the major classifications in the audited financial statements, and approved by the board.

Since July 1, 1988, all NCIB evaluations have been based on these standards. Full compliance with standards marked in brackets will be expected no later than January 1, 1991.

NCIB BASIC STANDARDS IN PHILANTHROPY
(old standards)

Philanthropic organizations have a high degree of responsibility because of the public trusteeship involved. Compliance with the following standards, with reasonable evidence supplied on request, is considered essential by NCIB:

1. Board: An active and responsible governing body, holding regular meetings, whose members have no material conflict of interest and serve without compensation.

2. Purpose: A clear statement of purpose in the public interest.

3. Program: A program consistent with the organization's stated purpose and its personnel and financial resources, and involving interagency cooperation to avoid duplication of work.

4. Expenses: Reasonable program, management, and fund-raising expenses.

5. Promotion: Ethical publicity and promotion excluding exaggerated or misleading claims.

6. Fund raising: Solicitation of contributions without payment of commissions or undue pressure, such as mailing unordered tickets or merchandise, general telephone solicitations, and use of identified government employees as solicitors.

7. Accountability: An annual report available on request that describes program activities and supporting services in relation to expenses and that contains financial statements comprising a balance sheet, a statement of support/revenue and expenses and changes in fund balances, a statement of functional expenses, and notes to financial statements, that are accompanied by the report of an independent public accountant. National organizations operating with affiliates should provide combined or acceptably compiled financial statements prepared in the foregoing manner. For its analysis NCIB may request disclosure of accounting treatment of various items included in the financial statements.

8. Budget: Detailed annual budgets approved by the governing body in a form consistent with annual financial statements.

☐ Appendix C ☐

CHARITIES-REGISTRATION OFFICES, STATE BY STATE

■ POTENTIAL CONTRIBUTORS WHO contact state offices requesting information about particular charities and nonprofit groups should be aware of several things:

1. Registration in a state office does not always require filing a copy of either an IRS form 990 or an independently audited statement. Often a state has a slightly different form (such as the NYS form 497 for New York State), tailored to its own needs for information. Other times, a state office may only require registration of minimal information (possibly without any financial data). If you are seeking financial information, rather than just a reassurance that a group is registered to solicit funds in your state, make that request clear when calling or writing a state office.

2. In the case of registered financial information, bear in mind that although a fiscal year ends in June or September, this does not mean that the latest filing will automatically be available at that time. Due to filing extensions and limited enforcement of registration rules, a given state office may not have information for the present year or the year immediately preceding.

3. Reproduction costs for copies of submitted materials vary, so ask about prices.

4. Many charities offices are understaffed. To make their job easier, please use the state registration numbers (when known) and, most important of all, be aware that their busiest times are at the end of March, June, September, and especially December.

ALABAMA
Attorney General
Consumer Protection Div.
Montgomery, AL 36130

ALASKA
Attorney General
Dept. of Law
1031 W. 4th Ave., Suite 200
Anchorage, AK 99501

ARIZONA
Attorney General
Tax Div.
1275 W. Washington
Phoenix, AZ 85007

ARKANSAS
Secretary of State
State Capitol
Little Rock, AR 72201

CALIFORNIA
Registrar of Charitable Trusts
Dept. of Justice
P.O. Box 13447
Sacramento, CA 95813

COLORADO
Corporations Dept.
Dept. of State
1560 Broadway, Suite 200
Denver, CO 80202

CONNECTICUT
Attorney General
Public Charities Unit
55 Elm St.
Hartford, CT 06106

DELAWARE
Attorney General
Civil Div.
Wilmington Tower
820 N. French St., 8th Fl.
Wilmington, DE 19801

DISTRICT OF COLUMBIA
Office of Licenses and Permits
N. Potomac Bldg.
614 H St., NW
Washington, DC 20001

FLORIDA
Dept. of Agriculture and
    Consumer Services
Div. of Consumer Services
Mayo Bldg., Rm. 209
Tallahassee, FL 32399

GEORGIA
Secretary of State
Business Services and Regulation
2 Martin Luther King Dr.
West Tower, Suite 315
Atlanta, GA 30334

HAWAII
Dept. of Commerce and
    Consumer Affairs
Business Registration Div.
P.O. Box 40
Honolulu, HI 96810

IDAHO
Office of the Attorney General
Consumer Protection Div.
Statehouse
Boise, ID 83720

ILLINOIS
Office of the Attorney General
Charitable Trust Div.
100 W. Randolph, 12th Fl.
Chicago, IL 60601

INDIANA
Attorney General
Consumer Protection Div.
219 State House
Indianapolis, IN 46204

IOWA
Attorney General
Consumer Protection Div.
Hoover State Office Bldg.
1300 E. Walnut
Des Moines, IA 50319

KANSAS
Secretary of State
Capitol Bldg., 2nd Fl.
Topeka, KS 66612

KENTUCKY
Attorney General
Consumer Protection Div.
Frankfort, KY 40601

LOUISIANA
Attorney General
Dept. of Justice
Consumer Protection Div.
Baton Rouge, LA 70806

MAINE
Professional Regulation and
  Financial Regulation Dept.

Div. of Licensing and
  Enforcement
Station 35
Augusta, ME 04333

MARYLAND
Office of the Secretary of State
Charitable Div.
State House
Annapolis, MD 21401

MASSACHUSETTS
Dept. of the Attorney General
1 Ashburton Pl.
Boston, MA 02108

MICHIGAN
Attorney General
Office of the Charitable Trust
  Section
P.O. Box 30214
Lansing, MI 48909

MINNESOTA
Office of the Attorney General
Charities Div.
340 Bremer Tower
7th Pl. and Minnesota St.
St. Paul, MN 55101
or
Charities Review Council
122 W. Franklin
Minneapolis, MN 55404

MISSISSIPPI
Attorney General
Carroll Gartin Justice Bldg.
P.O. Box 220
Jackson, MS 39205

MISSOURI
Attorney General
P.O. Box 899
Jefferson City, MO 65102

MONTANA
Secretary of State
Capitol Station, Rm. 225
Helena, MT 59620

NEBRASKA
Secretary of State
Corporations Div.
P.O. Box 94608
Lincoln, NE 68509

NEVADA
Secretary of State
Carson City, NV 89710

NEW HAMPSHIRE
Div. of Charitable Trusts
State House Annex
25 Capitol St.
Concord, NH 03301

NEW JERSEY
Div. of Consumer Affairs
Charities Registration Section
1100 Raymond Blvd., Rm. 518
Newark, NJ 07102

NEW MEXICO
Assistant Attorney General
P.O. Box 1508
Santa Fe, NM 87504

NEW YORK
Office of Charities Registration
Dept. of State
162 Washington Ave.
Albany, NY 12231

NORTH CAROLINA
Dept. of Human Resources
Solicitation Licensing Branch
701 Barbour Dr.
Raleigh, NC 27603

NORTH DAKOTA
Secretary of State
State Capitol
600 E. Boulevard Ave.
Bismarck, ND 58505

OHIO
Office of the Attorney General
Charitable Foundations Section
30 E. Broad St., 15th Fl.
Columbus, OH 43266

OKLAHOMA
Income Tax Div.
Oklahoma State Tax Commission
2501 Lincoln Blvd.
Oklahoma City, OK 73194

OREGON
Dept. of Justice
Charitable Trust Section
15 S.W. 5th Ave., Suite 410
Portland, OR 97201

PENNSYLVANIA
Bureau of Charitable
   Organizations
Dept. of State
Capitol Bldg.
Harrisburg, PA 17120

RHODE ISLAND
Dept. of Business Regulations
100 N. Main St.
Providence, RI 02903

SOUTH CAROLINA
Secretary of State
Public Charities Div.
P.O. Box 11350
Columbia, SC 29211

SOUTH DAKOTA
Attorney General
State Capitol
Pierre, SD 57501

TENNESSEE
Secretary of State
Charitable Solicitation Div.
Capitol Hill Bldg.
Nashville, TN 37219

TEXAS
Attorney General
Charitable Trust Section
P.O. Box 12548
Austin, TX 78711

UTAH
Dept. of Commerce
Consumer Protection Div.
P.O. Box 45802
Salt Lake City, UT 84145

VERMONT
Attorney General
Pavilon Office Bldg.
109 State St.
Montpelier, VT 05602

VIRGINIA
Dept. of Agriculture and
   Consumer Services
P.O. Box 1163
Richmond, VA 23209

WASHINGTON
Charities Div.
Office of the Secretary of State
Legislative Bldg.
Mail Stop AS-22
Olympia, WA 98504

WEST VIRGINIA
Office of the Secretary of State
Director of Charitable
   Organizations
State Capitol Complex
Charleston, WV 25305

WISCONSIN
Dept. of Regulation and
   Licensing
P.O. Box 8935
Madison, WI 53708

WYOMING
Secretary of State
Capitol Bldg.
200 W. 24th
Cheyenne, WY 82002

□ NOTES □

INTRODUCTION

1. Burton A. Weisbrod, "Nonprofits Crowd Private Sector as Public Pipeline Constricts," *Wall Street Journal,* November 14, 1988, p. A18.
2. Ibid.
3. *Giving USA: The Annual Report on Philanthropy for the Year 1988* (New York: AAFRC Trust for Philanthropy, 1989), p. 11.
4. Virginia A. Hodgkinson and Murray S. Weitzman, *Giving and Volunteering in the United States: Findings from a National Survey* (Washington, D.C.: Independent Sector, 1988).

2. CHARITY BEGINS AT HOME—HOW DIRECT-MAIL APPEALS WORK

1. $50 per thousand names for 107,114 "supporters of the president's space-based defense concept; average donation $26.42," a list of names owned by Steve Cram and Associates, Inc., dated August 8, 1988.
2. $55 per thousand names for 64,268 donors to "an appeal for stronger gun-control laws, including a complete ban on handguns; 55% men; average donation $16.00," a list of names brokered by Names in the News—California, Inc., dated May 24, 1988.
3. Walter H. Weintz, *The Solid Gold Mailbox: How to Create Winning Mail-Order Campaigns . . . By the Man Who's Done It All* (New York: John Wiley, 1987), pp. 107–20.
4. Francis S. "Andy" Andrews, *Billions by Mail: Fundraising in the Computer Age* (Lincoln, Mass.: Tabor Oaks, 1985), p. 314.
5. Mark Jacobson, "Do You Know Where Your Direct Mail Program Is . . . Or Where You Want It to Be?" *Non-Profit Marketing Insider,* vol. 2, no. 13 (May 31, 1986).

6. *The Household Diary Study, Fiscal Year 1987,* published by the Demand Research Division, Rates and Classification Department of the United States Postal Service (July 1988), p. VI-111.
7. "What's Working—and What's Not—in Direct-Mail Fundraising," *The Fundraising Forum,* reprinted in *Direct Response,* September 1, 1984.
8. Andrews, *Billions by Mail,* p. 182.
9. *The Household Diary Study,* pp. VI-95–98.

3. BURIED BY DIRECT MAIL—THE DEATH OF A CHARITY

1. United Cancer Council Annual Report 1988, p. 1.
2. Phone conversation with James S. Briggs, Jr., May 8, 1990.
3. UCC Annual Report 1988, pp. 4, 7.
4. United Cancer Council, Inc., IRS form 990, year ending December 31, 1988, Schedule A, p. 2, line 15d.
5. "Major charity spends 97 percent of budget raising funds," by Gayle Young, *United Press International,* April 13, 1987, PM cycle.
6. UCC, IRS form 990, lines 15b, c.
7. Gayle Young, "Major Charity Spends 97 Percent of Budget Raising Funds," United Press International, April 13, 1987; "Spent Majority of Money Raised on Further Fund-Raising," Associated Press, April 14, 1987.
8. "Charity Must Give Refunds to Misled Donors, AG Rules," Associated Press, undated 1983 story.
9. 1987 Agreement between American Institute for Cancer Research and the Watson and Hughey Company, March 17 and 20, 1987, p. 1.
10. David Johnston, "Research Institute Fund-Raising Thrives Despite Controversy," *Los Angeles Times,* April 16, 1985, Part V, p. 4.
11. American Institute for Cancer Research, IRS form 990, year ending September 30, 1987, Schedule A, Part III, line 2c (statement 5).
12. Ibid., Part IV, line 15d; AICR, IRS form 990, year ending September 30, 1988, Part I, line 12.
13. Ibid., Part IV, line b.
14. Ibid., Part II.
15. Johnston, "Research Institute."
16. AICR, IRS form 990, year ending September 30, 1988, Part I, lines 12–15.
17. 1987 Agreement between AICR and W&H, pp. 5–6.

18. Paul Nyden, "Two Charities Banned from Soliciting in State," *Charlotte Gazette*, June 11, 1987.
19. Full Service Direct-Response Fundraising Agreement by and between the Watson and Hughey Company and Committee Against Government Waste, dated July 19, 1984, Section 8, pp. 2–3.
20. New Jersey Charity Annual Report for Committee against Government Waste, Inc., 1987, Schedule 2—Professional Fundraisers.
21. Full Service Direct-Response Fundraising Agreement by and between the Watson and Hughey Company and the United Cancer Council, dated June 11, 1984, Section 8, pp. 2–3.
22. Letter from James S. Briggs, Jr., to the author, May 1990.
23. United Cancer Council, Inc., IRS form 990, year ending December 31, 1985, Part III, line b. Cited in NCIB report dated January 27, 1987.
24. Phone conversation with James S. Briggs, Jr., May 8, 1990.
25. Young, "Major Charity."
26. Barbara Carton, "Low Charity Return Is Alleged," *Washington Post*, April 18, 1987, p. A4.
27. Written testimony of James S. Briggs, Jr., submitted to the U.S. Senate Antitrust Subcommittee, December 15, 1989, p. 9.
28. Carton, "Low Charity Return."
29. Letter from Frank L. Gunther to Robert Cozzens of the New York Office of Charities Registration, March 21, 1987.
30. Agreement between W&H and UCC, June 11, 1984, Section 14, p. 4.
31. U.S. Postal Inspection Service News Release from T. W. McClure, Postal Inspector, Public Information Officer, Congressional & Public Affairs Branch.
32. *United States Postal Service v. Pacific West Cancer Fund, et al.* United States District Court for the District of Kansas, June 20, 1989. Civil Action No. 89-4026-R, Attachment B.
33. Phone conversation with Errol Copilevitz, July 23, 1990.
34. William Montague, "Charities' Sweepstakes Spark Many Complaints That Donors Are Misled," *Chronicle of Philanthropy*, November 8, 1988, p. 23.
35. Phone conversation with Errol Copilevitz, July 23, 1990.
36. Kate Ruddon, " 'Bonanza Sweepstakes' Bags Millions For Cancer Groups—How Much For Cancer?" *Journal of the National Cancer Institute*, vol. 81, no. 2 (January 18, 1989).

37. Rhonda L. Rundle, "A Crackdown on 'Charity' Sweepstakes," *Wall Street Journal,* March 6, 1989, p. B1.

38. Phone conversation with Errol Copilevitz, July 23, 1990.

39. Phone interviews with state charity officials in Connecticut, Iowa, Minnesota, New York, Tennessee, and West Virginia.

40. Assumption Agreement by and between the American Health Foundation, the Cancer Fund of America, and the Watson and Hughey Company, dated February 8, 1988.

41. Letter from James T. Reynolds to Rep. Thomas A. Luken, August 23, 1989. House Committee on Energy and Commerce, *Deceptive Fundraising By Charities: Hearing Before the Subcommittee on Transportation and Hazardous Materials,* 101st Congress, 1st sess., July 28, 1989, Serial 101-81, p. 27.

42. Rundle, "A Crackdown," and Montague, "Charities' Sweepstakes Spark Many Complaints."

43. United Cancer Council Annual Report 1988, p. 1.

44. Ibid., pp. 13–14.

45. United Cancer Council, Inc., IRS form 990, year ending December 31, 1988, Part I, p. 1, line 1.

46. Phone conversation with Margery Heitbrink, May 8, 1990.

47. Letter from James S. Briggs, Jr., to Pam Banks, Counsel of the U.S. Senate Antitrust Subcommittee, December 15, 1989.

48. Phone conversation with Errol Copilevitz, July 23, 1990.

49. Phone conversation with James S. Briggs, Jr., May 8, 1990.

4. USING PLASTIC FOR A GOOD CAUSE—HOW AFFINITY CARDS WORK

1. "Plastic Explosion," *Houston Post,* August 1, 1988, page unknown.

2. "Boom in Affinity Credit Cards Brings New Profits and Problems," *Non Profit Times,* September 1988, p. 1.

3. "Credit Cards for Causes," *Consumer Reports,* March 1988, p. 190.

4. Ibid.

5. "Plastic Explosion."

6. Affinity Group Marketing, Inc., promotional booklet, p. 7.

7. "MNC Top Issuer of Affinity Credit Cards," *Baltimore Evening Sun,* March 30, 1988.

8. "American Express, Creator of 'Cause-Related Marketing,' Fears That Imitators Are Harming Its Credit-Card Strategy," *Chronicle of Philanthropy,* November 8, 1988, p. 4.

9. "Boom in Affinity Credit Cards Brings New Profits and Problems," *Non Profit Times,* September 1988, p. 6.

10. "Credit-Card Tie to Nonprofit Groups," *New York Times,* July 5, 1988, p. D7.

11. "American Express . . . Fears . . . Imitators," p. 6.

12. Isadore Barmash, "MasterCard and VISA: Rival Donors," advertising column by *New York Times,* October 3, 1988.

13. "MasterCard Campaign Prepares to Repeat," *Fund Raising Management,* August 1988, p. 47.

14. Barmash, "Rival Donors."

15. "American Express . . . Fears . . . Imitators," p. 4.

16. "A Cautionary Look at Affinity Cards," *New York Times,* May 15, 1988, Business section.

17. Poster from Consumer Credit Card Rating Service, Inc., Santa Monica, California, © 1987.

18. "Credit Cards for Causes," p. 191.

19. "Enlisting Mets, Elvis in Credit Card War," *Newsday,* October 21, 1988, p. 55.

20. "American Express . . . Fears . . . Imitators," p. 4.

5. CAUSE MARKETING AND THE "BAND AID" SOLUTION

1. S. J. Diamond, "Firms Wrap Philanthropy in New Package," *Los Angeles Times,* July 22, 1988, Business section, p. 1.

2. Fritz Jellinghaus, "Profits Have a Place in Philanthropy," *New York Times,* March 29, 1987, Section 3, p. 2.

3. *Business Travel News,* June 23, 1986, quoted by Patricia Caesar in "Cause-Related Marketing: The New Face of Corporate Philanthropy," *Nonprofit World,* July-August 1987, p. 25.

4. "Traveling for Good," *Esquire,* April 1988; Larry Sterne, "Boom in Affinity Credit Cards Brings New Profits and Problems," *Non Profit Times,* September 1988, p. 9.

5. Nick Ravo, "Who's Hustling Whom? A Paul Newman Court Drama," *New York Times,* June 16, 1988, p. B6.

6. Diamond, "Firms Wrap Philanthropy"; "Charities in the Marketplace: A Look at Joint-Venture Marketing," *Insight,* Issue 2, 1987, p. 3.

7. Quad Marketing advertising supplement for *New York Times,* October 16, 1988.

8. Various color advertising supplements, including one for the *New York Times,* March 6, 1988.

9. Nathan Weber, ed., *Giving USA: The Annual Report on Philanthropy for the Year 1988* (AAFRC Trust for Philanthropy, 1989), p. 68.

10. "Marketing of Statue Alters Nature of Fund-Raising," *New York Times,* June 15, 1986.

11. Patricia Caesar, "Cause-Related Marketing: The New Face of Corporate Philanthropy," *Nonprofit World,* July-August 1987, p. 26.

12. Peter Goldberg, "A Dangerous Trend in Corporate Giving," *New York Times,* March 29, 1987, Section 3, p. 2.

13. Caesar, "Cause-Related Marketing," p. 26.

14. Ibid., p. 25.

15. "Cause Marketing Gets Good Marks," *Non Profit Times,* November 1988, p. 5.

16. "1990s Seen as 'Golden Years' for Giving and Volunteering," *Non Profit Times,* November 1988, p. 5.

17. Mary-Paige Royer, "Please Give Generously, Okay?" *American Demographics,* June 1988, p. 36.

18. "1990s Seen as 'Golden Years,' " p. 5.

19. Royer, "Please Give," p. 36.

20. Susan Calhoun, "Charities in Tune With the Times," *Foundation News,* January-February 1987, p. 34.

21. Robert Hilburn, "A Rousing Start for 'Human Rights' Tour," *Los Angeles Times,* September 5, 1988, Part 6, p. 7.

22. "Summer of Conscience," *Spin,* September 1988, p. 28.

23. "Ask and Ye Shall Receive, Believes Dallas Deejay Ron Chapman—Which Is How He Made $244,240," *People,* May 2, 1988, p. 65.

24. Roger M. Williams, "What Hath Geldof Wrought?" *Foundation News,* January-February 1987, p. 33.

25. Ibid., p. 31.

26. Calhoun, "Charities in Tune," p. 34.

27. Bruce Eder, "The Other Pop-Music Story from 1967," *Newsday,* July 1, 1988, Section 3, p. 13.

28. John Leland, "Talkin' 'Bout a Revolution: Rock's Summer of Conscience," *Spin,* September 1988.

29. Williams, "What Hath Geldof Wrought?" pp. 36–37.

30. Leland "Talkin' 'Bout a Revolution," p. 31.

31. Hilburn, "Rousing Start," p. 7.

32. Calhoun, "Charities in Tune," pp. 34–35.

33. Larry Sterne, "In Other Words: Nose for News," *Non Profit Times,* March 1988, p. 2.

34. Hilburn, "Rousing Start," p. 7.

35. Jefferson Graham, "Freedomfest Renews Anti-Apartheid Call," *USA Today,* June 10, 1988, p. 3D; Robert Keating, "Anatomy of a Cause Concert," *Spin,* September 1988, p. 72.

36. Calhoun, "Charities in Tune," p. 34.

6. CHARITY GOES ABROAD—LEARNING A NEW TRADE

1. Jonathan Burton, "Back to Nature—the Financial Way," *Banker,* December 1988, p. 25; Marjorie Sun, "Costa Rica's Campaign for Conservation," *Science,* March 18, 1988, p. 1367.

2. 1988 annual report for the Nature Conservancy; 1989 Annual Report for the World Wildlife Fund; John Walsh, "Bolivia Swaps Debt for Conservation," *Science,* August 7, 1987, p. 596.

3. Julia Michaels, "Fundraising Success of Brazilian Ecology Group Inspires Others," *Christian Science Monitor,* June 1, 1988, p. 8.

4. David Johnston, "Bad Debt Is Good Source of Funds for Some Top International Charities," *Non Profit Times,* September 1988, p. 15.

5. Ibid., p. 1.

6. Ibid., p. 17.

7. Ibid., pp. 15–16.

8. Burton, "Back to Nature."

7. HOW TO READ THE PROFILES

1. *Riley v. National Federation of the Blind of North Carolina, Inc., et al.,* No. 87-328, Supreme Court of the United States.

ABOUT THE AUTHOR

Howard Gershen was born in a Salvation Army hospital in New York in 1959. Since that time he has taught as a literacy volunteer, worked as a researcher-writer for a nonprofit public-policy think tank, and received a B.A. in English from Columbia (1981). His work has appeared in the books *The 80s: A Look Back, Hellbent on Insanity* (the best college humor of the 1970s), and *Reagan's Reign of Error,* and in the *Baltimore Sun,* the *San Jose Mercury-News,* the *Village Voice,* the Columbia *Jester,* and *Esquire* (where he first profiled fifty American charities).